D0788082

EARLY HUMAN KINSHIP

EARLY HUMAN KINSHIP

From Sex to Social Reproduction

Edited by

Nicholas J. Allen, Hilary Callan,
Robin Dunbar and Wendy James

Royal Anthropological
Institute

Blackwell
Publishing

© 2008 by Blackwell Publishing Ltd
except for editorial material and organization © 2008 by Nicholas J. Allen,
Hilary Callan, Robin Dunbar and Wendy James

BLACKWELL PUBLISHING
350 Main Street, Malden, MA 02148-5020, USA
9600 Garsington Road, Oxford OX4 2DQ, UK

The right of Nicholas J. Allen, Hilary Callan, Robin Dunbar and Wendy James
to be identified as the authors of the editorial material in this work has been
asserted in accordance with the UK Copyright, Designs, and Patents Act 1988.

First published 2008 by Blackwell Publishing Ltd

1   2008

Library of Congress Cataloging-in-Publication Data

Early human kinship : from sex to social reproduction / edited by
Nicholas J. Allen . . . [et al.].
     p. cm.
   Includes bibliographical references and index.
   ISBN 978-1-4051-7901-0 (hardcover : alk. paper)   1. Kinship.
2. Prehistoric peoples.   3. Human evolution.   I. Allen, Nicholas J.

   GN487.E33 2008
   306.83—dc22
                                                        2007047246

A catalogue record for this title is available from the British Library.

Set in 10/12pt Meridien
by Graphicraft Limited, Hong Kong
Printed and bound in Singapore
by Markono Print Media Pte Ltd

The publisher's policy is to use permanent paper from mills that operate a sustainable
forestry policy, and which has been manufactured from pulp processed using acid-free and
elementary chlorine-free practices. Furthermore, the publisher ensures that the text paper
and cover board used have met acceptable environmental accreditation standards.

For further information on
Blackwell Publishing, visit our website at
www.blackwellpublishing.com

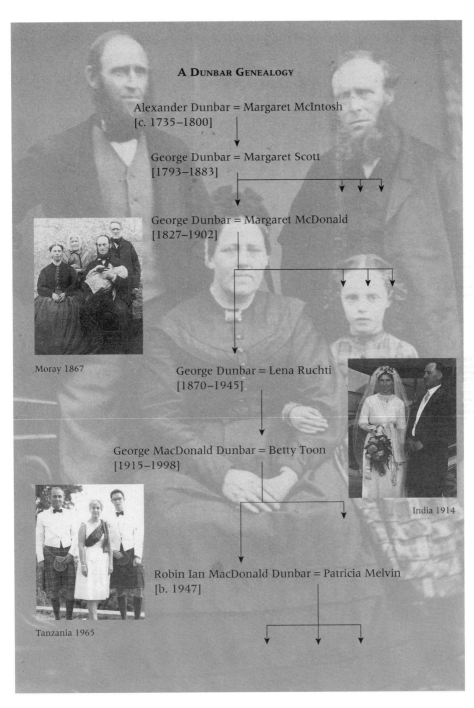

A DUNBAR GENEALOGY

Alexander Dunbar = Margaret McIntosh
[c. 1735–1800]

George Dunbar = Margaret Scott
[1793–1883]

George Dunbar = Margaret McDonald
[1827–1902]

Moray 1867

George Dunbar = Lena Ruchti
[1870–1945]

George MacDonald Dunbar = Betty Toon
[1915–1998]

India 1914

Tanzania 1965

Robin Ian MacDonald Dunbar = Patricia Melvin
[b. 1947]

Generations of a Scottish family. Background: the Dunbar family, Moray, c. 1872–73
(Lawson Collection, Royal Anthropological Institute)

Contents

Tables

Figures

Illustrations

Front cover: Copy of a later Stone Age rock painting from Kolo
                cave in the Sandawe region of northern Tanzania,
                interpreted by recent scholars as recording a shamanistic
                trance dance known as *simbo*. Some dancers may seem
                to take on animal form, while others need restraining
                from convulsions (compare anthropological accounts
                of 'spirit possession'). An older view was that this scene
                represented 'abduction'. It could equally well represent
                the ceremonial transfer of a girl, perhaps in marriage,
                from one side (represented by the round heads) to the
                other (represented by the narrow animal-like heads).
Back cover: Scale drawing of interacting male and female Dynamic
                Figures from a rock painting panel near the Mann River,
                central Arnhem Land, Australia. The male holds what
                appear to be three boomerangs in his right hand while
                the female holds a digging stick and wears a dilly bag
                from the forehead. Dots representing sound and/or
                motion were deliberately arranged near the mouths
                of both figures and the right foot of the female. The
                woman also appears to be grabbing the male's arm. The
                composition, and associated art style, is believed to be at
                least 10,000 years of age but a precise date has not yet
                been determined. We can only speculate on the nature

of the interaction: they may be fleeing something or someone together; she may be chasing him; they may be participating in a communal ceremony. Women are rare in Dynamic Style rock paintings and there are only a handful of compositions showing male-female interactions, so this image gives us a unique glimpse of an aspect of ancient Aboriginal Australian gender relations. (Drawing and original photograph by Paul S. C. Tacon, then at the Australian Museum, 1994; Mick Kubarkku and the Yikarrakkal community are thanked for access to the site and permission to use the image in publications.)

Preface

This volume introduces some new thinking on the emergence of typically human ways of organizing sex, marriage, parent/child and sibling links, and the consequent world of 'relatives' beyond. Although the chapters are all by specialists in one field or another of the human sciences, their findings are presented here in plain language as part of a set of accessible conversations.

While the academic topic of 'comparative kinship' might seem a little remote (and even to anthropologists a little 'out of fashion'), questions about how we find mates and call on others to help raise our children are of strong interest to us all. In this book the contributors debate how far the way in which we do these things, mixed up as it is with language, memory of the past, intentions for the future, and moral or even religious expectations, marks an important difference between ourselves as *Homo sapiens* and our earlier primate heritage. A good deal of popular writing and media programming has recently promoted the image of our closeness to the rest of the animal world, but here – without denying the evolutionary basics – we take a couple of steps back to consider again the nature of the *differences* involved. Even though we do not presume any single, simple transition to the family and kinship life of 'modern' humans, we do seek to specify elements of social and cultural organization that have fed into the tendency of us moderns to think in terms of aesthetically pleasing overall patterns, and to negotiate agreed ways of ordering our everyday worlds. Arguably this tendency may have provided survival advantages for groups of our ancestors in relation to their rivals. This is a complex story but, we think, one with wide appeal, not only to those eager to subsume human life seamlessly into the Darwinian paradigm, but also to those who have been used to thinking of human history as quite outside nature.

The volume is based on papers originally given at a workshop sponsored by the Royal Anthropological Institute, London (RAI) on 'Early Human Kinship', in collaboration with the directors and other participants representing the British Academy Centenary Project 'From Lucy to Language: The Archaeology of the Social Brain'. The workshop took place at the University of Wales conference centre at Gregynog from 20 to 22 March 2005. The aim of the project was to bring biological and social anthropologists together with archaeologists and historical linguists in order to produce a 'state of the art' discussion on the place of organized patterns of kinship in the emergence of language and modern human society. Participants paid particular attention to the relevance of symbolic, holistic models of 'imagined' kinship and social reproduction derived from the structuralist tradition, which had so far not been brought into line with recent advances on the bio-scientific side of anthropology or evolutionary studies.

Questions of 'kinship' have always been at the centre of anthropology. These questions certainly point to biological continuities and changes in a population, but also to the way the birth and socialization of new generations is shaped by the language and conventional practices of adult society, including specifically their existing rules governing sexual access and marriage. At the same time, the facts of physical reproduction have always lent themselves to evolutionary interpretation. Advances in the biological sciences today have prompted a new wave of interest in questions about the roots of human kinship behaviour and its long-term history. These studies, often seeking constructive inspiration from new work on the behaviour of other primates, or even more distant creatures, have sometimes been accused of setting 'culture' aside in their treatment of human life.

The present volume is the fruit of exchanges between leading scholars on all sides of the current debate. Coming from various disciplinary backgrounds, they share the basic view that we need to avoid any sharp distinction between nature and culture as such in understanding human behaviour and the forms of social life. Specifically, this collection emphasizes the long evolutionary heritage to which we are heirs, in both a biological and a cultural sense, but also draws attention to the key importance for human history as a whole of the relatively recent exodus of *Homo sapiens* from Africa (c. 60,000 years ago). All the elements of human understanding brought together under shared categorical ideas and practices redolent with 'symbolism' must have been in place well before that time of expanded human movement. A capacity to think and act, even empathize in an emotional sense, with reference to distant places, absent friends, potential mates, the living, the recently dead, and the generations to come, must have been well established before this time. This is the starting point from which we offer this book as a new set of interdisciplinary conversations in the debate over human evolution and the nature of society.

Acknowledgements

We are grateful to all those who attended the 2005 workshop which launched this project, particularly those who presented papers that could not in the end be included here – Bill Croft, and Clare Holden (who presented on behalf of herself and Ruth Mace). Robert (Bob) Parkin provided very helpful discussion at the meeting and subsequently. Steven Mithen was unable to take up his invitation because of fieldwork commitments, but has given us encouragement at several points in the evolution of the book. In the run-up to the workshop, we were very sorry to hear of the death of Per Hage, a specialist in the comparative history of kin terminologies, whose participation had been eagerly awaited. Several younger scholars and students were able to join us at the workshop and their responses played a key role in our deciding to take the project forward: Claire Cody, Iris Glaesslein, Anna Goodman, Matthew Grove, Hannah Hafezi, and Adam Newton.

Lord Runciman (W. G. Runciman), President of the British Academy when the Centenary Project 'From Lucy to Language: The Archaeology of the Social Brain' was launched, has actively supported our venture, and its aim of introducing a wider readership in fields of the humanities and social sciences to questions of long-term human history. The Centenary Project, while set within the disciplines of evolutionary psychology and archaeology, has engaged in a range of collaboration with other human sciences, specifically here with linguistics and various branches of anthropology. The Project contributed to the funding of our workshop, which was originally proposed and mainly sponsored by the Royal Anthropological Institute. Staff at the RAI have assisted in several capacities with the organization of the original workshop and the progress of the book. We would particularly like to acknowledge the help of Amanda Vinson in coordinating our efforts over the last three years, and Arkadiusz Bentowski for help in locating illustrations. In the final stages of preparation of the manuscript, we were greatly helped by the skills of Frances Kennett.

The editors, November 2007

Notes on Contributors

Nicholas J. Allen originally studied classics and medicine before qualifying in social anthropology at Oxford, undertaking fieldwork in Nepal. He lectured at Durham and, from 1976 to 2001, at Oxford, where he became Reader in the Social Anthropology of South Asia. He has published on the Himalayas, kinship theory, the Durkheimian School, and Indo-European Comparativism. The last three interests are represented in his *Categories and Classifications* (2000).

Alan Barnard is Professor of the Anthropology of Southern Africa at the University of Edinburgh. He completed his Ph.D. on Naro (Nharo) kinship at University College London in 1976. His books include *Research Practices in the Study of Kinship* (with Anthony Good, 1984), *History and Theory in Anthropology* (2000), *Hunter-Gatherers in History, Archaeology and Anthropology* (edited, 2004), and *Anthropology and the Bushman* (2007). His present research interests include the social anthropology of early hominins.

Hilary Callan has been Director of the Royal Anthropological Institute of Great Britain and Ireland since 2000. A graduate of the Institute of Social and Cultural Anthropology (Oxford), she has held academic appointments in anthropology in the UK, Canada, and the Middle East, and has also worked in the field of international higher education. Her research and publications in anthropology include work on biological and social anthropology, occupational cultures, and gender.

Robin Dunbar, formerly at Liverpool, is now Professor of Evolutionary Anthropology, and Director of the Institute of Cognitive and Social Anthropology, at the University of Oxford. He is Co-Director of the British Academy's Centenary Research Project ('From Lucy to Language: The Archaeology of the Social Brain'). His recent books include *The Human Story* (2005) and *Oxford Handbook of Evolutionary Psychology* (edited with Louise Barrett, 2007). His research interests focus on the evolution of sociality in mammals, and its cognitive and ecological underpinnings.

Christopher Ehret is Professor of History and Linguistics at the University of California at Los Angeles. His primary interests are the theory and application of linguistic methods in the historical reconstruction of human culture and economy. His recent books include *An African Classical Age: Eastern and Southern Africa in World History, 1000 BC to AD 400* (1998), *A Comparative Historical Reconstruction of Proto-Nilo-Saharan* (2001), and *History and the Testimony of Language* (in press).

Laura Fortunato studied biology at the University of Padua, and is currently working towards a Ph.D. in Anthropology at University College London. She uses theory and methods developed to explain behavioural variation in non-human species to investigate cross-cultural variation in marriage practices, focusing on Indo-European societies.

Clive Gamble is Professor of Geography in the Centre for Quaternary Research at Royal Holloway, University of London. When at the University of Southampton, he founded the Centre for the Archaeology of Human Origins. Among his books are *The Palaeolithic Societies of Europe* (1999, winner of the Society for American Archaeology Book Award) and *Origins and Revolutions: Human Identity in Earliest Prehistory* (2007). He is Co-Director of the British Academy Centenary Research Project 'From Lucy to Language: The Archaeology of the Social Brain'.

John A. J. Gowlett has his major research interests in the origins of design form as expressed in artefacts, and its relationship with art and other aspects of intentionality. Through fieldwork on sites such as Chesowanja in Kenya and Beeches Pit in Britain he also studies the origins and nature of early human fire use. Currently working in collaboration with Robin Dunbar and Clive Gamble in the British Academy Centenary Project 'From Lucy to Language: The Archaeology of the Social Brain', he is Professor in the School of Archaeology, Classics, and Egyptology, University of Liverpool.

Wendy James was Professor of Social Anthropology at the University of Oxford until 2007, and is now Emeritus Fellow of St Cross College, Oxford. She is a committed social anthropologist but with interests in the history of the discipline and its relations with other branches of knowledge. She has carried out ethnographic research in North East Africa, especially among the Uduk-speaking people of the Sudan–Ethiopian border. Her most recent books are *The Ceremonial Animal: A New Portrait of Anthropology* (2003) and *War and Survival in Sudan's Frontierlands: Voices from the Blue Nile* (2007).

Chris Knight is Professor of Anthropology at the University of East London. His main concern has been to help restore anthropology to its former status as a single discipline, re-integrating cultural and social perspectives with those of modern Darwinism. His many publications include *Blood Relations: Menstruation and the Origins of Culture* (1991), and he has recently edited or co-edited *The Evolution of Culture* (1999), *The Evolutionary Emergence of Language* (2000), and *The Prehistory of Language* (in press).

Amanda H. Korstjens is a Senior Lecturer in Biological Anthropology at Bournemouth University, UK. She investigates the social and ecological factors that determine the behaviour of humans and other primates. She did her Ph.D. (Utrecht University and Max Planck Institute) on colobine monkey behavioural ecology and has studied wild primates on all continents. As a postdoc at Liverpool, working with Professor Dunbar, she developed theoretical models of behavioural ecology.

Robert Layton is Professor of Anthropology at the University of Durham. Over a period of thirty years he has carried out a number of fieldwork projects in rural France and Aboriginal Australia. His research interests include social evolution, social change, art, and indigenous rights. Among his recent books are *An Introduction to Theory in Anthropology* (1997), *Anthropology and History in Franche-Comté* (2000), and *Order and Anarchy: Civil Society, Social disorder and War* (2006).

Julia Lehmann has qualifications in Animal Behaviour and Applied Statistics and a Ph.D. from Zurich in Behavioural Neuropsychology. She is currently Senior Lecturer in the Department of Human and Life Sciences at Roehampton University, London. Her main research interest is in the evolution of mammalian sociality (including humans), social bonding and social networks, with a particular emphasis on fission–fusion societies.

Kit Opie did a BA in Economics at Sussex University and an MSc in Human Evolution and Behaviour at University College London in 2004. His Master's thesis (2004) was 'Testing the Grandmothering Hypothesis: The Provisioning of *Homo erectus* Infants and Juveniles'. He is now a Senior Policy Adviser to the Department for Business, Enterprise, and Regulatory Reform in the UK Government.

Camilla Power completed a Ph.D. in Anthropology in 2001 at the University of London and is currently Senior Lecturer in Anthropology at the University of East London. Her research interests centre on Darwinian models for the evolution of cooperation, specifically sexual strategies in relation to the emergence of symbolic culture, art, and ritual. She has published extensively on the gender relations, ritual, rock art, and cosmology of African hunter-gatherers. Current research involving fieldwork with the Hadzabe in Tanzania focuses on women's initiation as 'costly signalling' in the evolutionary sense.

Introduction and Background

Why 'Kinship'?

New Questions on an Old Topic

Wendy James

Tremendous advances have been made in the biological sciences over recent years in our understanding of the evolution and early history of humankind. We have a new wealth of evidence about the complexity of our physical ancestry, the successive migrations of our forebears from the African continent, and the genetic connectedness of our modern species of *Homo sapiens* across the world today. Our species was the last of the hominins to emerge from Africa, and we now know this to have taken place relatively quickly and perhaps as recently as 60,000 years ago (see John Gowlett and Robin Dunbar's 'Brief Overview' of human evolution which follows this introduction). At the same time the vigour of classic Darwinian evolutionary theory has been strengthened by new work, not only in genetics, but in evolutionary psychology, environmental history, and field studies of animal behaviour, including primatology. The model of selection for the survival of an organism and its characteristics by virtue of its ability to reproduce its genes in the next generation is a powerful one, and in increasingly sophisticated forms drives a good deal of today's work in biologically based research. It has also made claims to explain aspects of social history and cultural transmission, though here there has been resistance from many mainstream scholars in the humanities. The issue of how far 'nature' expresses itself against, or through, 'culture' has deep roots and has surfaced in different ways in Western thought.

The conversations in this book revolve around the possible ways in which we could re-engage discussion between those coming from the science side, and those from the humanities, on the very important question of how evolutionary theory could or should take account of the *ordered character* of human organization, specifically in respect of how we try to manage patterns of male–female and parent–child relations, and thus the purposeful outcomes of our own reproduction. Among our contributors several put forward new ways of imagining the key turning points in our past. Clive Gamble makes some bold propositions about mobility, bodily techniques, and abstract thought as evidenced in the material record (ideas developed also in his recent synthesis,

2007); while Kit Opie and Camilla Power offer powerful arguments from the bio-ecological perspective for early female coalitions and the evolutionary rise of 'helpful grandmothers'. Chris Knight advocates a serious rethinking of some developmental anthropological theories of the nineteenth century, sadly swept aside by the Malinowskian focus on individualism and the present. Nick Allen draws inspiration from the structural-linguistic tradition in social anthropology in proposing the 'tetradic' model as a candidate for the earliest holistic representations of 'kinship and marriage' and thus of sociality as a field, almost a playing-field, of relationship-making. This model certainly encompasses several systematic principles along which the world's peoples have selectively developed agreed schemes of reproductive continuity and related marriage rules – often, as ethnographers keep pointing out, surprising to modern English speakers. For these reasons, though not all contributors are persuaded of the case for the historical primacy of the cultural logic behind the tetradic schema, we have found the model 'good to think with' in our collective effort to conjure up social life as it might have been in the earliest human times. Between them, other chapters offer up-to-date research and speculation on what light primate studies can throw on the comparative human question, on the range of evidence available about modern communities who practise, or practised until recently, hunting and foraging as their main means of subsistence, and on methods of probing the long-term continuities beneath today's linguistic and cultural diversity, with respect to kinship and marriage.

The 'Social Brain': From Genetic Kinship to a Capacity for Story-Telling

Biologists, and all those who approach the topic from a biological or evolutionary angle, use the ordinary English-language concept of 'kinship' to refer explicitly to the underlying genetic relatedness of individuals, whether human or animal. Amanda Korstjens makes the point particularly clearly in opening her chapter below: '. . . it is essential to note that when primatologists talk about kinship they refer to genetic relatedness . . . animals cannot tell you who their relatives are' (p. 151). And, of course, if they did talk about their relatives, would this necessarily match what the modern scientist means by genetic relatedness? Even when *people* talk about relatives, is this in fact what they mean? In the domains of everyday practice, and indeed the law, even the ordinary English 'kinship' can be used in several ways: for example, in the narrow folk sense of 'blood relations', but also in a more inclusive way to cover the concept of adoption, or relationship by marriage – what anthropologists call 'affinity'. Thus, in English law, for example, one's 'next of kin' can be an otherwise unrelated spouse.

The chapters by Korstjens and by Julia Lehmann in part III of this book show how powerful explanations of primate behaviour in terms of selective fitness can be, although Lehmann illustrates how difficult it is to apply the simpler versions of 'Darwinian' explanation to the complex range of behaviours observed among the great apes. 'Hamilton's rule', whereby animals favour their genetic close relatives over others (even where a naïve observer might identify an act as 'altruism') takes us a very long way, but sometimes has to be stretched to fit the cases observed. Robin Dunbar's chapter on the biological approach to kinship offers a very clear explanation of this rule, but also shows how we must in fact avoid a kind of teleology about genetic success and the continuity of social forms, and focus rather on the theme of strategic choice of action affecting survival and reproductive outcomes in all contexts. He also draws attention to the very interesting idea put forward by Austen Hughes (1988) that with respect to human kinship, it is important to recognize how people not only look back to past kin relationships but also look to the future, anticipating in strategic ways the crucial fertility of the current rising genera-tion of young people. This insight does help provide a bridge to the way that social anthropologists have focused on purposeful marriage strategies along with received cultural schemes of kinship classification.

What has become known as 'the social brain theory' proposes that a key factor for the success of human ancestors over other groups in primate evolution was growing brain capacity (for a short general account, see Dunbar 2004). Specifically it is suggested that the extra development of the neo-cortex (and especially the frontal lobes) of the brain, where inventiveness is seemingly located, has made it possible for individuals to make the most of social cooperation in local groups of increasing size. Primate groups maintain sociality among themselves through grooming; but something else enabled early hominins to live in larger cooperating groups than could be held together by inter-individual grooming. Here must lie elements of the beginnings of kinds of communication that would become more sophisticated and reach further – gesture, chorusing, singing; the more organized use of space, and time; a division of labour and increasingly 'symbolic' kinds of collective performance; language. These kinds of communication would make possible various strat-egic ways of keeping selfish members of the growing group ('free-riders') in line, as well as making for understood conventions in the group's relations with others. In evolutionary terms, this more sophisticated range of strategies for coordinated action, in relation to the resources of the environment as well as in relation to competing species, would give such early human ancestral groups real advantage. They would survive to pass on their ways of doing things, by example, to their biological descendants. Those groups including individuals with exceptional brain capacity would do particularly well and their offspring would inherit a further enhanced potential for complicated strategic activity – no doubt requiring from us what Dunbar develops here as a 'multilevel' approach to evolutionary analysis.

Robin Dunbar also develops a discussion of what he has dubbed the 'story-telling' capacity located in the frontal lobes of the brain. Here is the uniquely human imagination which can guess at the intentions of others and empathize with their emotional states – not only one individual other, but a chain of interacting characters all imagining each other's state of mind. This provocat-ive scenario of early human beings as story-tellers, and by extension dramatic actors and indeed stage managers, can only embolden the social anthropolo-gists in their own efforts to rethink some of anthropology's oldest questions, about, for instance, the performative, 'enacted' character of the earliest forms of human relationships between male and female, co-siblings, young and old, within cooperating groups. 'Kinship' is not mere story-telling – the term covers action as well as words, and in the human world much of the action is of a give-and-take character – as Hilary Callan reminds us in the Epilogue, a kind of game-playing. Exchange and communication are crucial to our social lives, not least to the way we try to reproduce ourselves.

In these chapters we reflect on the processes that led to our forebears being able to agree together on the various principles and modes of 'exchange' which define the making of human social relations, whether economic, material, kinship, or linguistic. How far can we propose models for what most of us would accept as a *qualitative* change, or series of steps, marking the transition from what we have to suppose is the animal condition of living in the here and now, to one in which the imagination is working possible action on a wider span of space and time – through story-telling and game-playing? One in which distant places, absent friends, strangers, the dead and the yet-to-be-born are part of a remembered and an expected order, one towards which present decisions about making useful relationships are directed? Such rela-tionships will be 'makeable' through material gifts or barter or the mutual learn-ing of techniques between specialists; through seasonal and no doubt festive regular contacts between groups in a region otherwise scattered for most of the year; with strangers as a result of movement in response to changing eco-logical conditions, including population pressures on resources.

The making of such relationships, by the older and wiser members of a community, is also likely to have included the option of making strategic arrangements over the giving or exchanging of youngsters in marriage, rather than losing them through the patterns of pragmatic dispersal we know from the primates. Here is the key point of emergence, perhaps, of what the social anthropologists speak of as 'kinship' in human society – there is an aspect of systematic give and take in mating arrangements and group affiliation; 'kinship' in this sense is on quite a different 'level', to borrow one of Dunbar's formulations, from genetic relatedness as such. It is inclusive of 'adoptees' or recruits within a group or category; and the whole 'system' pivots around the give and take of mating or indeed 'marriage' between such groups or categories. Where concepts, and terms, of kinship relationship – along with potential affinity, or intermarriage – are open categories, rather than labels attached to known individuals, they can in principle stretch out over distance and time, providing a framework for human mobility and newly extended forms of sociality. This in turn will have consequences for the biological repro-duction of a population, and the distribution of genotypes. Understanding the patterns of 'affinity', and the way they are locally set up, is surely the key to the way that genetic reproduction of a whole community, or set of regionally linked communities, will henceforth unfold. Whether this has consequences for the evolutionary 'fitness' of a given population is difficult to say, of course. But taking this point into consideration may well assist us in understanding how *Homo sapiens* was able to move so rapidly over the face of the earth around 60,000 years ago, and seemingly prevail over the earlier species of *Homo* who had long before reached Europe and Asia – not to mention coping with the great variety of climates, environments, and wildlife they met as they journeyed as far as Australia and eventually the Americas.

From Ego's Networks to Social and Spatial Form

It is against the background of this view of human history that the interdisciplinary conversations of this book take place. We do not write here of the 'origin of the family'. As Chris Knight explains in his chapter, the relatively recent focus on the 'nuclear family' as a universal (which he traces to the individualist approach of Malinowski) has been something of a red herring for comparative and historical anthropology. Knight argues that, rather, we should go back to the earlier agenda of late nineteenth- and early twentieth-century anthropologists, and in the interests of understanding global and long-term history focus rather on what Lewis Morgan (1871) called 'systems of consanguinity and affinity' – that is, the way in which 'kinship' has to be understood alongside the rules and patterns whereby marriages are made. Knight explains how such systems can be thought of as based on a few relatively straightforward principles. For example, in the first instance, we can regard a set of full siblings as the starting point for understanding how a wider 'classification' may be built up of the actual and potential relationships between people in a reproducing community. Siblings of the same sex are not a point of divergence in such a system; the image of solidarity between same-sex siblings is replicated as the classification unfolds, as, for instance, in cases where the offspring of such siblings – that is, two sisters or two brothers – are seen as being like siblings themselves and sometimes called by the same term. Anthropologists call them 'parallel cousins'. Like siblings, in many parts of the world they are not regarded as marriageable. Siblings of opposite sex, however, can be a different matter: they offer a primary image of gender contrast, and thus a starting point for differentiation within the realm of relatives. It is understandable that their respective offspring frequently regard each other as quite different from 'siblings'. Anthropologists call people in this relationship 'cross-cousins'. In many parts of the world they are free to marry, even in the case of 'first' cousins in the biological sense, though the logic of 'cross-cousinhood' may ramify at different distances and levels in a terminology and be associated with a general marriage rule applying to a category, rather than to any individual within it. We do have to bear in mind that the logic of kin terminology has its own momentum, and as we know even in English with 'second cousin three times removed', etc., it can depart completely from the physical life of communities on the ground. But kin terminologies do pervade the moral and political sphere close to home, and shape the material and productive life of real human groups. Knight, following the classic early anthropologists, shows how ideas of the logical and social equivalence of same-sex siblings, in particular, can be extended in many ways, for example to whole coalitions of 'sisters' or 'brothers' across a generation (in some cases conceived as descent groups or lineages).

The way in which the English language reckons kin relationship, of course, starts from 'ego' – one individual looking outwards, as it were, and counting the genealogical steps linking him- or herself through either parent equally to others. This is done symmetrically on either side of the family, regardless of the gender of each link, while 'relatives by marriage' are treated as somehow peripheral to real kinship. Knight makes the point clearly that we need to avoid the trap of thinking that this is how relationships are seen everywhere. He presses home his argument by giving new life to some of the older theories in anthropology which were once taken almost for granted – in particular, the long-term historical precedence of matrifocal domestic arrangements, and matrilineal ideology.

The Darwinian paradigm inevitably takes successful reproduction as its starting point for determining the future fate of populations, and has increasingly focused on the strategies of individual males and females of whatever species, humans included, in their efforts to raise healthy offspring to reproductive age. The focus on individual strategies – whether driven by 'genes' themselves or by some higher rationality – seems to engage easily, when applied to human beings, with that simple model of the nuclear family of which social anthropologists have been so wary. Modern Western ideas of relatedness and the 'natural' family have in any case themselves taken a few shocks in recent years with social changes and the startling new technical possibilities of the new reproductive technologies (Carsten 2004). In this volume we attempt to avoid taking this model for granted. We try to show how the more holistic conceptions of what used to be called 'consanguinity and affinity' could be made relevant to the concerns of today's evolutionary scientists. We therefore focus on the logical 'grammar' and necessarily hypothetical sociology of how such schemes of human relationship might have emerged, schemes which presumably do not exist in the rest of the animal world but were a new factor at some key stage of early human history. As Nick Allen's chapter argues, structuralist thinking in the era of Lévi-Strauss emphasized the lateral rules and relationships created by marriage, but paid less attention to the 'vertical' relations between a parental generation and their offspring and the way these may be systematically patterned over time. The tetradic model specifies minimal distinctions made both laterally and vertically between categories of immediate kin, which can at one and the same time specify the complementary parts of the social world – perhaps a small one, but perhaps also extendable in its application to neighbours and strangers, as is typical of those Australian marriage-class systems that echo the tetradic model most closely. In Part II I highlight an analogous mode of specifying alternating birth classes as the complementary, mutually life-giving categories of people in a society, a patterning that is widespread in northeastern and eastern Africa but has received little attention.

The key point lies, to a great extent, in language. Social anthropologists keep emphasizing that the kin terminologies we know from ethnographic research are connected to a particular imagined view of society as a whole, just as all language depends for significance on underlying grammar. That underlying grammar, arguably, never matches the genetic grid as defined by scientists (Fox 1967; Parkin 1997). Kin terms used in real life can actually mask the distribution of genetic relationships more than they reveal them. And yet they are not as arbitrary, optional, and malleable as might be thought by cultural relativists today – there are some remarkably persistent features, which do relate, for example, to the cross/parallel distinction that so often contradicts the biological view of relatedness (Godelier et al. 1998). This is a slightly different point from Dunbar's claim below that kin terminologies are not randomly related to the genetic matrix. While it could be argued that the detail of cultural terms for relatives does not matter to the biologist, the strategic way that kin terminologies distribute persons around the mating networks is surely important for understanding what will constitute the future population and its characteristics. These terminologies do not simply describe relatedness; it is much more helpful to think of them, at least comparatively, as mapping out the field of potential mates – in a 'story-telling' sort of way, thus trying to design the future.

Expansion from Africa:
Theories and Notes of Caution

We open this volume with two chapters by archaeologists, both seeking to throw light on the successive migrations of species of *Homo* from Africa. Special attention is paid to the preconditions that must have been in place before it was feasible for *Homo sapiens* to become dominant in Africa and then apparently expand to colonize the whole globe, at an unprecedented speed. Clive Gamble's speculations on the material contexts which fostered the growing human capacity for abstract and hierarchically organized thought are followed by John Gowlett's scanning of the hard evidence for this and many preceding periods. Spatial patterns in the material record are shown to indicate that the story of human sociality, perhaps including what the social anthropologists think of as 'intentionally organized kinship', may go very much farther back in time than previously thought.

Clive Gamble opens his chapter with the provocative question as to whether Neanderthals used to marry. We cannot actually answer this question; but by posing it, Gamble opens up some issues very sharply. Even if they had a statistical and biologically based tendency towards 'pair-bonding', would it be appropriate to call it marriage? Who would be marrying whom? Could the older generation perhaps have controlled the sexuality and fertility of their girls – and perhaps their young men too – through imposing requirements and rituals of initiation leading to approved adulthood, sanctioned 'marriage', and thus social, as distinct from biological, reproduction?

Gamble does emphasize the crucial changes in human capacity that must have occurred before the major migration of *Homo sapiens* out of Africa to settle across the world. Many archaeologists have previously spoken of the farming revolution of some 10,000 years ago as the major watershed to modernity for our ancestors. However, recently a few have emphasized the artistic achievements in various parts of the world that are dateable to around 40–50,000 years ago, and we now know that artistic activity can be put back beyond 80,000 years ago, as a result of the finds at Blombos cave on the South

African coast (Henshilwood et al. 2001). Farming may have had little to do with the full flowering of the modern human mind. If it is meaningful to posit a point at which we can say with confidence that *here* were human beings like ourselves, we know that Gamble would see such a revolutionary turning point as predating Blombos. As an alternative to any sudden revolution, however, he reflected at our original workshop on the long run-up there might have been to human 'modernity' – a creative period of 'sapiens-hood' or 'sap-hood', for short, in which elements of the final picture were coming into play piecemeal.

Gamble's chapter considers features in the material record from a number of angles, which might at first seem tangential to his opening question about Neanderthal marriage, but converge towards a striking picture of what the material culture record can suggest about early human society, or, indeed, the dynamics of 'sociality'. Specifically, for example, at some point in early history, ancestral populations moved on from using sticks and stones as instruments, and began to use material containers, something which the other primates are not known to do. Long before pottery began to appear in the archaeological record, containers would surely have been made from calabashes or coconut shells, from animal horns or skins, or leaves. To be able to use containers, to transport water, or food, or to carry infants, would enormously improve mobility – not to mention the later manufacture of boats. Moreover, the *idea* of the container, even more than the stick as an extension of the arm, lends itself to extended metaphor: not only to houses, or graves, where individual people are grouped and contained; but to dance and performance spaces; to the social circle of the hearth; and perhaps to more abstract concepts of people grouped by gender, 'kin', or generation, or attachment to certain strong leaders, by craft specialisms, or to special places. Groups and categories could even be marked as such through material or embodied symbolism, even before they were articulated and elaborated in language. Gamble's discussion thus outlines several imaginative ideas and possible scenarios for early human history. Would it not have been absolutely necessary for such features of our collective life, enabling shared understandings to survive over time and distance, to have been in place before we could become a diasporic species able to extend a network of connections over the globe?

Gamble has recently pursued a range of linked suggestions about the way that early material culture, including the making of hand-axes for example, entails the breaking up of natural materials and their re-arrangement, or wrapping in a new form (Gamble 2007). It is of course when archaeologists recognize that materials have been broken and reassembled that they know they are confronting human action. The actions of the hands and eyes in *breaking* and *re-making* objects from the materials of stone, wood, and so on, lead beyond utility and directly into the sphere of art. And could we take these insights a little further, perhaps also into the sphere of *design* in the making and marking of social relations, especially the embodied relations of sex and childbirth? One point to remember about human kinship patterns is that they are highly selective. From a 'biological' point of view, there is a re-arrangement of parts – some relationships from the biological matrix are picked out and given peculiar emphasis while others are discounted or seen as qualitatively different. As already mentioned, some systems, discussed in Nick Allen's chapter below and also my own, include the categorical separation of mother and offspring into permanently different, labelled elements of social arrangement beyond the domestic setting, to which they belong by birth or initiation. The parental link, which might appear the primary, and overriding, element of 'social' belonging, is here cut across by a wider set of linkages which organize the relationships of a much larger range of individuals, including not only prohibited sexual partners but also those explicitly available. What is being 'reproduced' here is perhaps qualitatively different from what might have been expected in a primate group.

While it is the case that we are looking for a qualitative change in the way that early communities reproduced themselves, a change linked with greater sophistication of modes of communication, it is impossible (at least on present evidence) to point to a single moment of transition, a particular defining revolution – a 'red bar' across the evolutionary curve. John Gowlett shows how difficult it is to trace patterns in the ancient material record, while arguing that pattern recognition 'above the individual level' is crucial in interpreting our remote past. Nevertheless, clues to an organized patterning of social activity, beyond what other living primates today could achieve, can be found at extremely early dates. These clues include, for example, traces of the early control of fire; the concentration of population at 'home bases'; and patterns in the spatial distribution of artefacts, suggesting transport from the source of raw materials to production sites and on through trading routes. In discussion at the original workshop, the important point emerged that while some patterns on the ground were the unintended fallout from human or even animal movements, others were the result of 'propositions', deliberate differentiation and ordering. The first would constitute zones of related phenomena, perhaps linked to mobility, while the latter would indicate distinctions created in specific sites or areas, for example through the spatial arrangement of objects, or apparent sorting based on size, colour, shape, technique, etc.

Gowlett emphasizes how fragile the evidence is, and uncertain in many cases, but nevertheless suggests in his chapter that there is evidence for patterned activity in concentrated sites from very early dates, preceding the emergence of anatomically modern humans. He discusses tentative models for interpreting patterns of movement and concentration, corresponding to the three major eras since stone artefacts first appear in the record. At about 2.6 million years ago, this evidence of early toolmakers adds a new dimension to the concept of a lived-in landscape. Gowlett points out that the beginnings of an 'economy' of manufacture and exchange might even here have implications for the emergence of the kind of reciprocities we assume go with social kinship. He also reminds us that the emergence of the concept of a home base near water, for which there is good evidence even at this early time, has a direct bearing on group organization. There is, moreover, recent evidence of a small-brained species of *Homo* who spread far across the Old World by 1.7 million years ago, pre-dating the classic era of *Homo erectus* of approximately 1.5–0.5 million years ago. *Homo erectus* not only followed the earlier out-migration from

Africa, but may well have acquired the 'hardware' for language, and certainly manufactured artefacts of a rule-governed kind, which themselves were transported over long distances and accumulated in favoured spots. Meat and fuel for fire was also transported in the later *erectus* period, as indicated by sites in several parts of Africa and Europe, and there was clearly collaborative effort, even a division of labour, as exemplified by the large fires and use of saplings for spear-making at Schöningen, 400,000 years ago. Modernity may have developed piecemeal over several hundred thousand years; it would be misleading, Gowlett suggests, to see the emergence of anatomically modern humans – perhaps from two hundred thousand years ago in Africa – as a sudden transition to the kind of social world we know today. Finely made blades had already appeared at sites in the Middle East and Kenya, while even our oft-demeaned Neanderthal predecessors in Europe had impressive skills, for example in hafting tools.

Gowlett shows how much we can immediately recognize as evidence of activity by people like ourselves, even in the remote past. Our 'modernity' in this sense may be older than we have assumed. On this basis, we should presumably be delighted but not astonished by the finds at Blombos; we might expect to find more evidence in due course of fully recognizable 'art' (and perhaps developed language?) from even much further back. What we know of art can be positively seen in material finds like this, but art as performance can only be inferred; Clive Gamble evokes here, as he has done in earlier works (1999, 2007), the image of a site of population concentration – such as a hearth or a settlement centre – as a sort of social arena, a stage for performances of some kind. Perhaps regular social gatherings, especially around the light of the evening fire, could have stimulated the development of all kinds of coded communication. But who were the people who tended to gather and re-gather at the old-style hearths or home bases, and who would have been the likely core residents, even the custodians, of such places?

'Home Bases': From Female Coalitions to Matrifocality

Older imagery of the prehistoric home base has tended to take for granted a domestic picture of 'Man the Hunter' who brings home meat for his mate and her offspring, as a kind of individual mummy-and-daddy exchange underlying pair-bonding. But recent discussion has focused more on the *sharing out* of meat, and even vegetable foods as they are prepared for meals. The core community of a home base would, moreover, be likely to consist of females, and a more transitory population of males, whether mates or offspring. This vision, and the hard evidence for assuming a key role for female coalitions in early human history, is presented in the chapter by Kit Opie and Camilla Power. A mother living in a female coalition would co-opt her 'sisters' and the child's 'grandmothers' into the care of infants, while the home-coming hunter would probably not only provide for his 'own family' – if this concept had a place at all – but contribute to a generally shared pool of food and other resources. This more collective image of an early community (though its dating is an open question) is compatible with evolutionary theories as to the reasons why modern women tend to outlive their biological fertility; there is an obvious evolutionary advantage to having grandmothers around for the increased years of care that human infants with their growing brain size but physical vulnerability have demanded. It is also compatible with some of the elaborate models worked out by Knight and Power (for example, Knight 1991; Power 1999) for the emergence of gender-based rituals as a crucial point in the invention of culture and symbolism generally.

Clare Holden, following in the path pioneered by Ruth Mace (1996), presented an argument at the original workshop for the persistence of matri-focality, and indeed the formalization of its principles as matriliny, in a comparative study of the Bantu-speaking regions of central and eastern Africa. She emphasized the continuing rationality of a matrifocal mode of social organization in the hoe-cultivating and foraging subsistence economies of the region, and supported earlier anthropological analysis indicating that the holding of cattle as family property tends to alter the strategic balance between the sides of a family, giving advantage to the principles of enhanced bridewealth transfers, patrilocal residence, and patrilineal grouping. While Laura Fortunato's chapter deals with a different part of the world, it also focuses on a region over which a particular language family has become dominant, in this case the enormous area of the Indo-European languages, and compares the long-term persistence of ways of representing gender relations, along with associated practices of wealth transfer at marriage. The principle of dowry, whereby wealth and property go with the bride, has proved strikingly robust in this language region, extending over large areas of Europe and the Indian subcontinent. Bride capture seems to have been the mode of marriage next in prestige in the Indo-European legal tradition, while the least prestigious mode was bridewealth transfer from the groom's side to the family of the bride (as we know it from so much of Africa). These cases, while focusing on relatively recent historical times, do illuminate the resilience of basic ideologies concerning gender and social reproduction within recognized language traditions, suggesting that these concerns lie very deep within the rather miscellaneous collection of practices and values that we tend to lump all together as 'culture'.

The Tetradic Model: and the Ethnographic Critique

Relative, and increasing, mobility of early human populations is a theme that underwrites all our chapters. We might suggest that whether mobility is a matter of individual dispersal, seasonal or longer-term patterns of fission and fusion of groups, or long-distance movement over years and generations which might imply intermittent or even permanent loss of contact between those who recognize each other, it is implicated in patterns of genetic and social reproduction. It is perhaps helpful to draw on imagery evoking a 'flow of life', not only over time but also over space. The setting up of mating patterns affecting the 'reproduction of life' would presumably have little consequence if limited to one proto-human hunting band but much greater consequence if they knitted together the future genetic fate of many small mobile groups. Given the global expansion of modern humans in particular, we have to think in terms not only of walking, or the use of boats, but of a 'flow of life' – a network of reproductive interconnections linking human groups over extending regions.

Biological scientists tend to think of a 'flow' of life on what Nick Allen below calls the 'vertical' axis, that is, from parent to child, child to grandchild, and so on. Social anthropologists focus more often on the 'horizontal' dimension, that is, how the mating link – whether marriage or some kind of concubinage or extra-marital affair – might have been set up in the first place, and what social or economic consequences might be entailed for the group-membership of the child. In Allen's 'tetradic' model, the biological 'flow of life' is cut through, re-arranged, and composed into a pattern of social reproduction which conceptualizes biological time as if it were an enduring alternation of complementary generations; but it has considerable capacity for lateral extension, spreading networks of connection between groups in the here and now, and no doubt implications for future patterns of biological inheritance. We are pointing here to the usefulness of the model not so much as a 'fixed' structure of a 'bounded' group, but, I would suggest, rather, as a set of emergent principles lending themselves to strategic deployment in the context of increasing mobility while enabling the development of a social whole, an ideology of connectedness with sets of 'others' over time and distance.

Current research on the mobility of group relations in the non-human primate world, and the patterns of both 'kin recognition' and 'fission and fusion' being studied in different species, does point to the special character of large periodic gatherings. Concepts of the 'social whole', and a scheme of agreed relations between its parts, might more plausibly be invented – and imposed? – at such times than during the seasons of dispersal when small bands live on their own, and deal all the time with known individuals. We recall Evans-Pritchard's seminal analysis of the Nuer system of 'segmentary' clans and lineages: these could proclaim common descent over a large geographical area when challenged, but at other times split into opposed factions emphasizing rival ancestors (Evans-Pritchard 1940). The idiom of 'descent' applied to enduring groups, and was not the same as personal kin networks traced out through parents, siblings, etc. (Evans-Pritchard 1951). The pattern of political fission and fusion echoed the smaller-scale movements of dry-season concentration at cattle camps (when the larger ceremonies were held) and wet-season dispersal. Such regular rhythms in human mobility have deep resonance with Durkheim's vision of the Australian corroboree. What environmental or demographic conditions in the remote past might have favoured large periodic gatherings? What advantages might accrue to groups who had discovered how to share regional resources on a basis other than violence between alpha males and the favouring of close genetic kin? Could it be that the invention of 'symbolic order' was part and parcel of the invention of political gameplaying beyond the face-to-face community, and beyond the welfare of the biologically closest of kin?

Allen himself does present his portrait of a 'tetradic' model in abstract and diagrammatic terms. We must remember that this model is put forward on the basis of a wide comparative study of the contemporary world's kin terminologies and related ideologies; it is not based on a study of today's hunter-gatherers. However, there are points at which we could attempt to relate the model to what are known from evolutionary and archaeological studies of the hunting-and-gathering conditions of life in early human times. For example, while Allen points out that the model would look the same whether from a male or female point of view, he himself explicitly starts from the point of view of a female ego and uses the device of individual genealogical specification to describe the system of categories. But as he points out, the model is at one and the same time 'sociocentric' as well as egocentric. It is probably helpful to concentrate on the likelihood that physical motherhood would be the only point of individual reference in the earliest systems; and that 'fathers' would be best understood under sociocentric categories. All the evidence one could assemble for the likely circumstances of a 'starting point' for human kinship indicates that we should not expect to find symmetry in relations between male and female, nor genealogical specification of individual fatherhood.

In the interests of further persuading the reader of the possible relevance of this model to the earliest era of 'deliberate' social organization, perhaps even before the full flowering of language, let us think about the following quite pragmatic scenario. Imagine first a localized community, whose core is an enduring female coalition – as we have seen this is very likely (a fairly common pattern among our fellow primates today). This small grouping does not live in isolation, but as one of several in a region, who have occasional contact (possibly on a seasonal basis). These are beginning to develop mutual links of 'exchange' with each other, perhaps of different foods or other material goods, including artefacts. Male adolescents disperse from the groups, go hunting (no doubt in their own groups), and use meat as a resource in seeking mates usually outside their natal group. Now, from the point of view of a female adult in this first group, how is her own community providing for its own continuity and security for the future? How can she keep her own daughter at home, where she already has the help of her ageing but still active mother, without the daughter simply being taken over by her own male partner? The daughter in this sense cannot just 'take the place' of her own mother. In some of the other primate cases, young females themselves disperse (as Lehmann describes), apparently in order to avoid the attentions of existing dominant males, including their own fathers. The role of long-lived grandmothers, already understood by the evolutionary scientists as perhaps crucial for the very survival of infants through a prolonged period of 'growing up', could also be a key to understanding how formal principles of ordering, even controlling, youth might have been invented. From our adult female's point of view, her mother and her children spend a lot of time at home together, even looking after each other, while she goes out foraging – when carrying large infants around is a real nuisance. When her own 'retirement' approaches, she will spend more time at the home base with her own grandchildren. It is easy to see how from a woman's point of view, her mother and her children who spend so much time together constitute a sort of category, different from herself and her own grandchildren. The grandmother may well play a role in monitoring the sex life of her growing charges.

In this scenario, we have posed a pragmatic, behavioural basis in which growingly clever, political, and imaginative early people might have tried out a more systematic set of practices, ordering not only the home community but its relations with others, incorporating into the 'exchange' principle a more organized way of 'dispersing' adolescents as appropriate mates to the neighbouring groups with whom they are already negotiating relationships. The home community already lends itself to a 'theory' of its own continuity through the cycle of replacement of the oldest generation not by its own offspring but by their grandchildren. A woman sees her children as 'replacing' her own mother and her cohort, as she herself will be replaced in due course by her grandchildren, over whose marriages she will no doubt have some say. Exchange between the communities will include the promotion of mating or 'marriage' between linked partner categories. Seasonal gatherings might well be the occasion for the performance of rituals which, in Allen's vision, were the scene in which crucial distinctions between categories of belonging, and the exchange relations between them, were set up as an abstract whole and signified through symbolism and embodied practice, such as dancing. The structure would not necessarily be realized as a whole in the intervals between these gatherings, when groups were fragmented and dispersed. My own effort in these paragraphs has been to propose a stronger link between the kind of overall structure that Allen proposes as formative of social kinship, and the pragmatic daily context of life in the smaller settings evoked by the archaeologists and palaeo-anthropologists – specifically, of home bases run by female coalitions. I think it also important that we visualize a hierarchy of nested levels at which 'groups' emerge as significant; the ceremonial emphasis upon overall structure would almost certainly be most prominent at the widest regional gatherings of the bands, but would be echoed in lesser ways down to the domestic level.

A further point has to be made in respect of the 'language' of kinship. It seems to me very unlikely that the earliest language of kinship was based on a *common understanding* of individual biological links and how they constituted the reproduction of the life of the community. A pragmatic scenario like that above would be consistent, however, with a common understanding based on the labelling of individuals, by everyone, according to the categories they 'obviously' belonged to – such as a generation set opposite to that of their mother, and thus the role they played, in the life and reproductive survival of the home community in its mutual dependence on others. This belonging of individuals to such publicly instituted categories, which could, as suggested, even have been pre-linguistic, is what is meant by a 'sociocentric' system. Within it, individuals might become increasingly differentiated by personal names, inter-personal relations as such, and more specific ways of theorizing and labelling inter-individual relations. It would seem a very strong possibility that pair-bonding or 'marriage' would stimulate more complex and 'genealogical' ways of reckoning relationship, through the concept of the 'individual father'. This concept, as distinct perhaps from 'individual pair-bonded mate', could scarcely have been part of the scene when the language of relationship first developed (again, see the chapters by Korstjens and by Lehmann for the problems associated with the determination of paternity in primate contexts, whether by zoologists or the animals themselves).

How far can we use modern hunter-gatherers as a guide to what might have been the earliest forms of human social organization? A large ethnographic literature has been produced since the mid-nineteenth century on such populations, especially in Australia and Oceania, parts of the Americas, and eastern and southern Africa, along with isolated pockets in Asia. There was a time when they were seen as direct descendants and representatives of the most 'primitive' forms. But their history, including linguistic and artistic history, has been as long as anyone else's (Wingfield 2005); they are 'our' contemporaries, and many of the modern hunter-gatherers have had to make their own accommodations with the spread of herders and farmers, quite apart from interacting with each other. Australia is the one continent where hunting and gathering was the only mode of subsistence until its 'discovery' by Europeans in the eighteenth century, hence acquiring its special place in anthropological speculation. Even there, however, what was discovered could be as well interpreted as a highly specialized set of social forms and practices elaborated after the original settlement of Australia as it could be evidence of the 'earliest' human times (and much of what the ethnography records was already a matter of memory by the time the anthropologists arrived). For various reasons, therefore, it is hazardous to regard today's hunter-gatherers as a direct guide to the reconstruction of the earliest ancestral periods of the beginnings of principles governing human language and ordered social life.

Robert Layton reminds us of the pragmatic individuality and fluidity of social relations which was a kind of disappointment to Lévi-Strauss when he arrived among the Nambikwara in the Amazon jungle, and this is something which he himself emphasizes for specific groups in Australia. Alan Barnard makes similar points for the Khoesan ('Bushmen') of southern Africa. But here we need to bear in mind three main points. First, there is no reason why a pragmatic kind of individual agency and 'labelling' of specific persons should not co-exist with an overall, sociocentric model of who is who. Second, the individuality of a person, or of an interpersonal 'relationship' term such as 'mother's brother', can only become significant in a *system* of distinctions, marking out other such persons from different viewpoints. It is difficult for us to imagine a pre-linguistic era in which such 'individuality' could begin to be elaborated, except as an outcome of an existing sociocentric way of labelling who people are: that is, to what part of a whole do they belong, as in, for example, the 'left-hand' or 'right-hand' generation moiety of a group. Although Barnard and Layton provide careful, evidence-based critiques of Allen's vision of the tetradic model as bearing on the kinship systems of the world today, with particular reference to various hunter-gatherer groups, we have to recognize that we are trying to ask questions which look back several hundred thousand years to times when our ancestors were just beginning to organize themselves effectively. We inevitably observe a kind of pragmatic individuality in the behaviour of our primate cousins. But does this translate directly into modern, social forms of individuality? Surely, Allen or James might reply, the first *social agreements* would have looked, rather, to significant *categories of belonging* as the basis of cooperation and the way these shaped behaviour. The organization of both sexual access and prolonged care for infants would have surely been part and parcel of that cooperative effort towards social reproduction, and some such forms would no doubt have been more successful than others, in the environmental and evolutionary senses.

Language, Human Movement, and Environment

Chris Ehret's chapter returns us specifically to Africa, and throws light on the importance of environmental factors and population mobility in understanding the way that the language families of the continent today have diverged from a fairly restricted area of what we know as the southeastern part of the Sahara where it adjoins the Ethiopian highlands. The expansion of the proto-languages of today's Nilo-Saharan, Afroasiatic, Niger-Kordofanian, and Khoesan groupings from here can be placed some 15,000 years ago. There had previously been a concentration of population in this relatively well-watered region of varied topography following the long dry period of the last glacial maximum from 21,000 years ago, when speakers of more ancient (and now unknown) languages may have retreated there. When improvements in the climate followed with the post-glacial amelioration, there was an increase and expansion of population, and those groups who were the most successful in taking advantage of the new opportunities spread out to re-populate many parts of the continent, taking with them the 'new' languages and some cultural ideas. The evidence for this scenario comes from the detailed working out of word correspondences, revealing both ancestral proto-terms and borrowing, within today's language families, and where he has available evidence, Ehret indicates some convincing histories of continuity in kin terms. He takes a rather different view from Allen in suggesting that primary terms of concrete reference for immediate 'family' later get extended to other kin, but admits that there is room for other ways of looking at this question, and that 'contraction' of specific reference can occur as well as 'extension'.

Although Ehret is not able to use his forensic tools to penetrate much beyond the major linguistic re-population of the continent from around 15,000 years ago, his methods and his findings help us formulate some good questions about earlier periods. Can we correlate the migration of modern humans out of Africa, from around 60,000 years ago, with a similar climatic cycle favouring first concentration, and then dispersal, of population groups – especially the 'successful' ones? Can Ehret's methods be pushed just a little further back in the hope of finding traces of those languages spoken before his four identified proto-languages? Since the Blombos cave discoveries, it has become a fascinating question to ponder what language or languages were spoken by their makers; not to mention what context of inter-community trading, group identities, personal adornment, and rites of passage, including initiation and marriage, might be inferred from this material record. The kind of questions discussed in this book certainly look back 'beyond Blombos', to those periods of time when as yet we still have to depend on imaginative modelling and indirect inference.

Alan Barnard offers one way of approaching this. Pointing out that nobody lives in 'half a kinship system', he rejects any idea of a creeping gradualism in the evolutionary build-up to the social life of *Homo sapiens*. He equally rejects the idea of a sudden major change. (Though no contributors would insist on this, Nick Allen does emphasize the balanced character of the tetradic model as an encompassing scheme likely to have been 'invented' as a whole, probably in large ceremonial gatherings.) Barnard, like Layton, extremely familiar from his own fieldwork with modern hunter-gatherers, proposes a kind of compromise, a sequence of distinct stages in the emergence of kinship 'systems', analogous to the three stages of Calvin and Bickerton's proposed stages in the emergence of language. The third of these would correspond to the appearance of 'elementary structures' of the Lévi-Straussian kind, which, of course, do 'exist' ethnographically. Barnard brackets the 'tetradic' model with these, though Allen's model addresses periods long before modern ethnographic evidence, which for him reflects only surviving, unfolding, and fragmentary elements of what had perhaps once been whole. Barnard and Allen agree, however, on the general dismantling of holistic systems in relatively recent historical times – at least in Europe. For the reconstruction of long-term world history, we still depend crucially on the evidence of comparative ethnography.

Conclusion

Our project started from an acceptance of the theory that increased population size in groups and contact between them was a factor in evolutionary selection for increased brain size in human ancestors. It goes on to ask 'who', in a social sense recognizable to us, even in a 'public' sense at the time, the members of such population groups were. As a minimum principle, the biological differences of sex and age would surely be elaborated in the processes of 'home'-making, coalition forming, production, sharing, and interchange. This returns us to older anthropological thinking on the topic of 'kinship' as reflected in the classic ethnography, literature in which general organizing principles of 'consanguinity and affinity' take priority over the somewhat restricted model of the nuclear family. Here we have taken as a working definition of what we mean by 'social kinship' the setting up of categories of relatedness, on the basis of which people engage mutually in a range of activities, both economic and 'symbolic' – but categories resting on the concept of the fertility of successive generations, crucially including a framework of approved and prohibited mating links into which newborn persons are accommodated. It is not necessarily a question of who paired with or gave birth to whom, but a general schema of reproductive logic. Cooperation, 'belonging', and productive labour within any human group are differentiated according to a dialectic of gender and generation in this sense (cf. James 2003: 156–80). Schemes of social kinship of increasing range, which might facilitate exchange relations with seasonally encountered others, would surely have been an 'advantage', whether in evolutionary or historical terms. They would also shape the way genetic characteristics were subsequently transmitted or selected for, as all invented games of human sociality have since impinged on biological processes.

Of course all speculation on the remote human past is a kind of myth-making, the telling of a story; but all history, all science, has an aspect of myth about it, and for this we need not apologize. The rapidly developing biological sciences of today have certainly produced a range of new evidence concerning our ancestry and our relation to the other primates. But as Hilary Callan argues in the Epilogue to this book, as she argued in a pioneering study many years ago (Callan 1970), the social sciences also have a useful toolkit to probe that past and to assist in the interpretation of that evidence. The topic of 'kinship' in reconstructing models of early human society is as central now as it ever has been in the history of debates in anthropology.

Acknowledgements

In revising this introduction I have depended on advice and input from my fellow editors, for which I am very grateful. At the same time, while we share a broad area of agreement over the main issues, they should not be expected to stand by everything said here.

A Brief Overview of Human Evolution

John A. J. Gowlett and Robin Dunbar

Early hominids began to appear in the Late Miocene (before 5.5 million years ago – in current abbreviation, 5.5 Ma), and flourished through the Pliocene (5.5–1.8 Ma). Somewhat confusingly, the Quaternary epoch – the period of dramatic ice ages, humans, and mammoths – begins at 2.6 Ma and runs through to the present day. It thus starts earlier than the Pleistocene period, which runs from 1.8 to 10,000 years ago (hence the frequent use of Plio-Pleistocene as a bridging term). Early Pleistocene is 1.8–0.78 Ma, Middle Pleistocene 0.78–0.125 Ma, and Late Pleistocene 125,000–10,000 years ago. Climatically speaking, the Miocene and Pliocene were predominantly warm and wet, with conditions being drier and more unstable during the Pleistocene. The great period of ice ages during the Middle and Late Pleistocene witnessed alternating intervals of relatively ice-free and ice-bound conditions on an approximately 100,000-year cycle. The last ice age (which began 80,000 years ago) came to an abrupt end around 10,000 years ago, when the massive ice sheets that covered the northern and southern hemispheres melted, causing sea levels to rise by about 120 m. The present Holocene warm period represents the early part of a warm interglacial which will eventually end in a new ice age.

The earliest known hominids are represented by three poorly known genera (*Sahelanthropus*, *Orrorin*, and *Ardipithecus*) from central and East Africa. By 4 Ma, however, we find a rapidly diversifying range of species, all of whom can comfortably be included in the genus *Australopithecus*. The best known of these are *Australopithecus afarensis* from East Africa and *A. africanus* from southern Africa. The period between 4 and 2 Ma finds the genus diversifying into a number of species and lineages, culminating in two major branches by about 2.5 Ma: the robust australopithecines (*A. robustus*, *A. boisei*, sometimes assigned to a separate genus as *Paranthropus*) and the earliest members of our own genus, *Homo*. The very earliest members of the latter lineage, the species *habilis* and *rudolfensis*, are shown in Figure 0.1 as falling within *Australopithecus*, although some taxonomies place them within the genus *Homo*. The diverse range of australopithecine species during the later period is especially noteworthy.

The appearance of the first true members of the genus *Homo* (*H. erectus* – some of the earlier African populations may also be referred to as *H. ergaster*)

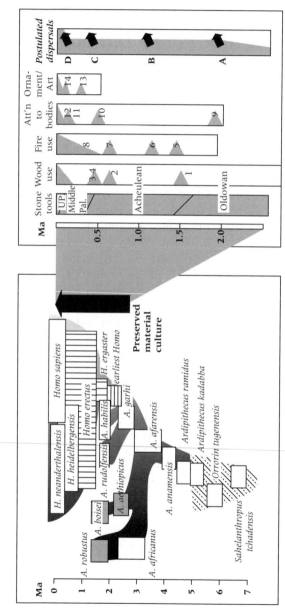

Figure 0.1 Overview of human evolution (© John A. J. Gowlett)

Key: The Material Record from 2.6 Ma (see enlarged diagram on right-hand side)

Wood use

1 Wear traces attributed to wood on stone tools, Koobi Fora: wood phytoliths on hand-axes, Peninj.
2 Polished plank at Gesher Benot Ya'akov, Israel.
3 Schöningen spears, Germany.
4 Kalambo Falls digging sticks, Zambia.

Fire use

5 Burnt patches/baked clay at Koobi Fora, Chesowanja, East Africa.
6 Burnt bone, Swartkrans, S. Africa, Taman Peninsula, Black Sea.
7 Hearths, Gesher Benot Ya'akov, Israel.
8 Hearths, Schöningen, Germany, Beeches Pit, UK.

Attention to bodies

9 Cutmarks on cranium from Swartkrans, S. Africa.
10 Cutmarks indicating cranial defleshing, Bodo, Ethiopia: deposition of bodies at Atapuerca, Spain.
11 Cutting and reshaping of skull at Herto, Ethiopia.
12 Burials, Es Skhul, Israel, c. 130,000 years ago.

Ornament/art

13 Berekhet Ram 'figurine', Israel.
14 Pierced shell beads, Es Skhul, 130,000 years ago.

around 2 Ma marked a sea-change in hominid evolution. Although the more robust *Paranthropus* lineages continued to survive in Africa for some time, the rapid geographical expansion of early *H. erectus* in Africa and its migration out of Africa across the Old World as far as China and what are now the Indonesian islands (then attached to the Indo-China mainland) introduced a new phase of hominid evolution based on a larger body, a larger brain, and a skeletal framework designed for striding travel over long distances.

   H. erectus proved to be an extremely successful and long-lived taxon that maintained a reasonable degree of anatomical uniformity across very large geographical distances and over a very long time period (about 1.5 million years), although taxonomists sometimes distinguish among the various subpopulations (*H. antecessor* in Spain, *H. georgicus* in Georgia). Indeed, in eastern Asia, *H. erectus* survived until as recently as 60,000 years ago, with some isolated island populations apparently surviving until as recently as 12,000 years ago. However, about 500,000 years ago, a new, larger brained species arose from the African *erectus* root and is now usually referred to as *Homo heidelbergensis* in Europe; similar African specimens may well represent the very first signs of *Homo sapiens*. These new appearances represent the first fully human species, with much enlarged brains and a generally lighter body build. These archaic humans (as they are generally named) gave rise to two new lineages: Neanderthals (*H. neanderthalensis*) in Europe (from around 300,000 years ago) and the much more gracile anatomically modern humans (*H. sapiens*) in Africa (from around 200,000 years ago). We now know from the genetic evidence that these two lineages were not directly related to each other, but rather sister species.

   The Neanderthals were an extremely successful lineage, occupying the whole of Europe and western Asia for the better part of 300,000 years, finally dying out as recently as 28,000 years ago. In contrast, the later lineage of anatomically modern humans blossomed in Africa, gradually displacing all later *erectus* populations. Around 60,000 years ago (but possibly as early as 130,000 years ago), they emerged out of Africa and spread rapidly along the coastal margins of southern Asia, reaching Australia soon after 60,000 years ago. The Neanderthals appear to have blocked their entry into Europe until about 40,000 years ago, when they entered Europe from the east. With the demise of the last Neanderthals around 28,000 years ago, the world stage was largely cleared for complete domination by *H. sapiens*.

   A terminological note. We here use the term 'hominid' for all members of the broad lineage leading to modern humans after the split from the great apes (i.e. the genera *Australopithecus* and *Homo* and their allies). Recently, some authorities have argued that the term 'hominid' should be extended to include the great apes, suggesting the term 'hominin' for the members of the human (as opposed to great ape) lineage. There is no current agreement on which usage is correct.

The Dispersals Out of Africa

There are four commonly postulated dispersals out of Africa by hominids, whose timings are indicated on the right-hand side of Figure 0.1 by the letters A–D.

A   The original Out of Africa dispersal by *Homo erectus* around two million years ago, demonstrated by findspots such as Dmanisi in Georgia, and the Nihewan Basin in China, both with finds dating to c. 1.7 Ma.
B   Possible expansion into Europe and other movements by *Homo erectus* populations around one million years ago.
C   Further dispersals before half a million years ago, leading to replacement of *Homo erectus* by more modern humans (e.g. *Homo heidelbergensis*) in most areas, and possibly to the occurrence of Acheulean hand-axes in new areas.
D   The final Out of Africa movement by early anatomically modern humans (AMHs, *Homo sapiens*), variously dated between 130,000 and 60,000 years ago, culminating in expansion through Neanderthal territories c. 50,000–25,000 years ago.

The Material Record

The earliest tools (usually based on cobbles worked to produce flakes and core-tools such as choppers) appear for the first time around 2.6 Ma in the African fossil record. Probably made by *A. habilis* and other late gracile australopithecines, they are usually referred to as the Oldowan industry. Around 1.5 Ma, this was replaced by the appearance of larger, more finely crafted hand-axes – the Acheulean tradition. Acheulean hand-axes remained remarkably consistent in size and shape for the better part of a million years over an immense geographical range in Africa and Eurasia. The use and control of fire appears at some time during the later part of this phase.

The appearance of archaic humans around 0.5 Ma coincides with significant changes in tool type and manufacture, with a much wider range of tool types as well as manufacturing designs (the Middle Palaeolithic including the Mousterian of Eurasia). Here, we find the first preserved evidence for the use of wood (e.g. thrusting spears) and bone/antler in tools. But the main emphasis is still very much on functional tools used in food capture and preparation. The appearance of anatomically modern humans after about 200,000 years ago witnessed a rapid cultural explosion associated with what, in Europe from about 40,000 years ago, has come to be known as the Upper Palaeolithic revolution. Not only do we now find a massive increase in the range of tool types (burins, projectile points, awls), but we also find new functional categories such as punches and pins, as well as purely decorative artefacts (beads in strings or stitched in quantities on garments, figurines, and even toys). There is a concomitant change in the fineness and quality of the workmanship, with many of the items requiring long hours of dedicated work. There is also evidence of extensive use of ochre, probably in body decoration (in Africa, from at least as early as 100,000 years ago). From about 28,000 years ago in Europe, there is evidence of multiple burials (decorated bodies, often accompanied by grave goods of one kind or another) and, of course, the famous cave paintings (best known from the well-preserved examples of France and Spain).

We show these broad patterns on the enlarged timeline on the right-hand side of Figure 0.1. Isolated early instances often precede the mass of evidence, of course.

Part I

Where and When

The Archaeological Evidence for
Early Social Life in Africa

Rustic Wedding: Pieter Brueghel the Younger, c. 1600 (Getty Images). A puzzled scholar (in black) looks on at the festivities.

1

Kinship and Material Culture
Archaeological Implications of the Human Global Diaspora

Clive Gamble

Did Neanderthals marry? Did they possess avoidance rules and did they recognize inter-personal relationships, both vertically (descent) and horizontally (generation), that form the axes for kinship? The questions are more interesting than just speculating about the time-depth of human institutions. They raise the issue of how recognition and possession of rules and relationships might have occurred when opinion is still divided about the antiquity both of spoken language and of the symbolic codes that organized social life and its cultural transmission.

Currently it is much easier to argue that Neanderthals did not marry because we can then analyse them through links to wider systems of animal kinship. Here the language of the genes speaks volumes, at least in the mathematical demonstration of mate choice and sacrifice for close kin, but at the expense of socio-cultural phenomena such as symbolism. Anthropologists have generally resisted such approaches, arguing that kinship is culturally constructed and only in the blood because consanguinity is a cultural rather than biological concept. Kinship is about the setting up of categories of relatedness through mutually structured activities, both economic and 'symbolic', but, as James explains in the introduction above, 'crucially including a framework of approved and prohibited mating links into which newborn persons are accommodated' (p. 40). Incest taboos, for example, are less to do with preserving the integrity of the gene pool than starting at home with the principle of exogamy enunciated so clearly by Tylor, long before genetics was formalized, as 'marry out or die out'. Marriage is about social and economic relationships and kinship has to be reckoned accordingly. The importance of marriage lies less in the gaining of a wife than, as Mead (1935: 84) pointed out some seventy years ago, in the gaining of a brother-in-law. The recruitment of affines to alliances, both social and economic, is central to the process.

My purpose in this chapter is to raise interdisciplinary issues rather than provide an origins account of marriage and kinship rules. My vehicle is the social brain hypothesis (Dunbar 1998, 2003), which suggests our social lives drove our evolutionary history as recorded both anatomically and culturally. The context in which this hypothesis is evaluated is the archaeological evidence for our emergence as a global species, which began some 60,000 years ago (Gamble 1993), associated with a recent Africa origin (Stringer and Mackie 1996). I will argue that this global human diaspora, which occurred late in human evolution, needed specifically human kinship as much as it required boats to get to Australia and the scattered islands of the Pacific. But I will also suggest that kinship structures, such as Allen's tetradic model (1998a; this volume), followed on from a gradual change over two and a half million years in the metaphorical use of material culture to express relationships and concepts grounded in the experiences of the body.

Kinship 'as-we-understand-it' was not the product of some revolution in human prehistory that produced either a Palaeolithic modern human (Klein 2000; Mellars and Stringer 1989) or, much later, a Neolithic farmer with a modern mind (Renfrew 1996; Watkins 2004). Instead, kinship emerged as a mode of establishing relatedness within the framework of a technology which was always social. Moreover, a different material basis for human identity, based on this social technology and eventually expressed as kinship, came to be recognized along a slow gradient of change.

Biological Kinship Is Not Kinship

Genealogy and kinship are currently in vogue thanks to routine Y chromosome (male-only inheritance) and mtDNA (female-only inheritance) testing to establish patterns of relatedness (*http://www.oxfordancestors.com/*), and to the Internet, which creates virtual sisterhoods and brotherhoods based on shared haplotypes. Such genetic kinship, as Nash (2004: 2) has shown, combines the security of the known and the excitement of the new. The result has been the geneticization of identity and the reduction of relatedness to a lottery of four letters, CGAT, so that 'genes are cast as keys to the essence of humanity in general and the uniqueness of each individual' (Nash 2004: 4). Our biological essence, as examined by Jones (1997), appeals to a primordial, ethnic identity contained 'in the blood' now supplemented by a genome that, we learn, 'underlies the fundamental unity of all members of the human family. . . . In a symbolic sense, it is *the heritage of humanity*' (UNESCO 1997: Article 1, emphasis added). According to Nash, this process of naturalization has been achieved by using the idiom of kinship and its components: generation, reproduction, ancestry, descent, offspring, maternity, paternity, and inheritance (2004: 25).

However, Marks reminds us that

> As anthropologists have known all along, kinship is constructed. . . . So in a literal, natural sense, relatedness is just a mathematical abstraction. It has no real, bracketable biological properties. In a cultural, meaningful sense, kinship is a way of defining social networks, establishing obligations, and organizing the transmission of property across generations. (2002: 251)

Ancestors who are invoked solely through genetic relatedness do not therefore represent a biologically determined, rather than a culturally constructed, kinship. The human genome may be a concept that we all share, but it does not relate us to each other through categories of kinship that social anthropologists such as Marks would recognize. However, his declaration that 'kinship is not a genetic property' (2002: 251) clearly goes too far. Kinship does have both biological and cultural aspects, and it is not possible to eliminate the difference between them. The problem, as Allen states (pers. comm.), is that kinship straddles the gap.

As a result, archaeologists cannot assume the existence of social kinship systems even though early hominins must have possessed genes and therefore biological kinship. But if we are looking for the thread of continuity from our earliest ancestors to the present, it will not be genes that establish such relationships, but rather the existence of a framework provided by socially based technologies that have consistently been used to manufacture relationships. These social technologies (Gamble 1999: 80–7; 2007) have ranged in sophistication from the workshops of the earliest stone tools, 2.5 million years ago (Semaw et al. 1997; Stout et al. 2005) to the workstations of the Internet. Consequently, human agency has always been implicated in networks of materiality through which categories of relatedness are revealed (Gell 1998; Knappett 2005). Kinship and material culture have therefore developed together.

Two Revolutions But No Kinship

But such hybrid networks are not usually part of human origins research. Here our evolving human endowment of genes, cognition, and culture is currently debated by archaeologists in terms of either a 'human revolution' that occurred sometime in the last 300,000 years, but with strong support for 40,000 years ago from the European evidence (Mellars 2005), or a 'Neolithic revolution' co-incident with farming at the beginning of the Holocene (Gamble 2007). At issue is the understanding of when we became human. Supporters of a Neolithic revolution point to the much earlier appearance during the Palaeolithic of art, burials, language, and rituals and ask why, once these gifts had been acquired, did it take upwards of 30,000 years for anything decisive to happen (Cauvin 2000; Renfrew 2001: 127)? By 'decisive', they are referring to the cultural advances brought about by a sedentary life and the added richness and complexity of symbols that then flowed. Indeed, they argue for the importance of a sedentary revolution that predated, by a few millennia, the appearance of domesticated crops and animals in Southwest Asia (Bar-Yosef 2001; Rocek and Bar-Yosef 1998). Watkins, for example, concludes from his survey of the built environment of these early mud-brick and stone villages that 'the world's earliest village communities were also the first to develop fully modern minds and a fully symbolic culture' (2004: 19). If such an extreme view was accepted, it would mean that Australian Aboriginal cultures were not 'fully symbolic' just because they were predominantly mobile hunters and gatherers.

Set against this view that settled life and agriculture made us who we are is the human, or symbolic, revolution (Bar-Yosef 2002; Klein 1995, 2000; Mellars 1994; Mellars and Stringer 1989). When judged by the long sweep of human evolution, this is a statement about human recency (Proctor 2003) that marries modern anatomy (Stringer and Andrews 1988), including genetic data, with archaeological evidence for symboling: colour choice, art, ornament, burials, and long-distance exchange (Barham 1998; Knight 1991; Roebroeks et al. 1988; White 1997). This novel cultural package was first identified in Europe, where incoming populations of Cro-Magnons replaced the resident Neanderthals (Stringer and Gamble 1993: Figure 74).

There have, however, been recent criticisms by those working in Africa (Deacon and Deacon 1999; Henshilwood and Marean 2003; McBrearty and Brooks 2000; Wadley 2001) of the significance of the European Upper Palaeolithic revolution. The evidence is compelling for much earlier instances of artefacts and sites that point to symbolic and ritual activity that is regarded as a hallmark of the modern mind (d'Errico et al. 2003). However, both groups of Palaeolithic archaeologists are united in their opposition to the notion that we became human during the Neolithic. They would therefore refute Renfrew's (1996) 'sapient paradox', which broadly translates in material terms as 'all dressed up but going nowhere for 30,000 years'. As Mellars (1990: 246) has remarked in a comparable context, the sapient paradox could equally be applied to the millennia of the Neolithic because metallurgy and writing only appeared much later during the Bronze Age.

Kinship rarely figures in discussions of either the human or the Neolithic revolution. It is not a symbolic category structuring social life that archaeologists regard as either amenable to investigation through the material evidence, or significant for understanding change in these early periods. However, along with language and symbolic representation, they would assume, if pressed, that kinship of a kind we would recognize as such did exist as soon as one or other of these revolutions ushered in the modern mind (Mithen 1996; Watkins 2004).

It therefore seems that kinship, as defined by James (see above), will never figure prominently if the main debate continues to centre on which revolution produced people like ourselves. The closest archaeologists are likely to get is through investigating concepts such as family and household, summed up, for example, in Hodder's (1990: 294) invocation of *domus*, and asking where in the Neolithic, the house, hearth, and pot became material metaphors for the domestication of society.

A Diasporic Species and Social Extension

There is, however, an alternative narrative concerning the archaeology of human evolution which does make space for a consideration of kinship as establishing categories of relatedness. This narrative concerns our emergence as a diasporic species with a global distribution (Cavalli-Sforza and Cavalli-Sforza 1995). It is less concerned with issues either of where we first came from, although inescapably that was somewhere in Africa as revealed genetically (Cann et al. 1987) and chronologically (McDougall et al. 2005), or when we first settled down in Southwest Asia (Bar-Yosef 1998; Bar-Yosef and Belfer-Cohen 1989). Instead it challenges the way we conceive of ourselves and how we marshall the evidence of the past to support that view.

Cresswell (2006), for example, has pointed out that contemporary values prefer the city dweller to the nomad, the resident to the refugee, and the homeowner to the tramp. He summarizes these preferences as a sedentarist metaphysics that has a long history in Western ideology. Against this background it is therefore unsurprising that the sedentary revolution has been championed in human origins research. Childe (1942: 55), for example, spoke of agriculture as an 'escape from the impasse of savagery' precisely because it allowed a sedentary life, while Braidwood (1957 [1948]: 122) dismissed Palaeolithic hunting as a time when people lived 'just like an animal' because they were peripatetic. If culture is to develop, then mobility must be tamed, a view that lies at the heart of the supposed sapient paradox (Renfrew 2001).

However, with a powerful sedentarist metaphysics it is easy to forget the singular discovery of the Age of Exploration that the entire globe, save for a few islands and Antarctica, was already populated before its rediscovery by Europeans. Moreover, the subsequent demonstration by archaeologists that this occurred late in human prehistory (Gamble 1993), but often long before farmers sent down roots, is downplayed. For example, according to Renfrew (2001: 127), the diasporas of hunters and gatherers that peopled the globe are to be described as nothing more than adaptive radiations.

The interesting point about the varied mobilities on land and sea that started with a global human diaspora 60,000 years ago is that it was not an immediate consequence of either a modern-looking anatomy with a large brain, dated to between 190,000 to 160,000 years ago (Clark et al. 2003; McDougall et al. 2005; White et al. 2003), or even symbolic representations, as seen, for example, in the surface alteration and use of ochre 80,000 years ago at Blombos Cave, South Africa (Henshilwood et al. 2002). Both of these instances of innovation and change occurred when *Homo sapiens* was still an Old World species and, moreover, limited within it by latitude, altitude, sea level, and landmass size. Moreover, the geographical distribution of the genus *Homo* was essentially the same over almost two million years of local speciation and multiple dispersals out of Africa and back again (Dennell 1998, 2003; Gamble 2001; Lahr and Foley 1994; Rightmire 2001).

The evidence that human mobilities had changed 60,000 years ago begins with the appearance of people in the Pleistocene continent of Sahul (Australia, New Guinea, and Tasmania linked by low sea levels) (Roberts et al. 1990; Smith et al. 1993). The 60,000 years that followed represents about one per cent of the time since the hominin/chimp split calculated using the molecular clock (Jones et al. 1993), or three per cent since the appearance of the genus *Homo*. Yet in that time some three-quarters of the earth's surface was inhabited for the first time. This included not only Sahul but also the interior of Siberia, the Arctic, North and South America as well as the islands and archipelagos of the Indian and Pacific oceans (Gamble 1993). Furthermore, when people reached Australia, the evidence shows that they immediately settled the desert interiors at a time in the Pleistocene when the red centre was hyper-arid compared to today and population numbers were extremely low (Smith 1989, 2005).

The mobilities that resulted in a global diaspora were assisted by new social technologies, including boats to cross oceans and domestic animals to pull sleds across Siberia. But these innovations (Fagan 2004; Troeng 1993), if indeed they were such, cannot be the only answer to the particularities of the process, just as labelling it an adaptive radiation explains neither the timing nor the sequence of landfall.

The global human diaspora that began as an African exodus was instead made possible by the extension of social life that depended on concepts that related people when they were apart. Elsewhere (Gamble 1999) I have examined the process using ego-based networks that are differentiated in size (Table 1.1) by the variable use of three resources – emotional, material, and symbolic (Toren 1999: 111; Turner and Maryanski 1991) – for the negotiation of social relationships.

The point about the extended network is that it differentiates the human from the primate community by allowing a social life that is not dependent upon co-presence. Such immediate and usually frequent interaction is the hallmark of an individual's intimate and effective networks (Table 1.1), and, in the case of the former, accounts for their very small size and the intense relationships that are constructed. By contrast, the extended network represents a release from proximity (Gamble 1998; Rodseth et al. 1991). By this phrase I mean that human trait of distributing our social selves across time

Table 1.1 Interactions and networks

Ego-based network	Principal resource	Size	Sample descriptors of modal size
Intimate	Emotional affect	3–7	Support clique
			Significant others
			Nuclear family
Effective	Material exchange	10–23	Sympathy group
			Colleagues and friends
			Minimum band, local group, clan
Extended	Symbolic 'positive style'	100–400	Friends of friends
			Dialect tribe, connubium, maximum band
Global	Symbolic 'negative style'	2500	Non-significant 'Others'
			Linguistic family

Sample descriptors for small-world societies are taken from the hunter-gatherer literature. The modal group sizes have recently been re-examined (Zhou et al. 2004) and a discrete hierarchy of modular group sizes has been recognized. A scaling ratio of three has been identified between these levels, but as yet is not explained, although it is possibly related to the processing of social proximity by the human brain.
Source: After Gamble 1999: Table 2.8 with references

and space, and where extended absence, the essence of ocean voyaging, does not necessarily result in the collapse of an individual's social networks. Absence is not only tolerated but encouraged (Helms 1988), and is increasingly celebrated as a nomadic metaphysics (Cresswell 2006).

Extension, however, would not be possible without social categories that were agreed, understood, and enacted. We may consider these in simple terms as 'friend', 'enemy', and 'stranger', and such categories, and the concepts that underpinned them, defined the appropriate response for those arriving and for those meeting the arrivals. Burch (1975: 25) provides a vivid, if extreme, example from the Arctic – one where failure to establish a prior relationship, however fictitious, could result in death when parties of hunters met.

The human global diaspora required novel technologies to cross oceans and inhabit deserts. But they also needed social categories such as friend, enemy, and stranger to overcome the requirements of co-presence by stretching relationships in time and space. Therefore, both the innovations, such as boats, and the relationships that made dispersal an intentional project were threads in well-spun networks of what I referred to earlier as a social technology. As a result, there would have been no substantial geographical dispersal 60,000 years ago without technical innovation and no social extension without the appropriate categories that related people when apart. Consequently, the change to our becoming a global species would not have happened at this time unless both aspects were involved. It is this closely entwined cable of technology and social categories that raises the question of what part kinship played in the human global diaspora.

The Social Brain, Language and Kinship Categories

The categories of friend, enemy, and stranger are not kinship terms. They do not carry the additional symbolic associations that give us aunts, cousins, and brothers-in-law, and which persist as categories irrespective of any friendship or enmity that might be felt towards individuals classified by such terms. As a result, such kinship terms will not necessarily coincide, as might be expected, with either an individual's intimate or effective network (Table 1.1) if they require either no, or little, emotional and material capital for their definition. The difference lies between a bottom-up approach to social interaction, outlined in Table 1.1, and the top-down categories of kinship, where, for example, a tetradic structure *precedes* the individual. These approaches can be further distinguished, and also resolved, by recognizing that the resource-based networks depend on negotiation to determine membership while kinship structures are determined by rules of recruitment. Negotiation to form alliances and cliques is a primate trait, and hence ancestral, while formal recruitment to pre-existing categories is not.

So where do kinship categories and the concepts they depend upon come from? Fox (1967: 31), for example, regards gestation, impregnation, domination, and the avoidance of incest as basic to all social organization and the base onto which systems of ideology, concerning true and proper relationships, are grafted.

More satisfying is James's discussion of the language and logic of the reproductive game. Using an analogy of section systems as dance teams (following
Allen 1982), she makes the point that kinship categories are about recruitment through marriage and alliance (James 2003:159–60). Instead of either
conjugal families or descent groups providing an inflexible model of affiliation,
what exists are socially created teams of individual recruits. Moreover, it is
the distinction between parent and offspring that generates these independent
sections, or teams within each generation moiety. Such a recruitment model,
as Allen (1998a) shows, presents the individual with a number of restricted
choices because endogamous generation moieties reduce by half the choice of
socially sanctioned mates in a society. Furthermore, it suggests that social life
might once have been organized according to clear game-playing principles,
as exemplified in the performance of dance and other ceremonies that embody
exchange.

But while these models recognize performance, they also emphasize how
dependent kinship categories are on language. The position is well expressed
by James, Allen, and Callan (2005):

> The evidence strongly suggests that some specific rules of the kinship game based
> on give-and-take are very ancient. It is possible that kinship terminologies,
> reflecting such rules and patterns, may be rooted in the very beginnings of
> language. Out in those primeval forests, you need to be able to talk about your
> mother in law, and who your daughter might marry, as much as about the need
> to find more witchetty grubs.

It seems to make little difference if you are extolling either the propriety of
the incest taboo or the logic of cross-cousin marriage: it is not easy to imagine
how there could be social organization based on kinship without language
(though see the arguments of Barnard, and of Callan, in this volume). It is
undeniable that the variety of human social forms known today, across which
kinship systems provide a measure of both their diversity and regularity, is
reflected in linguistic form.

But how does this emphasis on language differ from the geneticization of
identity discussed above? If some anthropologists are so emphatic that 'kinship
is not a genetic property' (Marks 2002: 251), then what makes them so sure
that it is primarily a linguistic one? Kinship has many aspects: lexical, jural,
statistical, and behavioural. Which, if any of them, has primacy is relevant
only when questions are asked about origins (compare Allen and Barnard in
this volume, for example). As an archaeologist, I feel more comfortable with
the proposition that kinship was never simply linguistic or genetic in origin,
but also material.

The alternatives can be evaluated, rather than asserted from different disciplinary perspectives, by examining the timing of the 60,000-year-old human
global diaspora. Was such a recent date in human evolution dependent on
the late appearance of language (e.g. Noble and Davidson 1996) that produced
kinship categories which permitted social extension? Or were technological
innovations required to make geographical separation possible?

Table 1.2 Community size predictions and language outcomes

Age in millions of years	Representative taxon	Community size	Communication
<0.1	Modern humans	150	Metaphor and technical
0.3	Neanderthals	120	Socially focused 'gossip'
<2	*Homo ergaster*	100	Vocal chorusing
5	Australopithecines	70	Primate grooming

Source: After Aiello and Dunbar 1993; Dunbar 2003

It is here that the social brain model can be brought into play. While it does not deal with the forms of social organization, it does address the consequences of changes in community numbers as predicted from a primate sample comparing brain and group size (Table 1.2).

The assumptions behind this developing pattern are that hominins benefited from living in larger communities, and that the benefits of community expansion selected for encephalization. These benefits might have been better defence against predators, increased foraging opportunities and reproductive success as measured against other smaller hominin communities. But we can go further, as argued by Dunbar (1993, 1996a, 2003), if we identify some principles for the regulation of these communities.

The consequence of increasing community size is that the primate mechanism of grooming which traditionally regulated relationships was no longer possible due to severe time constraints. With such strong selection for increasingly dense and complex social communities, the development of language from vocal chorusing becomes a strong possibility (Table 1.2). Words now supplemented fingers as the means to create socially negotiated bonds.

But the categories of social life were not always constructed using resources based on language because, as the social brain model indicates, coalition and alliance did not always need language to proceed (Table 1.2). Furthermore, data on hominin and primate encephalization appear to point to the presence of language long before the 60,000-year-old human global diaspora. Half a million years ago, group sizes show a dramatic increase in the numbers of people to be socially integrated (Figure 1.1) and selection for language would have occurred (Aiello and Dunbar 1993).

From the perspective of the individual, if we accept the social brain model, there would have been very different opportunities in hominin evolution for the recruitment of partners to those constructed kinship categories as championed by Allen (1998a, 2005) and James (2003). Using the analogy of the dance with its partners drawn from discrete categories, we see that the impact of language on recruitment to kinship categories will in the first instance be directed at the extended and global networks (Table 1.1) that an individual constructs.

Once language was present, it transformed negotiation in the smaller scale intimate and effective networks. However, even though language was selected

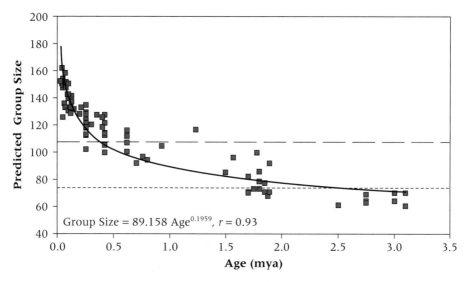

Figure 1.1 Fossil data on increasing brain size and group size during hominin evolution. Data reworked from Aiello and Dunbar (1993) with additions by Grove and used with permission. The implications of the data are assessed against primate grooming times, and where a limit of 30% (dashed line) is regarded as a daily maximum. This threshold was reached at least half a million years ago and hence indicates the appearance of novel forms of integration of which language is the most likely (Dunbar 1992b, 1993). The 20% threshold (dotted line) represents most primate grooming times. Using Aiello and Dunbar's (1993) equation, the lower grooming time threshold corresponds to a group size of 72 and the higher to 107

for by larger groups, the tiny intimate network continued to exert influence disproportionate to its size. As Milardo comments, the intimate network with a cross-cultural average size of five has a significant impact on an individual's decisions, psychological security, and network building in comparison to 'the sheer number of people contacted in the routine business of daily living and the breadth of opportunities they present or deny in terms of opportunities for social comparison, companionship and access to scarce resources' (1992: 455).

However, estimates of group size from the social brain model (Table 1.2) suggest that during earlier periods, recruitment, either to negotiated networks or to kinship categories, was from much smaller community sizes of hominins than are found today. In network terms (Table 1.1), these correspond to the intimate and effective networks and only to the lower end of the extended network (Gamble 1999). My point is that recruitment to some social categories, whether network- (Table 1.1) or kinship-based, was an ancestral trait and not necessarily dependent on the appearance of language. Neither does the appearance of language account for the global human diaspora 60,000 years ago since its presence is indicated at much earlier times. The question is whether formal recruitment to kinship categories represents a form of social extension that led to a global diaspora.

Material Kinship

If early hominin categories of kinship were not primarily linguistic, then what was their conceptual basis? Elsewhere (Gamble 2004a, 2004b) I have argued that the archaeological evidence which informs us about human evolution was structured by the use of material metaphors derived from the body. In particular the solid metaphors of *containers* and *instruments* (Table 1.3) derive their symbolic force from the head/trunk and limbs, respectively.

Anthropologists have consistently stressed the metaphorical use of material culture, and the house has proved an especially potent form that embodies social relations in architectural form (Bloch 1998; Carsten and Hugh-Jones 1995; Gell 1998: 252–3). By contrast, archaeologists have been more reticent in exploring the metaphorical connections between artefacts and social forms (but see Chapman 2000; Hodder 1990; Tilley 1999; Wengrow 1998), preferring instead the more familiar language of analogy and homology (Wylie 2002).

The purpose of metaphor, whether linguistic or material, is to understand and experience one thing in terms of something else (Lakoff and Johnson 1980: 5). The important word in this definition is *experiencing*, since Lakoff and Johnson argue that linguistic metaphors are not derived from cognitive processes alone. Our experience of the world depends on our bodies and our senses as well as our minds, and any division is unhelpful.

> The body is the ground or anchor by means of which we locate ourselves in the world, perceive and apprehend it. The centre of our own existence is always our body, as an axis from which spatiality and temporality are orientated: the human body *inhabits* space and time. Rather than mirroring the world, speech can be conceived as an extension of the human body in the world, a kind of artefact, by means of which we extend ourselves in the world, gain knowledge of it and alter it. Metaphor is an essential part of this process. Cognition is essentially a process of seeing something *as* something and this is the core of metaphorical understandings. (Tilley 1999: 34)

Metaphors allow us to express and categorize moods, emotions, relationships, and opinions through the physical experience that we have of the world, and this can be achieved through material culture as well as language and music.

Containers and instruments existed as solid, material metaphors, long before language elaborated on this manner of experiencing the world. Even without

Table 1.3 An embodied classification of material culture

Instruments (limbs, digits): knives, sticks, pestles, spears, ploughs, arrows, drills, chisels, axes, shuttles, looms, needles, chop-sticks, jewellery, brushes, pens, wheels, long-bones

Containers (head and trunk): bowls, pits, houses, barns, caves, pots, baskets, bags, quivers, mortars, blowpipes, rifles, clothes, moulds, jewellery, graves, tombs, masks, skulls

---

language, material culture, referenced to the body, supplied concepts for locating individuals in their social and physical worlds.

The reason for this is straightforward. Metaphors deal with relationships rather than rational assessments. For example, we cannot 'see' a concept such as the soul but that does not stop us from using an embodied metaphor to declare that 'the eyes are windows to the soul'. The metaphor is grounded originally in bodily experience rather than a rational judgement divorced from such an interpretive framework. I would argue in the same way that the cultural construction of kinship is metaphorically based on our bodily experiences rather than derived from any supposed rationality of the genes.

If, as discussed earlier, we focus on kinship as recruitment to culturally significant categories, then the metaphor of containment assumes particular significance for material culture. Many linguistic metaphors depend on the experience of being physically contained (Lakoff and Johnson 1980: 29–32), and the same cognitive approach to forming concepts can be extended to the material world.

For example, artefacts, in the form of either containers or instruments, acted metaphorically at times of community fusion to create social categories by referencing these material proxies, for example masks, rattles, drums, and percussion sticks, to the bodies of those engaged in the 'dance', and indeed to the organized shape of the dance space. It was at these gatherings that Durkheim's notion of 'effervescence' (Allen 1998b: 150) – forces that transcend the individual – emerged under the stimulation of rhythmic, coordinated action, dance, and music. Furthermore, containers and instruments can be traced through the social technologies of the past 2.5 million years since stone tools first appeared (Semaw et al. 1997; Stout et al. 2005).

But while containers and instruments have always existed as material metaphors, the artefactual record of the Palaeolithic is dominated by the latter. Containers are often made of perishable materials – bags, baskets, and clothing – and this has prejudiced archaeologists in their appreciation of the most ancient societies (Gamble 2004a). However, containers were always present in the form of bodily actions such as an embrace or an encircling dance that might leave nothing more than a well-stamped circle in the sand, and both examples can be described as an architecture without walls.

From this standpoint, we see how the long-run history of human technology records a changing emphasis regarding the use of social concepts to express relatedness. The metaphorical idiom in which these were most commonly articulated shifted over 2.5 million years from instruments to containers and with them changed the material basis of human identity (Gamble 2004a, 2004b). The gradient is most clearly seen in the move from implements to architecture.

But where does this leave kinship? I would suggest that Allen's tetradic model with its rules that govern recruitment and marriage is in fact primarily a material rather than linguistically based metaphor. Tetradic kinship is a container with four compartments. The partitions may not have architectural form, although this is not impossible, but rather they depend upon the activities of the effervescent gathering (Allen 1998b), those dances and rituals, to divide in such a manner that social life persists away from the concentration of community members. In other words, this was how the constraint of an individual's 'presence' for the *re-production* of social categories was transcended so that social relations could be stretched across time and space (Giddens 1984: 35): the release from proximity (Rodseth et al. 1991: 240) was achieved. Where social life was metaphorically expressed through instruments as material proxies for social categories, there was always a limit to the social and spatial extension of relationships. Since kinship categories are about definitions and rule-governed boundaries that rely on the idiom of the container, then it is expected that the global human diaspora after 60,000 years ago coincides with material metaphors expressing new relationships of boundedness. Boats and houses and well-dug graves now acquired importance, and, in time, sets of containers such as pots, baskets, villages, and towns came to dominate the metaphorical realization of the social landscape just as language now explained action.

Conclusion: Did Neanderthals Marry?

Social extension lies at the heart of the fundamental change that led to humans becoming a single hominin species with a global distribution and a language to order social relationships. But how did we become so culturally diasporic? As indicated by both the social brain hypothesis and the archaeological evidence for social technologies, we had language, a variety of visual displays, large communities, and environmental skills and knowledge from well before the start of the global journeys that began with the colonization of greater Australia 60,000 years ago. So why was the release from proximity delayed to such an extent? This is perhaps where a part is played by kinship, in the sense used by anthropologists with its recruitment to culturally determined categories, constrained by language.

I would suggest that Allen's (1998a) tetradic structure generates the rules not only for sociocentric kinship systems, but also for diasporic extension in a particular type of geographic space as well as time. The basic motor of demographic fission and fusion for hominin social organization seems inescapable, especially for Old World hominins who moved into northerly, seasonal latitudes. The key, as Allen (1998b) suggests, is the effervescence that comes from those moments of concentration and heightened interaction when emotional and material resources are literally fused into a social form. Since Durkheim's day, effervescence can be measured through the endorphin rush for those participating in the varied activities at such gatherings and where social behaviour is rewarded with emotional pleasure (Dunbar 2003). Any 'teams' that might have emerged at these times would not be random because what defined them was the distinction between parent and offspring. According to Allen, child-exchanging moieties were the first phase in building a tetradic structure, followed later by the splitting of each moiety into partner-exchanging sections. Allen's point is that this distinction provided the basis for the section system and was available for re-enforcement through ritual at social gatherings. However, the key concern is that 'identity and membership endure from one period of concentration to the next' (this volume, p. 110). Allen contrasts the effervescence of community fusion with the ordinary life of the fission phase. For example, when gathered together, Neanderthals might have been social in the sense of marriage and descent according to the tetradic model but pre-social, in Allen's terms, when apart from each other. I would suggest that it was here that the line between a biologist's notion of pair-bonding and an anthropologist's understanding of marriage becomes blurred. In my terms, Neanderthals had effective networks (Table 1.2) with classifications such as in-laws, thereby satisfying Mead's (1935: 84) understanding of the purpose of marriage. But these categories did not vire to their extended networks, where only strangers were defined, and so pair-bonding is a more appropriate description.

If correct, this interpretation suggests strong selection to occupy those habitats with resources that allowed more opportunities for fusion and social interaction rather than environments that required frequent fission and relative isolation. Neither ocean voyaging, nor living at population densities of one person per 100 km^2 – whether in hot deserts such as the Sahara or cold ones like Siberia – were conditions under which people can have preferred to live, even though in the case of Neanderthals they had language (Table 1.2). But more important than either language or their physical anatomy that classifies them as a separate species are the material metaphors that structured their experience. Neanderthal worlds were dominated by instruments rather than containers. A concept such as organized mating, and the recruitment of children to social categories, was not prevented by the lack of language, but it was limited by the structure of extended inter-personal relationships mediated by a social technology. It was not that material categories such as containers did not yet exist, but rather that their authority, as the means by which concepts of relatedness were produced, still had to develop relative to instruments as a much older material proxy for embodied relationships.

Hence three-quarters of the globe remained unoccupied by hominins until the process of expansion began 60,000 years ago. Kinship, which structured this intentional social process, is therefore the product of both material and linguistic metaphors. This conjuncture explains the timing late in human prehistory and indicates ways of forming the categories of social life that rely neither on genetic advantage nor on an exclusive facility with words, but instead on the power of things.

Acknowledgements

I am particularly indebted to Nick Allen for not only explaining kinship so clearly but also helping to clarify my arguments. I would also like to thank all those involved with the British Academy Centenary Project 'From Lucy to Language: The Archaeology of the Social Brain' for comments on earlier versions of this chapter: Fiona Coward, Robin Dunbar, John Gowlett, and, in particular, Matt Grove, who kindly allowed me to reproduce Figure 1.1. Financial assistance from the British Academy and the Royal Anthropological Institute is gratefully acknowledged.

2

Deep Roots of Kin

Developing the Evolutionary
Perspective from Prehistory

John A. J. Gowlett

Introduction: Deep Roots of Kin

The hominids arose perhaps eight million years ago, blossomed, and left the single dominant species *Homo sapiens*. Archaeology – an anthropology of the past – provides the main primary body of evidence about socio-cultural behaviour. Yet its books simply do not have chapters with titles like 'Kinship and Marriage'. Often archaeology confuses, even irritates, colleagues in other disciplines, because it can have the very highest of resolution in one area, yet fail to resolve even the most basic issue in some other. Here I am using a table that starts from Hinde's (1979) analysis of social structure to summarize what we can (and cannot) do (Table 2.1). It is only too easy to adopt projections from other disciplines and become 'the archaeology of expectation', writing fairy tales: the cautionary note was encapsulated in the subtitle of Lewis Binford's book, *Ancient Men and Modern Myths* (1981).

How do we work more rigorously towards asking credible questions about kinship in the deep past from archaeology and related disciplines? It will be necessary to find a conceptual framework, with models. For the record of hominid or hominin evolution, it is now evident that these must extend through some eight million years of time. They must address several grades of behaviour, numbers of species adaptations, as well as the notion of a gradient which leads in the end to modern humans (never forgetting that evolution is not teleological).

First I would like to establish two key points: how many models we need to work with, and what kind of social structure we can look at by means of past evidence. Then, the chapter uses specific archaeological evidence to outline models that have an emphasis on the ideas of kin.

Table 2.1 Comparison of conceptual frameworks involved in human evolution

*Primatology, Life Sciences**	*Anthropology*	*Archaeology*
Interactions – between individuals – observed	Interactions between individuals – observed, plus information gained from informants or material culture	Interactions – chiefly evidence of individual actions observed in material culture (with inference of interactions)
Relationships – observed from patterns of interactions	Relationships – observed from patterns of interactions observed between individuals, or apparent from other sources	Relationships – chiefly inferred from evidence of collective activities signalling shared intention
Social structure – inferred or abstracted from content, quality, patterning of relationships	Social structure – inferred or abstracted from content, quality, patterning of relationships	Social structure – inferred or abstracted from total material culture evidence

* The left-hand column follows Hinde (1979).

Conceptual Framework

For practical purposes, there is no point in letting the number of models get ahead of the resolution in data. Through millions of years the number of species and adaptations could be large (Turner 1986; Foley 1991; Tattersall 1995). Others argue for a relatively small number of species (e.g. Asfaw et al. 2002). Those shown in Table 2.2 are an absolute minimum, omitting the aspects of differently adapted species living side by side.

Recent research has concentrated remarkably on the idea of a 'human revolution' as an event, more than an extended process – to the point that it seems the primary task is to slide a bar of 'modernity' up and down the timescale until we find the best fit. This focus may hint at an emotional need to delimit groups, an 'us' of moderns and a 'them' of ancients, perhaps even reflecting the operation of an inference system of the kind discussed by Boyer (2001), but scientific detachment requires a more comprehensive view (see also Gamble 1999; this volume; Barnard, this volume). The analytical difficulty of 'before/after' is that the division may be just a convenient classificatory division, lacking true explanatory power. For kinship it would entail just modern kinship systems, or ancient simple ones.

The real challenge is to construct a framework that compares like and unlike, and it is recurrent in human evolution. The working solution is often to seek *some aspect* of continuity. For example, human bipedalism – upright walking – can be seen as an essential part of the hominid development. Apes do not have the same adaptations, and do not habitually walk upright. But, helpfully,

Table 2.2   The time-span

The Last Common Ancestor (LCA) in the background of the apes	(c. 10–8 Ma)
Models for the earliest hominids	(c. 7–3 Ma)
Models for early toolmakers	(c. 3–1.7 Ma)
Models for *Homo erectus*	(c. 1.6–0.8 Ma)
Models for *Homo heidelbergensis* etc.	(c. 0.7–0.5 Ma)
Models for modernization	(c. 0.4–0.05 Ma)

they are bipedal in a few situations, for a small part of the time. Similarly, fire use is universal in humans, and not known in apes. But evidence of fire habituation can be found, and apes can perhaps use fire in experiments. Language offers a more far-reaching case, and probably one that extends most strongly towards kinship. Language as we know it is unlikely to have been present in earliest (apelike) human ancestors – but they had means of communication. Could a system as portrayed in Nick Allen's model have existed before language? Could its rules be conveyed and appreciated, at least in a practical sense? This is not a trivial point, but essential to the modelling of an evolutionary gradient: the evidence will be introduced before discussion.

The Background of the Apes

The great apes are not merely relatives of humans with somewhat related social habits. The social context of apeness has existed for twenty million years (three times as long as hominids) and is the encompassing context for hominid developments. To link the living great apes requires an ancestral tree which encompasses some ten to fifteen million years. From this hominids emerge (Brunet et al. 2002; Goodman et al. 1989). Not only do all the great apes show strong features of social structure, but more and more complexity and variation are observed among these, for example the strong documented differences between chimpanzees and bonobos (White 1996; Wrangham et al. 1996, etc.). There are, however, some pervasive points. All the apes have:

- life in a community existence (apart from orang-utans, and possibly in them);
- a strong aspect of male dominance, but not usually such that one individual can exclude all other males from a group;
- across the ape species, few strong pair-bonds, except, temporarily, in chimpanzees and in orang-utans;
- fairly weak female bonding (except in bonobos).

Territorial environment is also a linking factor. Rain forests, the primary ape habitat, usually allow an ape social group to live in a territory about 4 km in diameter. Daily travel distances are then relatively small, of the order of a kilometre.

The scarcity of pair-bonding suggests at first sight little obvious relation to human kinship (cf. Nick Allen's formal model: this volume). Yet some continuities between human and ape systems can be sought out. In the case of a western lowland gorilla (such as Porthos), a single male with a small harem may be living very close to the structure of some human systems (Tutin 1996): the one male had long-maintained relationships with each of the females. It is perhaps a value-laden judgement to emphasize the pair-bond to the exclusion of other long-term mating bonds, or other long-term acquaintanceship bonds. In primates, even brief matings occur normally within a context in which two animals know one another, with emotional and cognitive aspects. Allen's model for humans prescribes certain rules for mate choice, regardless of duration of the relationship, or the number of relationships. It is thus highly specific, but also encompasses a great deal of variation (such as human polygamy). Key questions to resolve are (1) whether such rules can be recognized in the past and (2) whether other distinctive kinship patterns could be discernible (possibly not present either in apes or modern humans).

Models for the Earliest Hominids

The earliest hominids can be characterized simplistically but usefully as 'upright chimpanzees', and range through the period 7–3 million years ago. They became bipedal, had ape-sized brains and large teeth, although the canines became reduced. Recent developments include identification of *Sahelanthropus, Orrorin,* and *Ardipithecus*, all more than 5 million years old and in Africa (see, e.g. Brunet et al. 2002). They do not conform to an old idea linking them with savannah and the Rift Valley. The distribution is much more widespread, and environmental information suggests habitats of closed woodland more than open savannah. Leakey et al. (2001), however, emphasize the variety of habitats for *Australopithecus anamensis*. The emerging picture is of animals living in varied patchy habitats, outside the rain forests. Various authors have argued for a chimpanzee-like LCA (Last Common Ancestor) (McGrew 1992; Wrangham and Peterson 1996), but it may now be simplest to see the earliest hominids as simply the dry-country apes occupying vast swathes of territory that came to separate the remaining forests of Africa and South Asia.

Such habitats may have forced very rapid evolution. Hominid beginnings are possibly linked with the Messinian phase of the Miocene, between 7.7 and 5.8 million years ago, when there was major climate change. The Mediterranean dried up twice (Butler et al. 1999; Hilgen et al. 2000), probably implying huge areas of increased aridity where forest had formerly been continuous. Faunal movements occur at the same time, allowing possibilities of co-evolution. Horses and bovids may have helped to shape the hominid habitats.

In the absence of tools and living sites, these earliest hominids give us a suite of new physical characteristics which have implications both for social structure and subsistence adaptations (Table 2.3). Two remarkable finds give some small direct insight into early hominid sociality. One is the footprint trails at Laetoli in Tanzania, aged c. 3.5–3.8 million years ago. These show three

Table 2.3 Some main attributes of the record

Model	Anatomical features	Habitat	Archaeology
Models for modernity	Modern Cranial capacity: 1000–1600 cc	All including severe extremes	Upper Palaeolithic Parts of Middle Palaeolithic Art, ornament, decoration Burial Structured settlements Interlinking technologies
Homo heidelbergensis (and Neanderthal descendants)	Cranial capacity: 1200 cc upwards, (90–95% of modern)	All mainland Old World	Proof of wooden tools First hafting Fire Ochre use Structures Symbolic artefacts? Attention to dead?
Homo erectus	Cranial capacity: c. 1000 cc	All mainland Old World, except cold extremes	Stone artefacts (Acheulean, varied) Fire Structures?
Models for early toolmakers	Cranial capacity: c. 650 cc	Dry/varied	Stone artefacts Butchery 'Favoured places'
Models for the earliest hominids	Cranial capacity: 400–500 cc Habitual bipedalism Ape-size body and brain Greater sexual dimorphism Large teeth, but reduction in canines Long thumb (related to feeding, and perhaps tool use)	Drier landscape, bush	Larger exploitation territories Archaeology inferred only Footprints
LCA – Last Common Ancestor (human and chimp/bonobo)	Chimpanzee-like cranial capacity?	Rain forest Africa Small territories	None

creatures of different sizes walking together. Slightly less well known are the AL333 fossils at Hadar, which represent members of a band probably caught together by a flash flood, and argue strongly for the existence of multi-male, multi-female groups at 3 million years ago (Johanson et al. 1982; McHenry 1996).

For at least five million years the hominids retained ape-sized brains – until 2 million years ago, or later in the case of robust australopithecines. That fact might imply the continuation of an essentially ape-like social system, with the changes chiefly determined by resources, seasonality, and landscape. Most of the visible changes in hominids could be part of a single complex reflecting adaptation to the new environments. Apart from reduction of the front teeth (incisors and canines), the trend to massive molars is so strong around 3–4 million years ago that it points to primacy of dietary changes – away from fruits, and towards greater quantities of lower grade foods, including roots and tubers (cf. O'Connell et al. 1999; Walker 1981; Wrangham et al. 1999). The bipedalism may have been a feeding adaptation, as often argued, but it links with possibilities of tool use reducing the need for large canines in threat-displays and for defence.

Lovejoy (1981) argued that bipedalism helped reduce birth interval (certainly far shorter in modern humans), as infants can walk earlier, and be weaned earlier than is possible in an arboreal existence. These developments solve the 'reproductive trap' found in the apes, but predation risks may be greater on the ground, and juveniles may require more care from more individuals. Shorter birth intervals respond, however, by creating the likelihood of larger sibling groups who may be strongly bonded. If the ecological circumstances also hold the local group small, then individuals maturing within it may have very few mating opportunities, simply because siblings form too high a proportion of potential mates (cf. Lehmann et al. 2007 for ecological pressures).

Larger territories are undoubtedly necessary in drier and more seasonal climates. They force a subsistence using time and space differently – with prob-able effects on group structure. Populations cannot be evenly distributed, but will be more nucleated at times, and more dispersed at others. Mechanisms will be necessary both to exploit outlying areas and to allow breeding/mate exchange with neighbouring groups. There is probably a new diurnal cycle, with more time spent travelling, and a greater premium on fast, efficient feeding. Within a chimpanzee community, male groups and female groups may travel separately through the day, usually for quite short distances, keeping in touch vocally (Wrangham 1979). On a larger landscape with longer movements beyond any calling distance, there would be quite different pressures (Figure 2.1). If waterholes are at the core of band areas (true of many modern hunter-gatherers), then much activity would be concentrated within a local radius, but, concomitantly, larger distances would be exploited in the peripheral areas.

The small frame of Lucy is some direct evidence that sexual dimorphism, at least in body size, was greater than in chimpanzees or modern humans (McHenry 1996; McHenry and Coffing 2000). The high level of dimorphism has been attributed to a harem-like structure (Foley 1987). It creates a selec-tion pressure for small females, but presumably predation could make a

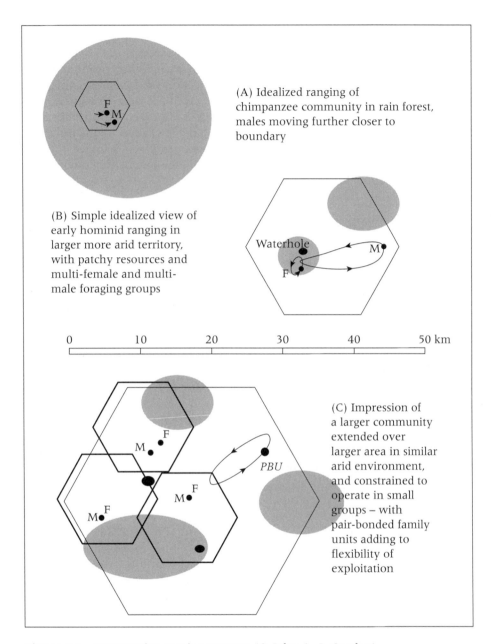

Figure 2.1   Comparative ranging patterns (© John A. J. Gowlett)

counter-pressure for greater size: the adult Lucy (at c. 3 Ma) was less than a metre tall. Such small hominids were obviously vulnerable, and the numerous occurrences of *Australopithecus* remains in South African caves which preserve carnivore traces tend to confirm the point. The smaller individuals might require protection in the form of larger males and group strength.

In chimps, feeding competition in females, usually for fruits, tends to increase in a harsher environment, reducing female bonding (which is much stronger in bonobos) (Wrangham et al. 1996). Hominids, however, eventually broke out from this gradient of pressures on females. In a harsher environment they may have bonded more, perhaps because protection for juveniles could best be offered by a different solution: multi-female groups foraging together. Male collaboration, present to a degree in chimpanzees, is effectively attested in strong form by the time of first tools (see below). Habitat change might force the initial developments, but ensuing feedback loops could easily lead to deeper socio-ecological change – including selection for a grandparent generation, with obvious implications for knowledge of descent.

Models for Early Toolmakers

When the first preserved artefacts appear at about 2.6 Ma, they immediately introduce a new dimension into the record – and we are close to the first appearance of *Homo*. Their hard evidence makes possible much more solidly based models. These are new ones, because such investment in artefacts changes the picture. The artefacts offer several great insights. They tell us about the spatial arrangements of localized activities; they tell us about the processes that people operated, and their durations; and they map human movements on a wider landscape, providing, as Isaac (1989) put it, 'visiting cards'. As material culture, the artefacts reinforce an idea of economy, bringing benefits and costs that are considerable and measurable. These concepts may well touch on kinship, given their collaborative nature, and the fact that later exchange systems are often tied in to kinship, as in marriage exchanges.

First, the artefact movements chart yet larger territories. At both Olduvai and Lake Turkana, most transport distances are less than 10 km, but some range up to 20 km. Movements of stone cannot be expected to map hominid movements fully. Nevertheless, these distances translate to habitual ranges of c. 80–150 sq. km, ten times larger than most ape territories. The quantities moved also entail 'delayed returns', as discussed by Woodburn (1968a, 1988) for modern hunter-gatherers; the costs of a stone-assisted economy make this inevitable.

The early toolmakers were responsible for dense artefact concentrations, sometimes found relatively close to water. These led to the idea of 'home bases', which were seen as contrasting with ape patterns of moving on each night. Home bases implied longer stays, and a geographical focus for systematic transport of food to be shared by the group (Isaac 1989). There came huge debate, driven especially by Lewis Binford's views that the association of stones and bones was not proven.

The Binford view (1981) that sites are mere hydraulic jumbles is no longer sustainable, but some authors remain unwilling to see the early concentrations as living sites. Rolland (2004), for example, sees the home base as a new arrival at 400,000 BP, made possible by fire use; O'Connell and colleagues (1999) argue that most of the sites are linked with kills and butchery rather than occupation. There is, however, a very strong case for seeing them in far earlier archaeological evidence, as originally envisaged by Isaac (1989). The idea that they require a cognitive step forward seems doubtful, as hamadryas baboons, for example, have home bases. It can be argued, too, that the whole of a small ape territory is effectively an extended home base.

The issue relevant to kinship is whether early humans had a definite knowledge of a home focus, which would affect group behaviour. The evidence for this is now strong: the concentrations of archaeological material are sufficient to indicate highly favoured places, right through the Pleistocene. Evidence of provisions brought to base systematically seems an important indicator of a more human social structure, and the consistent association of stone and bone (linked by cutmarks) far exceeds any random probability, occurring regularly even on the earliest sites (Semaw et al. 2003). Patterns of butchery indicate collaboration in transport, the freed skins perhaps becoming obvious simple carrying bags (see Gamble, this volume). Most important, the movements of stone do not simply relate to butchery. On many sites the numbers of cores and core tools are too large to relate to single butchery episodes. This point is very testable – toolkits from just such butchery episodes are very well known from a site like Boxgrove, and the tool numbers are vastly lower than on some of the earliest archaeological sites known in Africa. Schick and Toth (1993) record, too, that there were systematic imports and exports of part-worked tools on all of the early sites.

Let us hang onto this idea: a group of hominids select stones and bring them to a place where they knap them. The scatter occupies a patch perhaps 15 metres across, and there are around 60–70 cores or flaked pieces, with an average weight of about 0.4–0.5 kilos. Then, flaking studies show that many more cores have been part-worked on the site and transported out. How many people did this involve, on how many trips? It would seem to imply at least several adults, and patterns of organized activity running through at least two or three days.

'Home bases' remain a central issue for a study of social organization. In larger territories, permanent waterholes may have been an essential focus of activity, as for many modern hunters and gatherers; home bases may also involve important changes in a diurnal activity cycle – presaging elements studied for far later times by the Higgs group in the 1970s (Jarman 1972). That is, time out to resources and time back from resources has to be factored in, with c. 10 km/2 hour radii an important constraint on the daily cycle (in humans).

Even if the 'home' status of favoured places may remain in doubt, the presence of extensive artefact-and-bone concentrations from c. 2.5 Ma is effectively demonstrated, implying at the least a regime of time and resource sharing. O'Connell and colleagues argue for an early appearance of male coalitions and female coalitions, with the former concentrating on hunting and scavenging (sometimes with more symbolic than practical value), the latter on plant matter including roasted tubers. Thus, like Wrangham et al. (1999), they predicate fire use (O'Connell et al. 1999, 2002).

The chief argument for a gender division is that in these hazardous environments, as many individuals as possible had to be protected for as much of the time as possible. Chimpanzees may give a part-answer: the male groups tend to travel further, nearer the edge of the territory. Similarly, as hunting, carnivory, and butchery show a male bias, in both chimps and modern humans, it is most parsimonious to predict the same for early humans. Then the large numbers of stone tools associated with butchery sites are most easily seen as products of male collaborative ventures.

Are these gender-based social alliances *necessary* rather than merely plausible? For earliest hominids that is debatable, but the early toolmakers clearly show systematic cooperation in their activities, on a group scale. They demonstrate long distance ranging as fact. As apes and modern human hunter-gatherers are consistent in this respect, it is almost certain that this wider foraging would be done by males. The inference is that ecological factors enhanced gender-based roles.

Models for *Homo erectus* (and the Acheulean)

Early *Homo* – with relatively small brains – spread widely around the Old World as much as 2 million years ago (far earlier than was generally thought). The best evidence comes from finds from Dmanisi, Georgia, dated to about 1.7 Ma (Lordkipanidze et al. 2005; Vekua et al. 2002), but similar dates in China and Java indicate that a huge geographic area was colonized, including temperate latitudes in which fire may have been needed. The discovery of *Homo floresiensis* in Indonesia also points to early roots of *Homo* in Asia (Brown et al. 2004; Morwood et al. 2004). The presence of such small and small-brained (c. 700 cc) hominids can be linked with the idea of a very early spread of *Homo* right across Eurasia. Then, fairly quickly, appears classic *Homo erectus* – very widespread, homogeneous and long-lasting (c. 1.5–0.5 Ma). The developments could be seen as the first human revolution (cf. Barnard, this volume; Gowlett in press). The species has quite modern body proportions, and less size dimorphism than australopithecines – females from now on are relatively large.

That change may be linked with evolution of the pair-bond – to put it in perspective, *Homo erectus* is 90% of the time journey from LCA to modern human. In other primates it has been argued the pair-bond evolves for protection of juveniles, chiefly from other males (Alexander 1979; van Schaik and Dunbar 1990); in birds, it may arise because infants can survive only with care from two parents. In *Homo*, both arguments may pertain.

The most important new developments with social implications are spatial – a huge range for the species, large ranges indicated by artefact transport, varied habitats, and adaptations. The (shared) investments in artefacts are stupefying: transport of huge quantities for 10–15 km, and up to 100 km on several attested occasions – activities that were necessarily social or socially mediated.

Homo erectus also transported large numbers of heavy stone bifaces to favoured places. One can suspect that their strength and carrying capacity evolved for foraging as much as for moving stone artefacts or other materials. Other carrying certainly involved meat transport (cf. the modern Hadza: O'Connell et al. 1999). Eventually there must have been a corresponding transport of wood fuel for fire, which is well documented in the period 400,000–700,000 years ago, and may have started earlier (Goren-Inbar et al. 2004; Gowlett 2006; Rolland 2004 etc.).

The old idea that there was a long stasis in *Homo erectus* may be misleading – this species may well have acquired 'hardware' for language, and thus have undergone profound changes in social complexity. *Homo erectus* was certainly capable of handling quite sophisticated patterns of artefact manufacture, with rule systems, from before 1 Ma. – with possible implications that language origins date from the 'first revolution' already mentioned. It is a reasonable hypothesis that language implies or necessitates large groups (beyond the immediate band). The reduced sexual dimorphism may be the best clue for the beginnings of the pair-bond.

Overall, *Homo erectus* can be seen as powerful and efficient – not limited culturally, but rather with a tremendous capability for investment in culturally mediated activities, and with a major ability to adapt to varied environments. It appears nevertheless as a 'Mark 1' human, making large investments for quite large returns, but lacking the physical and intellectual leverage of more modern species (something of a gas guzzler).

Deep Roots of Modernity

Improvements in dating make plain that a more modern *Homo* had evolved about 600,000 years ago – *Homo heidelbergensis* in Europe, and initially very similar hominids in Africa and perhaps Asia. At these later times we are already more than 90% towards the present from hominid roots. *Homo erectus* were strong carriers throughout, but at the later time, we see efforts geared not just towards stone and meat transport, but centred on fire, as at Schöningen or Beeches Pit (Gowlett 2006, Gowlett et al. 2005; Thieme 2005). Large fires and high temperatures suggest that fire was maintained intensively, probably through division of labour. Artefacts such as the Schöningen spears were made from a tree trunk, parcelled down – another cooperative exercise. Specialized diets were a necessity in some regions, and part of the fire picture. Large sites with fires indicate well-established groups, quite large, with cooperation essential. Very thorough butchery, as at Boxgrove, suggests that meat was often taken off the bone.

The state of fire investigation mirrors those in other fields – for the beginnings, modelling is ahead of the evidence: the roasting of roots and habitation of the north should have required fire use, but that is not proof that it happened. For a middle period, the archaeological evidence becomes good, but only by hypothesis is the pattern distinctive. Inference says that the large hearths, and the requirements to keep them burning, placed emphasis on a larger group than the single family unit.

Modernity and Diversification

Increasingly it appears that modernity was reached gradually through the last several hundred thousand years. The anatomy of early *Homo sapiens*, in Africa in particular, traces the development. Large numbers of finely made flint blades from the recently discovered cave site at Qesem in Israel (Barkai et al. 2002) emphasize that the process of major cultural changes may have started as early as around 400,000 years ago. Hafting, seemingly mundane, is a key sign of extra leverage, and probably of cognitive advance. If so, it has to be admitted for Neanderthal ancestors, along with fire use, structures, and other special- ized technology. Similar advanced stone technology is found at Kapthurin in Kenya at 280,000 years ago; in Europe, Neanderthal ancestors were appar- ently less precocious, but their spears, their first use of hafting, and their fire use were all impressive aspects of the repertoire (Thieme 2005; Tryon and McBrearty 2002).

Through this period, here and there, come the first signs of classic behaviours once linked with the Upper Palaeolithic: self-adornment, other signs of symbolism (e.g. use of ochre), shaped bone tools, and hyper-long transport distances for artefacts. Although art-like phenomena appear to come only within the last 100,000 years, there is no single datum of appearance, in spite of dispositions to see an 'event'. Special attention to the dead, for example, may be shown in several scattered finds of cutmarks on skulls. The disposal of the dead in a cave gallery at Atapuerca in Spain, and the presence of one 'special' hand-axe, are perhaps together enough to indicate some feeling for identity and belonging and kinship at 0.5 Ma (Carbonell and Mosquera 2006). The pattern of deposition of many dead at Atapuerca may also indicate social collaboration (Gamble 1999). The cranium from Bodo in Ethiopia, dating to c. 0.6 Ma, has cutmarks on the brow; similar are seen on the remains of *Homo sapiens idaltu* from Herto at about 150,000 years ago (Clark et al. 2003; White et al. 2003). Individual burial comes only far later, at around 130,000 years ago on oldest present evidence.

Large brains show a steady development, but they were already modern in size by 200,000 years ago. Reduction of teeth and gracilization were partly there by 150,000 years ago (Herto/Idaltu), largely achieved in Middle East at 100,000, but the famed Cro-Magnons of the Upper Palaeolithic were also robustly built. Given their early occurrence, it now seems unreasonable to use stone blades as prime evidence of modernity. Art may remain as a key designator, but boundaries are now blurred by various degrees of 'specialness' in early objects. It also remains true that all key indicators are subject to sampling bias.

Finally, models for the 'modern' need not conform with some idealized Western notion of modernity – the range of modern behaviour includes many aspects requiring much explanation (cf. Opie and Power, Knight, this volume). The best modelling approach perhaps requires a turning round in perspect- ive – from their brain size and cultural evidence, humans of the last 200,000 years should be assumed first to be modern. Then we may ask what if any- thing clashes actively with notions of current behaviour, and seek to give it documentation.

Discussion

In this chapter, I have aimed to bridge the gap between biological perspectives (Dunbar, this volume) and those of highly complex later cultural behaviour

(Gamble, Opie and Power, Knight, this volume), with some emphasis on the importance of rule systems in shaping behaviour (cf. James 2003, this volume; Allen, Barnard, this volume). I stressed the need for a series of models, so that some factors affecting kinship can be drawn out. Admittedly, we often lack the resolution to say when some key change comes in, and then cannot (yet) use it in distinguishing the successive scenarios. Thus the model requirements (Table 2.4) are merely outlines, and the journey to working socio-ecological models will be challenging. Even so, there is sufficient evidence to show that past systems were different from those of both apes and modern humans; and material culture shows an increasing imposition of rules on the world.

Table 2.4 Major requirements for some social models in human evolution

Model	Model requirements
Models for modernity	Test for discrepancy from existing modern behaviour
Homo heidelbergensis	Pair-bonds Large networks Multiple layers of social organization Major investments in material culture, including fire use
Homo erectus	Large bodied meat-eating humans Medium-large ranges – up to c. 50–100 km Intensive investment Origins of pair-bond (putative)
Models for early toolmakers	Night bases close to water Ranges up to 10–15 km Considerable meat-eating with investment in carrying Local artefact transport Behaviour involving gender-separated activities in core and peripheral zones
Models for earliest hominids	Core areas; female bonding, escaping resource limitations Model 100 sq. km Needs to take into account diurnal pattern of socializing Male coalitions (cf. chimpanzee alliances?) Female coalitions with offspring (cf. bonobos?) Harem structure (cf. gorillas) Multi-male–multi-female consortia at dangerous times of day/travel Strong collaborative sibling groups No strong pair-bond
LCA – Last Common Ancestor (human and chimp/bonobo)	Probably more like chimpanzees and bonobos than gorillas or humans

As the physical individuals are usually absent from the record (the greatest potential comes from recent times where DNA is present in bodies in a cemetery), archaeology must work from a world of artefacts and the patterns of behaviour which they record. Site size and duration of occupation can be elucidated only generally, but transport distances are precise, providing good evidence about subsistence and network size. These allow us to get to grips with some requirements of the models above, and some major features of modern populations.

In hominid evolution, a key point – beyond appearance of the pair-bond – would be the transition from ape community to a multi-layer system with bands and superbands (dialect tribe) (cf. Wobst 1974). The main associated variables would appear to be changes in range area imposed by environment; change of diet (perhaps linked with fire use); and the consequences of language as a facilitator of 'cultural speciation'. In modern humans, the personal network size of about 150 (Dunbar 1993) can operate across these levels, in that individuals may have network connections far removed from the local unit. The known instances of hand-axe transport over 100 kilometres or more may hint that such interconnections were developed from more than a million years ago. In the context of such networks the addition of a grandparent generation affects longevity, relationships of care, and absolute numbers (Hawkes et al. 1998; O'Connell et al. 1999).

There is insufficient space to discuss these broader levels of 'kin', but the larger scale of numbers appears important in all senses, genetic, classificatory, and in social networks. Thus Barnard (1992) has commented on two different approaches to kinship among San: one that extends relatedness to everyone in its world; another that limits its real interactions to a world of 'true' relatedness. These notions would be impossible for chimpanzees: they depend on language. Hallowell noted somewhat similar views and constraints in the far-removed Ojibwa (Hallowell 1955 [1949]).

The overriding points for kinship seem to be about rules, language, and property. Here I return to the challenge of tracing continuities. There has been much emphasis on kin selection in primates (e.g. Hinde 1979). But if we seek to trace a line from kin selection in apes to kinship in humans, what similarities will there be? How formally does the system have to operate? We are not very good at modelling proto-systems (as I have argued for fire).

It seems reasonable to argue that patterns would be formed initially by local socio-ecological factors, then later reinforced (with abstraction) by a cultural system. You might have:

- a predisposition not to mate with siblings because of overfamiliarity;
- limited opportunities to mate within the local band, because of its small size;
- opportunities to mate further afield that are governed by practical contracts of proximity, neighbourliness, and territoriality – with perhaps a selective advantage in favour of better regulation (= exchange in some form);
- investment in material culture prompting an extended system and concepts of ownership.

These features could precede language. It is notable, though, that the rule content in artefacts increases markedly from 2 to 1 Ma. Again it is a reasonable hypothesis that foundations for social rules were laid at the same time.

One point to consider is that the hunter-gatherer band is not the ape community – it is more specialized, through its makeup of numbers of family groups which are often autonomous, with choices of fusion and fission (see Dunbar, Layton, this volume for further discussion). In archaeology, we might see this through multiple hearths, as in the modern Efe (Fisher and Strickland 1991), or for the late Palaeolithic at Pincevent (Julien et al. 1987; Leroi-Gourhan and Brézillon 1972). Our earliest actual hearths hint at larger communal arrangements, perhaps because continuous feeding of fires was essential (Gowlett 2006). Before 400,000 years ago, there is little precise information.

Superbands might be visible through artefact style boundaries. Such strong style is apparent within the last 100,000 years. Much archaeological attention has been paid to 'openness' or 'closedness' of cultural behaviour centred on groups, as evidenced by the artefacts (see Isaac 1989; Sackett 1982; Wiessner 1983). In larger territories, a lot of factors push towards discontinuities; the question is whether they can be recognized at particular timepoints, and related to kin. The most that can be said for earlier times is that local style features do exist, but all known artefact types also have broad geographic and temporal currency.

Marrying-in and marrying-out appears to be a major issue in constructing or reinforcing such boundaries. Archaeological variation cannot be used as a proxy without some understanding of the demographic issues. Kin selection studies show that many animals tend to breed with partners who are not too familiar, and not too dissimilar, yielding an optimum relationship of 12.5% shared genes – genetic first cousins in human terms (Bateson 1983; Crook 1980). Possibly significant here is that anthropologists insist on great precision in discussion of genetic and classificatory cousins. Distinctions of cross- and parallel cousins may have chiefly social rather than genetic significance, but the inherited effects of Y-chromosome, mitochondrial DNA, and even imprinted genes may mean that there are consequences to being related to a group through a female rather than male ancestor.

A greater degree of endogamy would seem to militate towards a smaller group that is more tightly related, and stronger boundaries between groups. Cultural concepts of 'universal relatedness' would seem to work in the opposite direction. Although issues of relatedness on the scale of network have been considered by Dunbar (1995; this volume) for various recent societies, the best approaches for very early societies are not yet elucidated, either in modelling population effects, or maximizing the information to be derived from the archaeological record. Subtle changes in the endogamy/exogamy parameters mentioned above could have a major effect on the information flows affecting continuity in artefact design. Archaeologists are largely constrained to exploring those situations where artefacts are complex enough and numerous enough to carry a good deal of information (as in the Acheulean), but other sources of variation have to be winnowed out. Complexity is perhaps the best primary sign of a society that has rule systems.

In the overall frame, language seems the vital determinant of possibilities. If in early stages it merely describes and formalizes the patterns that are tuned by natural selection (i.e. is primarily descriptive), later it could impose patterns. They would remain subject to natural selection, in that a group whose cultural norms departed too far from biological needs would be selected against. Small bands in large (probably arid) territories presumably may breed endogamously, *de facto*, but the group relying on endogamy to excess may reduce its chance to make alliances across a network, and may be vulnerable to elimination in hard times. Hence (one can argue), there is evolutionary pressure for a counter-mechanism of a marriage exchange concept – perhaps closely related to exchange concepts of other goods. For Lévi-Strauss (1977–8 [1958, 1973]), it is a fundamental of kinship that the men exchange the women. Language also seems the prime vehicle for allowing classificatory extensions of kin, enlarging support networks and responsibilities in a sort of retroactive symmetry.

Conclusion

Archaeology has the strength that it informs about the actual past, at specific moments. Other approaches tell us what 'must' have happened, but are vague on timings, and unable to handle issues of changes that were not consistently directional. This propensity to disentangle the elements of sequences is one of the major contributions that archaeology can make, alongside hominid palaeontology, which through its finds established (for example) the relative order of bipedalism and encephalization.

In kinship, these issues of ordering are of prime importance. Why should human kinship emerge? All other animals get by with mating systems that operate mainly at a biological level, perhaps with learned behavioural aspects. There are at least two possibilities:

1   The human system is like others, merely decorated with a cultural overlay.
2   A distinctive evolved hominid biological system has been tuned by language and culture, such that the present human system is now fundamentally sociological – largely replacing older systems for mate selection with a cultural apparatus.

The first view posits that a system like the human one could evolve in any species; when language came in later, it would simply label the existing components and practices. The latter view suggests that a unique hominid pattern arose over several millions of years for reasons that were more ecological than cultural; but that in the last million years or so, it became tuned through language and concepts of property and exchange, to higher degrees of formalization. Its rules would proscribe things that do in fact quite often happen, reflecting, as Bateson (1983) has suggested, the often strong feelings of those who observe a transgression. Kinship thus acquires a moral aspect. The last phase of formalization would take into account statements such as those of

Turnbull (1972), of the sociological being far more important than the biological in marriage among the Efe. The more cultural the species becomes, the more there is to know about other individuals, the more traits there are to take into account, the more these circumscribe mating choices. In this cultural game, increased sociality and formalization would be a key to successful harnessing of culture's opportunities.

In terms of sequencing, in hominid evolution the earliest evidence emphasizes range change and diet stress; large teeth were a more important immediate solution than large brains (Model 1). Then we can emphasize the start of higher quality diets, and greater size equality between sexes (Model 2), while Models (3) and (4) emphasize group collaboration. We may perhaps infer that coalitions were important first, and that from c. 2 Ma the pair-bond began to play a role. Fire has a highly significant role: first in allowing higher quality diet (modifying starches, fat, proteins); then in demanding organization and division of labour in return for its benefits; finally for its importance in marking ritual.

Archaeology has limitations, but it does record social information valuable to the anthropologist, and far more so where the evidence of material culture is sophisticated. Prior to that, the raw evidence (stone tools etc.) shows primarily *activity*, but it also shows its scale and costs, and so offers some proxy for other behaviour, even though it rarely reveals particular relationships. Archaeology does help precisely with some of the essential points in an evolutionary trajectory: such matters as size of range, existence of home bases, sharing of food brought to the point of consumption, site size, and existence of uniform styles of artefacts. All are relevant to kinship issues broadly defined. Biological information from fossils is also important, as has been seen: in addition to brain size, specific evidence is often available about body size, size of dentition, aspects of diet, sexual dimorphism, and longevity.

In hypothesis making and testing, the issues of kinship have some common points with 'simpler' matters such as the origins of fire use. Archaeology tends to struggle with an over-simple view of presence/absence, limited by the difficulties of modelling plausible proto-systems. Where we have not modelled, it is hard to be sure what we use our data 'for'. It seems absolutely vital now to move to construct working socio-ecological models in a series running through time. Then, shared analysis with anthropology can become particularly valuable, perhaps with a common emphasis on formal pattern, whether in tetradic classification or past 'activity' around hearths.

Acknowledgements

I am grateful to the British Academy for support within the 'From Lucy to Language' project; to my colleagues Robin Dunbar, Bob Layton and Clive Gamble, and especially to Wendy James and Hilary Callan, for the occasion of the Gregynog workshop.

Part II

Women, Children, Men – and the Puzzles of Comparative Social Structure

Child naming ceremony, Max and Bertha Farrars, Burma (1890–9) (Royal Geographical Society)

3

Early Human Kinship was Matrilineal

Chris Knight

It is said that kinship is to anthropology 'what logic is to philosophy or the nude is to art' – it is 'the basic discipline of the subject' (Fox 1967: 10). To ask questions about early kinship is to return to many of the fundamental historical and philosophical issues out of which anthropology emerged.

Humans do not tamely accept the 'facts' of their biological relatedness. They collectively shape and reconstruct those facts. Following the philosopher John Searle (1996), let's begin by drawing a distinction between 'brute facts' and 'institutional facts'. Birth, sex, and death are facts anyway, irrespective of what people think or believe. These, then, are brute facts. Descent group membership, marriage, and property *are facts only if people believe in them*. Suspend the belief and the facts correspondingly dissolve. But although institutional facts rest on human belief, that doesn't make them mere distortions or hallucinations. Take the fact that these two five-pound banknotes in my pocket are equal in value to one ten-pound note. That's not merely my subjective belief: it's an objective, indisputable fact. But now imagine a collapse of confidence in the currency. Suddenly, the realities in my pocket dissolve.

For scholars familiar with Rousseau, Marx, or Durkheim, none of this is especially surprising or difficult to grasp. Some kinds of facts are natural. Others are 'social' or 'institutional'. Since the inception of their discipline, however, anthropologists have been unable to apply such understandings to kinship. In Searle's terms, they have argued over whether the facts of kinship are 'brute' or 'institutional'.

What is it to be a 'son' or a 'daughter', a 'mother' or a 'niece'? Taking careful notes among his Native American informants, Lewis Morgan (1871) discovered to his initial surprise that an Iroquois child had several 'mothers'. Early in the twentieth century, Bronislaw Malinowski (1930) reacted against this idea, reshaping anthropology on the basis that it was patently absurd. No child could possibly have two mothers. Malinowski acknowledged that his Trobriand Island informants, like many other people, might systematically 'distort' the true facts of kinship. Two sisters, for example, might describe themselves as

'mothers' to one another's offspring, their children correspondingly address-
ing both as 'mother'. However, Malinowski insisted that such notions were
ideological fictions, not to be taken seriously. Correctly analysed, the facts of
kinship would always turn out to be at bottom (a) biological and (b) individual.

Classificatory kinship is anything but 'individual'. It expresses the principle
of 'the equivalence of siblings' (Radcliffe-Brown 1931: 13). It is the kind of
kinship we would expect if bonds of siblinghood consistently prevailed over
marital ties. Let me be more precise. It is the kind of kinship we would expect
if groups of sisters drew on support from brothers in periodically standing up
to husbands – a reproductive strategy aimed at enhancing female bargaining
power and driving up male mating effort (Knight 1991: 281–326; Power and
Aiello 1997; Power and Watts 1996). For obvious reasons, opposite-sex siblings
cannot always 'stand in' for one another in quite the same straightforward
way as same-sex siblings. But where kinship is classificatory, sibling unity in
general is accorded primacy over marital bonds.

Classificatory kinship is so widespread that modern social anthropologists
tend not to discuss it. Many prefer to assume that the readers of their monographs will simply understand all kinship terms in their classificatory sense.
For earlier generations of anthropologists, however, the whole issue was still
a novelty, and heated debates surrounded the significance of this seemingly
extraordinary and cumbersome mode of conceptualizing and classifying kin.
An unfortunate consequence of the recent lack of interest in this topic has
been that palaeoanthropologists and biological anthropologists remain almost
unaware of its existence, constructing their origin theories as if the task were
to explain kinship and marriage in forms assumed self-evident in modern
Western society.

Here, I will review some of social anthropology's basic definitions and
findings concerning classificatory kinship – findings that have never been
repudiated, but have in recent years become overshadowed by other concerns.
Although the sources may seem unavoidably rather dated, such a review of
the classical literature may help clarify the issues that a Darwinian approach
to the evolution of kinship should address.

The Equivalence of Siblings

The essence of classificatory kinship is that siblings occupy similar positions in
the total social structure. Their 'social personalities', as Radcliffe-Brown (1931:
97) put it, writing in this case of Aboriginal Australia, 'are almost precisely the
same'. Where terminology is concerned:

> A man is always classed with his brother and a woman with her sister. If I apply
> a given term of relationship to a man, I apply the same term to his brother. Thus
> I call my father's brother by the same term that I apply to my father, and similarly,
> I call my mother's sister 'mother'. The consequential relationships are followed
> out. The children of any man I call 'father' or of any woman I call 'mother' are
> my 'brothers' and 'sisters'. The children of any man I call 'brother', if I am a male,
> call me 'father', and I call them 'son' and 'daughter'. (Radcliffe-Brown 1931: 13)

By the same token, if a woman finds herself in a particular kinship relation-ship, any of her sisters may in theory join her in exercising the rights or fulfilling the obligations entailed. Since sisters are each other's equivalents, it follows that, theoretically, no mother should discriminate in favour of her own bio-logical children. All the children of a group of sisters should be addressed as 'daughter' or 'son' indiscriminately, all being considered 'sisters' and 'brothers' to each other.

In societies where siblings maintain solidarity in everyday life, the logic of all this becomes immediately apparent. Among the Hopi Pueblo:

> Sex solidarity is strong. . . . The position of the mother's sister is practically identical with that of the mother. She normally lives in the same household and aids in the training of her sister's daughter for adult life. . . . They co-operate in all the tasks of the household, grinding corn together, plastering the house, cooking and the like. . . . Their children are reared together and cared for as their own. (Eggan 1950: 33–5)

It is as if sisters were so close that they refused to discriminate between one another's children, each saying, in effect, 'My child is yours and your child is mine.'

Lewis Morgan's (1871) discovery and cross-cultural analysis of this seeming anomaly established social anthropology as a scientific discipline (Lévi-Strauss 1977 [1958] 1: 300). The basic principle – the formal equivalence of siblings – initially seemed incongruous and incomprehensible. As a certain Reverend Bingham wrote to Morgan from Hawaii:

> The terms for father, mother, brother, and sister, and for other relationships, are used so loosely we can never know, without further inquiry, whether the real father, or the father's brother is meant, the real mother or the mother's sister. . . . A man comes to me and says *e mote tamau*, my father is dead. Perhaps I have just seen his father alive and well, and I say, 'No, not dead?' He replies, 'I mean my father's brother'. . . . (Morgan 1871: 461)

Europeans typically concluded that the natives must evidently be confused. Sir Henry Sumner Maine felt moved to ask 'whether all or part of the explana-tion may not lie in an imperfection of mental grasp on the part of savages?' (1883: 289). To such Victorian savants, it was clear that genuine kinship was one thing, the imaginings of savages quite another. When Malinowski later adopted a similar approach – insisting that 'real' kinship must always be 'indi-vidual', regardless of native 'ideology' to the contrary – this style of thinking came to predominate within anthropology as a whole.

To ask whether a kinship bond is ideology or biology makes about as much sense as to ask whether a banknote can really be money when it is clearly a piece of paper. Writing of the puzzle posed by the very existence of classi-ficatory kinship, Robin Fox explained:

> It is because anthropologists have consistently looked at the problem from the ego-focus that they have been baffled by it. They have placed ego at the centre

of his kinship network and tried to work the system out in terms of his personal relationships. (1967: 84)

Classificatory kinship doesn't operate on that myopic scale. Its premises are not those of Western competitive individualism. Although it doesn't eliminate intimacy or individuality, classificatory kinship operates on a grander level – on which bonds of sisterhood and brotherhood create networks of interdependence, decisively overriding parochial attachments and aims. Contrary to Western prejudices, for example, no Aboriginal Australian hunter-gatherer could be said to have inhabited a 'small-scale community'. As George Peter Murdock long ago observed,

> a native could, at least theoretically, traverse the entire continent, stopping at each tribal boundary to compare notes on relatives, and at the end of his journey know precisely whom in the local group he should address as grandmother, father-in-law, sister, etc., whom he might associate freely with, whom he must avoid, whom he might or might not have sexual relations with, and so on. (1949: 96)

Establishing chains of connection stretching across thousands of miles, these Aborigines' mathematically elegant section and subsection systems – logical extensions of the simple principle of sibling equivalence – were built to a scale quite beyond the conception of scholars familiar only with kinship in its truncated Western forms.

A further expression of the equivalence of siblings is the levirate (or sororate) – inheritance by a person of his or her deceased sibling's spouse. Many Europeans are familiar with this primarily from the Bible:

> If brethren dwell together, and one of them die, and have no child, the wife of the dead shall not marry without unto a stranger: her husband's brother shall go in unto her, and take her to him to wife, and perform the duty of an husband's brother unto her. (Deuteronomy 25:5)

Both levirate and sororate seem to have been universal throughout Aboriginal Australia (Radcliffe-Brown 1931: 96). In the rest of the world, the tradition is so common that 'it is easier to count cases where the custom is positively known to be lacking than to enumerate instances of its occurrence' (Lowie 1920: 32).

In the levirate/sororate, a person steps into the marital role of a deceased sibling with little or no ceremony and as a matter of course. In a sense, the living sibling was 'married' to the deceased's spouse already, since siblings are kin equivalents and marital contracts are arrangements not between private individuals but between kin groups on either side. Among the North American Navaho, to take just one example, the payment of brideprice 'made each partner the potential sexual property of the rest of the clan', the ideal arrangement being for 'a group of siblings to marry another group' (Aberle 1961a: 126).

In Western Arnhem Land, Australia, the logic of a whole group of sisters exercising marital rights in a whole group of brothers yielded something quite unlike monogamy, although taking advantage of such rights tended to be reserved for special occasions:

> . . . a wife may have access to a number of tribal 'husbands', and 'brother-cousins' of her actual husband; while a husband enjoys the same privilege with his tribal 'wives', the classificatory sisters of his wife and wives and their female 'cousins'. Should the husband or wife object, or take steps to terminate such a union, this would be contrary to public opinion, and the protesting party is soon made to understand that he or she is part of an institution which legally sanctions such relationships. (Berndt and Berndt 1951: 47)

When Morgan spoke of 'group marriage', it was broadly this kind of arrangement that he had in mind.

In concrete social situations – at least in the contemporary ethnographic record – the equivalence of siblings is rarely carried through to its logical conclusion, which would be to give every woman tens or even hundreds of 'sisters' and a comparable number of 'brothers', 'husbands', 'mothers-in-law', and so forth. Day-to-day foraging constraints, marital bonding, emotional compatibility, distance or closeness of relationship, seasonally varying residence patterns, and other such factors make it impossible to treat siblings on all levels as identical. Darwinian anthropologists may with good reason object that hunter-gatherer mothers do tend to favour their own direct offspring, even if such favouritism is publicly played down. They may also note how people in reality certainly do discriminate between mates on biological grounds – again a 'brute' fact not highlighted in the institutional system, which proclaims all spouses to be equivalents.

Strictly speaking, however – that is, to the extent that 'classificatory' principles prevail – the logic implies that in each generation, those entering into relationships are neither individuals nor marital couples. They are self-organized coalitions of sisters/brothers. As Radcliffe-Brown put it: 'The unit of structure everywhere seems to be the group of full siblings – brothers and sisters' (1950: 87). In quoting this statement, Meyer Fortes offered his own opinion that it constituted 'one of the few generalizations in kinship theory that . . . enshrines a discovery worthy to be placed side by side with Morgan's discovery of classificatory kinship . . .' (1970: 76). He added that, like Morgan's initial discovery, this subsequent generalization 'has been repeatedly validated and has opened up lines of inquiry not previously foreseen.'

Radcliffe-Brown (1952: 19–20) noted that where 'the classificatory system of kinship reaches a high degree of development', the close conjunction of brothers and sisters necessarily entails a corresponding *disjunction* of husbands and wives. On a formal level – that is, where terminology and publicly professed ideals are concerned – husband and wife do not merge or combine their identities. Contrary to Malinowski's (1956 [1931]) claims for the centrality and universality of the 'individual family', the two spouses do not form a corporate unit in sharing relationships, property, or even offspring – which, in some formal sense, must always 'belong' on one side of the fundamental divide or the other.

To this picture of pronounced *separation* between spouses we may add that in many places, particularly in South America, Africa, and Oceania, spouses were traditionally not allowed to eat together – 'an arrangement', as Robert Lowie put it, 'almost inconceivable to us' (1960b [1919]: 122). In Africa, it is a common Bantu custom that 'the husband and wife do not eat together after marriage' (Richards 1932: 191). Among the Bemba, for example, it is 'considered shameful' for the sexes to eat together (Richards 1969: 122).

Very often, the rationale here is that for the sexes to share meals would signify their bond of kinship, with the corollary that any sex between them would be incest. In various parts of the world, menstrual avoidances, menstrual huts, post-partum taboos, in-law taboos, and 'men's house' institutions help ensure that gender distinctions are not blurred, incestuous confusion is avoided – and spouses are effectively kept apart for much of the time (Knight 1991). Uncomfortably for those who argue for the universal centrality of the 'nuclear family', in other words, we find that it is the disjunction of spouses, not their conjunction, which is the most strongly emphasized ritual and structural norm.

The Matrilineal Clan

There are good biological reasons why in any culture, a young infant might wish to stay close to its mother. Fathers, on the other hand, can come and go. Where brother/sister unity is preserved into adulthood at the expense of the marital bond, paternity certainty will be that much less likely and the scales will be tipped correspondingly toward matrilineal descent (Aberle 1961b; Kurland 1979).

The English adventurer John Lederer (1672) seems to have been the first to describe a matrilineal clan system accurately in print. His words refer to the Tutelo, an eastern Siouan tribe:

> From four women, *viz., Pash, Sopoy, Askarin* and *Maraskarin,* they derive the race of Mankinde; which they therefore divide into four Tribes, distinguished under those several names . . . now for two of the same Tribe to match, is abhorred as Incest, and punished with great severity. (Quoted in Tax 1955: 445)

Lederer's 'tribes' correspond to what would later be termed 'clans'. Note that endogamy – marriage within the clan – is prohibited irrespective of degree of relatedness.

Half a century later, Father Lafitau (1724) described in glowing terms the honoured status of women among the matrilineally organized Iroquois:

> Nothing . . . is more real than this superiority of the women. It is essentially the women who embody the Nation, the nobility of blood, the genealogical tree, the sequence of generations and the continuity of families. It is in them that all real authority resides: the land, the fields and all their produce belongs to them: they are the soul of the councils, the arbiters of peace and war. . . . (Quoted in Tax 1955: 445)

Some decades later, the Scottish moral philosopher Adam Ferguson remarked of 'savage nations' in general that the 'children are considered as pertaining to the mother, with little regard to descent on the father's side' (1995 [1767]: 126).

Johann Jakob Bachofen published his *Mutterrecht* in 1861. Drawing on ancient Greek historical texts and myths, he advanced the following propositions: (1) humanity once lived in a state of sexual promiscuity; (2) there could be no certainty of paternity; (3) kinship was traced through females alone; (4) women's status was correspondingly high; (5) monogamy emerged relatively late in history. According to Bachofen:

> ... mother right is not confined to any particular people but marks a cultural stage. In view of the universal qualities of human nature, this cultural stage cannot be restricted to any particular ethnic family. And consequently what must concern us is not so much the similarities between isolated phenomena as the unity of the basic conception. (1973 [1861]: 71)

The legal historian J. F. McLennan read Bachofen's book in 1866, having the previous year published his *Primitive Marriage*, which independently proposed 'kinship through females' as the 'more archaic system' (McLennan 1970 [1865]: 123). More effective in supporting Bachofen, however, was Lewis Morgan, who was excited to discover living matrilineal institutions among the Iroquois and other Native Americans. Morgan's *Systems of Consanguinity and Affinity of the Human Family* (1871) described comparable systems across much of the globe and marked the birth of the modern study of kinship. In this and in his subsequent *Ancient Society* (1907 [1877]), Morgan championed the historical priority of the matrilineal clan over patriliny and over the nuclear family. His authority was such that for several decades, almost all prominent scholars accepted the essentials of the Bachofen–Morgan evolutionary scheme.

Describing an Iroquois long-house, Morgan (1881: 126–8) wrote of its immense length, its numerous compartments and fires, the 'warm, roomy and tidily-kept habitations', the raised bunks around the walls, the common stores and 'the matron in each household, who made a division of the food from the kettle to each family according to their needs . . .'. 'Here', he commented, 'was communism in living carried out in practical life . . .'. When women in these matrilineal, matrilocal households needed to exclude a lazy or unwanted visiting male, they could reliably depend on their frequently returning brothers to ensure enforcement of their will. To illustrate the correspondingly high status of women, Morgan cites personal correspondence from the Reverend Arthur Wright, for many years a missionary among the Seneca Iroquois:

> Usually, the female portion ruled the house, and were doubtless clannish enough about it. The stores were held in common; but woe to the luckless husband or lover who was too shiftless to do his share of the providing. No matter how many children, or whatever goods he might have in the house, he might at any time be ordered to pack up his blanket and budge; and after such orders it would not be healthful for him to attempt to disobey. The house would be too hot for him; and, unless saved by the intercession of some aunt or grandmother, he must retreat to his own clan; or, as was often done, go and start a new matrimonial alliance

in some other. The women were the great power among the clans, as every-where else. (Morgan 1907 [1877]: 455n)

As Marx and Engels read all this, they excitedly concluded that Iroquois women must traditionally have possessed what modern trade unionists could only dream of – collective ownership and control over their own productive lives.

Engels and 'the Origin of the Family'

Engels elaborated and publicized Morgan's findings in his *The Origin of the Family, Private Property and the State*. 'The rediscovery of the original mother-right gens', he wrote ('gens' being at that time anthropological jargon for 'clan'),

> . . . has the same significance for the history of primitive society as the theory of evolution has for biology, and Marx's theory of surplus value for political eco-nomy. It enabled Morgan to outline for the first time a history of the family. . . . Clearly, this opens a new era in the treatment of the history of primitive society. (Engels 1972a [1891]: 36)

In the same passage, he went so far as to state: 'The mother-right gens has become the pivot around which this entire science turns. . . .' This was no hasty judgement. From their earliest days in revolutionary struggle, Engels and Marx had been wrestling with questions about sex as well as class. In 1844, Marx declared that the 'immediate, natural and necessary relationship of human being to human being is the relationship of man to woman', adding that 'from this relationship the whole cultural level of man can be judged' (2000a [1844]: 96). Marx took Morgan's work on the matrilineal clan as confirmation that an early form of communism must have preceded property-based class society and that its secret had been sexual equality. In *The German Ideology*, Marx and Engels contrasted this original egalitarianism with the subsequent dominance of 'property, the nucleus, the first form, of which lies in the family, where wife and children are the slaves of the husband' (2000b [1846]: 185).

According to Morgan, the rise of alienable property disempowered women by triggering a switch to patrilocal residence and patrilineal descent:

> It thus reversed the position of the wife and mother in the household; she was of a different gens from her children, as well as her husband; and under monogamy was now isolated from her gentile kindred, living in the separate and exclusive house of her husband. Her new condition tended to subvert and destroy that power and influence which descent in the female line and the joint-tenement houses had created. (1881: 128)

Engels added political impact to all this:

> The overthrow of mother right was the *world-historic defeat of the female sex*. The man seized the reins in the house also, the woman was degraded, enthralled,

the slave of the man's lust, a mere instrument for breeding children. (1972b [1884]: 68)

He continued:

The first class antagonism which appears in history coincides with the development of the antagonism between man and woman in monogamian marriage, and the first class oppression with that of the female sex by the male. (1972b [1884]: 75)

The Reaction

Around the turn of the twentieth century, virtually all those who had helped found the discipline of anthropology converged around the fundamentals of the Bachofen–Morgan theory. As Murdock (1949: 185) subsequently observed, the 'extremely plausible' arguments in its favour included (a) the biological inevitability of the mother–child bond, (b) the intrinsic difficulty in establishing biological paternity, and (c) numerous apparent survivals of matrilineal traditions in societies with patrilineal descent groups. 'So logical, so closely reasoned, and so apparently in accord with all known facts was this hypothesis', continues Murdock, 'that from its pioneer formulation by Bachofen in 1861 to nearly the end of the nineteenth century it was accepted by social scientists practically without exception.'

So, what changed everyone's mind? As we review the historical evidence, it becomes clear that political passions were never far beneath the surface and ultimately played the decisive role. With regard to the topic of 'primitive promiscuity', Engels commented: 'It has become the fashion of late to deny the existence of this initial stage in the sexual life of mankind. The aim is to spare humanity this "shame"' (1972b [1884]: 47). The reference here was to Edward Westermarck, scholarly defender of individual marriage and the family who was later to inspire the young Malinowski. Westermarck had chosen to turn public opinion against Bachofen's theory of 'primitive promiscuity' by associating it with modern prostitution. To this, Engels retorted: 'To me it rather seems that all understanding of primitive conditions remains impossible so long as we regard them through brothel spectacles' (1972b [1884]: 51).

Once Engels had incorporated Morgan's findings into the socialist canon, however, no one could write neutrally on such topics any more. Morgan's *Ancient Society*, as Robert Lowie was later to comment,

attracted the notice of Marx and Engels, who accepted and popularised its evolutionary doctrines as being in harmony with their own philosophy. As a result it was promptly translated into various European tongues, and German workingmen would sometimes reveal an uncanny familiarity with the Hawaiian and Iroquois mode of designating kin, matters not obviously connected with a proletarian revolution. (1937: 54–5)

Once Engels had endorsed it, Morgan's theory was destined to become a casualty of the central conflict of the age. Social anthropologists may like to

imagine that their discipline became shaped in its modern form quite independently of Marxism. It would be more accurate to describe it as moulded
specifically in reaction against the ideas of Engels and Marx. 'With Morgan's
scheme incorporated into Communist doctrine', observes Marvin Harris, 'the
struggling science of anthropology crossed the threshold of the twentieth
century with a clear mandate for its own survival and well-being: expose
Morgan's scheme and destroy the method on which it was based' (1969: 249).

Group Motherhood Versus the Ideology of the Family

A widespread consensus developed on both sides of the Atlantic that regardless
of the intellectual merit of Morgan's ideas, 'group motherhood' was in any
event too dangerous an idea to be allowed. A radio broadcast by Malinowski
revealed his state of mind:

> A whole school of anthropologists, from Bachofen on, have maintained that the
> maternal clan was the primitive domestic institution. . . . In my opinion, as you
> know, this is entirely incorrect. But an idea like that, once it is taken seriously
> and applied to modern conditions, becomes positively dangerous. I believe that
> the most disruptive element in the modern revolutionary tendencies is the idea
> that parenthood can be made collective. If once we came to the point of doing
> away with the individual family as the pivotal element of our society, we should
> be faced with a social catastrophe compared with which the political upheaval
> of the French revolution and the economic changes of Bolshevism are insigni-
> ficant. The question, therefore, as to whether group motherhood is an institution
> which ever existed, whether it is an arrangement which is compatible with human
> nature and social order, is of considerable practical interest. (1956 [1931]: 76)

While denouncing 'ideology', Malinowski nonetheless saw it as his scholarly
duty to 'prove to the best of my ability that marriage and the family have been,
are, and will remain the foundations of human society' (1956 [1931]: 28). He
insisted that 'marriage in single pairs – monogamy in the sense in which
Westermarck and I are using it – is primeval' (1956 [1931]: 42). It's worth
remembering here that the Finnish historian of marriage attributed 'marriage
in single pairs' equally to chimpanzees and gorillas, believing human marriage
to have been inherited from a primate precursor. Malinowski's assertion that
'monogamy' must be 'primeval' fits uneasily with declarations such as the following: 'I would rather discountenance any speculation about the "origins"
of marriage or anything else than contribute to them even indirectly. . . .'
(Malinowski 1932: xxiii–iv). Notable here is Malinowski's tactic of dissociating
himself from evolutionary research while specifying his opinion as to the 'initial situation' for human kinship. Throughout much of the twentieth century,
as Adam Kuper (1988) records, the strategy of smuggling in assumptions about
'origins' and 'initial situations' without having to justify them proved popular
among anthropologists of virtually every school. 'We do not know', wrote Lévi-
Strauss, 'and never shall know, anything about the first origin of beliefs and

customs the roots of which plunge into a distant past . . .' (1969a [1962]: 141). Following in Malinowski's footsteps, this didn't prevent him from propounding his own 'exchange of women' account of the origins of marriage, kinship, and much else besides (Lévi-Strauss 1969b [1949]).

The Case of the Kwakiutl Indians

In the United States, Franz Boas initially accepted the Bachofen–Morgan scheme, according to which descent systems invariably underwent historical change from matriliny to patriliny and not the reverse. In support of this was a 'complete lack of historically attested, or even inferentially probable, cases of a direct transition from patrilineal to matrilineal descent' (Murdock 1949: 190). Boas later came to believe, however, that he might discredit Morgan if he could find a single exception.

On Vancouver Island, the Kwakiutl were organized in groups known as *numaym*, which Boas translated initially as 'clan' or 'gens'. He explained that there was no consistent rule of descent: 'The child does not belong by birth to the gens of his father or mother, but may be made a member of any gens to which his father, mother, grandparents, or great-grandparents belonged' (Boas 1891: 609). Six years later, however, Boas changed his mind, attributing to the *numaym* now 'a purely female law of descent', albeit one secured 'only through the medium of the husband' (1897: 334–5). Despite this, anything short of a *purely* patrilineal system switching to a *purely* matrilineal one might still have allowed Morgan's evolutionist scheme to survive. Boas duly supplied the requisite categorical formulations. Although the Kwakiutl had today 'a purely female law of descent', he now proclaimed, the 'organization must have been at one time a purely paternal one' (Boas 1897: 334–5). For the very first time, a unilineal descent system had been found changing in the reverse direction from that stipulated by Morgan.

The loyalty of Robert Lowie to his great friend and teacher, Franz Boas, could hardly be in doubt. In 1914, however, even this ardent disciple admitted that the Vancouver Island data had been stretched to fit the case. Although 'the Kwakiutl facts are very interesting', as he put it, 'it is highly doubtful whether they have the theoretical significance ascribed to them' (Lowie 1960a [1914]: 28). Most awkward was the fact that the Kwakiutl *numaym* groupings central to Boas's entire argument were not unilineal descent groups at all. Neither 'matriliny' nor 'patriliny' was an applicable concept. 'For these reasons,' as Lowie put it, 'the Kwakiutl conditions do not seem to furnish a favorable test case.'

However, such scholarly reservations did nothing to stop Boas or his students from continuing to disseminate the myth. The 'extreme interest in Boas' handling of the *numaym*', as Marvin Harris comments in his historical analysis of the whole shameful episode, 'stems from the fashion in which he and his students seized upon this case to destroy the supposed universal tendency for patrilineality to follow matrilineality and at the same time to discredit the entire historical determinist position' (1969: 305). On the basis of this one drastically deficient case, there gradually diffused out of Schermerhorn Hall at

Columbia, through lecture, word of mouth, article, and text, the unquestioned dogma that Boas had proved that it was just as likely that patrilineality succeeded matrilineality as the reverse.

The Case of the Mother's Brother

Meanwhile across the Atlantic, A. R. Radcliffe-Brown (1924) intervened with his celebrated article entitled 'The Mother's Brother in South Africa'. It was this intervention which by general consent – at least among British structural-functionalist anthropologists – buried once and for all the evolutionist theory that the mother's brother relationship in patrilineal societies was a survival left over from an earlier matrilineal stage.

Radcliffe-Brown's specific target was a comprehensive monograph on the Thonga of Mozambique (Junod 1912). The following features (summarized in Murdock 1959: 378) seemed to require explanation:

- Although inheriting clan membership from their father, Thonga children on being weaned went to live in their mother's brother's village.
- A man without patrilineal heirs could require a sister to remain in his settlement, her male offspring continuing his lineage.
- Even when a man did have patrilineal heirs, his sisters' sons could claim items from his own estate.
- The maternal uncle had a share in the brideprice received for a sister's daughter.
- The maternal uncle and not the father officiated at the sacrifices in a young man's life-crisis ceremonies.

Junod himself interpreted these features as clear evidence that the Thonga were not straightforwardly patrilineal but were embroiled in a difficult and sometimes contradictory process of transition from matrilineal to patrilineal descent.

For Radcliffe-Brown, it was axiomatic that any such 'pseudo-history' had to be repudiated. The various components of a social system should instead be explained in structural-functionalist terms – that is, by invoking fixed laws on the model of physics and chemistry. He now proposed his celebrated structural-functionalist explanation. The involvement of the mother's brother in the upbringing of a Thonga (or Tsonga) boy has nothing whatsoever to do with past or present matrilineal descent. It's just an expression of a fixed and invariant sociological principle – the principle of 'the equivalence of siblings'. Since a woman and her brother are equivalents, any human child's feelings toward its mother will naturally tend to include her brother as well. Radcliffe-Brown termed this universal psychic mechanism 'the extension of sentiments', concluding after a few further observations that everything was now satisfactorily explained.

With the benefit of hindsight, what are we to make of this short essay? Let me begin by recalling David Schneider's (1961) classic survey of matrilineal descent systems. The essence of Schneider's argument is that a woman is faced with a choice. To put her brother first in her children's lives would be to put her husband second; conversely, if she puts her husband first, her brother must come second. It really is as simple as that: you can either have brother–sister unity as the fundamental principle or else you can have husband–wife unity, but you cannot have both at the same time. A corollary of this fact is that, contrary to Radcliffe-Brown, brother–sister unity cannot possibly be 'a universal sociological principle'. In fact, it is as much a variable as is matrilineal descent. It is easy to see that only a *matrilineal* descent group requires its male and female members to remain united following marriage. A patrilineal descent group requires no such thing. Patriliny requires husbands to let go of married sisters and monitor the fidelity of their wives. Where the husband's rights prevail, the wife to that extent yields control over her fertility to him and his kin, weakening her bond with her brother, enhancing paternity certainty, and thereby favouring patrilineal descent. Let us suppose, however, that after marriage, a woman chooses to remain primarily bonded to her brother. This can only be at the expense of her bond with her husband – reducing paternity certainty and hence favouring matrilineal descent. To sum up: Schneider's theoretical findings demonstrate that the very factor invoked by Radcliffe-Brown as an alternative to the matrilineal complex – namely opposite-sex sibling unity – turns out to be a covariant feature of that complex itself. To invoke 'brother–sister unity' as an explanation for the mother's brother relationship is no more than to invoke an aspect of the matrilineal complex while concealing it under another name.

Murdock long ago poured scorn on Radcliffe-Brown's whole approach:

> In the first place, the alleged principles are mere verbalizations reified into causal forces. In the second, such concepts as 'equivalence of brothers' and 'necessity for social integration' contain no statements of the relationships between phenomena under varying conditions, and thus lie at the opposite extreme from genuine scientific laws. (Murdock 1949: 121)

Ironically, Murdock's subsequent historical research on the Thonga confirmed that they were indeed in the throes of transition from matriliny to patriliny just as Junod had originally claimed (Murdock 1959: 378).

In conformity with Morgan's scheme, the rise of alienable property may be the crucial factor cementing marital bonds at the expense of brother–sister solidarity throughout much of sub-Saharan Africa. As one cross-cultural researcher put it: 'the cow is the enemy of matriliny' (Aberle 1961b: 680). Following in the footsteps of Murdock's cross-cultural comparative work, Mace and Holden's (1999) phylogenetically controlled analysis has confirmed a negative correlation between African matriliny and cattle owning. In their most recent analysis of matriliny as daughter-biased investment, Holden, Sear, and Mace comment that 'the two factors Morgan identified, heritable wealth and paternity uncertainty, remain central to our understanding of variation in matriliny and patriliny in human social organization' (2003: 110).

The Effect on Palaeoanthropology

Writing in 1965 about the evolution of religion, E. E. Evans-Pritchard felt
confident enough to declare Morgan-style origins research 'as dead as mutton'
(1965: 100). Except in the Soviet Union (where it became incorporated into
state dogma), Morgan's scheme was effectively suppressed – so thoroughly that
by the mid-1930s it had become institutionally impossible to re-open any of
the once highly charged debates.

Where did this leave palaeoanthropology and evolutionary theory? Morgan's
work on the matrilineal clan had led such influential thinkers as Engels, Freud,
and Durkheim to argue for fundamental discontinuity between primate and
human social organization. Classificatory kinship, exogamy, totemic avoidances
– in any but the most narrow and blinkered account of human origins, such
things simply cried out for explanation. But Morgan's suppression margin-
alized evolutionary questions and therefore sidelined social anthropology's
distinctive scholarly contribution to evolutionary science. From this point on,
the two branches of anthropology were hardly on speaking terms. As a result,
Darwinians became cut off from specialist knowledge about cross-cultural variability in human kinship arrangements and from processes driving historical
change. Forced to draw narrowly on their own cultural assumptions, would-
be Darwinian scientists recurrently mistook monogamy, paternal inheritance,
and other contemporary instantiations of Judaeo-Christian morality for core
features of human nature.

By default, as a gradualist theory, Darwinism tends to assume continuity
between primate and human life. Drawing on the primatology of his day, Darwin
himself had pictured primaeval man as a sexual tyrant jealously guarding his
hard-won harem of females to the exclusion of his rivals (1871, 2: 362). After
the Second World War, many professed followers of Darwin felt licensed to
weave popular narratives free of all ethnographic or anthropological constraint.
'Naked Ape' theory (Morris 1967) connected extant primates directly to the pair-
bonding preoccupations of contemporary Western culture. Eurocentrism was
the inevitable result, as middle-class English family values – or alternatively
US college campus lifestyles – became scientifically naturalized and projected
back into the evolutionary past. This trend continues today in much popular
literature produced by evolutionary psychology (e.g. Buss 1994; Miller 2000).

Leslie White and his students (Fried 1967; Service 1962; Steward 1955)
had attempted to salvage much of Morgan's evolutionist programme, with
the major difference that the 'patrilocal band' model of early hunter-gatherer
organization was now taken for granted. Against this background, Sherwood
Washburn and his associates launched the new discipline of palaeoanthropology,
their activities culminating in the 1966 interdisciplinary 'Man the Hunter'
conference (Washburn and DeVore 1961; Washburn and Lancaster 1968).
Among those present was Claude Lévi-Strauss, whose theory about the transition from nature to culture required acceptance of the doctrine that patrilocal
residence was a permanent and universal feature of all married life. The number of matrilocal systems, as he explained, 'is very limited':

Consequently, the only alternatives are, on the one hand patrilineal and patri-local systems, and on the other, matrilineal and patrilocal systems. The exceptional cases of matrilineal and matrilocal systems, which are in conflict with the asymmetrical relationship between the sexes, may be assimilated to the latter. (Lévi-Strauss 1969b [1949]: 116–17)

'Assimilating' matrilocal residence to its patrilocal antithesis means, of course, prioritizing 'exchange of women' doctrine at the expense of inconvenient facts. Hunter-gatherer ethnographers effectively demolished the patrilocal band model during the 1970s (Lee and DeVore 1968; Peterson 1976; Woodburn 1968b), but this has done little to prevent popular science writers from perpetuating it to this day.

Morgan Revisited

Most currently favoured scenarios for human evolution invoke paternity certainty as key to the process leading from Plio-Pleistocene hominin to modern *Homo sapiens*. In typical versions of the story (e.g. Alexander and Noonan 1979; Kaplan et al. 2000; Lovejoy 1981), paternal investment is linked directly to the sexual division of labour, food sharing, lengthy juvenile dependency, ovulation concealment, and continuous female sexual receptivity. The idea is that since the human female produces such unusually helpless and dependent offspring, her mate is necessary to provide long-term pair-bonding commitment and support. The catch is that no male should enter such a contract unless confident that his partner will be faithful to him in return. 'In evolutionary terms', as Terrence Deacon puts it, 'a male who tends to invest significant time and energy in caring for and providing food for an infant must have a high probability of being its father; otherwise his expenditure of time and energy will benefit the genes of another male' (1997: 388).

Dating from the 1960s and 1970s, this scenario has become in effect the Standard Model of Human Evolution (Beckerman and Valentine 2002). Robert Boyd and Joan Silk impute monogamy to *Homo erectus*:

Females may have had difficulty providing food for themselves and their dependent young. If H. erectus hunted regularly, males might have been able to provide high-quality food for their mates and offspring. Monogamy would have increased the males' confidence of paternity and favored paternal investment. (1997: 435)

Evolutionary psychologist Steven Pinker uses the same idea to explain why the sexual double standard is natural and inevitable:

Sexual jealousy is found in all cultures. . . . In most societies, some women readily share a husband, but in no society do men readily share a wife. A woman having sex with another man is *always* a threat to the man's genetic interests, because it might fool him into working for a competitor's genes. (1997: 488–90)

Partible Paternity

In response to such dogmatic statements, Stephen Beckerman and Paul Valentine have assembled counter-evidence from a substantial number of Lowland South American societies. In their book *Cultures of Multiple Fathers* (Beckerman and Valentine 2002), they demonstrate how – in direct refutation of Pinker – the paternity of a woman's baby becomes partitioned among multiple males. They quote this passage from a classical account of the Xocleng (previously Kaingang):

> 'Klendó's daughter, Pathó, is my child', said Vomblé. 'How do you know,' said I, 'since Klendó also lay with her mother?' 'Well, when two men lie with a woman they just call her child their child.' But not only do men feel that their mistress's children are their children, but people whose mothers have had intercourse with the same man, whether as lover or husband, regard one another as siblings. (Henry 1941: 45)

If such 'partible paternity' (as the authors term it) were found in only a tribe or two, it could perhaps be dismissed as an aberration. However, the institution is widely distributed across Lowland South America and found among peoples whose traditions diverged millennia ago – as evidenced by the fact that they live thousands of kilometres apart, speak unrelated languages, and show no indication of having been in contact for centuries. The authors continue:

> It is difficult to come to any conclusion except that partible paternity is an ancient folk belief capable of supporting effective families, families that provide satisfactory paternal care of children and manage the successful rearing of children to adulthood. The distributional evidence argues that it is possible to build a biologically and socially competent society – a society whose members do a perfectly adequate job of reproducing themselves and their social relations – with a culture that incorporates a belief in partible paternity. (Beckerman and Valentine 2002: 6)

Not only is the belief compatible with successful reproduction; it may even help babies to survive. Among the hunting and gathering Aché, children with one extra father are significantly more likely to reach maturity (Hill and Hurtado 1996: 444), a correlation confirmed by a longitudinal statistical study among the Barí (Beckerman et al. 1998).

Can a woman really help her baby by taking lovers during pregnancy? The answer seems to be yes. The explanation is probably that additional fathers contribute additional provisions and more protection against infanticide. It is not in a woman's interests to encourage the men in her life to engage in contests over biological paternity. From a woman's standpoint, the truth is that her current husband may become injured, die, or abandon her. In any event, she may have good reason to switch to a new man. If her new mate cares about not being the father, her existing offspring might suffer infanticide or abuse. Loss of a wanted child is enormously costly to any human mother, making it best not to divulge but precisely to *confuse* accurate paternity information, taking lovers to distribute illusions among multiple males. Whether these males contest or collude depends on the balance of costs and benefits involved. Where males strive to contest paternity, females may have an interest in driving up the costs.

Beckerman and Valentine view the range of variation as reflecting 'a competition between men and women over whose reproductive strategies will dominate social life'. In small-scale egalitarian societies, they continue,

> Women's reproductive interests are best served if mate choice is a non-binding, female decision; if there is a network of multiple females to aid or substitute for a woman in mothering responsibilities; if male support for a woman and her children comes from multiple men; and if a woman is shielded from the effects of male sexual jealousy. Male reproductive interests, contrariwise, are best served by male control over female sexual behavior, promoting paternity certainty and elevated reproductive success for the more powerful males. This profile implies that men choose their own or their sons' wives, and their daughters' husbands; that marriage is a lifetime commitment and extra-marital affairs by women are severely sanctioned; and that this state of affairs is maintained by disallowing women reliable female support networks, or male support other than that of the husband and his primary male consanguines. (2002: 11)

In humans as in other sexually reproducing species, neither sex is likely to succeed in imposing its strategies to the exclusion of resistance from the opposite sex (Gowaty 1997). Yet there are situations that may give the edge to one side or the other. When male strategies dominate in the human case, patrilineality and virilocality are the order of the day, with female autonomy correspondingly curtailed. However, as Beckerman and Valentine explain, the reverse outcome must be recognized if we are to grasp the parameters:

> Where women clearly have the upper hand, uxorilocal residence predominates; women's husbands are often chosen for them by their mothers, or they choose their own husbands; when a woman's husband dies, his children tend to be brought up by their mother, her brothers, and her new husband; women have broad sexual freedom both before and after marriage; the idea of partible paternity is prominent, with women having wide latitude in choosing the secondary fathers of their children; women usually make no secret of the identity of these secondary fathers; and the ideology of partible paternity defuses to some extent potential conflicts between male rivals – antagonisms that are seldom helpful to a woman's reproductive interests in the long run. (2002: 11)

Engels Revisited?

Beckerman and Valentine are Darwinian anthropologists who can hardly be accused of having Marxist sympathies. But I cannot help thinking that if Engels were alive, he might have been encouraged by their results. Here, for the record, is Engels on the subject of male sexual jealousy in evolutionary perspective:

... animal societies have, to be sure, a certain value in drawing conclusions regarding human societies – but only in a negative sense. As far as we have ascertained, the higher vertebrates know only two forms of the family: polygamy or the single pair. In both cases only one adult male, only one husband is permissible. The jealousy of the male, representing both tie and limits of the family, brings the animal family into conflict with the horde. The horde, the higher social form, is rendered impossible here, loosened there, or dissolved altogether during the mating season; at best, its continued development is hindered by the jealousy of the male. This alone suffices to prove that the animal family and primitive human society are incompatible things; that primitive man, working his way up out of the animal stage, either knew no family whatsoever, or at the most knew a family that is nonexistent among animals. (1972b [1884]: 49–50)

Engels accepts that a male gorilla might strive to hold on to any females he has succeeded in acquiring. But applied to the human case, mothers would then be denied access to any but the most isolated and intolerant males. The point stressed by Engels is that only a decisive social breakthrough could have solved this problem:

For evolution out of the animal stage, for the accomplishment of the greatest advance known to nature, an additional element was needed: the replacement of the individual's inadequate power of defence by the united strength and joint effort of the horde. ... Mutual toleration among the adult males, freedom from jealousy, was ... the first condition for the building of those large and enduring groups in the midst of which alone the transition from animal to man could be achieved. And indeed, what do we find as the oldest, most primitive form of the family, of which undeniable evidence can be found in history, and which even today can be studied here and there? Group marriage, the form in which whole groups of men and whole groups of women belong to one another, and which leaves but little scope for jealousy.

As I have argued elsewhere (Knight 1991; Knight and Power 2005), not all of Engels's revolutionary speculations look out of place today.

Kinship Theory in Crisis

'I believe', said Sir Edmund Leach half a century ago, 'that we social anthropologists are like the mediaeval Ptolemaic astronomers; we spend our time trying to fit the facts of the objective world into the framework of a set of concepts which have been developed *a priori* instead of from observation' (1961: 26). Anthropologists since Malinowski, he wrote, have imagined 'the family' in the English-language sense of this word to be the logical, necessary, and inevitable pivot around which kinship must revolve. But the fact is that human kinship becomes unintelligible when viewed from that perspective. Owing to its false initial assumptions, Leach concluded, the mental constructs of modern kinship theory appear as bewildering and futile as the cycles and epicycles of those Ptolemaic astronomers who insisted that the sun circled a motionless earth.

Some years later, in an evaluation of the contemporary state of kinship theory, Needham expressed a similar verdict. 'The current theoretical position', he observed, 'is obscure and confused, and there is little clear indication of what future developments we can expect or should encourage.' He concluded, in tones indicating a mood close to despair:

> In view of the constant professional attention extending over roughly a century, and a general improvement in ethnographic accounts, this is a remarkably unsatisfactory situation in what is supposed to be a basic discipline. Obviously, after so long a time, and so much field research, it is not just facts that we need. Something more fundamental seems to have gone wrong. What we have to look for, perhaps, is some radical flaw in analysis, some initial defect in the way we approach the phenomena. (1974: 39)

During the final decades of the twentieth century, most social anthropologists responded to their disciplinary predicament by abandoning the study of kinship altogether (Bloch and Sperber 2002). Intellectual bankruptcy on this scale is the price paid, I think, when autonomous science is prevented from shaping and informing politics, uninformed politics instead shaping and constraining the revolutionary potential of science.

Some Concluding Notes

Early kinship may have been simple; alternatively, we may imagine something more complex. Let's take simplicity as our starting point. For a woman, her kin come first. Once a brother, always a brother – unlike sexual partners, who may come and go. As a woman gives birth to children, she can turn to male kin for long-term commitment and support. The reason she must resist sex with such brothers is that she needs them precisely for support in the event of conflict with a sexual partner. She must, therefore, keep the two opposed male roles categorically apart. Since out-group males are a valuable source of mating-effort, she can encourage their provisioning activities but without giving them permanent control.

The logic outlined so far does nothing to prohibit father–daughter incest. However, mothers seeking to maximize male mating-effort will have good reason to bar existing spouses from additional access to their daughters. Now apply the principle of sibling equivalence. To the extent that they are acting in solidarity, mothers will be shielding *their own and one another's daughters* from the sexual advances of fathers. The parties on either side, however, will be of various different ages. At what precise point does a female become too young to count as 'sister' or 'wife' and a male become too old to count as brother or husband? The logic of siblinghood will prompt mothers to draw a categorical boundary between females in any one generation and their 'fathers' taken as a whole. In the sense that fathers and their offspring will now be defined as vertically related kin, the result might be conceptualized as a patrilineal dual system cross-cutting an already-established division into matrilineal moieties.

But however it is conceived, we now have the simplest possible version of what Nick Allen (chapter 5) terms a 'tetradic' system. From this point of departure, every known kinship structure in the world can be derived.

The section and subsection systems of Aboriginal Australia rest on just such a mathematically elegant foundation (Lawrence 1937; Maddock 1974; Testart 1978). As is well known, extant hunter-gatherers are usually more flexible about the rules, local decisions about residence and affiliation representing pragmatic compromises between various conflicting demands. Whatever the precise outcome, however, it is impossible to explain the details – whether we are dealing with Australia, Africa, or the Americas – without taking both sexes and their distinctive strategies into account. No sense can be made of the range of variability by one-sidedly assuming patrilocality, paternity certainty, or male sexual control.

Embarrassingly for proponents of the patrilocal band model, genetic data on sub-Saharan African hunter-gatherers indicate a matrilocal residential bias. Studies of mitochondrial versus Y-chromosomal dispersal patterns show that hunter-gatherer women across this region have tended to reside close to their mothers following marriage, migration rates for women being lower than those for men (Destro-Bisol et al. 2004). A census among the Hadza showed 68% of monogamously married women whose mothers were still alive residing with them in the same camp (Woodburn 1968b). 'Across all societies', concludes Marlowe on the basis of a careful cross-cultural study, 'the greater the dependence on gathering, hunting, and fishing, the less likely that residence is virilocal.' Hunting has the strongest effect and, contrary to proponents of the patrilocal band model, results in less virilocality, not more (Marlowe 2004: 80). Alvarez (2004) has reviewed the evidence behind the standard doctrine that patrilocality is characteristic of known hunter-gatherers. Most of the widely used classifications turn out to have been based on totally inadequate data and ignore insightful discussions that took place in early anthropology. The few ethnographies in which camp data are available support the view that individuals use a variety of kin and other links to decide where to live, the only discernible statistical bias being in favour of *mother–daughter links*.

One advantage of Marlowe's study of hunter-gatherer residence patterns is that it acknowledges variability through life history. A husband who has already helped provision a child might then be trusted sufficiently for his wife to agree to move with him to his natal camp. But this shouldn't obscure the fact that residence among hunter-gatherers tends to be initially matrilocal. Whether in Australia, Africa, or the Americas, a young bridegroom must not only visit his bride in her camp but also work strenuously for her, surrendering to his in-laws whatever game he catches. This, after all, is the essence of 'bride-service' – the fundamental economic institution in any hunter-gatherer society. To maximize incoming provisions, the young hunter's in-laws will strive to keep him under close supervision and control. It therefore comes as little surprise to find that, cross-culturally, males 'contribute less where residence is virilocal and more where it is uxorilocal' (Marlowe 2004: 281).

Females, then, obtain the best deal when they remain following marriage with close kin. On what grounds can it be claimed that this residence pattern was likely to have characterized early human kinship? According to the 'grandmother' hypothesis (O'Connell et al. 1999; Voland et al. 2005; Opie and Power, this volume), the selective advantage of distinctively human post-menopausal lifespans is that it enabled older women to assist their adult children in caring for and provisioning grandchildren. In genetic terms, a woman can never be as certain of her son's offspring as she can of her daughter's. For grandmothers to invest preferentially in their descendants through sons, therefore, would not be an evolutionarily stable strategy. It comes as little surprise, therefore, that a recent analysis of 213 Hadza camp compositions found that a woman over 45 with grown children is more likely to be in camp with her daughter than with her son, more likely to be with her daughter if that daughter has children under age 7 years, and more likely to be with her daughter if that daughter is suckling a baby (Blurton Jones et al. 2005). Of course, advocates of the patrilocal band model might counter that grandmothers could somehow find ways to encourage or enforce fidelity in their sons' wives. But unless they can explain how certainty of paternity could have equalled or exceeded certainty of maternity during the evolution of postmenopausal lifespans, we must conclude that the grandmothering hypothesis tips the scales decisively in favour of matrilocal residence and matrilineal descent (Knight and Power 2005).

Turning to the emergence of modern *Homo sapiens*, it is now widely accepted that our species evolved recently in Africa. From about half a million years ago, brain size began increasing exponentially (De Miguel and Henneberg 2001; Ruff et al. 1997). An infant with an outsized brain imposes heavy burdens on pregnant and nursing mothers (Foley and Lee 1991). If *Homo sapiens* mothers proved able to afford to raise such extraordinarily slow-maturing, ultra-dependent offspring, this fact alone testifies to the success of their alliance-building and reproductive strategies. The question arises: what new source of energy were they exploiting?

The spare provisioning capacities of the evolving human male might in principle have been available for exploitation by females, but it is important to recognize the difficulties. It is unknown for non-human primate males systematically to provision pregnant or nursing females. In the case of chimpanzees, adult males are interested mainly in females who are displaying an oestrus swelling. Where a female is nursing an infant, there is some danger that males who are unlikely to have fathered that infant may attempt to kill and eat it (Hamai et al. 1992; Hiraiwa-Hasegawa and Hasegawa 1994). The effects of primate male infanticide on female fitness and on population size and viability are for obvious reasons not positive (Butynski 1982; Janson and van Schaik 2000). Where male reproductive differentials and corresponding levels of intra-male conflict are high, nursing mothers must divert scarce energy and resources away from direct offspring care into fighting off harassment and guarding against infanticide. A primate or hominin population whose females had to cope with such behaviour might head towards extinction, even as a minority of its males achieved short-term reproductive success.

But the converse equally applies. According to current models, the ancestors of extant humans comprised a small population dwelling somewhere in

4

Alternating Birth Classes
A Note from Eastern Africa

Wendy James

Revisiting 'Generation Classes'

Age grading and age-sets are well known from the African ethnography. Less well known or understood are the systems of 'generation sets' (also sometimes called 'classes' or 'moieties') found quite commonly in the eastern parts of the continent. Although often assumed to be something to do with ageing, the 'generation sets' are rather different. They are the outcome of a particularly rigorous application of a simple principle (itself found in many parts of the world) which first sorts out one generation from the next, that is between parent and child, and then reverses the distinction in the succeeding generation, thus associating grandparents and grandchildren. Malcolm Ruel has shown, for example, that this way of distinguishing 'alternating generations' is typically found in many parts of Bantu-speaking eastern and southern Africa. He argues that this is by contrast with West Africa, where successive generations are typically conceived of as unfolding chains of 'parents' or forebears, each generational level marking successive steps in a series of links of essentially the same kind (Ruel 2002). These two markedly different ways of representing the significance of the parent-child-grandchild succession do not necessarily occur in isolation from each other. A recent collection shows what potential interpretations the grandparental connection may develop in various parts of Africa (Geissler et al. 2004). This kind of evidence shows how important it is for comparative anthropology to think outside the box of the nuclear family, or any over-simple model of 'parental investment' as explaining the principles whereby society reproduces itself over time.

The principle of alternating generations cuts across the naturalistic idea of parent-child continuity. Rather, it allocates each newborn child to a different category from one or both of its parents. In its most formal application, it confers individual identity as part of a set of siblings within a matrix of interpersonal, gendered kinship categories. As it takes its point of reference from the event of birth, I propose to avoid the term 'generation' here and to speak

rather of the principle of 'alternating birth classes'. Some systematic applications of this principle, where the model is applied well beyond 'families' to
'society as a whole', can be found in eastern Africa. These include a number of
cases where Bantu languages are spoken today by communities whose history
may have roots in the Cushitic or other (pre-Bantu expansion) linguistic-
cultural traditions of the region. Malcolm Ruel's studies of the Kuria of the
Kenya-Tanzania border provide one of the clearest accounts we have of
this institution in Africa (1962, 1997; cf. review by James 2000a). I return
to this case below.

I should first recapitulate what is commonly meant by 'age-organization'.
Here, an individual may achieve marks of personal status in the course of the
life-cycle itself; or boys initiated together into an age-set may advance in
concert through grades such as warrior, family head, ruler, and elder. Girls,
too, may be initiated into similar or corresponding sets. The names of successive age-sets can form an unending series, or may return to a starting point
within a long cycle, and this can provide a set of reference points for talking
about 'history', about past wars or famines or leaders by situating them in the
context of the ruling sets of the time. The description and study of these institutions, which in the clearest case could be seen as having a 'purpose' or function, has in practice tended to become peculiarly complicated. This is not
only for obvious reasons such as demographic unevenness, or historical lag
in the proper time intervals, or the multiplicity of ways in which people apply
the 'age' principle as such. It is, in some cases, also because ethnographers
have confused this with another principle, based on an assumption of almost
'natural' difference between parent and child, in addition to the 'natural' difference of male and female. It is clearly impossible to give an ordered account
if one assimilates the principle of generation distinction to one of age-grading,
even if informants themselves try to do this; nor can a survey of the existing
group-memberships of a given population necessarily reveal the principles
at work. A good example of a dedicated comparative analyst who took this
pragmatic approach is Frank Stewart (1977; see esp. 42–75). He tended to assume
a congruence between the steps of the age-set/grade series and the alternations of the generation classes as identified in the literature. The maximum
confusion has occurred among scholars who have tried to give a compre-
hensible account of the classic case, 'the' *gada* system of the Boran Oromo.
Here one has to accept that there are several competing dimensions in the
cosmological patterning of time, counterpointing and syncopating each other's
rhythms as they shape the marriages, births, and social history of the people
– and look for help from a philosopher rather than a pragmatic sociologist.
This was pointed out by the Ethiopian anthropologist Asmarom Legesse many
years ago (Legesse 1973), and is echoed by recent specialists (Megerssa and
Kassam 2005).

The event of birth, rather than ageing or the passage of time, is the best
starting point for grasping what anthropologists have usually described as the
'generation classes'. To focus on birth, even the anticipation of the unborn
and how they are to be fitted in to existing society, is a fresh and useful
perspective in any study of 'kinship'. In my first ethnography of the Uduk

people of the Sudan–Ethiopian border, I found it helpful to write of 'women and birth-groups' rather than take on the heavy baggage which had accumulated around the proper use of the expression 'descent groups', here matrilineages (James 1979; cf. 1978, 2007). I have also drawn attention to the specific theme of the way that social identity is fashioned for the as-yet-unborn, in a range of ethnographic cases and also very evidently in the context of the new reproductive technologies in the advanced West (James 2000b). The event of birth and its associated concerns gives us a sharp focus on what 'kinship' might mean, not only for the persons in question but also for anthropologists – and a point of possible convergence between the interests of those approaching from the biological and social ends, respectively.

Certainly the principle of alternating birth classes, while fundamental to social identity among those who practise it, is based directly upon the facts of actual bodily reproduction. The principle itself is well known from Australian ethnography – see, for example, the way that Pitjantjatjara people in Australia's Western Desert belong either to the 'sun side' or the 'shade side', even without further formal organization of marriage classes (Layton, this volume). This complementary distinction is directly echoed in the Kenyan case of the Meru, described by Anne-Marie Peatrik, whose analysis I return to below – their alternating birth classes fell into two 'streams', those of the sun and the rain, respectively (Peatrik 2005: 287). It is also a particular instantiation of one principle enshrined at the heart of Nick Allen's 'tetradic model' as a vision of the earliest form of human kinship, consonant with his comparative work on kin terminologies (see next chapter). He emphasizes the congruence, in his model, between the personal or egocentric perspective and the publicly agreed or sociocentric divisions of the community. Of course, the very general principle of association between the grandparent and grandchild, whether in ideological, religious, or practical contexts, is widely resonant throughout the world. Classic anthropological treatments include Lévi-Strauss's structural analysis of 'marriage classes' as found in Australia with emphasis on the sociocentric relations of affinity they could establish at a society-wide level (1969b [1949]: 73–4, 152–67). By contrast, Radcliffe-Brown's well-known discussions took the familial relation of individual grandparent and grandchild as a starting point, assuming that this could be generalized and extended to the point where moieties were distinguished (1952: 68–70, 96–100). His comparative discussion was, however, based on how 'relatives' behaved to each other and how individual labelling by kin terms could be rationalized by looking out from an ego's point of view across a series of individual connections in a chain to other persons, as though everyone everywhere shared a fundamental understanding of the individual-to-individual links of the Western imagination of 'kinship' – in the folk sense as well as the geneticists'. But to grasp the essentials of the principle of alternating birth classes, among other institutions of pre-modern society, we need to defamiliarize ourselves from what immediately might seem normal and reasonable about family relations or kin networks in the current Western context (as Knight has argued in the chapter above). We need to take seriously the language, indeed 'discourse and practice', of unfamiliar kinship worlds.

Alternating Birth Classes

If we disentangle the simple principle of alternating birth classes from 'age-based' modes of organization, and also from the even more standard 'descent groups' of the anthropological literature, we can recognize its importance and relevance to 'kinship and marriage' in the eastern African region. The well-known Kikuyu people of Kenya provide an example – there, everyone is either Mwangi or Maina, from birth taking the opposite category from the parent (see references cited in Ruel 1962). It would be as if the children of, say, indoor, musical people were automatically outdoor, athletic types, while their children in turn would be musical – so that the one 'kind of people' could be seen as giving birth to the other, much to the satisfaction of grandparents, who would find recruits to their own kind not from their own children but from their grandchildren. If we think in terms of a local model, with a starting point, over time it would not be sensible to call the musical and athletic types 'generations', because each community would soon acquire the same age profile. The succession within a given family would indeed represent a time sequence, but across the country at large this idea could only be applied metaphorically. At the 'family' or domestic level too, the rule that there should be no sexual contact or marriage between the different kinds of people would rule out parent/child incest for a start. But it might apply across the board, banning sex and marriage between the musical and the athletic communities. So then, who can the musicians, or athletes, for example, marry? They could either arrange reciprocal marriages with musical people in another locality; or they could subdivide among themselves – singers and composers? runners and jumpers? – which would produce a full-blown 'four-section' system (as we know it from the ethnography of Australia, in particular). We can see that the concept of 'kinds of people' is more than an individual's outlook on society, or a tracing of genealogical steps away from ego. 'Society' has pre-ordained the place of ego within an encompassing system, one which might provide him or her with individual relationships over wider spatial distances and variety of fellow-humans than the step-by-step method of genealogical calculation. The schema could arguably lend itself to conditions of migratory expansion, or exchange relations with similar communities, as well as to intermarriage and an overall pattern of social reproduction larger than the immediate core group of co-resident kin.

The logic of alternating birth classes is not always pushed through to this degree of explicitness. At least as far as the African evidence goes, it seems often to have been overlaid or cross-cut with other principles, mainly specifying 'kinship' relationships in the jural, political, and economic domain – justifying collective rights and their transaction in land, animals, and over other persons. Its trace may be found, nevertheless, in areas of the continent where it remains concerned with the intimate ritual specification of gendered persons, but it has often been neglected or misinterpreted in the anthropological literature of the functionalist period.

Alternating birth classes in modern Africa are not in the normal sociological sense 'corporate groups', with collective rights or shared resources like the kind of descent groups typical of agricultural or herding communities, nor are they part of a division of labour relating to the material world of property and economic production. They constitute an extending matrix of inter-personal relations based on categorical conceptions of gender, sexuality, and bodily reproduction. Personal identity, 'who' you are, and perhaps feel yourself to be, emerges within this larger patterning – you can locate yourself in relation to others even when away from your immediate circle. It provides a map of the wider world specifying among other things what 'kinds' of people are sexually out of bounds, and those who are available. Some individuals you meet for the first time will identify themselves, or be pointed out, as the same 'kind' as your own parents and children, while yet others can be claimed as your own kind – parallel cousins and therefore like your own siblings; or otherwise as those 'cross-cousins' – a different 'kind' you may eye as potential partners.

Again by contrast with modes of reckoning relationship by age-sets, genealogy, or descent lines, alternating birth classes do not provide a model for cumulative 'historical' memory, working as lineages do (such as the Smiths or the Joneses) steadily backwards in time or unfolding seamlessly into the future with the birth of new generations. Differentiation in time is well marked within the lifetime of persons, with the birth of children. But with the arrival of grandchildren, the pendulum swings back. Successive generations within the immediate domestic group provide a renewal of the here and now, as the flow of life back and forth between the 'kinds' does for the social whole.

The logic of alternating birth classes thus cuts across what is widely supposed to be the 'natural' side of social reproduction. It cuts across the common descent supposed between parent and child, assigning these to quite separate and opposed, ontological kinds. In theory, alternating birth classes and descent lines are rather different conceptions of continuity. But they do occur together in practice, and ethnographers have therefore tried to represent their workings – 'hybrid' systems as often as not – as functional wholes based on a common logic. This is why both the primary ethnography and secondary commentaries are so complicated.

The Kuria Case

An admirably clear account of the principles and logic of alternating birth classes has been provided by Malcolm Ruel for the Kuria, who are found mostly in Tanzania but straddle the border with Kenya (Ruel 1962 and 1997). He has shown how, up to the 'ethnographic present' of the 1950s, this system still had a direct bearing on inter-personal and sexual/marriage relations between people of the different categories. He also showed how the formal patterning was invoked and clarified on ritual occasions, while in practice other principles might be more evident in everyday contexts. Privileges were conferred periodically by the older members of each class upon their own younger members and upon the next class in the cycle, transferring a kind of seniority to the whole class, which gave the superficial impression that the classes themselves were based upon 'age'. Ruel made clear, too, how individuals could be re-ascribed to different classes when the demography had got out of joint, or when there had been breaches of the sexual and marriage code. His first detailed account (1962) was followed by a more recent compact summary in which the main points are still clear (1997), but in which he records the declining importance of the birth classes. The following account in the present tense is based on the original field research of half a century ago, itself partly a reconstruction.

Kuria country consists of fifteen traditional provinces cut through by the modern international boundary. The scattered communities within each province pursue a mixed farming economy and raise cattle, which are used in bridewealth (itself a transaction helping to give a 'corporate' character to local patrilineages). Family homesteads include the house of the family head and perhaps those of a couple of his married sons, but the grandsons will leave on adulthood to build elsewhere. Each individual among the Kuria is born into one of a cycle of four classes, succeeding that of their father. These are known as *amakora* (sing., *irikora*), translated by Ruel as 'generation classes', which I would regard as a type-case of 'alternating birth classes'. One's place in this classification is quite specific, and permanent – it 'determines the status of any individual person *vis-à-vis* others' (Ruel 1962: 17).

A relation of 'respect' or avoidance obtains between parent and child: for example, between a father who belongs to class A and his children who are born into class B. When a boy of B in turn becomes a parent, his children will constitute new members of C; a boy of C will father children who replenish class D, and then the cycle returns to A. 'Respect' should thus be observed between individuals of adjacent generations within the immediate family, and congruent with this model, 'respect' should also hold across the community – whether of the province or Kuria country itself and beyond – between adjacent birth classes. This 'respect' includes a ban on sexual relations or marriage. However, relations between alternate generations in the family circle or between the larger populations of the paired birth classes (A & C or B & D) are free, intimate, and 'equal'. Ruel notes: 'The equation of alternate classes is recognized by Kuria who speak of their members as being "one class" (or "one generation", *irikora remwe*)' (1962: 18). The community – 'imagined community', if you like – is thus constituted in effect of two halves or 'moieties': those you respect, to which your own parents and children belong, and those whom you regard either as 'fellows' or as sexual or marriage partners. 'Marriage or sexual intimacy (whether intercourse or any other kind of sexual approach) is forbidden between the members of classes who "respect" each other; it is permitted only between persons who "do not respect" each other' (Ruel 1962: 19). Although not fully merging egocentric and sociocentric categories, this case resonates with the classic tetradic model; it is an instantiation close to what Allen has described as 'the elaborated tetradic model, four level type', in which the generation moieties are split into 'submoieties' (Allen 1998: 324, and Fig. 14-8C; see also the next chapter).

Before giving a little more substance to this sketch, we should note that in practice there are in fact two self-contained and similar cycles of alternating birth classes in the homeland of the Kuria. Some are well represented in one province, and some in another. People say that these two cycles were once practised separately at two specific hills, but today their everyday activities often merge, especially where one cycle is strongly represented. Where one is less strongly represented, individuals can be assimilated into the class corresponding to their own, and parallel classes can be referred to as 'brothers'. However, on special ritual occasions, they each conduct their ceremonies separately, excluding members of the other cycle. The two cycles are known as MonyaSaai, 'the house of Saai', and MonyaChuuma, 'the house of Chuma'. The former is represented as senior to the latter, the relationship between them being thought of (metaphorically) as two matrifocal households of the wives within a polygamous homestead. For the sake of economy I will just list the four classes of the MonyaSaai cycle here:

1 abaSaai.
2 abaNyambureti.
3 abaGamunyere.
4 abaMaina.

This numbered list (Ruel 1962: 18) reflects what people describe as an unfolding order of seniority (which of course would always be evident within the immediate domestic circle). However, Ruel's own diagram to illustrate the recurring cycle (Figure 4.1) captures better the sense of a return to present times and the co-eval nature of the classes when viewed across the land of the Kuria (1962: 19; 1997: 241).

The diagram also makes it very clear that the rules of the *amakora* are not really concerned with seniority or age as such, but rather with regulating sex, gender, and reproduction not only within the immediate family circle (in purely biological terms, the avoidance of incest between close kin), but also across the community. Terms of address (in various ways) always indicate a recognition of the other person's place in the fourfold system, and class norms 'dovetail with and are subsumed by all kinship relations'; while the formal terms for

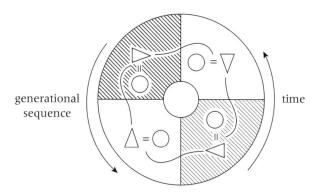

Figure 4.1 Kuria generation classes: the basic model (Ruel 1997: 241)

the birth classes were 'occasionally' used when referring to kinsfolk (Ruel 1962: 28). Ruel wrote later that within the domestic homestead, both men and women referred to each other by terms that related to age-status but added a possessive pronoun.

> One of the characteristic features of Kuria culture is the use of the same terms for age-status and family kinship, the kin-terms being dependent for their meaning on the appropriate possessive adjective. An *omogaaka* is a homestead or family head, but more generally an elder. *Omogaaka wane*, 'my omogaaka', means 'my husband'. (1997: 246)

Similarly, a general word meaning a young man or warrior-youth, with the possessive added, becomes 'my son' when a man or woman is speaking, and 'our (or my) brother' when a sibling speaks. Moreover, such terms, including words for father and mother, 'were used classificatorily across all members of a community so that all were brought into a continuous age-cum-kinship network' (1997: 247). Other examples are given, and although there is no distinction in ordinary kinship terminology between cross and parallel relations, we understand from Ruel that at the most abstract level, the class terms are available for use (which would result in 'Dravidian' distinctions, together with equations between alternate generations).

One class would periodically 'hand on' privileges to its successor in the imagined overall cycle. Some of the key rituals performed by the respective classes locally in their own provinces were dedicated to the initiation of children, and then via subsequent steps to maturity and 'retirement' of the class as a whole. At these points representatives of the appropriate 'fathers' or 'wives' of the class played a role (Ruel 1962: 21–2). These rites of passage did not confer material or public status on individuals, but signalled their personal ritual maturing, as well as the 'growth' of their class as a part of the overall religious schema and orderly prosperity of the country. The greatest ceremony marked the 'retirement' of a class, at which fines could be imposed for inappropriate sexual conduct, and individuals could even be reclassified to correct a situation *post hoc*. There was much feasting and dancing on these occasions, attended by members of the other three classes of the cycle (though members of the parallel cycle were excluded). At the time of Ruel's fieldwork (1957), the first two classes of the MonyaSaai cycle had recently completed their sequence, though in the MonyaChuuma cycle the last class had completed its retirement ceremony about 1940. In Renchoka province in Kenya, the last such ceremony was probably held about 1895. Ruel did observe the ceremony in Bureigi province in the 1990s (pers. comm.) but this was something of an anomaly.

The model of parent–child–grandchild–great-grandchild, which Ruel presents as a Kuria view of the whole social world, was thus applied in various contexts: the literal context of individual families, the wider context of the handing on of at least ritual seniority between the four *amakora* of a cycle, and the even wider context facilitating relations with other Kuria cycles or even with those of neighbouring peoples. The alternating birth-class principle encompassed all. 'The *amakora* established marriage classes that were as important in separating the generations in their procreative activities as in the determination of whom might marry whom' (Ruel 1997: 248). Kuria used to recall, in the 1950s, the prediction of a dream prophet that one day the *amakora* system would break down and there would be only two classes: males and females – with the implication that all regulation of sexual relations and marriage would have been lost. 'Ordering by generational succession, each class distinguished by behavioural norms and marriage regulations, would then have disappeared' (Ruel 1962: 15). Sadly – at least for our present purposes – by the 1990s Kuria 'could only give a garbled account of the system, commonly confusing the named classes with lineages' (Ruel 1997: 248). In the personal sphere of kin interaction, however, the alternating principle is still relevant.

Karimojong Comparison

I would like to draw a couple of comparative points from Neville Dyson-Hudson's study of a similar system among the Karimojong of northern Uganda, though he gives us very little information on marriage (1966; again, an ethnographic present of the 1950s). While the Kuria language belongs to the Bantu family, Karimojong belongs to Southern Nilotic, a branch of the Nilo-Sarahan family. Here we find four 'generation-sets', according to our ethnographer each constituted of five age-sets into which boys are initiated in cohorts over time. Each boy is normally initiated into the generation-set following that of his father. Like our alternating birth classes, these appear to have an ontological character which places them outside the kind of initiation required for the component age-sets. The four are named in a recurring sequence of Zebra, Mountains, Gazelles, and Lions, paired alternately – like Kuria, and I believe many Australian cases, there is an easy slippage between representing these systems as having two, or having four, classes. In the Karimojong case their identities are clearly signalled in the material culture: Zebra and Gazelles only use the colour yellow/white in their ornaments (e.g. brass) and can be known as Yellows; Mountains and Lions use red (e.g. copper) and are known as Reds (Dyson-Hudson 1966: 156–9, 176). In a variety of ways these principles echo those of the Kuria system. Though Dyson-Hudson tends to write of a two-generation system, because at the specific time of his observations only two were well represented among adult people, he writes that 'the system is a four-group system, not a concealed moiety system', and that each generation-set is said to 're-enter the place of their grandfathers' (1966: 158). From his few references to marriage, it appears that a child takes the generation-set membership following that of its father when bridewealth has been properly paid, but that following its mother's set if this is not the case – for example, if she is inherited by a man as his deceased father's younger wife. A woman may be described as 'a female Zebra', and while the source seems to assume this follows the husband's set, it would appear that she might have had this name all along.

The four sets of the Karimojong cycle are celebrated in every way, including song. In conclusion I quote a song 'of the wives of the people named after the [M]ountains' (a formulation which suggests they might actually be from a different class, or classes; Dyson-Hudson 1966: 177):

> *They were, even long long ago.*
> *And they endured, appearing strong*
> *They were, even long long ago*
> *Striped mountains, children of our grandfathers.*
>
> *They were, even long long ago*
> *And they clashed, appearing strong.*
> *They were, even long long ago*
> *The striped mountains, the children of our grandfathers.*

The Mountains are strong and enduring like the mountains; 'striped mountains', we learn, is a beautiful image to the Karimojong, referring to their distant view of cloud-shadowed and sun-struck mountains from the plains, a permanent point of reference within their own landscape. The refrain 'children of our grandfathers' recalls the continuous replacement of the people in this alternating manner, as does the emphatic effect, even in translation, of the repetition of the verses (no doubt in performance much extended and elaborated).

In conclusion, I might note that both anthropologists I have drawn on reflect on the way that the four-category classificatory system lends itself to the making of social links beyond a local community, to strangers perhaps with similar systems on the basis of which mutual recognition and possibly exchange can be established, even where there may be deep differences of language. Historically the central regions of the eastern African highlands have seen much coming and going of populations, and the inter-connectivity of these patterns of identity is certainly of historical relevance. Recall how the ethnographer Daisy Bates travelled across the northern parts of Western Australia as an honorary member of the Booroong, a class mutually recognized within the local four-class systems of many different Aboriginal groups; and when she later took the young Radcliffe-Brown with her, she identified him for convenience and the avoidance of gossip as a member of the Paljeri Division, and hence a classificatory son (Needham 1974: 146, 148, quoting Salter 1972: 136). This ruse worked. I would like to endorse Ruel's call for a more thorough investigation of the social history of alternating birth class systems in eastern Africa (1997: 250–1), and their regional, inter-linguistic, and historical relationships. These are likely to open up a range of new issues for research and discussion across the sister disciplines of anthropology, archaeology, linguistics, and evolutionary psychology.

Comparisons: Regional and Historical Speculation

I should emphasize the way in which the principle of alternating birth classes occurs in a geographically fairly compact zone of northeastern and eastern Africa but cases are reported among a number of geographically separate groups speaking languages belonging to very different families. Thus, for example, among Bantu-speaking groups (Niger-Kordofanian major linguistic family) Kikuyu, Embu, and Meru all had a form of cycling generations (though Kamba did not), similar in form to those of the Kuria and their southern neighbours, even sharing some generation class names. The Kalenjin peoples (Southern Nilotic speakers, like Karimojong, part of the Nilo-Saharan family) have cycling age-sets which also share similar proper names, to the point where Ruel (following Ehret 1971) backs the idea of a common Cushitic source (indicating the Afro-Asiatic linguistic family). He draws attention especially to the cosmological and ritual ordering of the world in the Boran Oromo system, which he sees as parallel to the Kuria case (Ehret 1997: 249–50). It is a puzzle which invites us to consider very long historical perspectives indeed upon language and socio-cultural continuity (compare Ehret, this volume). Could we speculate on the significance of a shift from hunting and gathering to a settled farming existence, as part of a process which helped marginalize the alternating birth classes and favour the rise of 'descent' lines related to rights in cultivable land and the formation of matrilineal or patrilineal localized descent groups? Whatever priority we may give to alternating birth identity as a 'general' principle of human society, as Radcliffe-Brown did (along with the unity of the sibling group, and the unity of the lineage group – see his various essays on these themes, 1952), its cultural emphasis, and its sociocentric materializations, are always to be understood within their historical specificity, and the circumstances of their historical transmission.

The relevance of 'generational' idioms is by no means confined to ethnography books gathering dust on library shelves, or to speculations on early human history. The categorical distinction between generations sometimes surfaces in surprising, and contextually very different, ways in 'modern' Africa. Anne-Marie Peatrik has published a detailed book in French on the age and generation system of the Meru of central Kenya, and also a shorter English paper which summarizes many of her findings (Peatrik 1999; 2005). It was only gradually in the course of her work among the Meru that she became aware of the resilience of the old system of alternating birth classes, which formed the two streams associated with 'sun' and 'rain' that I have mentioned above. They seemed to have lost public importance among a plethora of other institutions (many based on age as such), though every son knew which of the eight revolving names (two interleaved sets of four) they personally belonged to, different from their father's. Women could not marry into their father's class but could marry into a number of specified others, upon which they would join 'the class of the spouses of their husband's class'.

In the light of her careful sifting through archives as well as field research, Peatrik has been able to throw light on an extraordinary event which took place shortly before her fieldwork. One night in July 1991, the boys at a local mixed secondary boarding school (St Kizito) ran amok. The boys had decided to stage a strike against the headmaster, but the girls had refused to join in. Some 270 girls locked themselves in a dormitory, and 306 boys invaded and attacked the girls. Nineteen were killed, seventy-one assaulted and raped, and more than a hundred injured. There were many contributing causes, but Peatrik highlighted the fact that the boys had sung traditional songs and insulted the watchmen, demanding to know why they were preventing them from meeting their 'wives'. Previously, it was known that some adult teachers had had love affairs with some of the girls, and one had been made pregnant – though she was allowed back by the headmaster. The ensuing chaos was sparked by a sense of outrage at the untimely, 'abominable' behaviour of the older men who acted as 'incestuous monsters' to the girls in their care (evoking quite a lot of powerful vernacular terminology). It was indeed a limbo period between the closing period of one generation and the opening of the next: 'Everything happened as if this school acted as a stage for a traditional generation class performance which turned into a modern generational nightmare' (Peatrik 2005: 295). The older ideas, no doubt emotionally loaded ones, about the proper alternations of the flow of life between the generations were not far from the surface. A possibly very ancient image indeed of the proper relation between fathers, as a class, and daughters, as a class, had fed into the passions of that day of rioting and rampage.

Concluding Questions

The African continent is now recognized to be a key region for discovering the origins and sources of the whole world's population in a biological sense. However, Africa has been neglected by those traditions of social and cultural anthropology that have sought the universals or beginnings of human institutions. The continent scarcely figures in the massive writings of the Durkheimian school, for example, or the corpus of Lévi-Strauss on kinship or even myth – the French tradition has previously sought the elements of human society and culture rather in Australasia and the Americas (for a commentary on this odd lacuna, see James 1988a, 1998b). The ethnography of kinship and marriage in Africa has been dominated by the mid-twentieth-century interest in lineage and age principles, their relation to economic life and political authority, and in the jural aspects of marriage. There has been less attention to the ideological and ritual aspects of relatedness, and until recently very little attention has been paid to the linguistic domain – kinship terminologies. However, a recent paper in *L'Homme* by the late Per Hage (2006) draws attention for the first time to the existence of Dravidian kinship systems in Africa, focusing primarily upon the case of the Yao people of Malawi, but also other Bantu-speaking cases such as Burundi. He also finds equations between relatives in alternate generations in the Yao terminology, and reflects on the relevance of the 'tetradic' model (Hage 2006: 402–4).

If the right kind of questions are asked of kinship in Africa, some important answers may well be found, helping us to ponder the legacy of a common African heritage among the world's people not only in a bodily sense, but in a socio-cultural sense as well. Where a particular feature of social organization in eastern Africa seems to resonate with a theory of human fundamentals, there is a good reason to revisit the topic.

Acknowledgements

I am grateful for very helpful comments on an early draft of this chapter, especially from Nick Allen, Alan Barnard, Robin Dunbar, and Clive Gamble. Malcolm Ruel kindly read a later draft, providing both further background and a detailed commentary which helped me polish the argument

5

Tetradic Theory and the Origin of Human Kinship Systems

Nicholas J. Allen

Tetradic theory is an approach to kinship that developed in the 1980s. Encouraged by my supervisor, Rodney Needham, I had studied closely certain Himalayan kinship terminologies belonging to Tibeto-Burman languages, and this experience fermented together with insights derived from Mauss, Granet, Hocart, and Dumont. The early papers were addressed to social anthropologists in general (Allen 1982, 1986, 1989a) or to linguists (1989b), and in the 1990s the same basic ideas were repackaged for kinship specialists (1998) and for students of the Durkheimian tradition (2000a: 61–89). The present essay tries to address palaeoanthropologists of any disciplinary background.

The theory was taken up here and there by ethnographers or analysts. In particular it was applied to the deep history of kinship systems in certain language families (e.g. Mayan – Hage 2002; cf. Hage 2006).[1] The theory has, however, been doubted or rejected by some (e.g. Jamard 2000: 744; Layton, this volume) and has not been widely discussed. I am thus particularly grateful to Wendy James for giving it greater currency both in her book (James 2003) and via the Gregynog conference, for which her initiative was decisive.

The theory has two main aims: to characterize the original human kinship system (or, more precisely, the type of system to which it belonged), and to indicate the main lines of development that led from there to the range of systems we observe today. Since the second aim is less relevant to this book, we shall be concentrating on the first, starting from selected features of attested kinship systems and working backwards from there. As I shall argue, to start with primate systems and try to work forward would lead to an impasse, and the archaeological record contemporary with early humans offers little help with the relevant problems (Gowlett, this volume).

For anyone interested in extrapolating backwards towards human origins, kinship systems are a particularly attractive domain. This is because such systems lend themselves to the construction of formal and logical models which are less arbitrary in their assumptions and less speculative than would be the case with, say, economic, political, or religious systems. The quasi-mathematical aspect of kinship, which is much less a matter of statistics than of the logic of relations, makes it possible to answer the question 'what is the simplest logically possible kinship system?' The same question can of course be posed about other societal systems, but with them the chances of giving convincing answers are smaller. Of course, too, the claim that X is the simplest kinship system of the general type one expects to find among humans is different from the claim that X is the original human kinship system. Nevertheless, until counter-evidence or counter-arguments are advanced, the equation of simplest and earliest remains the most economical hypothesis.

Although tetradic kinship is logically simple, those who come to it for the first time often find it difficult to grasp. The paradox arises because its way of organizing relationships is so different from what we are accustomed to and take to be natural. A small number of technical terms are unavoidable, familiar words such as 'generation' have their meanings stretched in unfamiliar ways, and concepts of time and family history are relativized (cf. Testart 2000). Nevertheless, those without a background in social anthropology need not be deterred. I believe that for anyone seriously interested in early human kinship, if the argument presents a challenge, it will be a rewarding one, and I hope that for some it will also prove enjoyable.

In view of the potential difficulties, the priority will have to be clarity in presenting the theory, and little space can be devoted to relating it to other work in social anthropology, for which see chapters by Knight, Layton, and Barnard (this volume). However, by way of introduction, I take up three topics that are familiar within the discipline.

In thinking about human origins, we have to envisage small-scale societies with total populations probably in the order of two hundred (see Gamble on 'extended networks', or Barnard, citing Dunbar, both in this volume). Whether or not it is ethnographically realistic, it is convenient for purposes of exposition and model-building to think of a society as forming a totality and so as being in some sense bounded; but the important point is that in many small-scale societies every member of society is regarded as a relative (Barnard 1978a). The domain of relatives ('kinship') is thus coextensive with society. It follows that divisions made within the domain of relatives *could*, under certain circumstances, be congruent with divisions of society as a whole. To think clearly about this, we need to distinguish two ways of identifying entities. Divisions of society, e.g. clans, are ordinary entities such as can be identified by a name (perhaps totemic), which can be known throughout the society. Such entities are sociocentric. Categories of relative are different. One cannot know who is being referred to by the kinship term 'uncle' unless one knows *whose* uncle is meant – i.e. to use the jargon, unless one knows who is ego. Kinship categories are egocentric. The difference is roughly between absolute names for things and relative names.

My second introductory point concerns the notion of exchange. Adapting Mauss, Lévi-Strauss applied the notion to marriage: as he saw it, that institution and, with it, human society arose from the exchange of women. Without pausing to consider the objections that have been raised to this formulation, e.g. by Godelier (2004 – a massive work, with many virtues), I note only that neither author discusses the exchange of children, which is fundamental to tetradic theory. The idea will be explained later, but it does *not* refer to anything like an English and French family exchanging teenagers in the hope of improving their language skills, or even to the exchange of foster-children.

Finally, a quick word relating to the shape of the chapter. Most of the space has to be devoted to the mechanics of tetradic societies (or rather to the type of tetradic society that merits most attention), and is inevitably somewhat austere and abstract. Let me emphasize at once that tetradic societies have never been found by ethnographers. The theory proposes that such societies once existed but have now disapppeared, leaving behind enough survivals for us to be able to reconstruct them. The components of the model are in fact by no means new: they are sufficiently well established to need no documentation, and the novelty lies only in the consistency and economy with which they are brought together. But once the functioning of the model is clear, the question arises, towards the end of the chapter, how early humans could have invented it. The answer seems not to lie in modification of the pre-existing biologically based reproductive arrangements, and instead I turn to the theory propounded by Durkheim (1915 [1912], with input by Mauss) about the origin of religion. I propose that tetradic structures first arose not in ordinary life but in those creative ritual gatherings that Durkheim described as 'effervescent'.

Social Continuity and the Need for Rules

An animal collectivity cannot endure unless the members who die are replaced by new members who are born. In the simplest models the new members are the offspring of the old members, rather than outsiders; thus the continuity of the group results from birth, copulation, and death. These biological facts are the raw materials that humans have elaborated into kinship systems by establishing more or less explicit rules. The rules have been expressed and transmitted in language, and may be put into practice with varying degrees of rigour, but the simplest kinship system is the one with the simplest rules.

What sorts of rule does a kinship system need in order to be recognizably human? Probably the first such rule that comes to mind is one governing copulation: it will prohibit incest by dividing ego's relatives into the categories of permitted and forbidden sexual partners – the latter to include parents, siblings, and children. For the purposes of the present chapter we can leave a great deal unspecified: the relation between biological factors, such as the prolonged helplessness of human infants, and the incorporation of males into mother–child groups; the relation between such incorporation and the human institution of marriage; the different forms of sexual partnership such as monogamy (serial or lifelong), plural marriage, and concubinage; and rules of residence. We need only say that a recognizably human society needs some sort of marriage rule.

It may seem that the simplest society could function with a marriage rule alone. Indeed, with some effort, one can imagine a group of humans among whom parents produce children, but these children lack socially recognized links with previous generations. The biological condition of child would be associated with no filial role, and parents would lack any obligation to give their children names and a position in society. New members of society would be simply that, or (a slightly less extreme case) they would be given some more specific social identity but on grounds unrelated to their parentage. It would be as if all children were foundlings. Such a group could indeed endure, but is it recognizable as a human society, let alone as the sort of society one expects among very early humans? Societies seem always to have made some attempt to link new members of society with particular predecessors or categories of predecessors, and to have done so by building on the biological link between parents and children. Therefore the rules of our simplest imaginable human society will need to cover not only 'horizontal' relations (marriage) but also 'vertical' relations, for which 'recruitment' is a convenient general term.

To introduce the notion of kinship systems it is convenient to separate the horizontal and vertical rules, treating them as distinct dimensions – they are often contrasted as alliance versus descent or affinity versus consanguinity. However, the two sorts of rule are not necessarily independent, and in tetradic models they form a single complex such that neither can be fully expressed without the other.

Kinship Terminologies and a Tetradic Diagram

To carry the argument further, I move from rules to language. A distinction is needed straight away between the 'target' language used by participants in a kinship system and the meta-language used by analysts to discuss the target language. The analysts themselves of course participate in their own native kinship system, but the everyday language they use in that capacity is most unlikely to constitute a satisfactory meta-language. At the least it needs to be supplemented by a certain number of technical terms and devices.

For a start we need precise ways of talking about how target languages lexicalize the domain of relatives. Each language includes a kinship terminology, a set of single words distinguishing different types of relative, but the distinctions and assimilations operated by terminologies vary widely between languages across space and time. Of course kinship terms may have functions other than classifying relatives, but this minimal function will suffice here. Let us also simplify by assuming that a language has only a single set of terms.

To analyse the variation we need symbols for the elementary or primary relations, and Table 5.1 provides one of the conventional notations (supplied with a few mnemonic tips).

A relation, of course, usually links two things – two poles – which are not necessarily commutable. In the case of relatives, the two poles are the individual ego and the person (alter) to whom ego is related, and one conceptualizes the relation as starting from ego. Consequently, since we read from left to right, it makes sense to read the symbol M (for mother) as if it has immediately on its left an invisible symbol for ego. Usually this virtual ego need not be written, but it becomes relevant in certain contexts: for instance, the

Table 5.1 Symbols for primary relatives

Sex-neutral		Sex-specifying	
Parents	P	M	F
Siblings	G	Z	B (G: cf. Latin *germanus*. Z: cf. Dutch *zuster*)
Children	C	D	S
Spouses	E	H	W (E: cf. German *Ehepartner*)

relation of female ego to her mother can be distinguished from that of male ego to his by writing fM≠mM. Moreover, when we move from the primary relatives, those indicated by a single capital letter, to remoter ones (secondary, tertiary, etc.), the additional links are shown to the right, i.e. further from ego – whatever the grammar of the genitive in the analyst's native language.

Using this notation, we can make some elementary empirical observations about kinship terminologies, which will give us an idea of the direction in which simplification is to be sought. When seen in world-wide perspective, English, like other European terminologies, is not very typical. Thus, where English *aunt* assimilates the two sorts of parent's sister (i.e. it makes the equation MZ = FZ), most languages discriminate them (MZ≠FZ). Very commonly too, languages assimilate same-sex siblings (ssG), so that M = MZ, F = FB, and they do this not only when the sibling link comes at the end of a chain. Thus one often finds Z = MZD = FBD, B = MZS = FBS, and so on. Expressed in sex-neutral symbols, these formulae amount to G = PssGC: in other words, the terms for siblings also cover parallel cousins. However, the coverage is not limited to first cousins, since the G within the formula PssGC can itself be replaced by PssGC, and the replacement can be repeated as often as one likes. The terms covering this class of relative can then be referred to in the meta-language as 'classificatory siblings', and if the assimilation is carried through consistently, the terminology as a whole is called classificatory. It is this sort of terminology that I shall be concerned with unless otherwise specified.

Among such terminologies a good number, represented in all continents apart from Europe, have a separate term or terms assimilating maternal and paternal cross-cousins (MBD = FZD, etc.); in short, parallel cousins are distinguished from cross-cousins (PosGC, where os stands for opposite-sex), and in that case the society sometimes has a 'positive' marriage rule, prescribing that every ego should marry a cross-cousin of appropriate sex. Because the terminology is classificatory, the prescription does not necessarily concern a *first* cross-cousin. The logical and empirical concomitants of such kinship systems are described in text-books, and are difficult to grasp without the aid of genealogical diagrams. But since these systems are not our target, we can move on.

Occasionally, and particularly in terminologies which accord with the simplest cross-cousin marriage diagrams, one also finds a tendency towards the assimilation of alternate genealogical levels. In attested terminologies such

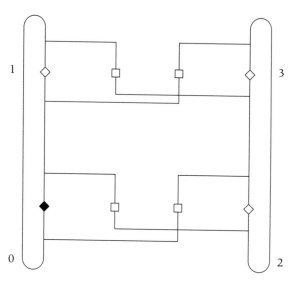

Figure 5.1 Genealogical diagram for focal tetradic society (© Nicholas J. Allen)

assimilation seems always to be partial or patchy, but it would be logically simpler if it were total and consistent. This is the point where we leave behind the structures that have been reported by ethnographers or envisaged by earlier historical linguists, and enter the tetradic domain. The result is again best grasped with the aid of a genealogical diagram, and the one I present (Figure 5.1) is in some ways conventional.[2]

Thus, as is usual (but not invariable), relationships are shown by the longer vertical and horizontal lines, and those between whom the relationships hold are shown by the little closed shapes or symbols. Ego is represented by the filled-in symbol (a diamond), parent–child links are shown by long verticals, brother–sister links by horizontals a little above the symbols, and marriage by horizontals a little below them. The two symbols represent the two sexes. Since we are talking about a classificatory kinship system, where same-sex siblings are assimilated to each other, all the sibling pairs shown in the diagram are of opposite sex. Thus the diamond representing ego is to be read as covering ego's same-sex siblings (among many other relatives), and all the diamonds and squares covering alters are similarly to be read in a classificatory manner. The symbols do not indicate individuals, as they would in a family tree. They indicate types of relative recognized by the system.

The diagram departs from convention in two ways. Normally triangles are used for males and circles for females, but I shall give below my reasons for avoiding this usage. Which symbol is allotted to which sex in Figure 5.1 does not matter, but it is easiest to take one of the options, and for purposes of illustration I shall make ego a female. The second unconventional feature is the presence of two filiation lines on each side of the diagram. One of them, the inner, connects ego directly to her same-sex parent, and in a normal diagram one expects to find another filiation line directly below ego linking her

to her same-sex child: normally, one generation is followed by another as the
eye moves down the page. In this case, however, there seem to be only two
generations – until one takes account of the cycling filiation line round the
outside. Let us concentrate first, not on interpreting its essence, but simply on
how to read it. Followed from ego downwards and outwards, it leads round
to ego's children, who are represented by the diamond and square in quadrant 1: one might supply the line with an arrow pointing in this direction,
to indicate that, despite moving up the page, the eye is moving in the direction in which time advances. However, the line can equally be read in the
opposite direction: trying to follow the filiation upwards from ego's mother
and backwards in time, one is carried round the outside and back to ego's
diamond, which thus also covers ego's MM. Whether one traces it upwards
or downwards, the female line simply shuttles back and forth between the
diamonds in quadrants 0 and 1. It is easy to see that the square in 2 covers
not only ego's husband (the relation resulting from marriage), but also her
FZS and MBS (a relation that existed even before the marriage). It is less
obvious on the diagram, but one finds that ego's mother, like all the other
females, also has as husband a bilateral cross-cousin (PosGS). As an exercise
(not compulsory!), to increase familiarity with the notation, it may be worth
working out which symbol covers FMBDSSWBDH (answer in note[3]). The point
of the exercise is to emphasize that, provided the marriage and recruitment
rules are obeyed, no genealogical chain, however long, can carry one outside
the diagram. All possible relatives are accommodated within it.

Because ego can reach an alter via an indefinite, indeed infinite, number
of genealogical paths, from one point of view the domain of relatives that the
model organizes is not the same sort of thing as the domain of relatives in
contemporary Britain. A computer print-out of hypothetical genealogies from
a functioning tetradic society would differ objectively from a print-out of British
genealogies. But from another point of view, the difference between the domains
disappears. Ego's relatives are those with whom she is linked by a relation
or series of relations of filiation, siblingship, and marriage, and the rules of
recruitment and marriage that create the multiple paths to a single alter make
no difference to this definition of relatives.

It was attested kinship terminologies that led us to the diagram, and we can
now return to them. We have already mentioned kinship systems that pre-
scribe cross-cousin marriage and the genealogical diagrams that relate to such
systems. In the simplest cases, a single symbol in the diagram corresponds to
a single kinship term. Applying the same principle to our eight-symbol diagram
gives a theoretical eight-term terminology covering all possible relatives – past,
present, or future. The question arises whether yet further simplification is
possible. It is. One can easily postulate a single base lexeme per quadrant and
distinguish the sexes either by two suffixes or by a single one for the sex that
is 'marked' (in the linguists' sense); and conceivably a human society could
operate with four sex-neutral kinship terms, entrusting the determination of
sex, in those contexts where it was relevant, to other methods, linguistic or
extra-linguistic. But this is the limit: we shall find that further reduction below
four takes us outside what is humanly plausible.

Implications of the Diagram:
Egocentric and Sociocentric Readings

Let us call the diagram the 'focal tetradic diagram' – tetradic because it consists of four quadrants, focal because, out of the various four-quadrant genealogical diagrams one can draw, it is on this one that, for various reasons, I focus the discussion (the most obvious variant has each quadrant consisting of a wife–husband pair, rather than a sister–brother pair). We are now in a better position to see what it is that the diagram represents.

It is not enough to say that the symbols it contains represent classificatory relatives, so that, say, the square in quadrant 3 represents a classificatory father. The statement is true, but more fundamentally and more abstractly, what the square represents is one component in a structure. Let us say that a structure (of any sort) is a totality whose components are linked by relations which remain constant when the content of the components changes – whether because the content changes over time, or because the structure is applied in a new context. As regards content, over time the individuals covered by the 'classificatory father' square change as old ones die off and new ones are born, but the relation with the other components remains unchanged. As regards context, relatives are people, kinship terms are words – entries in a dictionary; but when we shift from the one domain to the other, the diagram loses none of its relevance. The diamond now represents one word among the (let us say) eight that make up the hypothetical terminology, and the diagram shows its semantic relations to the others. One can also say, emphasizing solely the meanings (the signified as opposed to the signifier), that the diamond represents one slot within the semantic field of relatives.

What is to be said about the rules that give order to this field? Firstly, the rules eliminate marriage with any primary relative. Ego cannot marry her father in quadrant 3, her son in 1, or her brother in 0 – or indeed their classificatory equivalents; she can only marry within quadrant 2. A model with fewer than four categories cannot rule out marriage with all three types of primary relative and thereby becomes implausible.

Secondly, we need to consider the nature of the rules. We introduced the marriage rule via the empirical observation that societies quite often require ego to marry a classificatory PosGC, and we then introduced the less clearly attested rule prescribing *systematic* assimilation of alternate genealogical levels. Applied to the female ego of our focal model, this recruitment rule entails her assimilation to MM and DD, not to mention remoter relatives, such as those in the female line from more distant even-numbered generations; in sex-neutral language the assimilation is to ssPssP and to ssCssC. Applied to ego's husband, the rule entails his assimilation to ego's MF and SS (among others), and the model allows her to marry these relatives, either in the minimal or in the classificatory sense (incidentally, being secondary relatives, MF and SS are closer than PosGS, who is tertiary). In other words, the tetradic marriage rule cannot be properly stated without taking account of the recruitment rule, and the converse is also true: the category to which ego belongs includes not only MM but also, because of the marriage rule, FFZ (osPssPosG), represented by the same diamond. The marriage and recruitment rules are interwoven, or, more precisely, they are the horizontal and vertical implications of the unitary structure. Moreover, although it seems natural to introduce the structure as the *result* of rules, the perspective can be reversed: the structure *generates* the rules, which are merely its expression in a jural idiom.

So far we have been looking at the diagram from an egocentric perspective, viewing it as a way of organizing the domain of relatives. Recalling that in the model this domain is coextensive with society, we can now shift to a sociocentric perspective and view the diagram as showing one way of segmenting a society. The meta-language we need at this point has been developed mainly by students of Australian Aboriginal societies: we need the concept of a society divided into halves or moieties (French *moitié*) and of a society divided into quarters or sections. The problem lies in grasping the relations between the four quadrants of the diagram, which represent four categories of ego's relatives, and four sections, which are sociocentric entities.

The problem can be addressed by starting with binary structures. The lower half of Figure 5.1, which contains ego, can be labelled ego's 'generation moiety', but since it also contains members of all even-numbered generations, ascending and descending (grandrelatives, great-great grandrelatives, etc.), it can also be called the even-generation moiety. It stands in opposition to the upper half of the figure, which represents the odd-generation moiety. But the diagram also has a left half and a right half. If we continue to read diamonds as female, the left half represents ego's matrimoiety (since ego belongs to the same half of society as her mother, not her father), and the right half represents the other matrimoiety. However, the reading of diamonds as females was only one of the two options. If we read diamonds as males, the left half represents ego's patrimoiety (ego belongs to the same moiety as his father, not his mother). From a formal or logical point of view the two readings are equally valid, and it is to emphasize this that Figure 5.1 avoids the conventional circle–triangle notation. The latter notation can scarcely help introducing a bias, for even if matrilineal and patrilineal diagrams are drawn side by side the one on the left is encountered first and thus gains a shadowy priority. It is important to see that both forms of descent moiety are implicit in the structure *in equal measure*; the cross-cutting of generation moieties with one form of descent moiety necessarily generates the other. Those who think matriliny preceded patriliny in prehistory must put forward arguments that lie outside tetradic theory. Tetradic structures are totally symmetrical between the sexes. If they are thought necessary, ideas of unilineality must be introduced explicitly as a logical complication, as a departure from maximal economy.[4]

As regards sections, Figure 5.1, which was devised to explain a kinship system, is not ideal (for a sociocentric diagram see, for instance, Allen 2004: 223). There is no problem in the even level where the quadrants represent two of the four sections, but the difference between female and male viewpoints introduces a complication in the odd level. Female ego and her brother share a mother, but from ego's point of view the mother is a same-sex parent falling in quadrant 1, whereas if her brother is taken as ego the mother is an opposite-sex parent falling in quadrant 3. But a single individual can only belong in a single section. Thus the quadrants in the odd level do not exactly represent sections. Using Figure 5.1, one has to envisage the odd-level sections changing sides according to sex of ego. This formulation has of course nothing to do with movements on the ground; it is about locating individuals within kinship space and social space.

Moieties and sections are not only unavoidable but positively useful for analysts of tetradic societies, but it is not clear that members of a tetradic society would need to name these units, let alone have abstract generic nouns for them. Theoretically, the kinship terminology would suffice to identify them.

Moieties are particularly useful when one tries to formulate sociocentrically the relationships within the structure. This is where the notion of exchange becomes so helpful. A generation moiety is endogamous (all its members marry within it). But the children conceived in the wombs of ego's generation moiety are given to the other generation moiety to constitute its membership, as is shown by the two cycling filiation lines; and the prestation is reciprocated, as is shown by the two ordinary filiation lines. The descent moieties, both matri and patri, are exogamous (all members marry outside their natal moiety). They can thus be said to exchange partners, as is shown by the four marriage lines. In fact the structure is simply an expression of cross-cutting vertical child exchange and horizontal partner exchange.

It is clear by now that an isomorphism exists between (a) the vocabulary, rules, and behaviour in the domain of relatives and (b) the structure of society as a whole, and that this isomorphism arises because in all cases we are dealing with realizations of a single underlying structure. One can also envisage the structure being applied to other domains: within the realm of kinship, to the patterning of attitudes towards different categories of relative (familiarity, avoidance, respect and joking – to cite a long-established list of 'prescribed sentiments'), and outside it, to the construction of a cosmology. In some Australian languages the social structure even interacts with the grammar, affecting the choice of pronoun (Heath et al. 1982).

We can also now see more clearly the essence of the cycling filiation lines. They not only enable ego's generation moiety to make a return to the other for the new lives it receives, but also enable the system to function perfectly, given sufficient population (it is for demographers to model tetradic societies and suggest what would be sufficient). A sociocentric generation moiety is of course very different from an egocentric generation: in an ordinary kinship system one's parents' generation eventually dies off, whereas in the tetradic society ego's parental generation moiety (call it A) cannot die off, since it is constantly replenished by the children of ego's generation moiety (B). Reciprocally, A constantly replenishes B. It follows that, in theory, ego will always be able to find an appropriate spouse within B. Since both generation moieties are constantly being replenished, they both contain the full range of ages present in the society. Neither is older than or senior to the other; and if I draw A above B rather than below, it is only because one has to choose one or other layout and because ego starts out in life having parents but not children.

In contrast, textbook genealogical diagrams illustrating cross-cousin marriage in non-tetradic kinship systems take for granted generations in the ordinary sense of the word. Essential though they are for many analytical purposes, such models cannot be perfectly realized by a demographically and socio-logically realistic population. This is because there will always be some egos who cannot find a cross-cousin within their generation. In a tetradic system, a generation is continuous with, or runs on into, the next generation but one – as can be neatly shown by a double-helix model (Allen 1989a: 49–51).

Logical Simplicity and Historical Priority

Since tetradic kinship systems are so remote from our own experience, they may not be simple to grasp at first reading, but even so, and even without a formal definition of simplicity, the fact that they *are* logically simple is probably intuitively clear. The simplicity derives partly from the small number of categories that suffice to classify the whole domain of relatives/society without ambiguity or overlap, but there is another factor, at least as important. Under tetradic theory a single structure shapes a multiplicity of contexts that to us appear to be separate. Our relatives, scattered here and there across the map; the kinship terms with which we identify them as relatives (somewhat complicated by the decline of marriage, family breakdown/recombination, and new reproductive technology); the laws against incest; the results of marriage, especially the immediate appearance of a new set of affinal relatives, who previously were simply not relatives; a social structure that consists of vaguely or arbitrarily defined socio-economic classes, and the statistical tendency towards class endogamy – some such picture presents an obvious contrast with the tidy unitary structure of tetradic society. The worry might arise that this tidiness is due to the level of abstraction at which the analysis has chosen to operate, that the argument is circular, since if one simplifies by abstracting, the end-point will be simple. Not so: a system under which a single structure is reflected in a whole range of phenomena, including the domain of relatives and the articulation of society, really is simpler than one in which separate descriptions are needed for each of them.

One naturally asks whether the process of simplification can be carried further – some have speculated that human society began when two hordes met and started exchanging women. We have already touched on this problem. It is not possible to reduce a tetradic society to moieties (to 'dual organiza-tion') while retaining the prohibition on marriage with primary relatives *as an implication of the rules of social structure*. Whatever arrangement one tries, it will always be necessary to add a rule formulated in non-classificatory lan-guage to eliminate one or other primary relative. This new rule, so alien to the classificatory style that elsewhere pervades the system, nullifies, indeed reverses, the apparent gain in simplicity achieved by reducing four sections to two moieties. A *double* dichotomy is the ultimate simplification of the domain of relatives/society, if one wants to remain within what is humanly plausible.

One possible use for the tetradic model is as pedagogic device. Understanding the model helps one think clearly about kinship systems in general, much as understanding non-Euclidean geometry or imaginary numbers can help one think about space or arithmetic. Moreover, to approximate to a system such as we meet in the real world, the abstract model has of course to be enriched with all sorts of features (spatial and domestic organization, response to the breaking of rules, legal fictions and rituals such as adoption or blood-brotherhood, step-relatives, marital choice, local beliefs about reproduction, kinship, and gender . . .), and to appreciate this is to perceive the gap that has to exist between models and reality. Again, conceptualizing the transformations that are needed to bring the model into line with attested systems facilitates thinking about historical transformations of particular kinship systems. All of this is worthwhile, but my focus here is on the world-historical question with which the chapter started. Were the first specifically human kinship systems tetradic? Can the idea that simplest equals earliest be supported by empirical evidence or by types of argument we have not yet raised?

That we have been looking in the right general direction is suggested by various anthropological commonplaces. Tetradic society conforms to the generalization that small-scale tribal societies are 'pervaded by kinship', and it embodies or subsumes incest rules, which have so often been taken as a or the crucial step in the origin of human society. Moreover, to revert to points made earlier, the individual features that enter into tetradic society are all well established in the ethnographic record. This applies to bilateral cross-cousin marriage, terminological equations between alternate genealogical levels, societies with four sections, and generation moieties – even permission to marry grandrelatives. What has *not* been found is their synthesis into a single system of maximal economy.

Though it may be less widely known, another common finding is forms of assimilation between alternate generations additional to those made by kinship terminologies. Many societies name grandchildren after their grandparents, and among them a good number associate the name with a soul, thereby postulating reincarnation of individuals in the generation after next. Such phenomena can be readily interpreted as continuing the assimilation originally expressed in tetradic terminologies and social structures.

No doubt the strongest lines of argument have to do with historical change. One useful approach is to consider the motivations and mechanisms of semantic change in terminologies. The tetradic terminology contains three different types of equation: alternate generation equations (associated with the vertical dimension of kinship), horizontal equations resulting from the marriage rule, and classificatory equations based on same-sex sibling assimilation. Since all of these occur outside the model, opponents of tetradic theory need to offer explanations of how they arose. For instance, they might argue that languages which at one moment distinguish the real mother from classificatory mothers (so that M≠MZ) become so obsessed with the idea of ssG equivalence that they lose the distinction. Being based on the visible event of parturition, the distinction must always be relevant to some speakers in some contexts, and its retention would not be incompatible with the use of the ssG equivalence principle elsewhere in the terminology. Even so, the critic must argue, one or other of the two separate words (presumably the one for MZ, the less salient) becomes obsolete and disappears, so that the language now has M = MZ. Equally implausible changes are needed to explain, for instance, the replacement of H≠MBS or FZ≠ZD with the corresponding equations. Such problems do not arise if the equations are present from the start.

Another approach is to engage with the analytical literature. As Trautmann puts it,

> There is a remarkable uniformity of tendency among theorists in the 20th century to assume that the beginning point for the evolution of kinship terminologies was a system something like the Dravidian, and that the overall directionality of change in terminologies is towards something like the kinship terminology in English. (2001: 270–1)

The tendency is exemplified, for instance, by Fox, with his 'rock-bottom' nine-term terminology (1967: 245–6) or by Godelier (2004: 511–33). But a Dravidian terminology can be seen simply as a tetradic terminology which has 'unfolded' vertically, so as to rupture the alternate generation equations and thereby recognize generations in the ordinary sense.

It is worth noting the objections to tetradic theory raised by Trautmann (2001: 280–4) and Godelier (2004: 549–51). Trautmann, who doubts the Dravidian-origin consensus and favours envisaging a multiplicity of starting points, emphasizes firstly the lack of correlation between kinship terminologies and stages of economic or political development. But tetradic theory, although it is concerned with the directionality of changes, is not committed to a view on their causation, the study of which must take account of local factors, no doubt multiple and various. Secondly, Trautmann raises two historical phenomena: the development of terminological equations such as one finds in English or French, and the appearance of Dravidian equations in languages of immigrants to South India who would not have made the equations before immigrating. Tetradic theory accommodates these phenomena in different ways. The dominant diachronic trend for terminologies, it claims, is the rupture of equations that were initially present, but the world has also seen the appearance of 'counter-tetradic' equations such as were not initially present. For instance, Latin retains MZ≠FZ, as in the tetradic model, while its descendant, French, has the counter-tetradic *tante* MZ = FZ, presumably reflecting a decline in the social significance of the difference between the mother's and father's side of the family.[5] The South Indian case is a good example of a sub-stratum effect (specifically allowed for in Allen [2004: 234], where I had Sinhalese in mind).

Godelier (2004), too, is worried about counter-tetradic equations, but more interestingly he thinks that the congruence of egocentric and sociocentric in tetradic systems is unrealistic. This is partly because of certain historical claims by Australianists, partly because he denies that societies can be 'founded on kinship' (2004: 516–17); societies always need in addition, not only a territory, but also some sort of politico-religious glue to give them cohesion.

But although tetradic theory uses some Australianist analytical vocabulary, Australian data are not essential to it. If all Aboriginals had been wiped out by epidemics or genocide before the advent of ethnographers, one or other tetradic structure would still be the simplest way to organize a society where everyone is related to everyone else. It is a matter of logic. Moreover, there is no reason why a structure combining the egocentric and sociocentric should not underlie politico-religious phenomena *as well*.

Alternatives to a tetradic starting point all raise problems. The obvious rival theory would start with a terminology covering only primary relatives and then postulate extension to secondary ones and remoter ones. At its simplest this process leads to a terminology without equations, which then have to be introduced by processes whose implausibility was noted a few paragraphs back. Moreover, one has to suppose that the formation of the equations was guided by a vision of marriage and recruitment rules, but then it becomes hard to see how this vision originated in the absence of terms in which to express it. One cannot rule out the possibility that the first kinship terms were for one or more primary relatives (cf. Barnard, this volume), but the impasse lies in the transition from there to the classificatory terminologies characteristic of most of the non-Western world.

An extension hypothesis is also unnecessary. Since kinship is usually thought of in terms of relatives and their lexical classification, that was how we started on the path that led us to the tetradic model. But other paths are no less possible. Those already familiar with the idea of a four-section system can reach the same end-point simply by attaching to the system an isomorphic egocentric nomenclature; and one can introduce four-section systems by talking of cross-cutting moieties and their exchange-based rules of marriage and recruitment without referring at all to cross-cousins and the like. Approached in this way, the kinship system becomes an implication of the social structure, one among the ways in which the structure is manifested. If we can propose an origin for the social structure, we do not need a separate origin story for the egocentric terminology. This is what we shall now attempt. In doing so, we can accommodate Godelier's view that kinship considerations alone are not sufficient to make a society.

Origin of Tetradic Structures

Hunter-gatherer societies spend much of their time living in small bands with up to a couple of dozen members, but from time to time they assemble, typically for ritual purposes. We can thus contrast phases of dispersal and phases of concentration. It is more likely that a whole group will divide itself up – give itself a social structure – when it is gathered together in one place than when it is dispersed. But it is not enough to identify the social context in which such structuring arose – one would like to go further and model the processes that led up to cross-cutting generation and recruitment moieties. This will inevitably be speculative, but the association of demographic concentration with ritual offers a clue.

Rituals and similar activities quite often require the division of participants or congregation (dancers, singers, actors, contestants . . .) into two or more sides or teams, so the problem lies less in explaining holistic divisions of society than in seeing how these divisions could relate to rules of marriage and recruitment. Since the aim is to explain the origin of the rules, we have to make the effort to imagine that they do not yet exist. For convenience I talk of division of 'the society', but infants, the sick, and the decrepit elderly are unlikely to be fully involved in rituals. Thus the division probably applied primarily to active members of society, who were taken to represent it as a whole.

Suppose, then, that the society, understood in this way, splits into two teams. It does not matter how the teams are selected (e.g. randomly or on the basis of bands), provided that their identity and membership endure from one period of concentration to the next. Suppose, too, that, as part of the ritual, couples within each team pair off for sexual intercourse. Let us say that this relationship is socially recognized, even though it is confined to the ritual context. We might even think of it as proto-marriage, and of the ritual as constituting or including a sort of proto-wedding. But so far team A does not necessarily contain the parents and children of team B: we now have somehow to incorporate the vertical dimension of kinship. So, in due course, the time comes to initiate new members of society (whether or not they were conceived in the proto-marriages does not matter), and the collective initiation also takes place during a period of concentration. But the newcomers are initiated not into the team of the mother who bore them but into the other team (prototype of a recruitment rule). In this way the initial allocation of individuals to teams gives way, in the ritual context, to something like child-exchanging generation moieties. Since these units are not yet endogamous outside the ritual context, one cannot exactly say that the society possesses generation moieties.

Suppose that the ritual now becomes more complicated. The two teams are each bisected, randomly or otherwise, but in such a way that each individual within an established ritual couple belongs to a different half-team, newcomers to the team being allocated to one or other half. Any random element in the allocation can again in due course be phased out, the new participant being allotted to the half-team of his or her mother's mother. I talk of MM rather than FF because the identity of an individual's mother is always clear while that of the father need not be (probably, in this case, will not be); it is not necessary at this point to refer to descent moieties. (Logically, the allocation could as well be to the other half of the appropriate team, the half that contains not MM but FM. This will result in a tetradic structure of a non-focal type, a topic treated in my other papers.)

So far, nothing has been said about marriage or recruitment during the dispersed phase, and one cannot assume that what happens in the concentrated phase is immediately transferred into ordinary life when the assembly breaks up into bands. The bands could for generations, centuries, even millennia follow whatever non-tetradic arrangements have been transmitted from their primate or hominin past. During the transitional period the dispersed and concentrated phases would contrast, in our terms, as nature to culture; only gradually would the innovations developed in the context of ritual come to dominate tribal life as a whole. One need not assume total replacement of the habits of the dispersed phase, which among other things surely included male–female asymmetries (e.g. helpful grandmothers – Opie and Power, this volume). Perhaps one can think of the aesthetic elegance of tetradic structures, alongside their cognitive simplicity, as playing some part in their initial development and subsequent spread. There could also have been socially sanctioned selection pressures operating against non-conformists and in favour of those who, by virtue of their genes, were best able to grasp the new rules of ritual and kinship and most willing to follow them.

Once tetradic structures are invented, what happens next? Presumably the descendants of the inventors multiply and disperse, so that assembling for a single ritual gathering becomes impractical. But spread by diffusion can also be envisaged, whether via emigrants or via temporary visitors from outside. As to monogenesis or polygenesis, the question remains open and perhaps insoluble.

Wider Questions

This speculative little story about the origin of tetradic structures is less important in my argument than the ritual context and the derivation of the classificatory terminology from the social structure. I suppose, without having investigated the literature, that it is cognitively simpler to master a set of absolute names for sociocentric entities than to master a set of relativistic kinship terms, much as a toddler called Joe will at first refer to himself as Joe rather than using the first-person singular pronoun.

As regards the terminology, one can remain agnostic about the early existence of terms for primary relatives, or for some of them, especially mother – provided it is clear that these terms did not serve as a nucleus from which the terminology gradually expanded its coverage. However, there is still a deeper question, namely whether a tetradic society needs to possess a full spoken language at all (cf. Barnard, this volume). Since we started by working backwards from societies possessing terminologies, we have not really faced the question. After all, to operate the system in a minimal manner, ego only needs to know two things: into what section she can marry (horizontal dimension), and in what section her children belong (vertical dimension). But section membership could be signalled by non-linguistic means such as haircut, body painting, or ornamentation (what Dunbar [this volume] calls 'social badging'), or even perhaps, within the ritual context, by posture or position in space (position on the terrain of dance?). The relativistic categories would be present implicitly, and perhaps acted out, but they would not be lexicalized. Thus in theory at least, language is not essential. One might object that the organization of teams and half-teams is difficult to envisage without something resembling spoken language. On the other hand, such doubts may simply express a lack of imagination, caused by our own immersion in language.

This leads to the problem of how the invention of tetradic theory can be related to other palaeoanthropological innovations, and hence to absolute dates. On some issues, such as the origin of the nuclear family, the theory has nothing to offer. Since kinship systems typologically close to the focal tetradic model are so well attested in Aboriginal Australia, the model surely developed before the human settlement of that continent some 60,000 years ago; but since systems throughout the world are also derivable from tetradic ones, presumably the invention preceded the dispersal from Africa. Moreover, since it is so difficult to imagine a fully human society that lacks a rule-based kinship system, I suspect that the innovation was earlier still, but how much earlier, I do not know.

In any case, on one issue a more confident note seems justified. No satisfactory account of human origins can ignore the domain of kinship and social structure, and no satisfactory account of this domain can ignore the tetradic framework, within which alone these two aspects of society can be perfectly congruent and integrated.

Notes

1   We had hoped that Per Hage would come to the Gregynog conference, on whose proceedings this volume is based, but sadly he died in 2004 just before invitations were sent.

2   To understand the theory it is worth investing a little time in learning both to draw the diagram and to read or 'navigate' it. For drawing I recommend the following order: the four sister–brother or brother–sister pairs, the ordinary filiation lines, the marriage lines, the cycling filiation lines; finally fill in ego and add quadrant numbers.

3   The answer is the square in quadrant 0. Tip: write out the formula and under each letter write the quadrant.

4   A technical point (insufficiently clear in my earlier writing). Even if male and female tetradic egos use the same kinship terms and use them to make the same separations within the domain of relatives, this does not uniquely specify the model. The argument here has implied that in quadrant 1 of the four-term terminology ssP(G) = C (read: 'ego's same-sex parent and the latter's siblings are equated with ego's children'). An alternative has M(G) = ZC, where (by virtue of ssG equivalence) ZC reduces to fC for female ego. In this case, changing ego's sex entails swapping over the kinship terms applied to odd-level quadrants, but a sister and brother use the same term for a particular parent (e.g. for their shared mother). The two systems await satisfactory names. For this and other points relevant to tetradic theory, cf. the discussion by Testart (2006) of Australian and other data. For instance, his objections to the generalized 'parallel-cross opposition' can be compared with those of Allen (1998: 326–8).

5   English and French terminology is sometimes classified typologically as 'Eskimo' but, as Morgan himself was aware (1871: 275–7), Eskimo terminologies are classificatory, not descriptive: for instance, lineal grandrelatives are equated with collaterals (Dole 1960).

6

What Can Ethnography Tell Us about Human Social Evolution?

Robert Layton

Introduction

Anthropology and archaeology are now returning to discuss questions of long-term social evolution that were popular during the nineteenth century (cf. the chapters by Knight and Barnard, this volume). More evidence is available to answer these questions, and advances in theory provide a better appreciation of what 'social evolution' means. Exciting as this opportunity to revisit the big picture is, we must keep in mind the weaknesses of the earlier, more speculative theories that led to their rejection by twentieth-century anthropologists such as Malinowski and Radcliffe-Brown, and ensure that in our excitement about the rediscovery of the Big Questions, we do not fall again into old traps. Contributors to the present volume offer two complementary approaches to the reconstruction of early human kinship. Allen takes a cognitive approach, asking what minimum number of categories must be conceptually recognized to enable the construction of an ordered human society. Opie and Power take a behavioural, or adaptive, approach that asks what forms of social interaction would be most likely to enable viable reproduction in hunter-gatherer bands. This contribution looks critically at the insights and limitations offered by both. The chapter is divided into three sections: the first outlines some general issues; the second discusses whether Allen's tetradic kinship systems are likely to represent the earliest forms of human kinship; while the third reconsiders Opie and Power's argument that matrilineal continuity in local groups preceded patriliny.

What Is 'Social Evolution'?

Defining social evolution

Social evolution can be conceived in two ways. Prior to the Darwinian revolution, evolution was equated with progress through a series of stages in social organization. In the neo-Darwinian sense, however, it means the selection of social strategies that are adaptive in a specific ecological context; strategies that enhance their bearers' reproductive success under particular circumstances when measured against the available alternative strategies. It has long been recognized (Marx 1930 [1867]) that property and exchange create a dynamic in human society that may lead to progressive change, but 'progression', in this sense, should be used to refer simply to an increasing divergence from the society's previous condition. Such progressive change will, moreover, always be limited by the viability of any social system in its natural environment. Over-exploitation of resources or climatic deterioration can cause the collapse of complex societies.

Malinowski's theory of social behaviour was congruent with Darwinian evolutionary theory. He defined the function of a custom as 'satisfying [the individual's] primary biological needs through the instrumentalities of culture' (Malinowski 1954: 202). Malinowski saw the Trobriand Islander of the Pacific as a reasonable man, manipulating the possibilities in social relations to his advantage, although unaware of the total network of relations to which he contributed. The difficulty with Malinowski's argument was his inability to explain cross-cultural variation. The pre-eminent school of functionalism led by Radcliffe-Brown therefore set out to define types of society, and discover the distinctive forms of social behaviour associated with each type. Unfortunately this school subsumed the interests of individuals to the supposed need for 'the social system' to ensure stability (Radcliffe-Brown 1952: 178–9). Radcliffe-Brown's approach risks committing the 'group selection' fallacy, of assuming individuals who 'altruistically' subordinate their self-interest to the common good will do better than the selfish (see Trivers 1985: 79–84). If such social behaviour is genetically determined, for example, those individuals who forgo their own reproductive interests to benefit others will not transmit their altruistic genes to the next generation. Altruism will indeed be displaced by selfishness. By analogy, the same outcome will apply where people act through rational self-interest: the selfish will flourish at the expense of those who sacrifice their own interests to benefit 'society', or 'the group'. It must therefore be proven that altruism serves self-interest.

What are the 'elementary forms of human society'?

The quest for the elementary form of human society started with thinkers confronted by the breakdown of the *anciens régimes* of Europe. Two theoretical starting points can be identified. Rousseau started with the solitary individual, supposing the first human to have been answerable to no man, 'satisfying his hunger at the first oak, and slaking his thirst at the first brook' (1963 [1767]: 163). Adam Ferguson took the opposing view that humans are a social species, that behaviour can only be understood in terms of interaction. Ferguson argued that a wild man caught in the woods would be as defective an organism as an eye that had never seen anything: '. . . mankind are to be taken in groupes, as they have always subsisted' (Ferguson 1995 [1767]: 10).

Despite the speculative nature of seventeenth- and eighteenth-century theories, the recent study of hunter-gatherer and chimpanzee social behaviour supports some of the key ideas developed during the Enlightenment, and there is clearly value in returning to these large questions. Neo-Darwinian theorists frequently take the individual as their unit of analysis, yet Adam Ferguson's insight that humans have always lived in groups is supported by the discovery that apes and monkeys are social species, and the consequences of individual strategies depends on the social ecology created by interaction.

Foley and Lee (1989) present an elegant, logical analysis of possible pathways for human social evolution based on ways males and females may have mapped onto food sources in the landscape, and onto each other as reproductive resources. Following Ferguson's lead, however, I propose that human evolution has been characterized by interaction in larger groups. Humans are particularly dependent on social interaction for their individual survival. The consequences of sharing or hoarding food procured by hunter-gatherers, where the quantity exceeds the immediate need of the foragers who obtained it, illustrates this point. Kaplan and Hill calculate that among the Ache of tropical lowland South America, the sharing of honey alone increases the individual's nutritional status by 20%, sharing of meat alone increases it by 40%, while all observed food sharing increases nutritional status by 80% (Kaplan and Hill 1985: 233). If a set of individuals hunt and gather independently, pooling their catches at the end of the day will compensate for variations in each actor's personal catch. Every individual benefits from altruism, as each person's generosity is repaid on another occasion (Trivers 1985: 361–6). In low-latitude forest, savannah, and semi-desert environments, storage is impracticable and hunting success is unpredictable. Any surplus would go to waste, and there is no benefit from keeping it all for oneself. Sharing the surplus from large game is common among low-latitude hunter-gatherers (for a review of cross-cultural evidence, see Layton 2005). As long as they can be identified and punished, people who refuse to share will suffer where hunting success is variable and unpredictable. If a recurrent form of social organization is found in small-scale societies, however, the first question for a neo-Darwinian to ask is not 'is this evidence for the original human condition?' but 'how are people using this type of social strategy to enhance their survival and the transmission of their genes in the particular environments where it is practised?'

The minimal unit of human society

The sort of food sharing outlined in the previous paragraph takes place not at the level of the pair-bond of husband and wife, but in the more inclusive band (see Dunbar, this volume). The band is a flexible unit with often fluid membership. Humans and chimpanzees share a type of social organization that is unusual among non-human primates. This is known as the 'fission–fusion' community, where small sets of individuals within the residential community regularly split off to form temporary, task-specific parties before rejoining other members of the local group. Among chimpanzees, parties typically consist of between four and ten individuals, while the larger community has between twenty and a hundred members. Among human hunter-gatherers occupying the same low-latitude forest environment as chimpanzees (*Pan troglodytes*), foraging parties typically consist of two or three to ten men or women, while the band generally numbers between around twenty to seventy-five individuals.

There are nonetheless some important differences that caution against equating the band with the chimpanzee community and treating chimpanzee social life as the original human condition (e.g. Wrangham and Peterson 1996: 63). Chimpanzee parties sleep wherever nightfall finds them. Among human hunter-gatherers, the band reassembles each evening at a regular camp site. Whereas chimpanzees eat meat at the site of the kill, any large game that hunter-gatherer men have caught is brought back to camp and divided between house-holds. Most importantly, the band belongs to a wider regional community of several hundred people (see data in Layton and Barton 2001, Table 1), whereas the chimpanzee community is self-sufficient. Males defend its boundary and attack members of adjacent communities they encounter in boundary zones. Female chimpanzees may transfer at puberty, but males can only transfer on the rare occasions that adult females transfer with young male offspring (Emery Thompson et al. 2006; Lukas et al. 2005).

Even before chimpanzee society was observed, social anthropology equated hunter-gatherer society with the band (Radcliffe-Brown 1931; Steward 1936). Men were supposed to remain in the same band all their lives, while women transferred from one band to another at marriage. This model continues to inform some recent reconstructions of the evolution of human society (e.g. Foley and Lee 1989 and commentators on Hawkes et al. 1997; Layton 2005). In most recent hunter-gatherer societies, however, the band is a much more fluid and permeable grouping than Radcliffe-Brown and Steward appreciated. Human adults of both sexes often freely change band membership. Whereas male chimpanzees defend their troop's territory against neighbouring groups, among low-latitude hunter-gatherers neighbouring bands acknowledge mutual rights of access over each other's territories. This leads one to ask whether the regional community, rather than the band, should be equated with the chim-panzee community. Such an interpretation is more consistent with Dunbar's prediction of group size from brain evolution (Dunbar 1993). Bands and their base camps would in this view be seen as trends that crystallized within the wider fission–fusion community, emerging as social bonds of cooperation and reciprocal exchange between individuals became stronger during the evolution of modern hunter-gatherer strategies. The capacity to move between bands would, in this view, persist from the earlier pattern of fission–fusion within the wider community, but be enhanced by specifically human traits such as language, and gift exchange with friends in other bands. Mauss (1954 [1925]) argued that gift exchange was fundamental to human social organization, and it may indeed be that exchange enabled the human communities to persist even as their members dispersed over far larger areas than are occupied by chimpanzee communities.

Some cautions

Given these rather exciting developments in the understanding of human social evolution, it is appropriate to pause, recalling why Malinowski and

Radcliffe-Brown repudiated nineteenth-century grand narratives of human progress and set out to establish social anthropology as a discrete, self-sufficient,
and ahistorical discipline. First, they both insisted that social anthropology would
only become a science when it could deal in testable hypotheses. Radcliffe-
Brown rejected, for example, Junod's argument that the relaxed relationship
between a man and his mother's brother in native South Africa was a survival
of an earlier, matrilineal phase in social evolution (Radcliffe-Brown 1952: 24–5).
A sufficient explanation could be found in the present functioning of social
relationships, i.e. the function of the reserved relationship between a man and
his father was to avoid compromising the transmission of property from one
to the other. This consideration did not affect the relationship between a man
and his mother's brother, between whom relations were therefore relaxed (but
see Knight, this volume, for a defence of Junod).

The second reason for rejecting the study of long-term processes was that,
in the 1920s and 1930s, the archaeology of non-Western societies scarcely
existed, and only hypotheses about the present organization of small-scale societies could be tested. Malinowski thought it likely that oral traditions on the
Trobriand Islands, which he had collected at the time of the First World War,
might well contain useful information about successive waves of Pacific island
colonization, yet he dismissed any attempt to reconstruct the history of colonization from such sources as 'a mental game, attractive and absorbing . . .
but always remaining outside the field of observation and sound conclusion'
(1954: 125).

A new synthesis?

There are two reasons for reconsidering whether the functionalists' attempt to
establish social anthropology as a discrete subject is still justified. The archaeology of non-Western societies has advanced hugely over the past half-century,
and social theory has developed beyond the disregard for individual strategies
that characterized structuralism and Radcliffe-Brownian functionalism. In my
view the post-structuralist theories of Giddens and Bourdieu are compatible
with Darwinian evolutionary theory and its focus on the individual as the unit
of analysis.

Bourdieu rejected the reality of a collective 'culture', dismissing it as a
construction of the analyst who generalizes from observation of individuals'
behaviour and listening to their explanations. Bourdieu argued that each individual carries their own *habitus*, the individual's reconstruction of the rules,
tactics, and meaning of social life deduced from others' actions. Children acquire
their habitus by watching adults, and act it out as they grow up. Each habitus
is a variant of those learned by other members of the community and it
requires social effort to achieve a degree of consensus. Habitus can generate
an indefinite variety of dispositions and behaviours but tends over time to converge with 'objective' conditions (Bourdieu 1977: 109). Habitus is therefore
consistent with Darwinian modelling of the evolution of learned behaviour
via selective transmission between individuals (e.g. Boyd and Richerson 1985;
Cavalli-Sforza 1971; Durham 1991).

For Giddens, *agency* is the ability to act in particular ways, where more than one course of action is possible. Giddens regards social structure as a secondary, emergent phenomenon, generated by the interaction of informed agents. Few strategies can be carried to conclusion by individual agents. Most depend on chains of relationships stretching across and out of the community, a process that Giddens describes as *structuration* (1984: 33–5). Giddens emphasizes power, but cooperation and reciprocity are equally important in 'stretching' agency through social networks. Ideas developed in evolutionary theory can explain why there are limits to the possibilities of structuration. Axelrod (1990) demonstrated that reciprocity between individuals can only be sustained under conditions that facilitate mutual trust, while Ostrom (1990) extended this insight to explain what conditions are necessary successfully to allow a community to manage common resources. Cultural strategies may therefore be subject to selective pressures that enable evolutionarily stable solutions to persist in the face of competing behaviours. The case of sharing versus hoarding has been discussed above; Ostrom shows how variation in the incidence of collective versus individual ownership of property can also be explained as adaptive in different but specifiable conditions.

Pitfalls to avoid

I believe there are, nonetheless, some important lessons to retain from the functionalist era:

- Avoid looking for a universal 'original human condition'. Even the original human condition was an adaptation: modern humans adapted to a semi-arid environment in Africa and (perhaps later) to tropical coasts, while Neanderthals adapted to temperate Europe. Even if the modern human adaptation was achieved with distinctive cognitive skills such as gift exchange and the capacity for grammar and tense in language, we must give due emphasis at all times to local adaptations, and avoid thinking in terms of stages of progress.
- Don't return to the speculative reconstructions of the nineteenth century; in other words, do not seek to explain the known as a product of the unknown, to explain the present in terms of a speculative reconstruction of an alleged preceding condition.
- Don't put more weight on the archaeological evidence than it can sustain – it is very easy, in our excitement at rediscovering the big picture, to over-interpret ambiguous evidence, as in claims for home bases in the Olduwan (Isaac 1978a) or shamanism in the Upper Palaeolithic (Clottes and Lewis-Williams 1996). It is more helpful to future research to live with insecurity, not knowing, for example, whether archaic humans had proto-language or rudimentary art, than it is to obscure the unanswered questions with over-ambitious theories.

In the remainder of this chapter I comment on two of the issues debated elsewhere in this volume in the light of the theoretical framework outlined above:

- the proposition that tetradic systems are the earliest form of human kinship;
- the hypothesis that matriliny preceded patriliny in the structure of hunter-gatherer bands.

Do 'elementary kinship systems' reveal the earliest form of human society?

Allen argues that 'the equation of simplest and earliest remains the most economical hypothesis' (above, p. 97). In this section of the chapter I suggest that the logical elegance of cross-cousin marriage and tetradic systems, as described respectively by Claude Lévi-Strauss and Nick Allen, is not necessarily evidence for their historical primacy over other kinship systems. The most elegant and parsimonious cognitive models may not translate into the simplest patterns of social interaction 'on the ground'.

Lévi-Strauss defined 'elementary structures of kinship' as those where the whole social universe of a small-scale community was divided into categories of kin. The simplest is a four-category (tetradic) system defined by two lines of descent and two generation levels (see Allen above for a detailed account, and James, this volume, on 'birth classes'). Table 6.1 corresponds to Allen's Figure 5.1, but represents the system in its patrilineal variant.

In this structure, there are only four basic positions. Ego's children belong to the same generational moiety as ego's parents. Grandparents and grandchildren belong to ego's own generation level. Women are exchanged reciprocally between the moieties to maintain alliances. Ego's spouse is thus the child of his father's sister and mother's brother. 'Wife' is synonymous with mother's brother's daughter and father's sister's daughter (ego's cross-cousins). If ego's father had a brother, he would have married the mother's sister. Their children (ego's parallel cousins) will belong to ego's moiety and generation. They are therefore called 'brother' and 'sister'. Even the closest kinship relationships are thus determined by the structure of the system, and more distant relationships are equally defined by the position of the individual in the system. Radcliffe-Brown had argued that kinship is extended from closer to more distant relatives, such as extension from father to father's brother, or sibling to parallel cousin. Lévi-Strauss countered that kinship terms only gain their meaning in opposition to other kinship terms in a four-part structure (cf. Allen above on extensionist and classificatory kinship).

In the Kariera section system of Western Australia, each of the four cells in the tetradic system is named, allowing strangers to establish their relationship to each other, and therefore their mutual rights and obligations, even where they have no known kin relationship. Throughout the large area of northern

Table 6.1 Patrilineal moieties and generation levels

Generation level	Patrilineal moiety A	Patrilineal moiety B
Other	[1] Father and Father's sister	[3] Mother and Mother's brother
Own	[0] Ego and siblings	[2] Spouse and sibling-in-law

and central Australia where the Kariera system and its more complex relation the Aranda system are followed, territorial groups consist of local patriclans. Table 6.1 is, or was, manifested in local group organization. Among the Kariera, clans belonged to one or other of the two patrilineal moieties. Marriage exchanges tended to take place between neighbouring clans in opposite moieties, so that people married their actual cross-cousins, or people classified with them (see figures in Layton 1995: 226 and McConvell 1997: 208–9).

The Aranda system divides each of the four cells in the Kariera system into two, creating four patrilineal lines of descent out of two. McConvell's fascinating linguistic reconstruction of this process suggests that the Aranda system originated not later than 1500 years ago through the integration of two-four section systems that already existed in different parts of Australia (McConvell 1997: 209–16). Here, there is clear evidence for the evolution of a more complex kinship system from a simpler one.

Is the logically most elegant kinship system necessarily the earliest? In *The Elementary Structures of Kinship* (1969b [1949]), Lévi-Strauss is careful to avoid following Durkheim and Mauss's (1963 [1903]) attempt to reconstruct the progressive evolution of social structures. He rejects speculation as to whether moieties or cross-cousin marriage appeared first (Lévi-Strauss 1969b [1949]: 143–4). Although Lévi-Strauss's tripartite classification of kinship systems into 'elementary', 'intermediate', and 'complex' implies evolutionary progression, the concept of 'elementary kinship structures' is a logical and not necessarily an historical construct.

Lévi-Strauss's fascination with kinship was stimulated by the discovery that strikingly similar marriage rules exist among historically unrelated peoples in Australia, Asia, and the Americas. The structure of the Australian Kariera system is the same as that of the Yanomamö on the borders of Brazil and Venezuela in as much as both are based on bilateral cross-cousin marriage. In both cases, patrilineal descent groups are linked by marriage exchange. A man should marry his mother's brother's daughter/father's sister's daughter and cannot marry his mother's sister's daughter or father's brother's daughter. All such societies were characterized by rules that decree an individual should marry into the allied lineage containing his or her *cross-cousins*.

I suggest it is more likely that cross-cousin marriage has repeatedly been rediscovered among human societies of a certain complexity, not that it represents the original human condition. This was Lévi-Strauss's own position: the binary character of human logical thought led to the repeated discovery that cross-cousin marriage provided an elegant solution to sustaining reciprocal exchange between groups (Lévi-Strauss 1969b [1949]: 70, 144). Any social system which depends on regular marriage alliances can specify cross-cousins as the ideal marriage partners and forbid marriage with parallel cousins. Cross-cousins function as 'markers' who, even if they do not themselves become *ego's* marriage partners, signal the identity of the group into which he or she should marry.

Cross-cousin marriage is not universal among hunter-gatherers. Many recent hunter-gatherer societies – the !Kung San of the Kalahari (Ju/'hoansi and other speakers of Ju languages in the Kalahari; Barnard 1992: 268–71), the

Mbuti of central Africa, the Inuit of the Arctic – have a more flexible group structure, lack unilineal descent-based lineages, and do not practise cross-cousin marriage. Like Western European kin terms, northern San and Inuit terminologies make no distinction between parallel and cross-cousins. In fact, anthropologists have classified French and English kinship as belonging to the 'Eskimo' type, on the grounds that no terminological distinction is made between relatives on the mother's and father's side (but see Allen, note 5, this volume). The majority of recent hunter-gatherer communities have bilateral kinship systems. The Ethnographic Atlas Crosstabulations compiled by the Anthropology Department at the University of Kent (*http://boas.kent.ac.uk/ethnoatlas/*) show that where hunting exceeds 36% of economic activity, three-quarters (18/23 cases) have bilateral kinship or descent.

While Aboriginal Australia is famous for its examples of various types of cross-cousin marriage (Kariera, Aranda [Arrente], Murngin [Yolngu]), in central Australia, a simpler, more flexible form of social organization is found among the Pitjantjatjara of the Western Desert. The Pitjantjatjara recognize two generational levels, referred to as 'shade side' and 'sun side'. If I belong to the 'shade side', so do my grandparents and grandchildren. My parents and children belong to the 'sun side'. However, an individual is free to join either their mother's or their father's local group. Each local group therefore consists of a mix of people related through the father or the mother. Both cross- and parallel cousins who grow up together address each other as siblings. A distinction between cross- and parallel cousins would not predict who belongs to one's own group or who is an ideal marriage partner, and there are no descent-based moieties. The marriage rule states that one must marry someone from a distant group, and kinship defines all one's adjacent groups as 'brothers' and 'sisters'. This system is almost certainly a response to the harsh and unpredictable environment of the Western Desert, where flexibility of movement and an open network of social relationships is essential (see Layton 1995).

There is no tendency for alliances between specific groups. On the contrary, the safest strategy in an unpredictable desert environment is to spread one's network of kin as widely as possible. People in neighbouring local bands among the Pitjantjatjara are defined as 'siblings' and those in distant bands as 'in-laws' (see Layton 1995). The status of any band in this classification will depend on the viewpoint of ego's own band. Adults from distant groups in the opposite generational moiety to ego are therefore classed as classificatory mother's brother or father's sister. Hence Dousset (2005) translates the term for members of one's own generation in distant groups (*watjirra*) as 'cross-cousin' (see also Dousset 2002). Purely linguistic evidence might therefore imply that even the Western Desert people possessed the kind of elementary kinship system described by Lévi-Strauss, but the categories are not realized in local groups, as they are (or were) among the Kariera and other north Australian communities. Pitjantjatjara kinship terminology has the 'double dichotomy' required by Nick Allen's hypothesis: it distinguishes 'siblings' from 'in-laws' and it distinguishes adjacent from alternate generations. In this sense it *is* a tetradic system, but it does not have the elegant, logical neatness of a four-section system in which the four categories are given sociocentric labels that remain the same regardless of where ego's own clan is positioned. (The sociocentric system of the Alawa – typical of a large part of Australia's Northern Territory – is described in Layton 1997a.) Moreover, when the Pitjantjatjara's western neighbours the Pintupi began to adopt a four-section system that depended on patrilineal continuity in local groups and its concomitant practice of cross-cousin marriage, from the more northerly Warlpiri, this was hindered by the flexibility of local group membership (Myers 1986: 183–7). A linguistic distinction between parallel and cross-cousins does not necessarily signal a social system of the Kariera/Yanomamö type.

The Pitjantjatjara system may represent the slackening of rules in a four-section system in order to adapt to the sparse and unpredictable distribution of subsistence resources (although such an argument would be difficult to sustain in the Kalahari; see Barnard 1992: 234). Pitjantjatjara kinship may, on the other hand, represent the northerly limit of a simpler system character-istic of southeastern Australia that persisted because the historically documented spread of section systems was halted by the barrier of a desert with which it was incompatible. (For a reconstruction of local group recruitment in south-east Australia see H. Allen 1972: 104–7.) Linguistic evidence unequivocally links the Pitjantjatjara with the spread of Pama-nyungan speakers from the north to the centre, but Western Desert art shows continuities in style with the ancient 'Panaramitee' rock art tradition of the southeast (Layton 1997b).

It is no coincidence that matrilineal or patrilineal moieties and clans, cross-cousin marriage, and elementary kinship structures go together, since all are facilitated by a rule of obligatory descent through one parent. Their emergence in Australia, as represented by the Kariera, may be reflected in changing pat-terns of camp formation and rock art production over the last five thousand years that appear to signal more stable links between people and country (Layton 1997b). These changes first appear on the north coast of Australia and spread southward, reaching central Australia around 1500 years ago. They may have been triggered by the flooding of large coastal areas by rising seas after the last Ice Age.

The archaeological evidence for the origin of clan totemism on the North-west Coast of North America suggests a similar picture. The first human settlers on the Northwest Coast probably arrived before 13,000 BP, at least one thousand years before the now familiar forest cover returned. Rising sea levels rendered the estuarine environments along the coast unstable, preventing the accumulation of shellfish beds and making rivers and lakes unsuitable for spawning runs by fish. The earliest inhabitants of the Northwest Coast therefore probably lived in small, nomadic, relatively egalitarian bands. Stable settlements resembling those recorded in the eighteenth and nineteenth centuries only emerged after the sea level stabilized at about 3500 BC, while the familiar totemic art style (analysed by Lévi-Strauss in *La Voie des masques* [1979]) developed after AD 500 (Ames and Maschner 1999).

Thus, as noted earlier, while a case may be made for an internal dynamic in society, perhaps driven by the elaboration of exchange networks, ecology places a limit on what is possible, and in the last resort social relations must provide effective adaptations to local conditions.

Did Matriliny or Patriliny Come First?

The notion of the patrilineal band as the original form of human society has dominated anthropology since the days of Radcliffe-Brown (1931) and Steward (1936). Steward (1936: 333) argued that men's hunting success was key to survival, and sons inherited their fathers' hunting territories because that was the country they knew best. He accepted that matrilineal bands may arise where women play an important role in subsistence (Steward 1936: 343). In their chapter in this volume, Kit Opie and Camilla Power argue that the role of grandmothers as foragers for, and care-givers to, their daughters' children were critical to the emergence of hunter-gatherer social adaptations. Thus, by inference, the earliest human groups coalesced around matrilines comprising women, their daughters, and daughters' daughters. It is true that in all hunter-gatherer societies women make an indispensable contribution to the diet. But I question whether that justifies disregarding the men's contribution, and its potential effects on social organization. I propose, based on the model sketched in the first section of this chapter, that the band is a social unit of fluctuating membership, its composition at any time based on both male and female members' efforts to balance conflicting social ties.

The Hadza of Tanzania provide vital ethnographic support for both of Opie and Power's hypotheses, since O'Connell and his co-workers argue that Hadza grandmothers help forage for their grandchildren while their daughter is caring for a newborn infant. Men's hunting, on the other hand, does not support their own children, but is apparently undertaken to gain prestige among other members of the band. Research into the role of female grandparents among the Hadza has prompted an interesting hypothesis for the evolution of women's longevity beyond the menopause. Hawkes et al. (1997) found that Hadza mothers reduce the time they spend foraging at the birth of a new child. Older, weaned children too young to support themselves will therefore suffer. This is where the grandmother steps in: grandmothers spent most time foraging when their infant grandchild is youngest and their weaned grandchildren are receiving least from the mother. Gurven and Hill (1997), in their comments on Hawkes et al. (1997: 566), point out that only two of the eight older women tracked in the study were mother's mothers, but five out of the eight were matrilateral relatives, and there is therefore evidence for the adaptive value of adult daughters living with maternal relatives. The specific value of the maternal grandmother's role has since been supported by Sear et al.'s (2000) study of infant survival among subsistence cultivators in the Gambia.

O'Connell et al. (2002), however, describe two apparently contradictory aspects of Hadza behaviour: on the one hand, meat contributes an estimated 50% of the mean caloric intake among those who are full-time foragers; on the other, meat is rarely shared in ways that favour the hunter's own family. The latter observation leads them to conclude that the object of hunting cannot be to contribute to the hunter's own children's survival and, therefore, male provisioning of children cannot have figured in early human social evolution. Hawkes and Bliege Bird (2002) do not dispute the practical value of meat – they argue that this makes it more valuable as a way of signalling status – but they also question whether hunting benefits the hunter's own household. The large game animals that men hunt are widely distributed in camp, 'producing more calories for the group than for their own households' (2002: 59). The crucial fact for Hawkes and Bliege Bird is that Ache, Hadza, and Meriam data show the good hunter never gets back as much as he gives. They conclude that 'meat is a medium of communication through which the hunter transmits information to potential mates, allies, and competitors' (2002: 60–1).

Both O'Connell et al.'s and Hawkes and Bliege Bird's papers overlook the function of meat sharing described above, as a means of reducing the risk that an individual hunter will, as he often does, return empty-handed (Winterhalder 1990, 1996). As long as a successful hunt yields more than a single family can consume and future success is random, it is more adaptive to share, so long as recipients can be required to repay their debt on a later occasion when they have good luck in the hunt. It is true that the successful hunter may himself only receive a minimal share of his kill, but he will benefit when he is repaid by others. Hawkes et al. write unequivocally that 'meat makes up a large proportion of *everyone's* diet' among the Hadza (1997: 573, my emphasis). Lee reports that among the !Kung:

> Many good hunters did no hunting at all for weeks or months at a time, while their wives and children waited patiently and ate the meat distributed by other hunters. . . . A period of hunting inactivity allows the hunter to enjoy the benefits of some of the reciprocal obligations he has built up. (1979: 248–9)

There is no doubt that some men are more successful hunters than others. Of 127 !Kung men in Richard Lee's sample, thirty-seven had never killed a Kudu, whereas 79% of Kudu had been killed by 34% of the men (1979: 243). But hunting is risky, even for good hunters. Male and female foraging strategies are different, and must be interpreted within a lifetime perspective. Women can gather effectively into old age, but successful hunting demands good eyesight. Among the !Kung, age is an important factor in hunting success, although not the only one (Lee 1979: 243–4). Hawkes et al. write that among the Hadza, older women spend significantly more time foraging than females in any other category, whereas the male pattern is quite different: '. . . *the peak for males comes before marriage*' (1997: 555, emphasis added). They also write: 'Males of all ages *except adults*' (i.e. juvenile men!) spent more time foraging than females (1997: 557, emphasis added). As Nic Peterson long ago pointed out to me apropos his fieldwork in Australia (pers. comm.), a young man's best asset is his hunting ability, whereas one of the best assets an older man has is a marriageable daughter. Here is a much more explicit link between male hunting and reproductive success than vague hypotheses of prestige and surreptitious affairs (e.g. Kaplan et al. 1990). Thus, to quote Lee again,

> With the killing of his first buck, the young man is considered much more favourably as a potential son-in-law. . . . Traditionally, the prime characteristics parents of a girl sought in a son-in-law were proved hunting ability and a

willingness to live with his in-laws and provide meat for them for a number of years. (1979: 240)

Note that this behaviour depends on distinguishing between generation levels, and between lineal relatives and in-laws, the basis of tetradic systems.

Interestingly, the strategies of the best documented hunter-gatherer societies differ. Among the !Kung, 'The camp core of older people want to encourage the sons-in-law to stay with the group permanently, as more hunters mean more meat' (Lee 1979: 242), and many stayed for between three and ten years. The Tiwi of northern Australia adopt a similar strategy: a man might bestow his infant daughter on someone he wanted as an ally, or he might bestow her on a younger man as 'old-age insurance', in which case he would look for a younger man in his late twenties or thirties who showed signs of being a good hunter and fighting man (Hart et al. 1988: 19). 'The meat, fish and game provided for the large household of an old man was provided by the young men', both sons and sons-in-law (Hart and Pilling 1960: 34).

The Mbuti and Ache, however, seem to take a more relaxed attitude. Turnbull implies that a single kill is sufficient: the suitor, having slept with the girl and asked her parents' permission to marry, 'now only has to prove himself as a hunter, and the act of betrothal is sealed by his killing one of the larger antelope and presenting it to the girl's parents, perhaps also with some other gifts' (1965: 140). A small Mbuti band will want to keep the incoming partner, but a large band wants to lose the resident one, so there is no consistent pressure on the son in law to stay. Hill and Hurtado (1996: 228) describe marriage among the Ache, before settlement on reservations, as entirely a matter for the couple. Women preferred men who were handsome and kind, good hunters and hard workers but not killers, since killers were liable to mistreat their wives. While the Ache lived as foragers, good hunters had both higher fertility and better offspring survival into adulthood than did poor hunters.

Parents' success in both hunting and gathering would affect their children's survival, although Hill and Hurtado (1996) note that, while the Ache were full-time foragers, they would not have got all the food they needed without sharing. Evidence for the benefits of sharing among the Ache was cited above.

The contribution of game to hunter-gatherer diets ranges from 25 to 100% (Marlowe 2001). The relative status of the sexes undoubtedly varies accordingly, with greater equality where women's contribution is greatest (Friedl 1978), but, as Marlowe notes, as long as men can obtain more than they need to consume, they can increase the nutrition of women and children.

What effect will following the kinds of strategies outlined above have on local group recruitment among hunter-gatherers? Hawkes et al. (1997), followed by Opie and Power (this volume), argue that the grandmother's role points to an adaptive advantage for women remaining in their natal group, and men transferring to their wife's group at marriage. Participants in this debate, equating the human band with the chimpanzee community, infer a radical reversal from patrilineal to matrilineal group continuity during human evolution. Several commentators on Hawkes et al. question whether such a radical switch in behaviour would be possible (Hawkes et al. 1997: 568, 569, 572–3).

If, however, it is the regional hunter-gatherer community that corresponds to the chimpanzee troop, then the flexible band structure seen among recent hunter-gatherers is the outcome of choices between competing social strategies for improving inclusive fitness, including pair-bonding, male hunting, and female grandmothering.

Such flexibility in human behaviour has been demonstrated through a comparison of swidden cultivators and livestock herders. Holden and Mace (2003) demonstrate the statistical probability that the adoption of cattle by Bantu groups led to a shift from matrilineal to patrilineal continuity in household recruitment and inheritance. Bantu who practise swidden cultivation tend to transmit rights to land through matrilineal descent. Holden and Mace argue that matrilineal descent is often associated with swidden cultivation, because women typically do much of the productive work in the fields. Cattle, however, are vulnerable to theft and must be defended by men. Patrilineal descent is a more appropriate form of inheritance among livestock herders. Both forms of descent are adaptations to particular economic regimes. Goldschmidt (1979) has earlier noted the same functional correlation between pastoralism and patrilineal descent. Holden and Mace do not, however, make any claims about the *original* type of inheritance among Bantu speakers:

> It is uncertain whether they were matrilineal or patrilineal. . . . The reason why we cannot infer descent rules among early Bantu-speakers with certainty is probably because descent rules are highly variable across equatorial African populations today, and also change relatively rapidly. (2003: 2429)

In the second section of this chapter, I argued in support of Lévi-Strauss's inference that cross-cousin marriage had originated independently on different continents. The same is almost certainly true of patrilineal and matrilineal descent. Domestication of crops was invented independently in the Americas; the earliest humans to enter the Americas were hunter-gatherers and therefore, on the balance of probabilities, had a bilateral kinship system. The Iroquois (who first stimulated Morgan's – 1907 [1877] – theory of evolutionary stages in human kinship from matriliny to patriliny) were swidden cultivators who practised matrilineal descent. This almost certainly came about as an *independent* adaptation to cultivation, supporting a Darwinian approach to the evolution of human kinship systems but not a theory of evolution through universal stages of progress.

Conclusion

As indicated in the introduction to this chapter, I consider that after a century of meticulous scholarship archaeology and anthropology are ready to readdress the big questions that excited Victorian scholars. It is precisely because the potential for advancing our understanding of those issues is still so exciting that I contend we must not overreach ourselves. In this chapter, I have argued that humans and chimpanzees have flexible forms of social organization that apparently derive from a shared evolutionary history. The significance of parallels between the two species depends upon whether the hunter-gatherer band is equated with the chimpanzee community or (as I argue here) with the transitory fusion episodes during which individuals within the chimpanzee community come together. I hypothesize that customs such as unilineal descent and cross-cousin marriage followed earlier, more transient forms of association in the fission–fusion communities of our ancestors, appearing as social adaptations to specific ecological circumstances made possible by uniquely human forms of cognition and behaviour. Each custom should be evaluated for its adaptive consequences in the specific environment in which it is practised, but there may be limited scope for cumulative processes of change generated by the dynamics of interaction within hunter-gatherer communities.

Acknowledgements

I am indebted to Filipo Aureli for introducing me to the concept of fission–fusion societies, and to participation in a recent workshop organized by Robin Dunbar at Liverpool University for the development of the approach that postulates evolutionary continuity between the hunter-gatherer band and fusion episodes in the chimpanzee community. I thank Nick Allen for his good-humoured tolerance of my efforts to critique tetradic theory, Alan Barnard for refining my statement about San kinship, and Sean O'Hara for providing the references to Lukas et al. and Emery Thompson et al.

Part III

Other Primates and the Biological Approach

A chimpanzee female coalition in action at Arnhem Zoo, The Netherlands. Marka and Monique, daughters of the high-ranking Mama, confront third-ranking male Fons. Photo copyright Kathelijne Koops

7

Kinship in Biological Perspective

Robin Dunbar

Introduction

My aims in this chapter are twofold: first, to describe as clearly as I can what a biological (and hence Darwinian) view of kinship constitutes, and, second, to set this conventional biological view on kinship into the context of more recent work on multilevel selection. The first is necessary because non-biologists rarely have a well-informed understanding of contemporary evolutionary biology. The second is important because it promises to provide the basis for a convergence of view between biologists and social scientists.

Before I embark on this, however, let me first clear up one common misunderstanding. Since the mid-1970s, it has become widely appreciated that evolutionary explanations of behaviour involve what has become known as the 'selfish gene' approach. However, most non-biologists seem to assume that this has something to do with the genetic determination of behaviour. This is an understandable conclusion, since the selfish gene approach focuses on selection for genes, and its arguments are usually explicitly phrased in terms of 'the gene for [. . . a particular behaviour]'. Unfortunately, however, the conventional conclusion does not follow from the premises on which it is based. While it is, of course, perfectly possible that individual genes for individual behaviours could exist (and may conceivably do so), it is important to appreciate that the link between genes and behaviour in the Darwinian equation is at best indirect. Almost no species has its behaviour determined in the simple sense implied by the conventional genetic determinist view. Indeed, not even the anatomy and physiology that make us what we are have this kind of simple genetics. This does not, however, stop us from using the gene's-eye view as a convenient metric for costing out the evolutionary processes and the way they act on the organism. In a nutshell, the Darwinian approach is not about the role that genes might have in determining behaviour (that would, in any case, be the remit of developmental biologists, not evolutionary biologists); rather, it is about strategic thinking.

By strategic thinking, I refer to the fact that the way evolution works is directly analogous to the way we might think about choosing between options. This does not, of course, imply that evolution (or the gene) acts in any conscious sense to weigh up the pros and cons of different alternatives, but rather that the process of natural selection inexorably results in those traits that yield the highest fitness (i.e. the largest number of descendents bearing that trait) being favoured. In other words, those traits that enable an organism to reproduce itself more successfully will be the ones that come to be represented most often in future generations. This approach is termed 'strategic' because natural selection has to 'choose' between alternative forms of a given trait on the basis of which is the most efficient in terms of genetic replication. This is all that the theory of natural selection entails.

One more point is worth making. Biology is a complex, multi-layered discipline, and its concerns span a wide range of questions. Known as *Tinbergen's Four Why's*, these can be broadly classified into questions of function (the teleonomic question: what role does a phenomenon play in an organism's life?), questions of mechanism (how is that phenomenon produced physiologically or psychologically?), questions of ontogeny (what are the respective roles of genes and the environment in guiding the development of the phenomenon?) and questions of phylogeny (what is the historical sequence that led up to the present condition?). These questions (first enumerated, albeit in reduced form, by Aristotle in his biological writings) are logically independent of each other (hence, the answer to one question does not prejudice the answer to any of the others), but can and ought all to be answered (at least, if we are to say that we have genuinely understood the nature of the phenomenon we are considering). Within biology, sub-disciplines tend to focus on one or other of these questions, although organismic biologists (in other words, those who make most use of the Darwinian approach) are commonly forced to consider all approaches together. In contrast, most other disciplines concern themselves with just one or two of these questions (psychologists with mechanisms and ontogeny, physiologists with mechanism, molecular biologists with ontogeny, and so on).

The reason this distinction is important (in fact, crucial if we are not to make egregious errors in understanding what biologists do) is that the term 'gene' appears in two separate places – once in functional explanations, and once in ontogenetic explanations. However, the *sense* in which this term is being used is very different in these two cases. When evolutionary biologists refer to genes in functional contexts, they mean 'the consequences that a trait has for the future structure of the species' gene pool', whereas when developmental biologists or molecular geneticists refer to genes, they mean 'those bits of DNA that are instrumental in producing a trait during the course of an organism's development from the point of conception'. Unfortunately, these two senses often get confused, especially in popular discourse – probably because biologists do not usually bother to specify which sense of gene they are referring to (it is usually obvious from the context, and is not in itself a particularly interesting issue for them). The distinction, however, is important, because they do not refer to the same thing. This is so for two reasons.

First, there is no necessary reason why whatever it is that determines a trait in the ontogenetic sense should be the same identical thing that is propagated into future generations. This is because almost no behaviour is so rigidly determined by genes in the way such a claim would presuppose. It is easy to see why this should be so. The capacity to make efficient decisions about how to behave is determined by the brain's ability to make the necessary calculations (which is mainly a function of its size and structure, features that undoubtedly have a genetic basis). Efficient decisions allow you to survive or reproduce more successfully, and that in turn allows the genes for your big brain to be propagated more successfully into the future. But it does not follow from this that your decisions about how to behave are determined by the genes that underwrite your big brain. Indeed, in evolutionary terms, the whole point of having a big brain is to allow the organism to respond in a more context-dependent way to the vagaries of the world; since the future cannot be predicted, flexibility of behaviour and decision-making is critical. Having your behaviour locked in by your genes in this way would be a recipe for rapid extinction and evolutionary disaster (unless your rate of reproduction is so fast that you can track changes by genetic change alone faster than the environment can change – something that is probably only possible for viruses and bacteria).

Second, although the word 'gene' is used in both contexts, the term in actual fact refers to two quite different entities. The genes of ontogeny are bits of DNA, but the genes of function are Mendelian genes. Now, the important thing about Mendelian genes is that they are traits or characters rather than bits of DNA. Of course, in some cases, there is some kind of direct relationship between Mendelian genes and the underlying bits of DNA that give rise to them (eye colour is a well-known case in point), but in many cases this relationship is so indirect that it doesn't make a lot of sense to view this as a form of genetic determinism. Mendel did not know about DNA or even genes when he did his experiments on peas and developed his ideas about inheritance, any more than Darwin himself did. Instead, he couched his entire argument in terms of 'fidelity of copying' (the extent to which offspring resemble their parents on a particular trait).

This was rather fortuitous, as it turns out. Although biologists have inevitably been interested in the hardware of life and the mechanisms that produce this, in fact nothing in either Mendel's theory of inheritance or Darwin's theory of natural selection (the two complementary strands that make up the modern neo-Darwinian theory of evolution) specifies that the gene is the actual or only mechanism of inheritance. Since the issue is simply the fidelity with which traits are copied from one individual to another, learning is just one of many ways in which traits can be passed on in a Darwinian world. Learning is a process of selection between options in which one survives at the expense of the others – which is all that is meant by natural selection. Thus Darwin's theory of natural selection does not depend in the general case (even though it may do in particular cases) on which particular mechanism of inheritance happens to meet the requirements of Mendel's theory of inheritance. It is this that allows us to have Darwinian theories of cultural evolution (see Boyd and Richerson 1985; McElreath and Henrich 2007) that are not based on genes.

In sum, in most cases, evolutionary biologists use the word 'gene' in their explanations as a shorthand for the rather complex processes of inheritance. The mechanism of inheritance is not necessarily of any particular interest, especially if their main focus is on the strategic aspects of behaviour: in this case, their core question is 'To what extent do evolutionary considerations drive behaviour?' By that, they mean the extent to which the interests of maximizing genetic representation in future generations structure and guide an individual's choices among alternative behavioural actions in the here and now. The mechanism of inheritance (when this is DNA or learning, or any of the many other possibilities) merely determines how fast a trait is inherited, and how easy it is to effect changes.

It is perhaps worth reminding ourselves that to answer an evolutionary question requires that we understand the context in considerable detail, because the optimal strategy (that which maximizes fitness) depends on the balance of costs and benefits for the various alternatives that individuals (or natural selection) have to choose between. It is the particular context that an individual finds itself in that determines the costs and benefits of the particular options it has, and part of that context is its own past history. In that respect, the need to have a very deep understanding of the particular context is crucial for any evolutionary analysis – a point that is, of course, very much in the spirit of the anthropologist's traditional ethnographic method.

I won't elaborate any further on this, since it is all pretty much standard biological theory and practice, and further details can be found in any basic textbook of evolutionary biology or behavioural ecology (for recent summaries, see Barrett et al. 2002; Dunbar et al. 2005). So with these preliminaries taken for granted, let me now turn to the more specific question of what kinship means to evolutionary biologists.

Biology, Evolution, and Kinship

The foundations of biological kinship lie uncompromisingly in genetics. So I will begin with the simplest possible situation, namely what biological first principles have to tell us. I will go on to show how this can (and, indeed, does) become more complex, but it is usually considered heuristically helpful in biology to begin with the simplest possible situation. The issue here is very straightforward. By virtue of the processes of biological reproduction, individuals inherit genes from their biological parents. Although there is some variation across the biological world in the basis of this process, humans share with all mammals a relatively simple pattern of inheritance in which each parent contributes an approximately equal share of genes to each offspring. We thus share our genetic make-up in varying proportions with our relatives by virtue of descent from a common ancestor. The proportions in any specific case (a half in the case of full siblings, a quarter in the case of a grandparent and grandchild, an eighth in the case of cousins, etc.) reflect the number of reproductive events that separate the two individuals in question (for more detailed explanation, see Barrett et al. 2002: 26–8). It also, of course, partly depends on whether you have an endogamous or exogamous mating system: in the former case, two cousins, for example, may be related through several routes in the pedigree, and thus have higher relatedness than will be the case when matings are strictly exogamous.

Although others had recognized the significance of this before him, W. D. Hamilton (1964) is generally credited with the first comprehensive explanation for how this shared genetic history might influence an organism's behaviour. His explanation (known as the theory of kin selection, and enshrined in what is now referred to as 'Hamilton's Rule') begins from the fact that we have a defined probability of sharing a particular gene with another individual that is a simple function of our relatedness within a pedigree. This allowed Hamilton to show why a notional gene for altruism might evolve in a Darwinian world. Hamilton's Rule states simply that (and I paraphrase) 'a gene for altruism will spread whenever the benefits of aiding a relative to reproduce more success-fully exceed the costs incurred by lost personal reproduction'. When the costs and benefits of action are measured in terms of numbers of future offspring born or forgone, the coefficient of relationship (the probability of sharing a given gene by descent from a common ancestor) determines the balance of the equation. In principle, individuals that are genetically more closely related are worth more to each other in fitness terms, where fitness is technically defined as an individual's genetic contribution in future generations. (Note that fit-ness is not an absolute quantity: it is always defined relative to the average contribution for all individuals in the population as a whole. It is also strictly speaking the property of a gene, or a behavioural strategy, rather than of an individual.) Individuals that further a relative's reproductive interests will, on average, inevitably leave more descendants than those that do not, providing that action does not detract too much from their own success at reproducing, because copies of the gene in question will find their way into the next generation through their relatives (given that they share that gene). In the limiting case, an individual might sacrifice its own future reproduction entirely in order to enhance that of a relative if the benefit is great enough (as in the famous case of honey bees, whose sterile workers are females that have for-gone all possibility of future reproduction in order to help their sister – the queen – reproduce).

It is important to appreciate three things about Hamilton's Rule. One is that it does not state that we should always be more generous to more closely related individuals. Rather, it states that *all else equal* we should be more generous to close relatives. (Note that the word 'should' here carries no moral force: it is strictly an economic imperative – if you want to maximize your fitness, this is what you should do.) The issue here is the trade-off between the benefits that accrue through enhancing a relative's ability to reproduce and the cost to me in terms of my own ability to reproduce. If I gain more in terms of personal reproduction by aiding an unrelated individual (or even just by refus-ing to help a relative and saving my resources for myself), then Hamilton's Rule specifies that helping the stranger (or being selfish) is the evolution-arily optimal decision. The issue hinges critically around the magnitude of the reproductive benefits to the relative and the cost to me in terms of lost opportunities for future reproduction (my so-called 'opportunity cost', or 'regret') when these are discounted by the coefficient of relatedness. The second issue is that Hamilton's Rule is not optional: it is an unavoidable consequence of the way biological reproduction works (whatever that may happen to be). Its consequences follow come what may: actions that facilitate investment in relatives will always benefit one's fitness; those that do not will always harm fitness. That will tend to result in relatives having priority under most circumstances, unless other constraints or considerations militate against them. Consequently, where biological and social kinship do not coincide, this should alert us to ask what extra has been added in that has resulted in their decoupling at those particular points where they are decoupled. Finally, Hamilton's Rule is not the only biological explanation for the evolution of altruistic behaviour, but it is important because it reminds us that genetic kinship always provides the baseline in any biological analysis of behaviour and that the unit of cost accounting has to be genes.

When biologists speak of kinship in animals, it is this genetic sense that they mean, and nothing else (see Korstjens, this volume; Lehmann, this volume). But how well does this biological conception of kinship translate to the human case? Anthropologists have consistently pointed out that social kinship as conventionally exemplified in human societies does not always correspond to biological kinship. Notoriously, kinship categories often do not coincide in different terminologies (in the case of Omaha and Crow classification systems, for example, they may even be mirror images of each other). Other, more subtle differences seem to cut directly across what might otherwise look like points of convergence between biological and social kinship classifications. The offspring of parallel cousins, for example, are commonly placed into a different category from the offspring of cross-cousins in many (though not all) kinship systems, even though, biologically, there is more to distinguish the offspring of daughters from the offspring of sons (because sons inevitably face some measure of paternity uncertainty: they can never guarantee that their wives' offspring are their own).

There are two questions we need to ask here. One is whether this lack of correspondence is so intrusive that it cannot reasonably be said that there is any useful correspondence between biological and social kinship. The other is how much any lack of correspondence actually matters.

The first is essentially an empirical issue. The fact is that, even taking some of the more exotic kinship naming practices into account, kinship systems around the world represent only a very small sub-sample (on most accounts, a mere half dozen or so generic typologies) of what would theoretically be possible. People do not classify their relatives in a completely random way, but rather tend, in broad terms, to agree about the categories they use. To sustain the claim that there is no correspondence between biological and social kinship requires us to show that the one is a random mapping onto the other, and so far – despite some impressive (but perhaps not altogether surprising) individual naming practices like the habit of referring to one's mother's sister as 'mother' as in Crow-type kinship systems – this seems not to be the case. In general, kinship classifications do correlate with each other in broad terms even though they do not do so in detail – certainly a great deal better than we would expect if they were completely random and unrelated to any underlying genetic reality.

The second issue is a purely statistical one: does it matter if the correspondence between biological and social kinship (as expressed in a genealogical grid) is not perfect? The short answer is: only if the mappings from one to the other are completely random. If there is *any* degree of consistency between social and biological kinship, no matter how small, then, from an evolutionary point of view, investing in one's social kin will have the consequence, on the long-term average, of investing in one's biological kin. Evolution is a statistical process, not a deterministic one, and a very great deal of statistical slop can often be tolerated. When biologists state that bigger organisms live longer, they do not mean to imply that *all* big organisms live longer than all small ones. The fact that, on average, more do than do not is sufficient to drive evolution. The only effect this issue really has is on the *speed* of evolution: the more highly correlated the two kinship systems are, the faster will any trait that is dependent on kinship evolve (i.e. come to typify all members of the population or species); conversely, the less well correlated they are, the slower the trait will evolve. It does not affect the question of whether or not evolutionary change will occur.

Nonetheless, there is plenty of empirical evidence to suggest that, irrespective of the importance of social kinship, biological (i.e. genetic) kinship does play an important background role in the decisions that individuals make on how they should treat each other. In an analysis of Icelandic Viking sagas, for example, my colleagues and I (Dunbar et al. 1995) showed that individuals were significantly less likely to murder close relatives (those related to ego as paternal cousins or better) than less closely related individuals (for a similar analysis of the English kings and queens, see Johnson and Johnson 1991). More importantly, their willingness to murder relatives was modified by the value of the action to the murderer: they were willing to murder distant relatives for trivial benefits (e.g. in a drunken brawl), but close relatives were only murdered if the gains were very high (e.g. by doing so, they inherited an earldom or land). Similarly, the Vikings were more willing to form alliances (or to make loans of ships, supplies, or men for expeditions) with close relatives than more distant ones, and when they did so were less likely either to demand explicit reciprocation or to renege on the agreement later.

Note that it does not matter much how the Vikings themselves construed their patterns of kinship in these cases: these findings are based entirely on pedigrees constructed out of declared paternities. While the Vikings may have occasionally made mistakes about paternity, as we all do, paternity (and maternity) were important to them because they were associated with rights to land. These paternities are, of course, all taken from the Vikings' written records, the sagas that were composed and/or written down mainly in the thirteenth century to provide records of individual family histories. As with all historical records, we might ask whether we can rely on them: after all, victors in history tend to colour the accounts they give with their particular view. There are, however, three relevant circumstances in this particular case.

First, these accounts were written for public consumption by a very small community (medieval Iceland) where most people were intimately familiar with both the events and the characters described (in most cases, their own immediate ancestors): they would not have hesitated to say so if Snorri Sturluson (who was responsible for composing a great many of the Icelandic sagas in the 1220s and 1230s) had made too many egregious errors. Second, the Vikings themselves were very clear on real paternity (as best as they could define it biologically): despite the fact that fostering was a major feature of their world (as it continued to be into quite recent times throughout northern Europe), they made a clear distinction between foster-sons or foster-brothers and real sons or real brothers. Foster-sons could inherit land from a foster-parent if the parent so chose, but they did so by right of adoption and not by birth-right. Finally, even if the stories are complete fiction, we can still ask: did the Vikings compose their stories in such a way that they followed biological prescriptions?

The Vikings provide us with a second intriguing example of the role of biological kinship in the life of a pre-modern community. One of the features of the Viking world was the phenomenon of the *berserker*, an individual whose fearsome reputation on the battlefield was often associated with shape-changing, the use of psychotropic drugs, and a great deal of myth. *Berserkers* were at the same time both feared (they were extremely dangerous when roused, and as often as not caused mayhem in the community when back home) and admired (for obvious reasons, they were invaluable on a raiding expedition, and many of the Scandanavian kings employed *berserkers* as bodyguards). An analysis of Icelandic sagas revealed that whether or not the family of a murder victim accepted blood money in compensation or insisted on a revenge killing (they were entitled to a free choice between the two) depended heavily on whether or not the murderer was a known *berserker*: revenge killings were preferred against ordinary mortals, but blood money was the more common choice against a *berserker* (Dunbar et al. 1995). The reason is fairly obvious: *berserkers* were simply too dangerous to take on. But why should these individuals and the phenomenon they represented have been tolerated? The answer seems to be that, directly or indirectly through their reputations, they provided protection for their extended families. Families that contained a known *berserker* lost only about half the number of adult male members to brawls and vendettas compared to families that were not so blessed (Barrett et al. 2002: 262), despite the fact that the *berserkers* themselves were often short-lived. In other words, being related to a *berserker* was quite a good thing in fitness terms, and *berserkers* themselves had significantly higher inclusive fitness (measured as the number of surviving male family members in the following generation, devalued by their degree of paternal relatedness to the *berserker*) than the average for men in families that lacked a *berserker*.

Another example of the way biological kinship intrudes into everyday life is provided by Madsen et al. (2007). They asked individuals from two different cultures (the UK and South African Zulus) to undertake a painful isometric skiing exercise for the benefit of relatives (who received a monetary or food reward that was directly proportional to the length of time for which the exercise was maintained). In five replicates of the experiment, the duration (and hence reward value) declined with declining relatedness to the subject. In this study, considerable care was taken in drawing up lists of potential beneficiaries to ensure that they were biological relatives of the specified degree. While there was inevitably a great deal of variation across individuals, the bottom line is that, on average, closer relatives did better than more distant relatives (or even children's charities) across four degrees of relatedness (self vs siblings/parents vs grandparents/uncles/aunts/nieces/nephews vs cousins). When real sacrifice is involved (the exercise becomes excruciatingly painful the longer one does it), altruism is titrated by genetic relatedness.

There is considerable observational and ethnographic evidence to show that relatives are more likely to be benefited, treated better, helped (without expectation of return), trusted, and invested in than non-relatives (for summaries, see Barrett et al. 2002: esp. 45–66; Salter 2002). For example, close biological relatives are more likely than unrelated individuals to take each other's side in disputes (Chagnon and Bugos 1979; Hughes 1988), offer emotional and material support (Barber 1994; Berté 1988; Betzig and Turke 1986; Dunbar and Spoors 1995; Hames 1987; Hill and Hurtardo 1996), help each other out under catastrophic circumstances (Grayson 1993; McCullough and Barton 1991; Morgan 1979) as well as combat situations (Shavit et al. 1994), live together or stay together when communities fission (Chagnon 1981; Hurd 1983; Koertvelyessy 1995), engage in labour exchange or other kinds of assistance without expectations of reciprocity or payment (Berté 1988; Hames 1987; Oates and Wilson 2002; Panter-Brick 1989), share food (Betzig and Turke 1986), exchange information (Palmer 1992), provide protection against infanticide (Hill and Hurtado 1996), help out with childcare (Bereczkei 1998; Burton 1990; Ivey 2000; Judge 1995; Pennington and Harpending 1993; Silk 1990; Stack 1975), and invest in others both as grandparents (Euler and Weitzel 1996; Gaulin et al. 1997; Hawkes et al. 1989; Hill and Hurtado 1996; Pashos 2001) and through *post mortem* bequests (Judge 1995; Smith et al. 1987). Grandmothering, in particular, has risen to prominence as a peculiarly human trait (Lehmann, this volume) that has had enormous influence of the reproductive strategies, and hence fitness, of human females (Opie and Power, this volume).

Of course, humans do not figure out genetic relatedness by assaying for real shared genes any more than any other animals do. Rather, we use an array of cues, including familiarity, co-residence in childhood, physical similarity (including both appearance and olfactory cues), and even (at least in the case of humans) instruction to figure out who is related to whom (Hepper 1986; Madsen et al. unpublished data). Of these, emotional ties based on childhood co-residence are invariably much the most important because they provide intense emotional bonds that are hard to override (Korchmaros and Kenny 2001). This does not mean that it's impossible for any of these mechanisms sometimes to mislead us (as in cases of adoption), but rather that, statistically speaking, they are robust enough to give us a rough guide to the underlying biological kinship that works well enough most of the time.

It is equally important in this context to be clear about what is being claimed here. The claim that our behaviour is underpinned by the implications of biological relatedness does not mean that we do not use social rules to guide our behaviour. Social and biological kinship rules are not mutually exclusive kinds of explanations, but, rather, different ways of viewing the same thing. No species explicitly uses biological relatedness; rather, they use proxy rules that work well enough most of the time. In humans, social kinship functions in part at least in just this way. This is not to say that it cannot be elaborated into more complex structures or used for other purposes. It is simply to say that, if you use social kinship to structure your behaviour, that will have the effect most of the time of allowing you to invest in kin.

This said, there are some important differences between biological and social kinship systems. Cronk and Gerkey (2007) point out that social anthropology has traditionally considered two separate modes of relatedness (namely kinship and descent) that play different roles within societies. In this case, descent groups are all the individuals that are descended from some identified ancestor, and these may have quite varied kinship relationships with some target individual (the ego that forms the epicentre of all kinship classifications, both biological and social). Most human societies pay attention to both types of schema, and sometimes descent groupings can override kinship groupings. Cronk and Gerkey argue that there is no real equivalent in biology for the descent groupings that are such a prominent feature of most traditional societies (although this may be arguable in the special case of intensely social species like primates, where matrilineages or patrilineages stay together to form cohesive social groups: see Korstjens, this volume; Lehmann, this volume).

Alvard (2003) provides an example of this in respect of whaling crews among the Lamalera of Indonesia. Whaling crews predominantly consist of members of the same patrilineal descent group, and this ought to result in tensions between biological relatedness and 'relatedness' by co-membership of a descent group. Alvard was able to show that descent lineage was a better predictor of crew membership than genetic relatedness. He argues that this reflects the fact that individuals gain important benefits from being members of a lineage that spread beyond the simpler returns to inclusive fitness from relatedness. Among these are the availability of a wider pool of skills and resources that help to reduce the risks of whale hunting. It is important to note that individuals are still maximizing their inclusive fitness, but they are balancing the costs (losing inclusive fitness by investing in less closely related individuals than they could choose) and benefits (gaining inclusive fitness by improving the chances of a successful hunt and reducing their own risks of death or injury) across a wider biological framework. That said, of course, descent lineages do consist of related individuals, so this clearly provides some additional fitness payoff in terms of biological relatedness: individuals do not often choose to crew with wholly unrelated individuals. This example thus provides us with a nice reminder that the biological issue of relatedness is not all-or-none: it is a matter of fine-tuned balance between alternative options where kinship is one dimension under consideration. That was well understood in Hamilton's original conception of inclusive fitness.

Thornhill (1991) offers another example of an apparent mismatch between biological and social kinship in relation to incest avoidance rules. Most societies have rules about who can marry whom, and these rules often underpin social kinship terminology. Certain categories of relation are defined as not being marriageable. Inevitably, perhaps, biologists have given this a particular gloss in terms of the avoidance of inbreeding depression: reproducing with closely related individuals incurs a high risk of deleterious recessive genes coming together and being expressed in the offspring. The result will be reduced fitness for the parents, and thus we might expect evolution to produce mechanisms that enable organisms to avoid mating with close relatives. But, in humans, mating prohibitions can extend to cousins and even beyond, and, more confusingly, can vary widely between societies (or even, within a society, over time). Thornhill pointed out that the risk of inbreeding depression really only applies to very close relatives (between parents and offspring, or between full siblings) since genetic similarity falls off very rapidly with each reproductive event separating two individuals. Hence, she argued, the genetic reasons against marrying relatives should only apply to these very close relatives, and not to the many other more distant classes of relative that feature in the marriage rules of many societies. Moreover, there is a perfectly good biological mechanism for preventing very close relatives (especially parent–offspring and siblings) reproducing with each other that is widespread among the primates as well as humans: growing up together tends to depress sexual interest – the well-documented Westermarck Effect (for details, see Barrett et al. 2002: 222). Consequently, there should be no particular need for any social rules prohibiting mating between these categories of very close relatives. The only categories that would require rule-based prohibitions would be more distant relatives, but these would not be a problem in biological terms (the risks of inbreeding would be too low to worry about). Using a large ethnographic database, Thornhill (1991) was then able to demonstrate in a seminal quantitative analysis that most of the marriage prohibitions recorded in different societies are in fact mainly the product of competition between elites and their attempts to control the way in which resources are inherited across generations.

Having said this, however, it is important to appreciate that this biological conception of kinship is in itself a simplification – and it is a particular simplification in those species like humans that have extended lifespans and live in complex multi-generational societies. This point was made very eloquently in a mathematically rather difficult book by Austin Hughes (1988). Hughes pointed out that the central point of Hamilton's Rule is not just any old reproduction but *future* reproduction. As Hamilton (1964) himself made clear (but people often fail to appreciate), past reproduction is irrelevant: you cannot influence that by the way you behave now, and it comes for free no matter what you do. It is future reproductive opportunities that we have to worry about. However, when we think of future reproduction, something else comes into the equation, namely Fisher's (1930) concept of 'reproductive value'. Reproductive value is essentially the number of future offspring an individual can expect to produce at any given age, relative to the average produced over their entire lifetime by all individuals. This means that age becomes a crucial part of the question, and all relatives are then no longer equal in Hamiltonian terms. Since reproductive value is an inverted-J shaped function of age (peaking around the age of first reproduction, with a long tail to the right), very young and older individuals are worth less in fitness terms than those at the peak reproduction – because the latter are likely to produce most future offspring.

Hughes (1998) argued that this has crucial implications for human kinship. He suggested that when humans make judgements about kinship, it is not simple genetic relatedness that they are thinking in terms of, but rather common future fitness interests, and this might explain why social kinship does not always seem to correspond to simple biological relatedness. His argument boils down to the suggestion that when humans cost out kinship relationships, they do not do so purely in terms of pedigree relationships (i.e. the pattern of past births), but in terms of how reproductive value is cashed out with genetic relatedness to produce *future* descendants (or, rather, copies of some arbitrary gene in the next generation). In effect, he argued, we specify many of our patterns of behaviour in terms of shared future reproductive interests rather than past genetic relationships. He analysed a number of classic ethnographic examples of kinship (including both kinship naming and co-residence patterns) and demonstrated that they were indeed better explained by shared future reproductive interests than by conventional pedigree relatedness.

Hughes pointed out that, if this is the case, then it inevitably raises a paradox: the foci of shared kinship interest commonly tend to lie with the currently pubertal generation (those about to reproduce), but this set of individuals is not stable over time: instead, it shifts with each generation and stage of ego's life-cycle. What was in my best interests when I was young will no longer be focused on the same generation (or even set of individuals) when I am older, or for those who come after me. Hughes argued that this inherent instability might explain why humans make so much of past pedigree history, since this at least provides a stable point off which to hang current interests. More importantly, the genetic past has the interesting property that it fades very fast: the processes of biological reproduction mean that the probabilities of sharing a gene by descent from a common ancestor decline precipitously with each generation back, such that within just a few generations related-ness becomes 'smeared out' across the whole population – most individuals are pretty much equally related to each other if you step back far enough. This has an unexpected advantage: it doesn't matter too much whom you hook your pedigree from, since almost everyone will be related to them. In fact, it doesn't even matter that much whether or not these individuals ever actually existed – and Hughes was able to show that you get exactly the same patterns of relatedness foci for a set of real individuals even when you include the moon or green cheese as the apical point in a pedigree of any depth. The key point is that maintaining a claim of descent from some fictional ancestor allows us to keep better track of changing current patterns of shared genetic interest without introducing unnecessary complexities due to the natural temporal dynamics of pedigrees. Hughes's argument thus converges on the conventional social anthropological claim that kinship is all about marriage arrangements (see also Allen, this volume; Knight, this volume), and thus future reproduction.

Hughes adds one further point of interest in this context. He reminds us that paternity is always uncertain: women know whom they have given birth to, but men can never be absolutely certain whom they have sired. That being so, there is a natural asymmetry in kinship patterns that will tend to shift the balance in favour of female descent. (As much modelling work has shown, there should be – and, up to a point, is – some tolerance of paternity errors on the part of men: their fitness interests may be better served by focusing on both future sirings and the welfare of their true offspring, even if as a result they make some mistakes. They should worry about the average risk rather than the precise paternity of every putative offspring.) However, when paternity certainty is always low (i.e. promiscuity is high), then there is no advantage in descent systems that emphasize the male line: far too much investment will go astray. Hughes showed that, in these cases, a kinship terminology that takes cognizance of biological reality would result in a kinship terminology diametrically opposite to that produced by a paternal or a bilateral descent system. He then shows that the contrast in the kinship terminology between the matrilineal Crow and patrilineal Omaha is exactly that which would be optimal (in terms of identifying foci of relatedness) when paternity certainty was 0% versus 100%, respectively. As seems so often to be the case in evolutionary biology, natural selection gives rise to rules of thumb that do the job well enough without necessarily having to worry about getting all the details exactly right.

Prosociality and Multilevel Selection

Hitherto, biological interests have, perhaps inevitably, focused on the vast majority of organisms that are neurologically rather simple and which thus live in simple social systems. However, biologists' growing understanding of the basic principles of behavioural evolution have gradually drawn attention to an important issue in the nature of sociality, namely the fact that group-living is itself an adaptation carrying costs and benefits in fitness terms. Animals that do more than simply aggregate around food sources or refuges use social groups to solve the problems of survival and reproduction more efficiently than individuals can do on their own. A classic case of this would be cooperative hunting, such as occurs in many large carnivores (including lions, wolves, and hyenas). Here, cooperation allows a set of individuals to bring down much larger prey than any individual could do on its own. In the case of lions, for example, a pride acting together can bring down a giraffe, whereas, on her own, a lioness would have to make do with a gazelle (Schaller 1968). The giraffe is worth much more meat per individual hunter than a gazelle. Primate societies, by the same token, are attempts to solve the problem of predation cooperatively (Dunbar 1988; Shultz et al. 2004), and a similar argument can be made with respect to small-scale human societies (although, in this case, the predators may be other humans: Johnson and Earle 2001).

The issue is the same in all these cases: in order to gain the added marginal benefits of cooperation, group members have to be willing to compromise on their more selfish interests. This has been termed group-level, or multilevel, selection: selection acts at the level of the group (how well it functions to solve some key fitness problem), but the fitness benefits still accrue at the level of the individual (or, to be more precise, the gene). These mechanisms seem to become especially important as the possibility of gaining benefits through group-level cooperation increase, but this may only be possible for species that (a) are long-lived, (b) have overlapping generations, and (c) have the cognitive abilities to appreciate the longer term consequences of their actions.

One important consequence of this is the fact that, in humans, lineage survival seems to become the key to fitness maximization (Barrett et al. 2002): ensuring that the lineage (and, in agricultural societies especially, the land or other resources needed to achieve this) survives through time. Inevitably, perhaps, lineage survival gives the upper hand to the parental generation, who may manipulate their offspring so as to maximize the parents' fitness, even though this is not necessarily in the immediate interests of the offspring. This amounts to managing one's offsprings' reproduction (e.g. by arranging marriages) or by allocating resources to some offspring at the expense of others. Mace (1996), for example, shows how, among the pastoral Gabbra of northern Kenya, family resources (camels) may be concentrated into the older sons, who are then able to afford the brideprice required to marry. Similarly, Bereczkei and I were able to show that Hungarian Gypsies invested more heavily in their daughters than in their sons because the fitness payoff (measured in terms of the number of grandchildren produced) was higher through daughters than through sons (Bereczkei and Dunbar 1997). Among the Tibetans, polyandry allowed parents to ensure that the family farm (the economic basis for lineage survival) did not become split up into ever smaller (and eventually uneconomical) units across the generations, despite the fact that polyandry irked the younger sons, whom it severely disadvantaged (Crook and Crook 1988). Similarly, Deady et al. (2006) showed that, among the farmers of Co. Limerick, Ireland, during the late nineteenth century, sons from families with more than the average number of boys were most likely to end up in seminaries training for the celibate priesthood (i.e. just those cases where partitioning the farm too many ways would reduce its economic value). The medieval Portuguese nobility solved the same problem over partitioning estates in a different way: they persuaded younger sons to seek fame and fortune in expeditions abroad (one reason for the initiation of the Age of European Exploration in the fifteenth century), while placing younger daughters into nunneries as 'Brides of Christ' (from where they could easily be extracted if required for a political marriage or the older sister died prematurely; see Boone 1988). The fact that some offspring are forced to become non-reproductive also makes these cases of kin selection: some family members forgo reproduction in order to enhance the effectiveness with which their siblings can reproduce, so that all of them benefit more in the long run. However, all also have the effect of maximizing lineage survival because those who forgo reproduction enable their siblings to survive and reproduce more effectively precisely because the family's economic basis is not dissipated.

In human societies, of course, families (extended or otherwise) are but one level in a hierarchically inclusive series of levels of grouping (Zhou et al. 2005).

The community itself is not merely the context in which individuals make their fitness decisions, but also part of the solution. A community is, implicitly or explicitly, a form of social contract that individuals make so as to enable them to survive and reproduce more effectively. Social systems of this kind are based on trust: individuals cooperate with each other in the social contract on the implicit understanding that everyone will honour their debts. However, this inevitably creates a tension between the opposing forces of pure selfishness (the default condition for all biological systems) and pure community-directed altruism (the *sine qua non* for maximum community cohesion and functionality). The problem is that there is always something to gain by freeriding (taking the benefits of sociality without paying all the costs). Freeriding threatens the fragile balance of the contract because individuals who trust indiscriminately are liable to find themselves paying a disproportionate share of the costs. When that happens, the economy of the selfish gene will naturally tend to reassert itself and individuals will withdraw from the social contract rather than be exploited too often. Indeed, experimental studies of humans have demonstrated that, faced with too much exploitation by freeriders, individuals will spontaneously bail out and join another group where freeriding is policed more heavily (Gürerk et al. 2006). The danger is of total social collapse as individuals withdraw from spontaneous cooperation with each other, even at the expense of losing out on the benefits that would otherwise accrue from the social contract. The only way to prevent this is to evolve mechanisms to control freeriders and enforce the social contract. And the greater the benefits of cooperation, the greater will be the pressures to do so. This will not eliminate freeriding altogether, but evolutionary processes are usually satisfied as long as freeriding is kept to a reasonable level.

Humans seem to have a particularly large number of mechanisms for enforcing commitment to the communal project. These include a psychological sensitivity to abuses of the system (so-called 'cheat-detection mechanisms': Cosmides and Tooby 1992; Mealey et al. 1996), the use of various forms of social badging (observable declarations of group membership), various mechanisms apparently designed to enforce commitment to the group (for example, religion and other social bonding rituals like dance and music), altruistic punishment (the proactive punishment of those who offend against the social mores of the group even though the punisher may not themselves directly benefit from their action: Fehr and Gaechter 2002) and a level of prosociality (willingness to adhere to the group norms) that is quite exceptional outside the social insects (where such behaviour is chemically imposed). Most of these have been studied in some detail by evolutionary anthropologists and evolutionary psychologists (for a general overview, see Barrett et al. 2002; Dunbar et al. 2005).

Social badging is particularly interesting in this context because it makes a statement about group membership, and one that, in traditional human societies, is often explicitly related to rules about marrying in or marrying out. Badges of this kind imply something about shared values, about adherence to socially agreed norms of honesty and reciprocity, of commitment to the community project. However, conventional forms of badging (such as the adoption of certain forms of clothing or particular hairstyles) are always open to cheating: there is nothing to prevent me wearing the same special hat as you and claiming to be a member of your community, even though I am completely new to the area and fully intend to renege on the duties that community membership entails. There is a great deal of evolutionary theory and empirical research on animal behaviour on the topic of 'honest signalling': the burden of all this work is that signals of status or ownership are more likely to be honest statements of the signaller's real condition or intentions if they impose a cost on the signaller. The same should be true of signals of group membership. This appears to be so: Sosis and Alcorta (2003), for example, have shown that, in nineteenth-century US millennial cults, the more demanding the cult was in terms of what members were required to give up, the more successful it was (in terms of how long it lasted). Cheap signals of commitment are too easy to cheat. Since there will always be pressure for the population at large to test the honesty of signallers by calling their bluff, difficult-to-fake signals will always be more successful. Scarification is a perfect candidate in this respect because it imposes pain (perhaps even the risk of infection and death) and is permanent – I cannot easily disguise my origins if I try to switch communities.

Dialects provide another example of a difficult-to-cheat badge of community membership. Dialects are by no means unique to humans (they occur in bird song and whale song, as well as in primate vocalizations), but human dialects seem to be unique in their extensiveness and their speed of change with time. Considering that language exists to allow us to communicate effectively with each other, it seems at best perverse that evolution should have produced a system of communication that is so fragile that it consistently produces small communities between whom communication is all but impossible. Dialects have two properties that make them especially interesting in the present context. One is the fact that they change very fast (on the scale of generations, such that parents and offspring sometimes seem to speak mutually incomprehensible languages). The other is that they are learned very young: once past puberty, it becomes increasingly difficult to change one's dialect. You are indelibly marked for life as a member of the community in which you grew up (and hence, presumably, that into which you were born: see Nettle and Dunbar 1997).

One reason why this is interesting is precisely that it adds a dimension of kinship to the whole process. In the context of traditional societies, where mobility is more modest than in contemporary societies, growing up in a community means growing up with your biological kin. Kinship adds two safeguards against freeriders: one is that there is a wider group of individuals with sufficient interest in your particular behaviour that they will be willing to police it; the other is that even if you do renege on your promise to pay me back, the cost to me of my generosity is greatly reduced if I am investing in a relative (and hence gaining back through kin selection at least some of what I lose in helping you).

The role of dialect in marking communities can even be seen on the wider scale of languages. Daniel Nettle (1999) showed, for both Africa and the

Americas, that the number of speakers of a language (and, conversely, the number of different languages spoken per unit area) correlate with latitude, and specifically with the length of the growing season. In effect, on the equator, where there is little seasonality and crops can be grown throughout the year, language communities tend to be small in size and geographically confined; at higher latitudes, where the climate is more seasonal and the growing season limited, language communities tend to be large and widely dispersed. He argued that this essentially reflects the need to maintain trading networks in more seasonal environments at high latitudes. Languages facilitate reciprocal exchange of resources in several ways, of course: they allow people to communicate about their needs, but they also allow them to create trading networks. Speaking the same language immediately identifies you as a member of a wider community that has shared values and obligations.

Being able to specify kinship provides a more precise mechanism for specifying community membership. In addition, it also provides a mechanism for exhortation: calling someone by an explicit kin term may engage psychological mechanisms of attachment even when, strictly speaking, this is not warranted. Kinship is not entirely something that we wear on our foreheads (although personal smell, which *is* genetically determined through the MHC gene complex, does provide one such mechanism, even in humans). So, like most animal species, we rely to a large extent on knowing who was a member of our community when we were very young. But it should be no surprise that humans exploit the opportunities provided by language to acquire information that is otherwise hidden from animals, such as folk knowledge of deeper pedigrees.

It is important to appreciate that multilevel selection is not the same thing as group selection. In group selection, it is the group that is the unit of reproduction and the individual's (or gene's) interests are subservient to the interests of the group (or population or species). Kin selection comes closest to this in that a family can collaborate to ensure the successful reproduction of just some members. Indeed, some evolutionary biologists (including E. O. Wilson) have incorrectly referred to kin selection as group selection. In kin selection, the final arbiter of what happens is the gene, not the group as an entity, and hence it requires no new mechanism of evolution other than standard Darwinian processes (Maynard Smith 1964, 1976). In multilevel selection again, the unit of evolutionary cost-accounting is the gene, and not the group. Group-level processes are intended to facilitate the successful replication of the individual member's genes, not to facilitate the successful replication of the group. The distinction is subtle, but crucial.

Some Cognitive Constraints

Finally, let me end by saying a little about the role of cognition in managing kinship structures. I noted earlier that there seems to be a natural limit to the size of human groups (at about 150) and that this limit may be imposed by cognitive constraints on the number of individuals we can know as persons

(Dunbar 2004; Zhou et al. 2005). It is significant in this respect that, if we assume endogamy and the patterns of reproduction found in contemporary and recent natural fertility populations, the value of 150 turns out to be exactly the number of living descendants (i.e. the three current living generations) of an apical pair five generations back from the current offspring (i.e. youngest) generation (Dunbar 1996a). What makes that interesting is that this apical pair is the current grandparents' grandparents, or about as far back as any living member of the community will be able to remember from personal knowledge who is related to whom through which particular descent routes. The currently living grandparental generation thus comes to occupy a pivotal position in the community, because they are the only ones who know how the various families and sub-groups that make up the community actually relate to each other historically. Without them to provide that knowledge, the second cousins of the youngest generation would soon lose any sense of why they belong to a community, and so quickly drift apart. Grandmothers thus play two important roles in human societies – a direct one through the impact they have on their daughters' fitness (see Opie and Power, this volume) and an indirect one through their capacity to act as a group memory for extended kinship knowledge and the effect that this has on maintaining community-wide social cohesion (as well as regulating marriage arrangements).

This leads us naturally into an important aspect of human cultural behaviour that is very germane to the question of pedigree histories, namely our propensity for story-telling. Telling stories round the camp fire, as it were, not only continues to be a source of endless entertainment for us even now, but has always played a central role as a mechanism for bonding small-scale traditional communities. In this respect, it provides an important mechanism for creating a sense of community and belonging, and hence acts as one of the many processes designed to control freeriding. However, not only does story-telling provide enjoyment and create that sense of camaraderie on which social bonding depends, but it also serves as a store place for knowledge about a community's history (origin stories are, after all, a major industry in all cultures) and, more importantly in the present context, kinship relationships. Story-telling (and maybe pedigree construction) is dependent on advanced cognitive abilities that come under the general label of mindreading (or mentalizing). The base form of this is so-called 'theory of mind', the ability to understand another individual's mind state ('I believe that you think . . . X'). Theory of mind is really the second tier in a reflexive hierarchy of mentalizing levels, usually known as the orders of intentionality ('intentionality' being the technical term in philosophy of mind for those mental states associated with verbs like *believe, desire, intend, understand, suppose*, etc., that suggest an understanding of one's own state of mind). In this respect, theory of mind is second-order intentionality.

Normal adult humans seem to have a natural limit at fifth-order intentionality ('I *believe* that you *intend* that I *understand* that you *want* me to *suppose that* . . . X') (Kinderman et al. 1998; Stiller and Dunbar 2007). Indeed, most complex stories and plays tend to involve at most four key characters and their mind states, so that the audience has to be able to manage five orders of intentionality (remember: the listener has to *believe* that . . .) in order to keep track of the events on the stage (Dunbar 2004). Importantly, of course, the story-teller has to manage one level higher, because he or she 'has to *intend* that the listeners *believe* that . . .', which means that good story-tellers have to be able do better than the average for the population as a whole (and so tend to be somewhat special in the cognitive skills they have).

We do not really know very much about how the cognitive demands of constructing kinship relate to these kinds of endogenous constraints. However, it seems intuitively plausible to suggest that telling stories about the community that specify who is related to whom might be especially important in the context of sociocentric kinship systems, and may thus provide a crucial cognitive underpinning for Allen's tetradic kinship structures (this volume). This might also explain why kinship is both shallow and limited in its sideways extent in most animal species, including the great apes (see Lehmann, this volume). Without language and the capacity to tell stories, animals can only know what they see. Owing to life's vagaries, different individuals will inevitably see only a selection of the key events as they happen, and so any set of individuals will end up with several different constructions on possible patterns of relatedness. Since the resulting pedigrees would be only partially correlated at best, this would be a poor basis on which to found anything but the very simplest alliance or marriage arrangements.

It may be no accident, then, that the upper limit on our mindreading capacities (fifth order) just happens to be the same as the limit on the number of generations we typically have to deal with in pedigrees. (This is not to say that pedigrees, at least in the lineal sense of 'X begat Y, who begat Z . . .' sense cannot be longer: what I refer to here is the number of generational levels required to bed everyone in the community as it currently stands into a network of relatedness to everyone else.) We don't really know much about the cognitive (e.g. memory) demands of recounting pedigrees and lineages. However, memory is clearly an issue here, because, as Ellison (1994) has pointed out, keeping track of bilateral descent will be infinitely more demanding than keeping track of unilateral descent, which may explain why unilateral descent systems are much more common than bilateral ones. Bilateral kinship systems in which equal weight is placed on both maternal and paternal descent lines are relatively rare outside modern European societies. Ellison has suggested that this may be a consequence of the demographic transition: because families sizes are now much smaller than was traditionally the case, we can manage to keep track of both sides more easily. Bilateral is always more accurate *if* you can do it, but when family sizes are large, we may just have to settle for unilateral systems because they are less demanding (and adequate in terms of their reliability).

Ellison has also noted that, in societies where the variance in male lifetime reproductive output is greater than the variance in female lifetime reproductive output (as it is in most polygamously mating societies), enumerating relatedness patrilineally may both be less taxing and encompass larger numbers of individuals than doing so matrilineally: because fewer men sire more of the children in each generation, paternity lines will converge in fewer generations than maternity lines will, and will thus be easier to construct in one's mind. This has practical implications: to the extent that kin usually make the most committed allies (thanks to kin selection, if nothing else), coalitions based on paternal descent will be both bigger and more shallowly nested (need to go back fewer generations to converge) than coalitions based on maternal descent. That should, Ellison argues, give patrilineal descent systems an edge over matrilineal descent systems, and ought therefore to make them more common.

Conclusions

My aims in this contribution have been twofold. One has been to spell out exactly what is involved in biological explanations of kinship. The other has been to show how such a conception of kinship can in fact generate just the kind of kinship systems one finds in human societies. The point is that kinship terminologies do not necessarily have to correspond on a one-to-one basis with biological or genetic kinship. They need do so only statistically to work as biological processes. More importantly, perhaps, kinship systems can easily become part of the complex of mechanisms that humans have had to develop to manage freeriders who would otherwise destroy social systems that are based on implicit social contracts. However, it is, I think, clear that much of this would not be possible without language and the capacity to create 'stories' (or 'tellings') that both help us keep track of large numbers of individuals' relationships with each other and allow us to pass this information on from one generation to the next. Schemas like the tetradic system that allow us to classify kin into categories may thus help ease the cognitive burden by reducing individuals to classes. An important implication may be that managing complex social relationships in large communities may only be possible if language-based mechanisms of this kind are available. Cognitive capacities may thus come to play an important role.

8

The Importance of Kinship in Monkey Society

Amanda H. Korstjens

The role of kinship in primate societies is especially evident when we study cooperation (where close relatives are preferred partners) and reproduction (where close relatives are avoided). In this chapter, I will review some studies on the role of kinship in monkey groups, while emphasizing the enormous variation in how much kin selection determines social relationships in primate societies (Chapais and Berman 2004). First, it is essential to note that when primatologists talk about kinship, they refer to genetic relatedness (see Dunbar's chapter above). Correspondingly, terms such as 'matrilineal' and 'matriline', which also play an important part in the analysis of human kinship, are used in primatology in a strictly biological sense. Furthermore, one has to keep in mind that it is not easy to determine relatedness among individuals: animals cannot tell you who their relatives are and only maternal relatedness can be inferred from association patterns between mother and offspring in the often promiscuous primate societies. Only long-term studies allow us to form a complete picture of matrilineal relatedness, and even then, in species in which females leave their natal group, one cannot be sure about the relatedness among adult females, only about relatedness between mothers and their immature female offspring. Paternity is even more difficult to assess because female monkeys often mate with multiple partners. Even if there is only one breeding male in the group, females can (and sometimes do) mate with extra-group males (e.g. Cords et al. 1986; Korstjens and Noë 2004; Reichard 1995; Sicotte and MacIntosh 2004). The closest we, and presumably most primates, can get to knowledge of paternal relatedness is an estimate of the most likely father, based on mating frequency and timing of mating, or phenotypic similarities. Fortunately, the recent advances in genetics are greatly improving our understanding of kinship.

Kinship and Cooperation

Cooperation is expected to arise when the costs of the cooperative act are less than the benefits. These costs and benefits need to be measured ideally in life-time reproductive success, looking at inclusive fitness (Hamilton 1964). This means that genetic success of an individual should be measured by looking at that individual's own survival and reproduction plus those of its closest genetic kin. Consequently, there are three scenarios which can lead to cooperation: kin selection (Hamilton's Rule) leading to kin-based alliances; reciprocal altruism, which is most successful among familiar individuals/friends that have formed long-term associations; and mutual benefits to both partners, which does not require strong bonds.

If all else is equal, inclusive fitness benefits make kin preferred coalition partners (Hamilton 1964). Obviously, the *potential* to cooperate with kin is constrained by their availability and whether they really are equal in other respects to non-kin (e.g. Dunbar 1988; Hill 2004). The presence of suitable rela-tives depends on group size, dispersal patterns, and life history variables (e.g. longevity, inter-birth intervals, and mortality). The suitability of kin as coali-tion partners depends on the context of the cooperation (e.g. support during conflicts, help in raising offspring, or predator detection) and the characteristics/qualities of the kin (e.g. competitive power, capability of carrying offspring, or alertness, respectively). When relatives are not available or less qualified, reciprocal altruism (i.e. a cooperative act is reciprocated by the recipient of the act, in same or different currency) is a likely explanation for cooperation. It is important to note, though, that reciprocal altruism is a successful strategy only when individuals have a long-term bond, they are 'friends', and they need to maintain this bond by making sure that reciprocation occurs.

One relatively basic form of cooperation is group-living. Aggregating can reduce predation risk or increase foraging efficiency (Alexander 1974), but *stable* groups, such as most primates form, can be seen as alliances of individuals that depend on cooperation for survival. Following the logic of kin selection, one would expect that individuals tend to form groups around families. Indeed, monkey groups that split up are likely to do so along kinship lines (e.g. Henzi et al. 1997; Hill 2004), and migrating individuals prefer to do so in the presence of relatives or will prefer to join a group that contains kin (Colmenares 1992; Gouzoules and Gouzoules 1987; Greenwood 1983; Silk 2002). Whether they are close kin or not, group-living primates cooperate: (1) as a group in defence against predators; (2) in inter-group competition; (3) during intra-group com-petition over food (females) or access to mating partners (males); and (4) in raising offspring.

(1) Cooperation in predator defence

It is often assumed that the tendency for group members to warn each other about danger and to cooperate in attacking predators has led to kin-based groups as a result of kin selection, but there is a paucity of empirical evidence showing that the likelihood of an individual to call is related to the presence of kin in the group (Silk 2002).

(2) Cooperation in inter-group competition

Female alliances can be important in inter-group conflicts, and the need for group-alliances with kin is thought to lead to female philopatry (Cheney 1987; Sterck et al. 1997; van Schaik 1989; Wrangham 1980). Philopatry is the term generally used in biology to indicate that an individual remains in its natal group throughout life. In primates, a philopatric individual will have the advantage of having kin around as possible coalition partners and in most cases it also means that the individual remains in an area where it knows hiding and feeding locations. Female- and male-biased philopatry correspond to the anthropological terms of matrilocal and patrilocal. Contrary to the theoretical link between female philopatry and the intensity of inter-group aggression, there are several species where inter-group aggression among females is strong but females disperse (Isbell 2004; Isbell and van Vuren 1996; Koenig 2002; Korstjens et al. 2005). This is probably due to the fact that female philopatry is costly in those species and that this type of cooperation can be easily maintained through the mechanisms of mutual selfish benefits and reciprocal altruism.

(3) Cooperation in intra-group competition

Monkeys also commonly cooperate to fight other individuals or coalitions within the same group. For females the most important form of competition tends to concern food, whereas for males it concerns reproductive opportunities (Trivers 1972). The dynamics (including the importance of kinship) of these two forms of competition are quite different and I will, therefore, discuss female and male cooperation separately.

Primate females are most likely to cooperate when contest competition over food (i.e. direct competition over food sources that can be monopolized) is strong and food items are large enough to be shared among coalition partners. Weak bonds among females are only expected when food is either not shareable (because patches are too small) or not worth defending (because it is distributed in small abundant patches or of very low quality; this being so, scramble competition prevails, in which food is not monopolizable and competition is the result of individuals sharing resources, thus individuals will not fight over food) (Isbell 1991; Sterck et al. 1997; van Schaik 1989). The best examples of primates with strong female alliances can be found among Old World monkeys that live in large groups, such as vervets, baboons, and macaques (Gouzoules and Gouzoules 1987; Hill 2004; Silk 2002). In these species, an individual's position in the dominance hierarchy (which often depends on the alliances it can form) influences reproductive success. Simultaneously, groups in these species tend to be large enough for females to form large matrilines. Individuals of one matriline rank adjacent to each other and they support each other so that every one of them dominates all individuals of a subordinate matriline. Consequently, an individual's dominance rank is determined by the size of its matriline and it is essential for females to remain in the group that contains their mother and sisters (i.e. females are philopatric). The strength of the dominant matriline increases disproportionately because its members have the highest reproductive success.

Many reviews of kinship focus on those typical matrilineal species, but to give a more balanced view of the importance of kinship in monkeys, I will also discuss red howler monkeys (*Alouatta seniculus*), a New World primate in which demography (in this case female dispersal and small group size) does not allow for large matrilines to form within groups. Red howlers are also an excellent example because they differ from vervets, macaques, and baboons by having relatively low levels of contest competition within groups.

New red howler groups are formed when two unrelated solitary females form an alliance to defend a territory. These females depend on each other's help for territorial defence since their nutritional intake is insufficient for reproduction until they own a territory (Pope 2000a). Kin alliances (i.e. sisters) are rare because groups are small and generally only one female leaves a natal group to start a reproductive life at any one time. Group size is tightly restricted by an upper and lower boundary: these arise because when there are too few females, they are unable to defend a territory, but when there are too many females, they are unable to find sufficient resources and are more prone to male take-overs and infanticide (Crockett and Janson 2000). Thus, there is no room for multiple large matrilines, but as a group matures, female relatedness in the group increases because only female offspring of the dominant female are usually allowed to stay in the natal group thanks to the mother's support. This kin support from the mother leads to faster reproduction for her daughter compared to that of the subordinate female's daughters, who have to migrate and team up with unrelated females to obtain a new territory. Consequently, reproductive success increases with the average female relatedness in a group, thanks either to a better defended territory or to the presence of better allomothers (Pope 2000b).

Pope shows that population density also influences the importance of kinship. In populations with high density, there is such intense territorial competition that it is difficult for females to establish a new territory, infant mortality is high, and the female reproductive rate is low. Consequently, the advantage of established groups with high relatedness is disproportionately stronger than in populations where new groups can easily find a good territory in which to reproduce. Therefore, average relatedness within groups is higher, and relatedness between groups lower, in areas with high compared to those with low population density (Pope 2000b).

Alliances among primate males are most often formed under four (non-exclusive) kinds of circumstances: (1) to maintain or obtain a position in the dominance hierarchy; (2) to gain access to mating partners; (3) in conflicts between groups (generally a result of male mating competition); and (4) in defence against predators. The potential for kin bias in male cooperation is often limited because males leave their natal groups in most primates, but it should be more common in male-philopatric species like the atelins and red colobus. Indeed, red colobus (*Procolobus badius*) males cooperatively attack predators and defend their group against male intruders (Stanford 1998; Starin 1994; Struhsaker 1975). In atelins (woolly monkey, *Lagothrix*, muriqui, *Brachyteles*, and spider monkeys, *Ateles*), males form strong bonds (associating and grooming together) and they cooperatively defend their territories/females against intruders (reviewed in Di Fiore and Campbell 2007). A kin bias in male cooperation is also less likely than in female cooperation because males often select coalition partners on the basis of competitive ability (Noë and Sluijter 1995). Strong unrelated allies will, thus, be preferred over younger siblings. This contrast with female relationships is due to the generally shorter duration of bonds among males because of their often shorter reproductive careers. Even in species in which males leave their natal groups, however, males tend to prefer to migrate with brothers or join groups in which male kin reside (Pusey and Packer 1987). Although the actual coefficient of relatedness of young males within one group may be low (due to promiscuous mating, short male mating tenure, and short male life expectancy), a male is still more likely to be kin with a male peer from his natal group than with one from outside it. In addition, there is always still the benefit of cooperating with a familiar over an unfamiliar individual. Males disperse also in red howlers, but male coalitions are important, especially in crowded conditions, for defending mating access to a group of females and defending the offspring against infanticidal attacks from other males (Pope 2000a). Despite this strong dependence on each other, genetic evidence shows that only one of the males in the alliance sires most of the offspring in the group, while the subordinate male gains few benefits from the coalition. In support of Hamilton's Rule, male coalitions that are composed of close kin are more stable than those consisting of unrelated males (Pope 1990). This leads us to the fourth common form of cooperation in monkey society, infant care.

(4) Cooperation in raising offspring

In primates, an infant's main caretaker is its mother, but some care is provided by fathers and other females (allomothers). Paternal care is generally limited to protection against predators and intruding males. Such male protection is essential for infants that risk infanticidal attacks from adult males.

Male infanticide (reviewed by van Schaik and Janson 2000) is a result of male mating competition. The intensity of this competition depends on population density (how easily can new groups establish a new territory), life history variables that determine the operational sex ratio (sex ratio at birth, mortality among males, age at first reproduction, breeding tenures, and female reproductive synchrony in groups), and the number of females that a male is trying to defend (Dunbar 2000). In groups with only a few males, competition can be fierce and males often have to expel a male from an established group in order to mate with females. Considering that a male's breeding tenure is often very short as a result, a new male has to reproduce immediately after entering the new group. He speeds up the moment at which females become receptive by killing the offspring of females that are still nursing (unless breeding is highly seasonal and females can only reproduce each consecutive breeding season, in which case he cannot speed up female receptivity by killing current offspring).

The importance of males in protecting their offspring has been suggested as the main cause for long-term male–female associations (Hamilton 1984; Palombit 2000). Indeed, groups sometimes split up when a new male joins the non-lactating females because the lactating females remain with the older male until their offspring is weaned (reviewed in Sterck and Korstjens 2000). Alternatively, sometimes the old male stays in the group as a subordinate male after being defeated (Crockett and Sekulic 1984; Dunbar 1984; Onderdonk 2000). Although infanticide is most often observed in one-male groups, it is probably also an important determinant of male protection in multi-male groups, where unrelated males are always around (Borries and Koenig 2000; Paul et al. 2000). In addition, savannah baboon males sometimes intervene in intra-group disputes on behalf of their offspring (Buchan et al. 2003), while males in other species may intervene when conflicts among juveniles become severe.

Lastly, paternal care is essential in marmosets and tamarins because females habitually bear twins and become pregnant during lactation (Digby et al. 2007). The females depend on males to perform all maternal tasks other than nursing (Digby et al. 2007; Goldizen 1987). Male relatedness to the infant is not a prerequisite because the females have post-partum oestrus. This means that soon after giving birth, the female is ready to be impregnated again. So infanticide would not shorten the time that a male has to wait before he can mate with the female (Dunbar 1995). Indeed, the best strategy for the male is to stay close to the female to ensure that he will be the sire of the next brood (possibly paying for his right to stay by parenting).

Non-maternal care can also come from other females (Mitani and Watts 1997; Nicolson 1987). In species with high levels of intra-group aggression among females (such as those with strong matrilineal groupings), the allomother is more often than not related to the mother (as an older siblings or aunt); in colobines, in which aggression levels among females are low and females occasionally disperse, allomothers are rarely related (Nicolson 1987). Interestingly, while allomothering is common practice in black-and-white colobus, it does not occur in the closely related red colobus genus (Fashing 2007). This difference may be a consequence of a lower degree of relatedness and familiarity among females in red colobus (who have larger groups and more regular female dispersal than is the case in black-and-white colobus) (Korstjens et al. 2007). Differences in intra-group aggression cannot explain this variation because aggression among females is less common in red colobus than in black-and-white colobus (Korstjens et al. 2002). Females that are not the mother of an infant also sometimes protect it against male infanticide, and kin are generally the best protectors (Borries and Koenig 2000; Smuts and Smuts 1993). In tamarins and marmosets, females depend on older siblings to carry, clean, and warm infants (Digby et al. 2007; Goldizen 1987). Sibling support is so important that female offspring of reproductive age often stay on in the natal group, even though by doing so they are unable to reproduce, due to physiological suppression by the mother (Abbott et al. 1997; Digby et al. 2007). A female cannot breed until it leaves its natal group or the mother disappears (Goldizen 1987).

This brief review of non-maternal care suggests that it would be worth exploring in more detail exactly how ecological and social conditions affect primate allomaternal care, and how any relationships observed in primates may be able to help explain the cross-cultural variation in childcare practices that we observe in humans. This would be especially interesting in the light of the positive effect that grandmothers and older children may have on human reproductive success (Hawkes 2004; Kramer 2005).

Monkey mothers (in their role of soon-to-be-grandmothers) can positively affect their maturing daughters' reproductive success (1) through rank (leading to coalitionary support during conflicts, access to preferred food) (Kapsalis 2004; Paul and Kuester 2004); (2) by protecting inexperienced daughters against male aggression (reviewed by Pavelka et al. 2002); and (3) by direct care and protection of the grandchildren. Mothers have a positive effect on a female's or male's reproductive success in particular through earlier age of first reproduction and shorter inter-birth intervals (Pavelka et al. 2002). Direct support of grandchildren is limited, but post-reproductive females have been observed to be important protectors of infants against infanticidal males in Hanuman langurs (Hrdy 1974).

I would like to suggest another, less often investigated, role of grandmothers: a role as the matriarch who keeps the multiple sub-matrilines of her daughters together. In that role, she ensures that each daughter is part of a larger extended matriline/family. Because the average relatedness between sisters (especially considering that each of them probably has a different father in most primate species) is less than that between mother and offspring, sisters that have no mother to bring them together would slowly lose contact while they look after their own offspring. Consequently, adult females that have no mother have a smaller coalition and will be lower in the dominance hierarchy than those that still have a mother. This is also a possible explanation for the grandmother effect in humans.

These examples on cooperation have shown why and when relatives are the best 'friends' and collaborators and why you would want to live with kin. There are situations, however, when you need to avoid close kin.

Inbreeding Avoidance

Inbreeding, i.e. breeding between close relatives, is often successfully avoided in primates both passively, because of a low average relatedness within groups, and actively, thanks to behavioural inhibitions (reviewed in Paul and Kuester 2004). Effectively, these mechanisms may display close parallels to marriage rules in human societies.

Low average relatedness among breeding individuals in a group can result from demographic factors, e.g. migrations, large group sizes, high mortality among infants, short male breeding tenures, or low reproductive rates. Inbreeding avoidance is often seen as the most important function of sex-biased natal dispersal in primates, and the fact that males often leave the group in species with female philopatry (Moore and Ali 1984). Female dispersal, ultimately reducing the chances of inbreeding, often occurs when daughters mature during their father's breeding tenure (Clutton-Brock 1989). In such a situation, the cost of inbreeding, in the sense of lost breeding opportunities, is less for the male, who can still mate with the older unrelated females in the group, than for his daughter, who risks failure of one of her few life-time breeding opportunities (Waser et al. 1986). Furthermore, the male may be even less inclined to move when an average male only gets one opportunity in his life to join a group of females. Thus, if the father has better breeding opportunities by staying in the group, but the daughter does not, she can only avoid inbreeding by leaving her natal group. Whatever function dispersal has, it generally leads to low average relatedness between individuals of the opposite sex. In addition, the chance of breeding among half-siblings is reduced by sex differences in age of first reproduction (generally earlier in females than in males) and mortality rates (generally higher in young males than in females). Therefore, the combination of dispersal, life history variables, and group size and structure are probably the most important causes of low rates of inbreeding in primates.

Occasionally, close relatives do get the opportunity to mate together, but there are many examples of primates that refuse or avoid mating with close or even more distant kin (reviewed in Gouzoules and Gouzoules 1987; Paul and Kuester 2004). This leads to the last question with which this chapter is concerned: can primates differentiate between related and unrelated individuals?

Kin Recognition

One can argue that for inbreeding avoidance and kin selection to occur, there must be some form of kin recognition in primates. In most cases this does not need to be a complicated mechanism: simple rules of familiarity can do the trick (Bergman et al. 2003; Cheney and Seyfarth 1999; Rendall 2004). Monkey females tend to prefer unfamiliar males over familiar ones as mating partners (reviewed in Gouzoules and Gouzoules 1987; Rendall 2004). However, some studies also suggest that there is some kin recognition based on phenotypic similarities (Silk 2002). In Barbary macaques, paternal siblings show signs of kin recognition even in a large multi-male society in which they cannot know their father or their peer's father on the basis of familiarity alone (Widdig et al. 2002). Another example is found among baboon males that support their own offspring despite a promiscuous mating system (Buchan et al. 2003).

Kin recognition in primates (particularly recognition of paternal relatedness) is, however, not expected to be extremely reliable because this would increase the risk of infanticide by males. Infanticidal males hardly ever kill their own offspring, but are more likely to accept unrelated infants in their vicinity because accidentally killing one's own offspring is a more costly error than leaving another individual's offspring alive (van Schaik et al. 2000). Therefore, it would be extremely costly to the infant if a possible sire could immediately be certain whether or not he is the father. As long as males can be fooled, females can use promiscuous mating as a successful strategy to avoid male infanticide (Hrdy 1979).

Conclusion

These examples show that biological kinship runs like a red thread through the social organization of primates and cannot be ignored. The examples also show that the importance of kinship in primates is probably very similar to that in humans, even though primates are unable to tell others whom they are related to. Individuals preferentially cooperate with kin at various levels, from sharing food sources to fighting competitors, to assisting in raising related offspring. However, in many cases, the actual opportunities to cooperate preferentially with kin are constrained by demographic variables (e.g. longevity, migration patterns, age at first reproduction, breeding tenure) and social variables (relative suitability of kin versus non-kin as coalition partners depends also on the social status and competitive strength of your kin relative to that of other potential partners). Close inbreeding is relatively rare in primates due to demographic factors (leading to low average coefficients of relatedness within groups) and direct avoidance of close relatives. Recognition of kin is mostly achieved by familiarity, but also to some extent by the capability of individuals to recognize kin based on (as yet largely unidentified) phenotypic markers. Primates may not develop complicated hierarchical kin structures with strict marriage rules, but they do often live in structured societies in which related individuals preferentially affiliate and cooperate together, but at the same time avoid mating with one another.

9

Meaning and Relevance of Kinship in Great Apes

Julia Lehmann

In human societies, kinship patterns are very important in structuring social relationships, but can we see similar patterns in our closest living relatives, the great apes? Do they have a concept of kinship, do they favour kin over non-kin, and how can we actually find out about kinship in apes? Contrary to those scientists who study humans, primatologists cannot ask their study objects about their social relations or about the criteria they use to distinguish kin from non-kin. Models, such as the tedradic model developed by Allen (this volume) or that of alternating birth classes as found in eastern Africa (James, this volume) are unlikely to apply to apes in the way they apply to humans. On the other hand, it may be possible to interpret notions such as moieties and age cohorts in ways that shed light on non-human primates as well as human societies (Widdig et al. 2001). In addition, the meaning and relevance of kinship in great ape societies may help us to understand how kin relationships might have been used to structure the societies of our own ancestors, the early hominids (Foley and Lee 1989).

In primates, kinship as such can only be analysed in the strict biological sense, i.e. kinship refers to biological relatedness, as it exists, for example, between siblings and half-siblings, or between parents and infants. Although mother–offspring pairs are usually easy to identify (at least in long-term studies), it has been in the past notoriously difficult to establish other kinship relations, such as relatedness between adults, in wild apes. Furthermore, the paternal side remained largely unknown, because all female apes mate with multiple males and behavioural observations are often unreliable indicators of paternity. Thus, until recently, most studies of kinship in primates have concentrated on maternal bonds, and the existence of matrilines. Paternal bonds, which in human societies are often very important (Fox 1967), remained in the dark for decades, since paternity and paternal half-siblings could not be identified. Therefore many theories about social structures and kinship preferences in primates remained untested or were based on rough estimates of paternal kinship. More recently, new non-invasive genetic methods have allowed us to analyse paternal as well as maternal kinship structures in wild animal populations more reliably. As a result, theories about how kinship affects group structure and social behaviour can at last be more fully tested, although research in this area is still in its infancy.

Why should animals care about kinship at all? Clearly, knowing kin relationships is important to avoid inbreeding, but this problem could also be solved by sex-specific dispersal patterns. Why do biologists expect kinship to play a role in animal social behaviour? Hamilton (1964) hypothesized that in many cases it should be advantageous for animals to support kin versus non-kin (see also Trivers 1971), because supporting related individuals can enhance one's own fitness (i.e. direct and indirect lifetime reproductive success). Known as kin selection theory, this proposal has found support from many species across the animal kingdom (for a discussion see Griffin and West 2002), and has provided a theoretical background with which behaviours such as cooperation and altruism can be explained. Numerous studies have shown that animals (including humans) often prefer to help relatives over unrelated individuals, and this remains true despite the fact that in some human societies the term kinship is not restricted to genetically related individuals but can include many other, non-related individuals (see also Dunbar, this volume).

So what does kinship mean for apes? Do they recognize and favour genetically related individuals? Or do they form social bonds based on other so far unknown criteria? In what follows I summarize what is currently known about the role of kinship in the social life of apes.

Kinship and Social Organization in Chimpanzees

Chimpanzees (*Pan troglodytes*) live in large multi-male, multi-female communities, in which males stay in their natal community while females disperse when they reach maturity. In the absence of empirical testing, it had therefore been hypothesized that males within a community are genetically more closely related to each other than females are. In addition, males of similar age have been considered to be paternal half-siblings because dominant males can monopolize a large proportion of all matings, and father the majority of the offspring sired during their tenancy (Boesch et al. 2006). The interpretation that males but not females are often kin seemed very much in line with the observed social behaviour: males, but not females, frequently form strong social bonds and coalitions, support each other in fights, groom each other preferentially, and share food amongst themselves. This seemed a classic case of kin selection: more closely related males exhibit strong social bonds while the virtually unrelated females mostly remain on their own.

However, since non-invasive sampling methods for genetic relatedness became available, it has been possible to test this hypothesis in greater detail. Are males really more closely related to each other? And is it really primarily (half-)brothers that demonstrate strong social bonds, as would be expected on the basis of kin selection theory? The short answer is 'no' in both cases: recent studies suggest that male chimpanzees are on average not more closely related to each other than females are (Lukas et al. 2005). This might be due to relatively high male mortality and incomplete reproductive control by the dominant male. Thus, paternal half-siblings are less common than previously thought and full siblings are even rarer, as a male's tenure as the dominant (and hence principal breeding) male is often shorter than the long inter-birth interval of about five years.

Furthermore, although maternal half-brothers have been observed to form strong social bonds, those are rare between paternal half-brothers (which are closer in age) and the majority of coalitions are actually found between genetically unrelated individuals (Langergraber et al. 2007); in other words, brothers or half-brothers are not more likely to become coalition partners than unrelated males (Mitani et al. 2000). Thus, kinship *per se* only plays a limited role in male chimpanzee affiliation patterns (Langergraber et al. 2007) and kin selection theory does not seem to explain the strong social bonds observed (Goldberg and Wrangham 1997), nor are the effects of nepotism easily observable among adult chimpanzees.

Because social bonds between chimpanzee males are so obvious, most research has so far concentrated on male social behaviour. However, as it now seems likely that male bonding is not solely driven by kinship, more and more researchers are beginning to look at the female side of the equation. In striking contrast to the apes, many of the monkey species are female-bonded with strong social bonds between females within and between matrilines (e.g. Bernstein et al. 1993) – after all, mother–daughter relationships are easy to observe, for researchers as well as for animals. Although chimpanzee females have always appeared to be rather asocial compared to males, as more studies are carried out on female behaviour, it has started to become apparent that females may also have strong and long-lasting social bonds which are maintained over many years and often ended only by death of one partner (Lehmann and Boesch 2008, Lehmann and Boesch submitted), despite the fact that they are usually unrelated. Thus, just as for males, female social relationships are not primarily driven by kinship patterns.

Strong female bonds have also long been known from the other *Pan* species, the bonobo (*Pan paniscus*). Since both *Pan* species are equally closely related to humans, comparing their social systems and discovering underlying evolutionary selection pressures might enable us to understand better where the social system of early humans has evolved from. Given the variety of social organizations and kinship patterns in human societies, it may not be so surprising that our closest living relatives have very flexible social systems. Good long-term data from bonobos, however, are still not available, but it appears that their social organization differs in several key parameters from that of the chimpanzees (see also Parish and De Waal 2000). As in chimpanzees, bonobo males remain in their natal communities, while females disperse. However, in bonobos, females appear to be dominant over males (Furuichi 1989; Parish and De Waal 2000) and bonds between females are among the strongest (White 1992), while male bonds are relatively rare. The strongest bonds in bonobos, however, appear to occur between the sexes, and often between mothers and their sons (Hohmann et al. 1999), hence between kin. Thus, as in chimpanzees, kin relations seem also to play a role in bonobo life. However, it is the strong bonds between (unrelated) females that have puzzled scientists, because this observation cannot be explained by kin selection theory.

Overall, then, evidence is accumulating that, at least in *Pan*, kinship only plays a limited role in explaining group structure as strong social bonds do not exclusively (or even preferentially) occur between related individuals, but can often be found between unrelated members of the group as well. We are therefore in need of new testable hypotheses as to why members of the genus *Pan* form these strong social bonds and on what basis they choose their partners. Is it, for example, that sociality enhances infant survival, as has recently been reported for baboons (Silk et al. 2003)? Or is it simply a mechanism to reduce within-group competition and aggression, as found in chimpanzee females (Lehmann and Boesch submitted)? Further studies are needed to investigate the functions and mechanisms of social relationships in *Pan*, now that kin selection theory has been shown not to explain the observed behaviour to its full extent.

Kinship and Social Organization in Gorillas

Most of our knowledge about gorillas (*Gorilla gorilla*) comes from mountain gorillas, as they are the best-studied subspecies. However, more recent work on lowland gorillas reveals that gorilla social systems can vary to a large extent between subspecies and populations. Generally, gorilla females associate closely with one male (one-male groups, as are typically found in the western lowland gorilla) or with several males (multi-male groups, as are more typical for mountain gorillas). In multi-male groups, there is usually a high reproductive skew and the dominant silverback sires most (but not all) of the offspring born (Bradley et al. 2005). Dispersal patterns in gorilla vary, but both sexes have been reported to disperse at least once in their lifetime.

In contrast to chimpanzees, gorillas do not defend territories, they live in smaller social groups, and they appear to be much less sociable than members of the genus *Pan*. They spend very little time engaged in social activities such as grooming (Watts 1988), and strong bonds between individual members of a group have not been reported. In mountain gorillas, groups usually consist of both related and unrelated females with one or more males. Although, in the past, males were thought to be related to each other as either father–son pairs or (paternal) siblings from the same natal group (Harcourt et al. 1976), a recent study has found that the two highest ranking males are usually not related (Bradley et al. 2005). However, males within a group rarely interact. Coalitions and bonds between males have not been reported among mountain gorillas. Females, on the other hand, appear to associate primarily with kin: maternally related females have been found to rest more together, groom more frequently, show more tolerance towards each other, and behave less aggressively amongst themselves, compared to unrelated females. Female paternal siblings show intermediate patterns (Watts 1994). The study by Watts (1994), however, is based not on genetic data but on inferred kinship relations, which, in gorillas, seemed reasonable.

In the light of the new evidence that males are not always related and that subordinate males also sire offspring, the data about kin preference need to be read with care. Nevertheless, social bonds in gorillas are generally weak and bonds between unrelated individuals do also occur.

A recent study on western lowland gorilla relatedness suggests that some kinship bonds may be functional over quite large distances, i.e. between groups. Bradley et al. (2004) found that males in neighbouring groups are more likely to be related to each other than are females. This suggests that females disperse over larger distances than males, while (related) males remain within the same area. Bradley and her co-authors have further suggested that such an extended kinship network can explain the observation that in western lowland gorillas, inter-group encounters are often (but not always) peaceful, without any aggressive displays. This is in striking contrast to mountain gorillas and chimpanzees, where inter-community encounters can be lethal (although, in bonobos, as is well known, aggressive behaviour is very rare). Thus, western lowland gorilla males can be viewed as patrilocal, as they appear to stay within the vicinity of their natal group and relatives, sharing this trait with chimpanzees and possibly early hominids (Bradley et al. 2004; Doran-Sheehy and Boesch 2004). (I use the term 'patrilocal' here in its biological sense: males remain as adults in the area where their fathers lived.) More studies on lowland gorilla social behaviour are needed to understand fully the flexibility of their social system and to discover if and how gorilla kinship networks work.

Kinship and Social Organization in Orang-Utans

Little is known about orang-utan (*Pongo pygmaeus*) social relationships, dispersal patterns, and relatedness. Orang-utans live a relatively solitary life but have largely overlapping home ranges. Although they occasionally aggregate in large fruit trees (McKinnon 1974; Schürmann and van Hooff 1986) and have been observed to travel in a coordinated fashion during fruiting seasons (Utami et al. 1997), adults do not normally interact. The only other time during which orang-utans have been seen to associate is during reproductive consortships, where mature adult males and females may stay together over weeks (Rijksen 1978); however, little is known about social relationships between adults other than during mating. Recent studies on individual relatedness suggest that both sexes disperse (Utami et al. 2002). Whether or not related individuals of the same sex remain in proximity is not yet known. However, given their solitary life-style, social bonds between kin other than between mother-dependent offspring pairs are not expected, although kinship networks such as those proposed for gorillas may exist also in orang-utans.

Can Apes Recognize Kinship Patterns?

A further factor has to be considered when discussing kin relationships in apes: how can individuals in such fluid systems where females mate with multiple males and where males do not provide paternal care for the offspring actually recognize their (paternal) kin? Proposed mechanisms include phenotype matching (matching physical similarity in facial or other features, or even in smell), social familiarity, and proximity in age (Holmes and Shermann 1982), their effectiveness depending on the species' social system. However, familiarity and age proximity can only be seen as 'rule of thumb' mechanisms for kin recognition and they are inevitably prone to errors. While such a general rule may be sufficient in gorillas (where one male monopolizes most of the reproduction within a given social group), it is unlikely to work in *Pongo* (where males are not around during infancy) or *Pan* (where females mate with many males). Mating with most or all of the group males has been suggested to be a possible female strategy for reducing the risk of infanticide by confusing paternity (Hrdy 1979). At least in *Pan*, females also appear to seek extra-community copulations (mating with males in neighbouring communities), thereby further diluting assumed genetic ties within the community. Thus, whatever the mechanism used, it may be in practice difficult for an individual to recognize paternal kin. The fact that they are unable to recognize paternal kin might explain the general absence of preferences for paternal kin in male chimpanzees, despite the fact that paternal kin usually belong to the same age cohort and hence have similar interests (Langergraber et al. 2007). Maternal kin, on the other hand, can easily be recognized based on familiarity and, in line with this, most kin preferences reported in apes occur between maternally related individuals, despite the fact that maternally related half-siblings are usually in different age cohorts due to the relatively large inter-birth interval in apes (approximately five years: Boesch and Boesch-Achermann 2000; Goodall 1986; Reynolds 2005). Preferences for maternal kin can already be found in young chimpanzees, who groom and play preferentially with maternal but not with paternal relatives (Lehmann et al. 2006). However, the same study also suggests that chimpanzee males might be able to identify their own offspring and invest preferentially in their socialization. Male-offspring recognition is presumably easier than recognizing paternal half-siblings (in the absence of paternal care). Paternal kin recognition has, however, been reported from some other primates. In macaques, for example, paternal half-siblings spend more time together than would be expected by chance (Widdig et al. 2001), suggesting that they can recognize paternal ties. Thus, at least in some primates, there may be potential for (paternal) kin recognition (see also Korstjens, this volume), although many further studies are needed in order to find the mechanisms behind this.

Implications for Early Hominids?

It has frequently been suggested that patterns of social structures and kin relationships of living primates can be used to reconstruct the possible social system of early hominids (Foley and Lee 1989; Ghiglieri 1987; Isbell and Young 1996). In this context, chimpanzees have proven to be of particular interest not only because of their close genetic relationship to humans (Chimpanzee

Sequencing and Analysis Consortium 2005), but also because many features of their social system appear closely to resemble that of traditional human (hunter-gatherer) societies (Ghiglieri 1987). In contrast, the social systems of gorillas and orang-utans bear little or no resemblance to those of modern humans. This is in line with the genetic evidence, which suggests that orang-utans split from the ape–hominid line about 14 Ma, followed by gorillas, who split from the Last Common Ancestor about 8 Ma; the chimpanzee–human split occurred only about 7 Ma (Purvis 1995).

Although human societies vary tremendously regarding their social structures and bonding patterns, extensive ethnographic comparative analyses have found a number of general trends: the majority of human hunter-gatherer societies appear to be patrilocal (Ember 1978; Seielstad et al. 1998); bonds between men are often stronger than bonds between women (Hrdy 1981); male coalitions are frequently based on kin relationships (Pasternak et al. 1997); and almost all human societies are territorial (Ember 1978). Interestingly, all of these traits are shared with chimpanzees (but not with orang-utans and gorillas). In humans, however, kinship bonds are often extended beyond the limits of biological kinship to individuals that belong to the same age cohort (see James, this volume). Based on Hamilton's kin selection theory, we would not expect to see such strong bonds between unrelated individuals in chimpanzees. However, recent data suggest that patterns similar to those in humans may occur also in chimpanzee communities, where strong social bonds and coalitions are observed between genetically unrelated individuals (Langergraber et al. 2007; Lehmann and Boesch submitted).

There are, of course, also a number of differences between human societies and apes: while promiscuous mating is common in apes, it is relatively rare in humans (although many human societies are polygynous: van den Berghe 1979). In addition, and maybe as a consequence of high paternity certainty, males in most human societies contribute to the raising of the offspring (van den Berghe 1979), whereas in apes such contributions are uncommon and rarely go beyond the level of territorial defence and protection against infanticide. Finally, we see a much larger variety in human social systems as compared to apes, although all ape species have social systems that are rather flexible and can vary somewhat between populations (presumably along ecological gradients).

In many human societies the nuclear family (parents and offspring) is at the core and stays in close proximity. However, such family units are usually embedded into a wider kinship network which includes also more distantly related kin, such as grandparents, cousins, and so on (Geary and Flinn 2001). It has been suggested that the presence of female kin and especially grandmothers played a crucial role in early hominid societies in that it allowed females to shorten their otherwise very long inter-birth intervals (see Opie and Power, this volume; Hawkes et al. 1998). This theory (known as the grandmother hypothesis) has, however, often been criticized as it is based on female philopatry, and it remains unclear how this shift from male philopatry (as found in chimpanzees) to female philopatry has occurred (see, e.g., Kennedy 2003). Although there are no studies in apes testing the importance of grandmothers to females, it is unlikely that we will find precursors for this in extant apes. First, females do not usually live beyond their reproductive phase, i.e. menopause does not exist, and hence ape communities lack the non-reproductive grand-mothers (although studies on captive apes suggest that females experience menopause when they live long enough: Caro et al. 1995; Peccei 2001). Second, in all apes, females usually disperse from their natal community on reaching sexual maturity, so females would normally not know their grandmothers because they are not present in the same group. Nonetheless, as long as they are in the same group, mother–offspring bonds are very strong and youngsters benefit from the social status of their mothers (Goodall 1986), while mothers have been suggested to benefit from the presence of older offspring (Reynolds 2005). However, we know very little about the potential effects that the presence of grandmothers could have on ape reproductive success, even in those rare cases where females remain in their natal communities. Given the long inter-birth intervals and late onset of reproduction in ape species, most females would not live to see their grand-offspring growing up, and collecting data on such effects is not an easy task.

Conclusion

Although better data on kinship and social relationships in apes are needed fully to answer the question of how important kin relationships are in apes, the evidence so far suggests that kin bonds may be not as strong and important as previously predicted. On the other hand, there is emerging evidence to suggest that apes show preferences for maternal kin (Harcourt 1979; Watts 1994), and that in some cases paternal ties can be recognized, such as in western gorillas (Bradley et al. 2004; Doran-Sheehy et al. 2004) and chimpanzees (Lehmann et al. 2006, Lehmann and Boesch submitted). This suggests that recognizing kin provides an evolutionary advantage and that kin relationships are important in some contexts (such as paternal care in chimpanzees and inter-group encounters in gorillas) but not in others (such as male–male coalitions, long-term friendships, and grooming behaviour). The preference for maternal kin might be related to the fact that maternal kin can easily be recognized while the recognition of paternal kin is uncertain and more prone to errors. Thus, investments into paternal kin relationships will be lower and based on a rule of thumb, such as age proximity. Bonding within age cohorts is also often found in human societies, and age similarity might be used as a basis for kinship bonds in the wider sense (i.e. not necessarily for genetic advantage). Alternatively, social interactions in humans as well as in apes may be used to establish bonds especially between unrelated individuals, as these are the group members with whom no other bonds exist. Further studies and efforts to bring together expertise from different fields, such as social anthropology, biology, archaeology, and linguistics, will be needed to shed more light on similarities and differences between early human and ape social systems and kinship relationships. Such cross-disciplinary integration will ultimately help us to understand the evolution of hominid sociality.

10

Grandmothering and Female Coalitions

A Basis for Matrilineal Priority?

Kit Opie and Camilla Power

Introduction

Two major opposing models have been advanced for the evolution of human life histories: the 'grandmother' hypothesis (O'Connell et al. 1999) and the 'diet, intelligence, and longevity' model (Kaplan and Robson 2002; Kaplan et al. 2000), also known as the 'embodied capital' theory (Kaplan et al. 2001). Both of these have different implications about possible pathways for emerging kinship systems. Basically, Kaplan and colleagues' model is predicated on male paternal strategies, stressing importance of paternity certainty for male invest-ment, with implicit assumptions of male philopatry – males staying close to natal territories and their own relatives. By contrast, O'Connell and colleagues' grandmother hypothesis requires a tendency or a switch to female philopatry – females staying close to their mothers and female relatives – when the strategy emerges. There are two major reasons why the grandmother strategy must evolve via mother–daughter matrilines in the first place. One is the issue of paternity uncertainty, diluting the benefits to a grandmother supporting put-ative offspring of her son; the other concerns age of first reproduction, which is generally later for males than females, implying a grandmother would need to live longer to be of help to her son. The matrilineal priority debates of the early twentieth century were superseded by assumptions of male philopatry associated with 'man the hunter' models by mid-century, but the recent work on the 'grandmother' hypothesis has rejuvenated the idea that early kinship systems originated from matrilocality and matriliny (Knight and Power 2005).

Another model, by Aiello and Key (2002), examined reproductive ener-getics of early *Homo* with a view to testing these two main possibilities for life history evolution. Aiello and Key's model provides important constraints on the timetable for evolution of life history change, associating body size change from the late Pliocene to early Pleistocene (c. 2 Ma) with the necessary emer-gence of allocare (investment in offspring by others than the mother). They also avoid assuming that male contributions or provisioning require paternity certainty, showing how these could emerge via male mating effort strategies.

This chapter tests the two main models using Aiello and Key's body size energetics, combined with data on productivity and consumption by chimps and modern hunter-gatherers. This will allow us to estimate constraints on reproductive and social strategies of early African *Homo erectus*. Female *Homo erectus* must have needed extra energy subsidies for reproduction, amounting to allocare, which could come from two places essentially: male mates/fathers of offspring or female kin. This chapter shows that male contributions alone (at the level of modern hunter-gatherer foraging) would not have been sufficient; older female kin contributions alone would not have been sufficient. Foraging effort by the female herself, plus contributions by older female kin and male mates, would have been needed. This has implications for the emergent kinship affiliations.

The Three Models

Kaplan and colleagues (Kaplan and Robson 2002; Kaplan et al. 2000) argue that aridification produced a change in the diet available to *Homo erectus* on the dry open savannah. The expansion of the savannah brought with it an increase in the availability of large ungulate prey. Kaplan et al. (2000) argue that hunting provided a much higher quality diet, dense with nutrients, but hard to acquire. Children, unable to acquire the new food, would need to be provisioned by their fathers throughout childhood. Hunting skills had to be learned, and although productivity was low while these skills were acquired, the investment was repaid by very high productivity in adulthood (Kaplan and Robson 2002). This led to increased longevity and reduced mortality, with, importantly, a payoff for increasing brain size. Females were less efficient at hunting because of reproductive demands and the extended period necessary to acquire hunting skills. Therefore they were dependent on males, with whom they formed long-term pair-bonds in return for paternity certainty (Kaplan et al. 2000). Kaplan and colleagues maintain that male provisioning of females and juveniles with a high-quality, meat-based diet provided the stimulus for the co-evolution of brain enlargement, long lifespan, and a long period of childhood dependence, ultimately leading to the modern human pattern seen in hunter-gatherer societies.

O'Connell and colleagues (Hawkes et al. 1998; O'Connell et al. 1999) agree that a change in *Homo erectus* diet was caused by a major drying of the climate. They propose that this prompted a change in habitat and resource use, with *Homo erectus* surviving on the underground storage organs of plants (tubers) as the main staple among other resources. Juveniles had neither the skill nor the strength to dig for tubers, and so were reliant on adults to provision them. Under these circumstances, an older female could enhance her own inclusive fitness, as her fertility declined, by providing food for her daughters' weaned offspring. This would have enabled the daughters to reduce their inter-birth intervals, becoming pregnant more quickly and increasing their fertility. O'Connell and colleagues (1999) contend that older females who were more vigorous would have had higher reproductive success, spreading genes for vigour in older age through the population. They argue that the decrease in mortality would have led to a longer growth period and a delay in maturity, while still retaining a period of fertility similar to great apes (Hawkes et al. 1997, 1998). This pattern, Hawkes, O'Connell, and Blurton Jones claim, can be seen in modern-day forager societies, exemplified by the Hadzabe of East Africa (Hawkes et al. 1997; O'Connell et al. 1999).

Aiello and Key (2002) argue that the increased body size compared to ancestral australopithecines would have meant an increased energy requirement for bodily maintenance, but, more importantly, would have increased the costs of reproduction for females. If *Homo erectus* had continued to follow an australopithecine reproductive pattern, thought to be similar to that of extant chimpanzees, female reproductive costs would have increased by 40% per reproductive event. Moving to a modern human pattern of early weaning would reduce energy requirements per offspring and increase the number of offspring. However, the difficulties of early weaning would have been exacerbated by a changed diet, inaccessible to juveniles. Aiello and Key suggest that *Homo erectus* mothers would have had to rely on other adults for help.

The first two models propose mechanisms of sexual and kin selection to advance alternative pathways for emerging kinship affiliation in *Homo*. Aiello and Key's model constrains the possible timetable for the life history changes in *Homo*. In the early presentation of their model, Kaplan et al. (2000) did not specify the particular period of encephalization during which male hunting and provisioning strategies emerged, the main alternatives being Late Pliocene/ Early Pleistocene (c. 2 Ma) associated with *H. erectus*, or Late Middle Pleistocene (from 500,000 years ago) associated with *H. heidelbergensis*. Aiello and Key's results compel Kaplan and colleagues to argue for the earlier period. This implies arguing for male 'paternal' strategies at an early date, a position similar to the old 'man the hunter' ideas. These have been strongly challenged by modern 'selfish gene' models which highlight the differential trade-offs for parental investment between the sexes. Male parental investment comes at high opportunity costs of mating other females (Trivers 1985); any model arguing for paternal investment needs to show why males would be prepared to forgo such opportunities (cf. Hawkes et al. 1995b). Another aspect which becomes questionable at this early date for onset of male provisioning is the level of productivity in the Early Pleistocene.

This chapter models production and consumption among chimpanzees and modern forager populations at different stages of life history for both sexes. These energetics models will be used to reconstruct costs of reproduction for female *H. erectus*. In the discussion, we consider whether *H. erectus* requirements constrain us to choose between the alternative models presented above.

Consumption, Production, and Provisioning of Offspring

For female anthropoid primates, energetic costs of producing a single offspring are calculated by breaking down a single inter-birth interval (IBI) in terms of costs of gestation, costs of lactation, and costs when resuming menstrual cycles after weaning (Key 2000: 337). By estimating the additional energy require-ments (net production) for a mother during gestation and lactation, above her own bodily needs, it is possible to assess the net consumption of an infant. This extra energy the mother must produce alone (as in the case of a female chimp) or by consuming what others produce (as forager women do).

Kaplan et al. (2000) directly compare productivity data from hunter-gatherers, including the savannah-dwelling Hadzabe of East Africa and the forest-dwelling Ache and Hiwi from South America, with chimpanzee data. This, they argue, supports their evolutionary hypothesis of male provisioning of females and their offspring two million years ago.

Chimpanzees

Chimpanzee infants in the wild are dependent, wholly or partially, on their mothers for food until they are weaned at about age 5 (Kaplan et al. 2000). As they approach weaning, they gather more of their own food, still in close physical proximity to their mother. They receive no food from any other adult, so chimp mothers must eat more than they need for themselves to provide for infants during gestation and lactation (Goodall 1986).

Kaplan and Robson (2002) use body size and calorific requirements to estimate that a chimpanzee infant's net consumption is 730 kcal/day until the age of 5 years. The same method is used to estimate that during this time a chimpanzee mother's net production is 300 kcal/day. However, without the infant being provisioned from another source, it is not clear how a chimpanzee mother would cope with an infant's energy demand of more than twice her net production. These data suggest that over the lifetime of an adult female chimpanzee, she could provide the energy required by 2.5 infants. However, this is only achieved because of the very long lifespan that Kaplan and Robson (2002) suggest for the chimpanzee mother. Indeed Kaplan and colleagues use other data (Kaplan et al. 2000, Table 10.1) to suggest that the expected age of death at 15 years for chimpanzees is 29.7 years. Providing for the energy requirements of an infant until age 50 would therefore be rare. If a chim-panzee mother survived to 29.7 years she would provide the required energy investment for only 1.4 infants. This would be a low reproductive rate and not sustainable across a population.

Key and Ross (1999) also use body weight to estimate energy requirements. They developed a formula for daily energy expenditure (DEE) of primates based on body weight, and multiples of that formula for the energy requirements of gestation (1.25 times) and lactation (1.39 times). Using the Key and Ross for-mula and an adult female chimpanzee weight of 33.7 kg, DEE is calculated as 1305 kcal/day. DEE is increased by 1.25 during gestation to 1631 kcal/day. During lactation DEE is increased by 1.39 times to 1814 kcal/day (Aiello and Key 2002). Averaging DEE over a reproductive cycle gives an estimate for the energy an adult female chimpanzee needs to produce for herself and to raise her infant from conception to weaning. Using an average adult female chimpanzee reproductive span of 19 years (Kaplan et al. 2000) suggests that her energy requirements are an average of 1713 kcal/day, 408 kcal/day above her own needs.

Taking an IBI estimate of 5.6 years (Galdikas and Wood 1990) and an average reproductive span of 19 years (Kaplan et al. 2000), and applying Key and Ross's body weight formula for DEE, a female chimpanzee is predicted to have 3.4 infants in her lifetime. This is slightly higher than the estimate of three infants per mother derived from observations of chimpanzees in the wild (Goodall 1986; Nishida et al. 1990), which suggests that a model based on the Key and Ross (1999) formula is more realistic than that used by Kaplan and Robson (2002).

Human forager populations

Kaplan et al. (2000) use body weight and total group production to estimate food consumption for forager adults and children. They estimate forager production by averaging across the Ache, Hiwi, and Hadza forager populations, weighting each group equally (referred to here as the 'Kaplan Group').

Women
Kaplan and colleagues' data suggest that forager women produce a maximum of 2950 kcal/day by age 51. But because their consumption averages 2600 kcal/day between ages 20 and 56 years, they only produce a surplus from the age 46 to 69 years, when their production is near its maximum and then as their consumption starts to fall. The overall lifetime net production for women is in deficit by 14.5 million kcal.

Kaplan et al. (2000), using data from four modern forager populations (Ache, Hiwi, Hadza, and the savannah-dwelling !Kung – properly known as Ju/'hoansi – from southern Africa), propose an average age at first reproduction of 19.7 years and last reproduction at 39.0 years. The model used here also assumes an inter-birth interval of 4 years, longer than Kaplan and colleagues' figure of 3.44 years. This gives more conservative estimates for the energy requirements of children. Our model suggests that the net energy demand (taking account of children's own energy production) of a mother's children peaks at 6245 kcal/day when a mother is 33 years old and her four children are aged 14, 10, 6, and 2 years. The total net energy demand of a mother's four children would be 33.4 million kcal.

Forager women would be heavily dependent on others throughout their child-rearing years to provision both themselves and their children. Assuming that a mother is no longer responsible for the energy needs of her children after the age of 18 means that she would be free of responsibility for all of her children when she reached 49 years. She would then be free to use her surplus production to help her daughters. However, from the age of 49 to 69 she would have a total surplus of 2.7 m kcal – only 8% of the estimate of children's energy requirements of one of her daughters. If these assumptions are correct, forager women would need to look elsewhere for help in bringing up their children.

Men
Kaplan et al. (2000) show that women look to men in order to make up their energy deficit. According to their data, a forager man produces a surplus from

the age of 19 to 59 years, with peak production of 6600 kcal/day at the age of 33 years. Over his lifetime he would produce a total net surplus of 21.7 m kcal. This surplus would be enough to provide for an adult woman's energy requirements from the age of 19 years for the rest of her life (4.8 m kcal), but only enough to cover half the 33.4 m kcal needed by her children. Kaplan and colleagues argue that men are essential to modern human forager populations and that they are the main providers of food. However, according to their data, one man could not meet the requirements of a woman and her children.

This modelling casts doubt on the reliability of data on these three hunter-gatherer groups. But, rather than the production data, it may be the assumptions about consumption that are problematic.

Consumption
Kaplan and colleagues' (2000) data suggest that adult females consume 2600 kcal/day and adult males 3200 kcal/day. These estimates are high compared to those of other researchers who have calculated daily energy requirements (DEE) ranging from 1712 to 1931 kcal/day for females and as low as 2085 kcal/day for males (Aiello and Key 2002; Leonard and Robertson 1997). Using lower adult DEE figures would increase the surplus available to a forager family. Alternative estimates for children's energy needs (based in Torun et al. 1995) are also well below Kaplan and colleagues' (2000) estimates.

Forager production estimates
Of the nine forager populations for which Kaplan et al. (2000) publish energy production data (see Figure 10.1), Kaplan and Robson (2002) use the data from three populations (the 'Kaplan Group'). Of these three, they include two populations out of the lowest three in terms of women's mean production (the Ache and Hiwi), and the only African group where men's mean production is higher than women's (the Hadza).

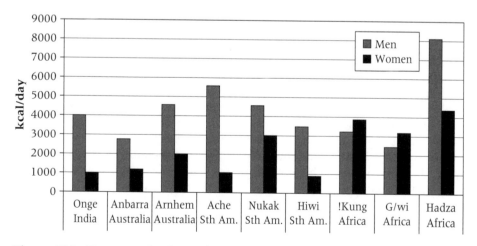

Figure 10.1 Energy production in forager populations (drawn after data in Kaplan et al. 2000, Table 2)

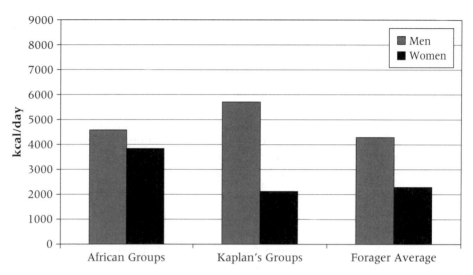

Figure 10.2 Production for selected groups of forager populations (drawn after data in Kaplan et al. 2000, Table 2)

Men's average daily total production for the 'Kaplan Group' is 5723 kcal/day (72.9% of total adult calories) compared to 4297 kcal/day (65.2% of total adult calories) for all nine groups (Kaplan et al. 2000). Women's average daily total production for the 'Kaplan Group' is 2123 kcal/day (27.1% of total adult calories) compared to 2292 kcal/day (34.8% of total adult calories) for all nine groups. Indeed, an averaging of the three African groups in the sample shows much higher women's production (3820 kcal/day, 45.5% of total adult calorie production), much closer to men's production (4574 kcal/day, 54.5% of total adult calorie production).

Figure 10.2 shows that using the average adult production estimates of the nine forager groups or the three African groups would alter the energy balance between men and women, and for a forager family.

!Kung net production
!Kung consumption and production estimates (Figure 10.1) produce net production estimates for both sexes. Higher adult female net production (2152 kcal/day) than for males (902 kcal/day) in the !Kung results from lower average consumption (1712 kcal/day for females, 2319 kcal/day for males) and higher production (3864 kcal/day for females, 3221 kcal/day for males) than males. Howell (2000) points out that female production is high among the !Kung because of the high calorie content of the mongongo nuts collected.

Using the model developed above, a !Kung woman and man would be able to provide the necessary energy resources for four children, except for six years (when they were 31–7 years old). During this time they would need additional resources. An older !Kung woman with high production and low consumption would be able to provide the necessary energy resources, if she was available.

Grandmother Availability: !Kung vs Hadza

The support adult females can expect from their mothers depends on the proportion of post-reproductive women in the population. Using the appropriate model life table as developed by Coale and Demeny (1983), we can estimate the ratios of different age groups, and how these might change with different levels of population growth.

For the !Kung, the number of children (aged 5 to 14 years) per 'grandmother' (women between the ages of 50 and 69) would be 2.7, if there was no growth in the population. A growth rate of 1% increases the number of children per grandmother to 4.3. A faster growth rate of 2.5% would increase the number of children per grandmother to 8.8.

If there was zero growth in the population, the !Kung model developed above would be in energy balance, with grandmothers having 797 kcal/day for each child. However, 1% growth in the population would mean grandmothers' provisioning (500 kcal/day per child) was not enough when needed. Population growth of 2.5% would stretch grandmothers' resources (245 kcal/day per child) too thinly to provision children adequately. Howell (2000) reports that the !Kung populations that she studied were scarcely growing. The level of surplus that a grandmother can provide to her grandchildren may act as a constraint on population growth for the !Kung.

The Hadza, however, are a fast-growing society (1.3%–1.4% per annum) according to Blurton Jones et al. (1992). Using the North 6 model life table (Coale and Demeny 1983) suggests that there are 2.3, 3.7, and 7.8 children per 'grandmother' at zero, 1%, and 2.5% population growth (respectively). Although slightly lower numbers of children per 'grandmother' than for the !Kung, these data suggest that Hadza 'grandmothers' would have to spread their resources among many children at high rates of population growth. However, older Hadza women have high-energy production (6169 kcal/day). Using Aiello and Key's (2002) adult consumption data suggests net production of 4238 kcal/day. At 1% per annum population growth 'grandmothers' could provide 1145 kcal/day per child. Even at 2.5% population growth, grandmother provisioning would, according to the model, still amount to 543 kcal/day per child. This, coupled with high levels of energy production by the children themselves (Blurton Jones et al. 1989; Hawkes et al. 1995a), may account for the high Hadza population growth rates.

Summary of Chimp vs Forager
Production and Consumption

Kaplan and Robson (2002) argue that a comparison of data derived from chimpanzee and modern hunter-gatherer societies is the most dramatic evidence in support of their male provisioning hypothesis. However, the modelling here has questioned the data used to support their argument. In particular, they used production levels from a sample of human forager societies not representative of the average, which tends to exaggerate the disparity between males and females. They also make a high estimate of consumption levels compared to those of other researchers.

The alternative model developed here has produced data on chimpanzee offspring numbers that reflect observations in the wild. For human forager societies, the data produced by the model fit with demographic data for the !Kung and the Hadza. Furthermore, the model suggests that the level of energy production of post-reproductive females may be an important determinant of population growth in those societies.

The *Homo erectus* Model

Having tested the model on living groups of chimpanzees and human foragers, we will now apply it to *Homo erectus*, making explicit assumptions about their life history. Kaplan and colleagues (2000), O'Connell and colleagues (1999), and Aiello and Key (2002) argue, based on Smith's (1993) work, that *Homo erectus* had a life history intermediate between modern humans and chimpanzees.

The modelling here will use the possible pattern of *Homo erectus* age at maturity, lifespan, length of fertility, and infant dependency to estimate the food energy that a *Homo erectus* mother would have to secure for her offspring at variable inter-birth intervals (IBIs).

Age at maturity and first birth

According to Kaplan and colleagues' data (2000), mean age at first birth for chimpanzee females is 14.3 years. This is 2.9 years after eruption of the third molar (M3) according to Smith (1993). For human forager females, mean age at first birth is 19.7 years (Kaplan et al. 2000), 1.7 years after M3 eruption (Smith 1993). To obtain an age at first birth for *Homo erectus* females for modelling purposes, we propose to average the period after M3 eruption for chimpanzees and humans. This would give an age of 16.8 years for age at first birth for *Homo erectus* females.

Lifespan

Human lifespan is considerably longer than that of chimpanzees. Smith (1993) suggests that *Homo erectus* may have lived about fifteen years longer than chimpanzees. Using Kaplan and colleagues' (2000) mean chimpanzee expected age of death at 15 years of 30 years suggests an age of 45 years for *Homo erectus*.

Age at last birth

The same source of data suggests that the average age of last birth in chimpanzees is 27.7 years, whereas the average of Ache, Hiwi, and !Kung women is 39.0 years (Kaplan et al. 2000). For the purposes of this model, the mid-point age of 33 years will be used for age at last birth in *Homo erectus* females.

If *Homo erectus* females lived on average to age 45 years, this would mean twelve post-reproductive years.

Childhood dependency: self-sufficiency and energy requirements

Chimpanzee infants are dependent on their mother until about age 5 years. This is slightly earlier than the eruption of M2 (6.5 years), the second molar associated with the onset of adolescence in primates (Smith 1993). Among modern human forager societies, children usually contribute little if anything towards their energy needs until approaching adulthood. However, among the Hadza, who occupy a similar environment to early African *Homo erectus*, juveniles can produce a higher proportion of their energy needs. Using children's energy consumption data and Hadza energy production data, Kaplan et al. (2000) show that at about age 12, a female forager may have achieved energy balance, thereafter producing a surplus. This is soon after the onset of adolescence marked by the eruption of M2 (age 11.3 years in Smith 1993). We propose to use the age at M2 eruption as the beginning of self-sufficiency in *Homo erectus*, suggested by Smith (1993) to be 9 years old.

As Hadza children begin to forage at about the age of 5 years, they reduce the level of provisioning required from others. Girls produce more at an earlier age while boys' production remains low until nearing adulthood, when it rises steeply. Using average children's consumption and girls' production until age 12, when self-sufficiency is reached, would mean an average energy requirement of 492 kcal/day. This figure is just higher than the additional energy requirement during gestation calculated by Aiello and Key (2002) for human females of 483 kcal/day.

We propose to extend the Aiello and Key (2002) model here with an average energy requirement for *Homo erectus* juveniles from the age of 5 to 9 years equal to the additional energy requirement for a *Homo erectus* female during gestation. With each of these explicit life history assumptions built in, the model calculates the total energy requirement of a *Homo erectus* female and her offspring (Opie 2004).

Results of energy requirements at different inter-birth intervals

Table 10.1 shows the results of the model: the energy required by a *H. erectus* mother to produce different numbers of offspring at different inter-birth intervals, assuming she provisions them up to age 9. It shows the percentage increase in these energy needs above the average production of contemporary female foragers, both throughout the reproductive lifespan and during the most energetically expensive years.

A *Homo erectus* female who cared for her offspring up to age 9 years before starting a new pregnancy would have energy requirements equal to the forager women's average production. But she would only produce two infants throughout her reproductive lifespan. The model shows that *Homo erectus* mothers with a chimp-like IBI (5 years), intermediate IBI (4 years), and human-like IBI (3 years) would have increasing energy requirements, to produce four, five, and six offspring, respectively.

Table 10.1 Energy requirements for *H. erectus* mothers by number of offspring and inter-birth interval

No. of offspring	Inter-birth interval, years	Energy required, kcal/day	Exceeds forager average, %	Exceeds average in peak years, %
2	9	2291	=	–
4	5	2546	+11.1	+22.7 (for 9 years)
5	4	2777	+21.2	+31 (for 15 years)
6	3	2951	+28.8	+47.4 (for 12 years)

Source: Opie 2004

A woman's average fertility among the Hadza is 6.2 births (Blurton Jones et al. 1992), whereas among the !Kung it is 4.7 births (Howell 2000). The former study (Blurton Jones et al. 1992) reports that Hadza women between the ages of 40 and 49, who may have finished reproduction, have an average of 3.5 children still alive. Although mortality is highest among the young, we can expect that a Hadza woman would incur the energy costs equivalent to bringing four to five offspring to self-sufficiency.

This suggests that the intermediate inter-birth intervals of four or five years might be applicable. This would have been a considerable burden for a *Homo erectus* female alone. During the peak years of energy requirements (nine years if IBI of five years, fifteen years if IBI of four years), when she was provisioning two or more dependent offspring, she would have to produce from 22.7% (five-year IBI) to 31.0% (four-year IBI) more than the forager women's average production. This level of production is not feasible. She would clearly have required help from other adults.

Help from grandmothers

O'Connell et al. (1999) suggest that it is grandmothers who would fulfil that role. However, Caspari and Lee's (2004) work suggests that the ratio of older to younger adults (OY ratio) only increased to modern levels in the Upper Palaeolithic. Their results suggest that the OY ratio for *Homo erectus* was 0.25. If this was the same as populations of *Homo erectus* when alive, this implies that there was one post-reproductive female to four reproductive females. This would mean that, if relying only on the help of older females, each reproductive *Homo erectus* female would on average be able to expect help equivalent to a quarter of the net production of a post-reproductive female. With this level of maternal help, a *H. erectus* female would still have to produce an average of 2676 kcal/day during the twelve hardest years, 384 kcal/day (17%) more than the forager women's average, to raise four infants (Figure 10.3). Producing five infants would require an average of 2907 kcal/day, 615 kcal/day (27%) above the forager women's average, during twelve of the fifteen hardest years, rising to 3002 kcal/day for the remaining three years.

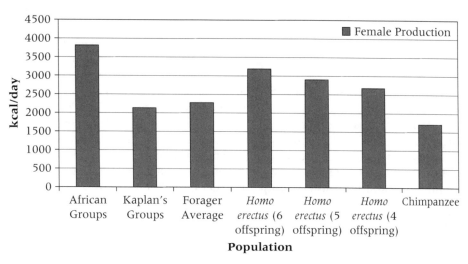

Figure 10.3 *Homo erectus* female energy requirements for different numbers of offspring, with support from post-reproductive females, compared to average production for selected population groups (© Kit Opie and Camilla Power)

Help from males

According to Kaplan and colleagues (2000), *Homo erectus* females relied on adult males for help. If a *Homo erectus* female produced at the forager women's average she would need a male to have high production levels. To provide for four offspring would require a male to produce an average of 2341 kcal/day, 71 kcal/day (3%) below the G/wi male average. For the nine most demanding years a male would have to produce 2608 kcal/day, 196 kcal/day (8%) above the G/wi male average. To provide for five offspring would require a male to produce an average of 2797 kcal/day, 385 kcal/day (16%) above the G/wi male average, for the most demanding fifteen years and 3040 kcal/day, 628 kcal/day (26%) above the G/wi male average, for the three peak years.

Discussion

How did *H. erectus* meet her energy budget?

If African human forager populations provide an accurate model, *Homo erectus* females, in a stable or growing population, may have been producing four or five offspring (to self-sufficiency) in their lifetimes. This would require them to produce food at 17% or 27% (respectively) above the forager women's average, for the majority of their adult lives, even with the support of post-reproductive females. In addition, fewer post-reproductive females would have meant less infant care, so that a *Homo erectus* female might have had to produce at this level with a number of offspring to care for as she worked. She would also have lacked modern technology and the skills available to a female with a modern human-sized brain. These production levels would most likely have been very demanding, if not impossible. It seems more likely that *Homo erectus* females would have found some mechanism for procuring provisioning from males.

The model used here suggests that if a *Homo erectus* female produced at the forager women's average she would need a male to have high production levels, as high as some modern hunter-gatherer men. But, *Homo erectus* males lacked the skills and technology that large-brained modern humans use. Hunting is a highly productive activity among modern foragers, however, it is not clear to what extent *Homo erectus* males engaged in hunting (see, e.g., Domínguez-Rodrigo and Pickering 2003; O'Connell et al. 1988, 2002), and, if they did, how productive they may have been. In addition, the mechanisms for cooperation between males necessary to secure the large prey required have not been explained. The model developed here suggests that the energy required by a *Homo erectus* female for her offspring would be more than she and a *Homo erectus* male could provide.

Homo erectus females may only have got enough calories for their offspring if they were helped in provisioning by both males and older females. Indeed, our model suggests that even if both a grandmother and a male were involved in supporting a *Homo erectus* female in provisioning her offspring, they would each have to produce 2430 kcal/day or 2542 kcal/day to provide for four or five offspring (respectively). Even the lower figure means that *Homo erectus* females were producing 138 kcal/day (6%) above the modern forager women's average, and *Homo erectus* males slightly (18 kcal/day) above the male G/wi hunter average production.

Females needed cooperation from both female kin and mates

The involvement of post-reproductive females and males in the provisioning of juveniles for the first time among great apes would have had major implications for social interaction and organization. If correct, these changes from the assumed australopithecine (chimpanzee-like) pattern would have amounted to a revolution in hominin social organization. We will now consider the implications for possible alternative pathways of kinship and affiliation in *Homo*. We do not assume residential 'home base' strategies, since these are not supported archaeologically in early African *Homo erectus*. The relevant question is who lives with and cooperates economically with whom?

If we assume the traditional standpoint of male philopatry from a phylogenetic heritage shared with chimps and australopithecines (cf. Foley and Lee 1989; Rodseth et al. 1991; Wrangham 1987), this deprives *H. erectus* mothers of support from available senior female kin. The only source of allocare support remaining would be from a male or males (as fathers of her offspring). The main questions raised here are: would *H. erectus* males in an Early Pleistocene hunting/scavenging economy, with primary access to large game animals doubtful, be able to produce at the level of a contemporary G/wi hunter armed with bow and poison arrows? Even if a *H. erectus* male could produce at an adequate level, why would he divert all his production to one female when she was non-fertile, if he had alternative mating opportunities?

Key and Aiello (1999, 2000) used game theory models (iterated Prisoner's Dilemma) to explore the conditions under which either females or males would cooperate with a mother to provision her offspring. Females would cooperate through reciprocal altruism (exchange of like for like) when female energetic costs were very high. Males would only become cooperative if their energetic costs of reproduction were significantly lower than female costs. This occurs where sexual size dimorphism is less than 50% (Key and Ross 1999). A male would then offer benefits, for instance high-energy food, to a mother for no more than a 50% chance of mating (Aiello and Key 2002: 561). So, a flow of benefits from males to females becomes more likely as sexual size dimorphism decreases. But there is no necessity of 'paternity certainty' in this model: the payoffs for male cooperative strategies are extra mating opportunities (50% of the time) and increased female fertility thanks to food sharing. Members of each sex are likely to 'trade' with more than one partner.

How can Key's abstract model be related to the actual fossil record (see Table 10.2)? Among earlier hominins prior to 2 Ma who retained significant climbing abilities, brains and bodies were relatively small, with high size dimorphism between the sexes. From about 2.5 Ma, some of these species began to encephalize while bodies remained quite small and apparently still highly dimorphic (McHenry 1996). This suggests increasing costs for females, indicating more pressure for female–female cooperation, while males still had high body-size costs and were less likely to be cooperative. These encephalized early

Table 10.2　Reproductive costs and cooperation between the sexes in relation to life history indicators

Hominin grade, date	Brain/body size	Sex dimorphism/ relative reproductive costs	Cooperation	Life history
Australopiths, pre 2 Ma	Small brains, bodies	High size dimorphism	Non-cooperative males	Ape-like growth schedules, mortality
Encephalized early *Homo*, c. 2 Ma	Brains increase, bodies still small	Still size dimorphic	Female–female cooperation	Ape-like
H. erectus, from 1.9 Ma	Bigger brains and bodies	Reduced size dimorphism, females relatively bigger	Onset of male cooperation	Intermediate between ape- and human-like, reduced mortality
H. heidelbergensis, from 0.5 Ma	Large brain, large robust body	Female costs increase with brain size	Male cooperation with females	Close to modern human life history

Source: Following Key and Aiello 1999; Skinner and Wood 2005

Homo species led to the emergence of early African *Homo erectus* after 2 Ma, the first hominin with body proportions like ours, bodies that were bigger and designed for walking not climbing (Wood and Collard 1999). Sexual size dimorphism had been reduced, largely because female *H. erectus* increased body size proportionately more than males (McHenry 1996). With female costs rising relative to males, significantly more cooperation by males with females can be expected from this time. But this is based on the prior evolution of inter-female cooperation.

Already in Early Pleistocene hunting/scavenging economies, males may have been giving females significant benefits – but we should be careful not to make assumptions about paternal investment by males. For *H. erectus* living in large multi-male, multi-female groups, probably as defence against predation (Aiello and Dunbar 1993) and for purposes of aggressive scavenging, paternity certainty may have been difficult for males to achieve. In that case, males may have competed for more mating opportunities rather than for higher chances of paternity from fewer matings. Efficient hunting and mate-guarding of fertile females by sexually competitive males are incompatible activities (cf. Gilby et al. 2006: 176–7 on effects of fertile females on chimpanzee hunting). If good hunters lose out on sexual access, males would not pursue that strategy. None of these issues is clarified by Kaplan and colleagues.

We need to consider the implications of female cooperative strategies as the basis for the emergence of male–female cooperation. Suppose daughters remained close to their mothers and female relatives, so senior female kin were available for allocare, whether extra provisioning of daughters' children or babysitting. Would *H. erectus* females have lost out on male production? Not necessarily. A prototype 'grandmother' strategy could have worked in positive feedback with males starting to increase production levels on the basis of mating effort. One of the main effects on females who had senior female kin support would have been reduction of IBIs. This implies earlier return to cycling and increased fertility, precisely the factors which encourage more male cooperation in Key's model. Those females who had senior female kin support would have received increased male attention in the form of mating effort. Recently weaned offspring of such females would have benefited both from nutritious meat gifts from males hoping to mate their mother, as well as from regular supplies of tubers provided by grandmother. Female foragers' returns are more predictable on a day-to-day basis, of great importance for supplying growing children with energy, compared with more 'risky' irregular male returns (Bliege Bird 1999; Hawkes et al. 1989, 1997). With reduced mortality rates, we have selection for longer lifespans, delayed sexual maturity, and post-reproductive lifespans in females. With the presence of female allocarers, we can also account for the apparent contradiction of slower life histories evolving in *Homo* combined with reduced IBIs (relative to chimps).

Only a female philopatry or matrilocal model permits allocare support from both female kin and male mates. The 'grandmother' model also gives us a parsimonious account of the emergence of key life history characteristics, including slowed early development coupled with earlier weaning, delayed sexual maturity, and post-reproductive lifespans, selected especially in females.

Kaplan and colleagues' model offers a piecemeal account of these life history characteristics. In particular, it is silent on preadaptations to menopause. In focusing on the issue of productivity of longer-lived males, it fails to explain why women tend to live longer.

The 'grandmother' hypothesis also has significant problems. One question critics have raised is whether enough older females would survive for long enough to contribute effectively to support of their daughters' offspring (cf. Kennedy 2003). A view that humans have only lived long lifespans in the recent historical past is untenable given what we know from extant hunter-gatherer and horticultural groups. Konigsberg and Herrmann (2005) cast doubt on the statistical methods used in palaeodemographic reconstructions to date, including that of Caspari and Lee (2004).

Another question for the 'grandmother' model is whether foraging by senior females, principally for roots and tubers, would provide adequate nutrition for hungry weanlings. Underground storage organs as a staple food are rich in calories from carbohydrates, but relatively poor in nutrients. Given their underdeveloped digestive systems, children require not only calories but also easy-to-digest packages dense with nutrients, ideally provided by animal-derived proteins, meat or fish, full of micronutrients (Milton 1999). Again, the combination of provisioning by senior females and by male mates can support children's requirements, while male foragers alone would be too risky, and female foragers alone offer too few nutrients.

The main argument pitched against the idea that male philopatric hominins could have switched to become female philopatric is the cost of inbreeding depression (Foley and Lee 1989). If the ancestral state is for males to stay while females disperse, then females who began to change strategy in order to stay close to female relatives would risk mating close relatives such as brother or father. However, a major feature of the changes implicated in the brain expansion of 2 Ma is increase in social network size, inferred from the increase in brain size. Group sizes predicted from estimated neocortex volumes for *H. erectus* are almost twice the mean group size for chimpanzees (Aiello and Dunbar 1993; Dunbar 1992a). If hominins had to bunch into larger groups to reduce predation risk in more open environments, this should dilute the risks of inbreeding by offering a wider pool of accessible mates. According to O'Connell and colleagues (1999: 468), as the climate changed and tubers became increasingly abundant, hominins, in particular females, would have been able to gather in larger numbers, since returns were limited by handling requirements rather than food availability. The benefits to females who could stay near their mothers to obtain help with weanlings would outweigh any costs of inbreeding risk.

The objections to the 'male-only' provider model are more profound. In this chapter, we have challenged the specific data used by Kaplan et al. in building their model. But the problems are more fundamental. Kaplan and colleagues ignore two decades of archaeological debate about whether Plio-Pleistocene hominins were able to hunt or scavenge. What we can be reasonably sure about is that male foraging strategies have altered much more radically since the Early Pleistocene than female strategies have. Technology used by Hadza women today for digging tubers like *//ekwa* may not have changed for over a million years. The same is not true for tools and weaponry used by African savannah hunters, which include very recent technological developments.

The 'grandmother plus man the cooperative hunter/scavenger' model also appears more realistic in relying only on male mating effort and making no assumption about paternal investment. Selfish-gene cost–benefit accounting predicts that males have a trade-off between effort put into mating access and effort put into provisioning extant offspring. While it is likely that some form of male care or paternal solicitude is ancient in primates as a guard against risk of infanticide, this is different from male parental investment (MPI) involving provision of energy to mother or offspring. The latter is not seen among non-human primates, and we have to account carefully for its evolution in terms of fitness benefits and costs to males. The work of evolutionary ecologists on hunter-gatherers today has undermined beliefs in MPI as the main motivation for men's hunting (Hawkes et al. 1991) *even in the present*. Instead, hunters may target valued foods that can be used either for mating or for parental effort according to opportunities (Bliege Bird 1999). In the Hadza case, a man's kill is distributed throughout a camp, not to one specific nuclear family, enabling him to 'show off' to a wide social audience. If men are not trading provisioning for pair-bonds and paternity certainty, we need different models for the emergence of a social division of labour (Blurton Jones et al. 2000; Hawkes et al. 2001). In the 'grandmother plus man the hunter/scavenger' model, the social division of labour begins as cooperation between generations of related females, but this encourages increased productivity by males through mating effort. This model can satisfactorily account for the actual relations of production among African savannah hunters to this day.

From grandmothering to female ritual coalitions and kinship

Allen's 'tetradic' model (this volume) offers a template for an initial situation of formal kinship which can most parsimoniously generate any extant system. The model is purely abstract, with triangles readily interchangeable with circles in kinship diagrams, indifferent to issues of 'matriliny' or 'patriliny'. However, the perspective of life history and reproductive energetics does not allow indifference to material constraints. As argued by Aiello and Key (2002), the necessary life history changes that arose with genus *Homo* some 2 million years ago would have forced females to adopt strategies of allocare that required complex social solutions involving both female kin and male mates. These can be viewed as unique primate social systems, rather than constituting any symbolic categorization of kinship at that stage. But importantly they constrain the possible pathways for the emergence of subsequent symbolic systems.

In the final phase of encephalization, from 500,000 years ago among *H. heidelbergensis*, female costs again rose steeply as mothers had to fuel the energy-hungry, larger brains of their offspring. During this phase of rapid encephalization (de Miguel and Henneberg 2001), strategies of cooperation between females would have remained central in ensuring male support and productivity (Key and Aiello 1999). According to Knight and colleagues (Knight 1991; Knight et al. 1995), female coalitionary strategies were needed to reduce male behavioural competition and promote economic cooperation, resulting in a sexual division of labour with 'home base' strategies. The 'sham menstruation' or Female Cosmetic Coalitions model argues that ritual and symbolism emerged through this female cooperation (Power 1999; Power and Aiello 1997; Watts 1999). To prevent philanderer males targeting females who were imminently fertile (that is, showing menstrual cycles) as against pregnant or lactating females, whole coalitions adopted a strategy of using cosmetics to scramble such information about fertility. Using red cosmetics, females signalled their resistance to philanderers. Investor males – big-game hunters who brought meat back to 'camp' for the whole coalition – came to favour these ritually, cosmetically decorated females as *Homo sapiens* evolved in Africa. The Female Cosmetic Coalitions model is the only current Darwinian explanation for the archaeological record of ochre use that arose with the ancestors of modern humans in Africa and spread with *H. sapiens* around the planet (Henshilwood et al. 2001, 2002; Hovers et al. 2003; Watts 1999, 2002).

As female reproductive costs increased with brain sizes in *H. heidelbergensis* and early moderns, these strategies necessarily drew on prior structures of female kin-bonding. In addition, male kin potentially played important roles in support of female relatives to 'exploit' male mates (Knight 1991: 302; 1999). Cosmetic rituals would delineate a boundary of kinship between groups: sons and brothers act defensively in support of female relatives who display to male outsiders – potential mates who must produce meat to be welcomed. Two fundamental rules should arise through this ritual performance. Firstly, to maintain security of the coalition, male allies, related matrilineally to any female member of the coalition, could not be treated as sex partners. With all insider males counting as 'sons' or 'brothers' in a classificatory sense to the female coalition (see Knight, this volume), this instigates a classificatory exogamous moiety system. Here, fathers and sons must belong to different coalitions. Secondly, to maintain economic productivity, mothers could not allow their own mates to have sex with their daughters as well; they need to recruit a new generation of hunters. Therefore rituals must bar classificatory husbands from access to daughters. This will put mothers and daughters into opposite age-classes even though belonging to the same coalition. Combining these two principles generates Allen's tetradic structure.

Evidence from molecular genetics suggests that an ancestral tendency of female kin to stick together persisted with the emergence of modern humans. Studies reveal difference in philopatry patterns between hunting and farming populations in sub-Saharan Africa (e.g. Destro-Bisol et al. 2004; Hammer et al. 2001). Alvarez's (2004) review of ethnographic evidence which has been claimed in support of patrilocality among recent hunter-gatherers found a lack of pattern, but statistical bias to mother–daughter links. Marlowe's (2004) study of marital residence in contemporary and recent historical forager populations shows characteristic fluidity with significantly more multilocality/uxorilocality compared to non-foragers, especially in 'warm-climate' samples. The greater the reliance on hunting in these populations, the less likely they are to be virilocal. But the direction of cause and effect in this needs investigation. One hypothesis is that females with kin support are in a better position to get males to work as a condition of sexual access – the general principle of brideservice. Blurton Jones et al.'s (2005) analysis of where older women lived from 213 Hadza camps revealed the strategic targeting by Hadza grandmothers. They were more likely to be in camp with a daughter than a son, and particularly with a daughter who had children under 7. But they were less likely to be with a daughter who had her own teenage daughter to help; or with an infertile daughter. They also favoured unmarried daughters with young children over married daughters. Grandmothers direct allocare to where it is needed most. A growing number of studies now demonstrate a real 'grandmother effect' – increased inclusive fitness either through improved child survivorship or raised fertility rates of mothers – in contemporary populations from hunting, farming, and urban industrial economies (e.g. Hawkes et al. 1997; Lahdenperä et al. 2004; Leonetti et al. 2005; Mace and Sear 2005; Sear et al. 2000).

Conclusion

This chapter has modelled reproductive energetics of female *H. erectus*. The results suggest that female *H. erectus* could not rely on her mother's help alone, or on the help of a pair-bonded male alone, if she were to raise enough offspring to replace the population. Females would have needed to draw on both these sources of allocare and help with provisioning. This implies that a *H. erectus* mother would need to live throughout most of her reproductive lifespan with female kin. Any tendency to male philopatry in early *Homo* would cut females off from such kin support. By contrast, a female philopatric model allows 'man the hunter/scavenger' to play his role. Grandmother and man the cooperative scavenger become mutually reinforcing, able between them to provide children with regular supplies of energy and high-quality nutrients.

Grandmothering appears vital to our evolution. The modelling in this chapter suggests that the availability of post-reproductive females remains an important determinant of population growth in contemporary hunter-gatherer groups. Selection of longer-lived females may have been critical in the emergence of lineages of encephalized *Homo* in the Middle Pleistocene, leading to *H. heidelbergensis*, ancestors of ourselves and Neanderthals.

Under the reproductive stress of encephalization, female kin coalitions developed ritual strategies underpinning the sexual division of labour and the first rule-governed kinship systems. We conclude that our ancestors, from early African *H. erectus*, through *H. heidelbergensis* to early moderns, were biased to matrilocality, forming a basis for matrilineal priority in the earliest symbolic kinship systems.

Part IV

Reconstructions

Evidence from Cultural Practice and Language

The Emir of Gorgoran and his harem, Nigeria: Tucker, 1935 (Royal Anthropological Institute)

11

A Phylogenetic Approach to the History of Cultural Practices

Laura Fortunato

Cross-Cultural Comparison and Galton's Problem

Examination of the spatial and temporal distribution of cultural practices can shed light on both their function and their development (Goody 1976: 2). However, human societies cannot be treated as independent data points in statistical analyses of the distribution of cultural traits: any pattern inferred by tallying societies in which the traits of interest occur runs the risk of being spuriously inflated or deflated (e.g. Dow 1993).

This issue, first recognized by Galton in objection to Tylor's (1889) cross-cultural analysis of marriage and descent practices, is known in anthropology as 'Galton's problem'. To address the analogous issue of the non-independence of species or other biological taxa, evolutionary biologists incorporate in their comparative analyses information on the historical relationships among the taxa (Felsenstein 1985; Harvey and Pagel 1991). Mace and Pagel (1994) advocated the application of this approach to the study of cross-cultural variation: within this framework, the issue of the non-independence of societies is addressed by identifying independent instances of change – the acquisition or loss of a cultural element, by original invention or by copying from another society – while controlling for the effect of shared history.

Besides providing a principled solution to Galton's problem, the phylogenetic comparative approach has proved particularly effective in reconstructing the history of practices related to kinship and marriage, which have left fragmentary information on their development in the archaeological and historical records. Most of the work in this area has focused on re-evaluating previous anthropological analysis, while controlling for historical relatedness in a rigorous manner. Holden and Mace (2003, 2005; Mace and Holden 1999), for example, used phylogenetic comparative methods to investigate the relationship between descent type and subsistence mode in sub-Saharan Africa; results indicate that matrilineal descent and the keeping of large livestock are negatively related. This association had been previously suggested by Aberle (1961b); the phylogenetic comparative analyses by Holden and Mace rule out the possibility that it is simply an artefact of historical relatedness. Further studies have used this approach to investigate the cross-cultural distribution of bridewealth and dowry (Cowlishaw and Mace 1996; Fortunato and Mace in press; Fortunato et al. 2006; Mace and Pagel 1997; Pagel and Meade 2005), the relationship between polygyny and variation in sexual dimorphism in stature (Holden and Mace 1999), between polygyny and sex ratio (Mace and Jordan 2005; Mace et al. 2003), and variation in East African family and kinship organization (Borgerhoff Mulder et al. 2001).

Below I provide a brief introduction to this approach, followed by a discussion of recent developments in its application to cross-cultural data. In the second part of the chapter, I illustrate its use with data on wealth transfers at marriage in societies speaking Indo-European languages.

Phylogenetic Approaches to Cross-Cultural Comparison

Phylogenetic comparative methods

The principle underlying the phylogenetic comparative approach is that all inferences must take into account the historical relationships among the societies under investigation; this is illustrated in Figure 11.1. The phylogenetic tree in Figure 11.1(a) is a model of the historical relationships among seven societies, which are represented by the tips of the tree. Internal nodes correspond to the hypothetical common ancestors of the nodes that descend from them; the root of the tree represents the hypothetical common ancestor of all other nodes, and is the oldest point on the tree. Figures 11.1(b) and 11.1(c) show the distribution of states for two traits, X and Y, across the seven societies; X and Y represent the cultural practices under investigation. Each trait can take two states: 0 and 1 for trait X, a and b for trait Y. A simple count would suggest a correlation between 0 and a, and between 1 and b, as these states always occur together; this corresponds to performing a cross-cultural analysis without controlling for the effect of history.

Now consider the two possible scenarios for the pattern of change in the traits shown in (b) and in (c). In (b), one change occurs from state 0 to state 1 in trait X, followed by a change from state a to state b in trait Y; changes are represented by horizontal lines across a branch. In (c), changes from 0 to 1 followed by changes from a to b occur in three independent occasions. Although the two scenarios result in the same distribution of states at the tips of the tree, only (c) can be taken as evidence that changes in traits X and Y are correlated.

Phylogenetic comparative methods work by inferring statistically the possible patterns of change in the traits, and by formally evaluating the validity of each scenario. Several methods are available, which differ in the statistical

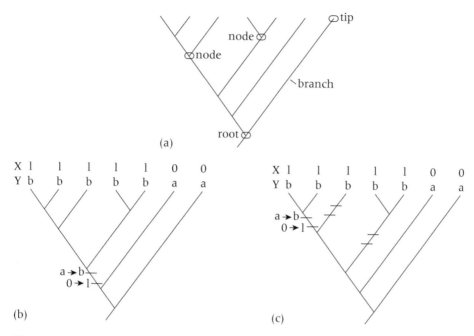

Figure 11.1 (a) Phylogenetic model of the historical relationships among seven taxa; time proceeds from the root to the tips. (b) and (c) show the distribution of states 0 and 1 for trait X, and of states a and b for trait Y. Horizontal lines represent changes from 0 to 1 for trait X, and fom a to b for trait Y. (© Laura Fortunato)

framework used to reconstruct the possible scenarios, and in the criteria implemented to assess them; they also differ in the type of data they can analyse (discrete or continuous). Below I discuss recent developments in the phylogenetic approach that are particularly relevant for the accuracy of cross-cultural analyses.

Phylogenetic Tree-Building Methods

The earliest applications of the phylogenetic comparative approach to cross-cultural data used trees derived from the linguistic and genetic literature as simple models of population history. Holden and Mace (1997), for example, used phylogenetic comparative methods to test hypotheses about the evolution of lactose digestion in humans. They used trees from Ruhlen (1991) and from Cavalli-Sforza et al. (1994) as models of the historical relationships among a worldwide sample of societies; on these trees they plotted information on lactose digestion capacity and degree of dependence on pastoralism for each society.

In recent years, phylogenetic comparative analyses of cultural traits have used trees obtained by applying phylogenetic tree-building methods to linguistic data. The tree-building approach is intuitively close to the traditional comparative linguistic one: both aim to reconstruct the relationships among a set of languages, based on the similarities and differences in lexical or structural features, and both model the relationships as branching rooted trees, with internal nodes representing ancestral entities. Unlike the traditional linguistic approach, however, the computational one makes use of explicit criteria to choose among the host of tree topologies: for a sample of fifty languages, for example, the number of possible configurations is in the order of $3 \cdot 10^{76}$ (Felsenstein 2004: 24). Further, formal tree-building methods enable researchers to quantify the degree to which linguistic relationships can be modelled as a tree rather than as a network (e.g. Bryant et al. 2005; Nakhleh et al. 2005); this addresses concerns that tree models may be inappropriate given the reticulate nature of human genetic, linguistic, and cultural history.

To date, phylogenetic tree-building methods have been applied to Austronesian (Gray and Jordan 2000), Bantu (Holden 2002; Rexová et al. 2006), Indo-European (Gray and Atkinson 2003; Nakhleh et al. 2005; Rexová et al. 2003; Ringe et al. 2002), and Papuan (Dunn et al. 2005) languages. Following traditional linguistic practice, most studies have used vocabulary data, which allow for time depths of approximately 8000 ± 2000 years; relationships resulting from over 10,000 years of divergence can only be inferred from structural features of languages, such as grammar and sound systems (e.g. Dunn et al. 2005).

Trees generated through computational methods have been used in phylogenetic comparative analyses of Bantu (Holden and Mace 2003, 2005), Indo-European (Fortunato and Mace in press; Fortunato et al. 2006), and Austronesian (Jordan 2007) societies; this procedure increases the accuracy of the analyses by including quantitative information on the relative degree of divergence of the groups. On the other hand, the temporal reach of the tree-building approach limits our ability to make comparative inferences beyond individual language families. We must rely on the lexical reconstruction of cultural elements for inferences further back in time (e.g. Ehret, this volume).

Trees as History

The use of phylogenetic trees as models of population history does not imply that the history of those populations was tree-like; a host of more complex scenarios is indeed more likely to capture the historical relationships of human populations. Trees, rather than networks, are used in phylogenetic comparative analyses because the methods currently available can only deal with strictly bifurcating trees. This simplification is justified on the grounds that by not using an explicit model of population history we implicitly assume that the groups under investigation are equally related to one another (Felsenstein 1985); this seems a worse approximation of the past than a properly constructed phylogenetic model, for biological and human groups alike.

Indeed, any phylogenetic tree is, by definition, a hypothesis about the historical relationships among the groups under study, and it is a well-known problem of the phylogenetic comparative approach that results may be affected by the phylogeny used (e.g. Martins and Housworth 2002). To address this issue, recently developed methods take into account the statistical uncertainty in the estimation of both the phylogeny and the parameters of interest to the comparative question (Huelsenbeck and Rannala 2003; Pagel and Meade 2005, 2006; Pagel et al. 2004). Huelsenbeck et al. (2001), Holder and Lewis (2003), and Ronquist (2004) provide accessible introductions to the statistical framework; below, I illustrate its application to cross-cultural data with a case-study of wealth transfers at marriage in societies speaking Indo-European languages, reported in Fortunato et al. (2006).

Wealth Transfers at Marriage in Indo-European Societies

Marriage is often accompanied by the transfer of resources, in the form of women, services, or property (Westermarck 1926: 156). Property may be transferred from the groom or his kin to the bride's kin (brideprice or bridewealth) or to the bride (indirect dowry: Goody 1973: 2), or from the bride's kin to the bride (dowry); alternatively, the families of the spouses may exchange goods in reciprocation.

Worldwide, bridewealth is common and dowry is rare; further, dowry is found exclusively in European and Asian societies (Goody 1973: 22). Based on this observation, and on the assumption that older traits are likely to be more widespread than recent ones, Jackson and Romney (1973) inferred that dowry is a relatively recent phenomenon. This line of argument corresponds to making inferences from the distribution of states at the tips of a phylogenetic tree: by similar reasoning, we would infer that state 0 of trait X appeared after state 1 in the example in Figure 11.1, because it is less common among the seven societies. As is clear from Figures 11.1(b) and 11.1(c), however, the distribution of states at the tips of a tree results from the branching pattern of the tree combined with the pattern of change in the trait.

My colleagues and I (Fortunato et al. 2006) used a phylogenetic comparative approach to reconstruct the most likely scenario for the pattern of change of these practices, while controlling for the effect of history. We used cross-cultural data on wealth transfers at marriage for a sample of societies speaking Indo-European (IE) languages; the comparative data were mapped onto a statistically justified sample of trees obtained from linguistic data, which served as a model of historical relationships among the societies under investigation.

Data and Methods

Collating the cross-cultural dataset
My colleagues and I collated the comparative data by matching speech varieties in Dyen et al.'s (1992) IE basic vocabulary database with societies in Gray (1999), in Levinson (1994), and in primary ethnographic sources. We then

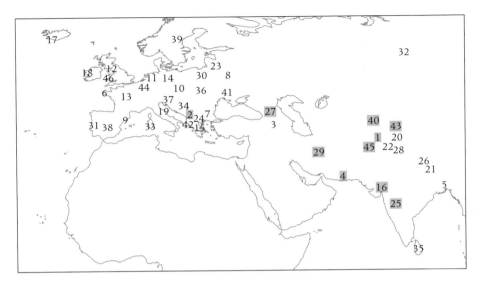

Figure 11.2 Geographical distribution and mode of wealth transfer at marriage of IE societies; black represents dowry, grey shading bridewealth. Societies are located at the mid-point of the language area, based on data from Gordon (2005). 1 Afghan; 2 Albanian; 3 Armenian; 4 Baluchi; 5 Bengali; 6 Breton; 7 Bulgarian; 8 Byelorussian; 9 Catalan; 10 Czech; 11 Dutch; 12 English; 13 French; 14 German; 15 Greek; 16 Gujarati; 17 Icelandic; 18 Irish; 19 Italian; 20 Kashmiri; 21 Khaskura; 22 Lahnda; 23 Lithuanian; 24 Macedonian; 25 Marathi; 26 Nepali; 27 Ossetic; 28 Panjabi; 29 Persian; 30 Polish; 31 Portuguese; 32 Russian; 33 Sardinian; 34 Serbocroatian; 35 Sinhalese; 36 Slovak; 37 Slovenian; 38 Spanish; 39 Swedish; 40 Tadzik; 41 Ukrainian; 42 Vlach; 43 Wakhi; 44 Walloon; 45 Waziri; 46 Welsh. (© Laura Fortunato)

used data from the linguistic database to generate a sample of phylogenetic trees for these societies, as described below.

Societies were coded as practising bridewealth or dowry based on the direction of the transfer (transfer from the groom's kin versus transfer from the bride's kin). Groups with evidence for both practices were coded based on the prevalent mode of transfer. The geographical distribution of the societies and their mode of transfer are shown in Figure 11.2.

To assess the effect of these coding decisions, we repeated the analysis using several alternative coding strategies. Specifically, in order to assess the effect of using binary coding (bridewealth versus dowry) we re-ran the analysis excluding societies with evidence of both practices, by recoding them as missing data points; the names of these societies are italicized in Figure 11.3. Further, we assessed the effect of coding the outgroup Hittite as practising dowry by repeating the analysis with Hittite coded as practising bridewealth, and as missing data point; the significance of adding Hittite to the sample is explained below.

This procedure allows us to assess the effect of coding decisions at the level of individual inferences. As such, it addresses concerns related to the coding of practices characterized by qualitative and quantitative variation, both within and across societies. Critics of the cross-cultural approach argue that cultural traits are integrated into a system, and that by coding them in discrete categories, we overlook the significance of the system as a whole. This is a persistent criticism of cross-cultural research (Levinson and Malone 1980: 10–11), yet one that we can dismiss empirically by showing the robustness of the inferences to the coding strategy used.

Obtaining a Model of Population History

Dyen et al.'s (1992) IE basic vocabulary database includes the meanings in the Swadesh 200-word list of items of basic vocabulary for 95 modern IE speech varieties (languages, dialects, and creoles), classified into cognate classes; two or more forms of similar meaning are cognate if they share a common origin. Swadesh lists consist of cross-culturally universal items of basic vocabulary such as pronouns, body parts, and numerals, which are less prone to innovation and borrowing than other meanings (Embleton 1986).

Linguistic data for Hittite were added to the sample of 51 IE speech varieties for which comparative information was available. Phylogenetic tree-building methods determine ancestor–descendant relationships among the groups under investigation, the 'ingroup taxa', through a procedure known as 'outgroup rooting'. This consists in including in the analysis one or more 'outgroup taxa', which provide information on the direction of change in the data by virtue of being distantly related to the ingroup taxa. Hittite belongs to the extinct sister-group to the IE languages, the Anatolian clade, and is commonly used as outgroup taxon in phylogenetic tree-building analyses of IE languages. Together, the Anatolian and IE clades form the Indo-Hittite language family (Rexová et al. 2003; Ruhlen 1991: 325). I will use the term 'Proto-Indo-Hittite' (PIH) for the hypothetical ancestor of Indo-Hittite languages, and 'Proto-Indo-European' (PIE) for the hypothetical ancestor of IE languages, and for the hypothetical 'proto-societies' that spoke them.

We generated a sample of 1000 trees from the linguistic data for the 51 IE speech varieties plus the outgroup Hittite, using the tree-sampling method described in Pagel and Meade (2004). Trees appear in the sample in proportion to their posterior probability, which is the probability of the tree conditional on the data, and can be interpreted as the probability that the tree is correct (Huelsenbeck et al. 2001). This can be illustrated with an example. Figure 11.3 is a summary of the 1000 trees in the sample. The Indic speech varieties share the same ancestor in 96% of trees; the probability that they are a monophyletic group is thus 0.96, given the data and the model of word evolution used in the tree-building analysis.

By using a large sample of trees, we are effectively considering a large number of hypotheses about the historical relationships among the groups in the sample; this addresses the concern that no tree is a perfect model of population history. Further, we ensure that the results of the comparative analysis are not dependent on any particular hypothesis about the historical relationships among the groups.

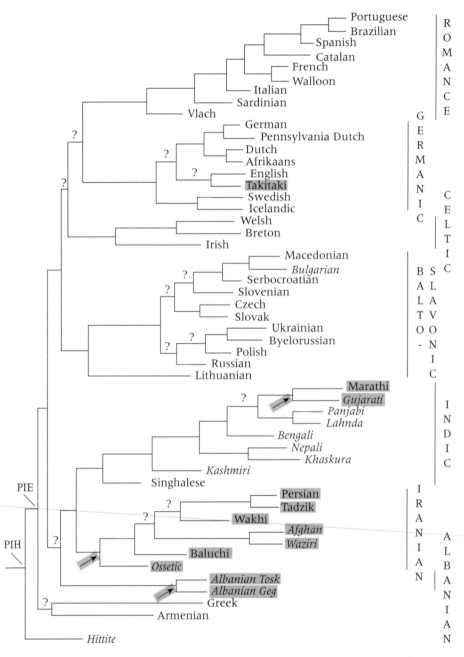

Figure 11.3 Summary of a sample of 1000 trees generated from linguistic data for 51 IE speech varieties plus Hittite. Black represents dowry, grey shading bridewealth; italics indicate societies with evidence of both practices. Arrows indicate nodes with a combined probability for bridewealth ≥ 0.70; unmarked nodes have a combined probability for dowry ≥ 0.70; question marks indicate nodes with combined probabilities ≤ 0.70 for both practices. PIH: Proto-Indo-Hittite; PIE: Proto-Indo-European. (© Laura Fortunato)

Reconstructing Ancestral States

We estimated the probability of dowry and bridewealth at each node across the sample of trees, using the phylogenetic comparative method developed by Pagel and colleagues (Pagel and Meade 2005; Pagel et al. 2004). This method works by estimating values for the parameters of interest to the comparative question, based on the sample of trees and on the comparative data mapped onto the trees. These parameters include, for example, the probability of change from bridewealth to dowry and from dowry to bridewealth, and the probability of each state at a given node.

This information is then combined with the posterior probability of each node obtained from the tree-building analysis described above, to estimate the probability that either state represents the ancestral practice at that node. An example will illustrate this procedure. The tree-building analysis returned a probability of 0.96 that the Indic speech varieties form a monophyletic group. The comparative analysis tells us that the probability for dowry at this node is 0.99; this is the mean value of the probabilities for dowry at that node for the trees in which the node exists, that is, 96% of trees in the sample. The 'combined probability' for dowry at this node is obtained by multiplying the two values, and equals 0.95. Within the Indic clade, the probability that Marathi, Gujarati, Panjabi, and Lahnda form a monophyletic clade is 0.68 (Figure 11.3). The mean probability for bridewealth at this node is 0.61; the combined probability for bridewealth is obtained by multiplying these values, and equals 0.42. The low value indicates that this reconstruction is uncertain. By reiterating this procedure for all nodes, we estimated a likely scenario for the pattern of change of the two states across the sample of trees; combined probabilities of 0.70 or higher represent reconstructions with a high degree of certainty.

This method allows us to combine the statistical uncertainty in the estimation of the phylogenetic relationships with the statistical uncertainty in the estimation of the comparative parameters. Any uncertainty in the reconstruction of a node limits the confidence that we can place in the reconstruction of the ancestral state at that node (Pagel et al. 2004).

Results

The standard elementary subgroups of IE languages (Albanian, Iranian, Indic, Slavonic, Celtic, Germanic, Romance), as well as previously suggested higher groupings (Indo-Iranian, Balto-Slavonic), were recovered as monophyletic with high posterior probabilities (0.96 for Indic, 1.00 for all others; Figure 11.3). Reconstructions of some of the higher level groupings were less certain, reflecting the difficulty encountered by both classical comparative linguistic and computational methods in resolving these relationships (e.g. Rexová et al. 2003; Ruhlen 1991: 325).

The results of the comparative analysis are shown on the tree in Figure 11.3. Arrows indicate nodes with a combined probability for bridewealth equal to or above the 0.70 threshold. Question marks indicate nodes with combined probabilities below this threshold for either practice; this can be due to uncertainty in the phylogenetic reconstruction, to uncertainty in the reconstruction of the ancestral states, or both. All other nodes have a combined probability for dowry equal to or above the 0.70 threshold.

Dowry is the most likely practice for nodes PIH and PIE at the base of the tree. The reconstructed pattern of change indicates that a minimum of four transitions from dowry to bridewealth is necessary to explain the observed cross-cultural distribution of the two states; the uncertainty in the reconstructions at some of the nodes suggests, however, that alternative scenarios cannot be excluded.

These inferences are robust to the coding strategy used. The reconstruction of dowry as the most likely state at the root (node PIH) was not affected by recoding Hittite as missing. Recoding Hittite as bridewealth reduced the combined probability for dowry at this node below the 0.70 threshold; however, even this strategy failed to retrieve a combined probability for bridewealth greater than the threshold value. Both coding strategies negligibly affected the reconstructions at other nodes.

Recoding of those societies with evidence of both practices as missing affected the reconstructions for the Albanian and Indo-Iranian clades, which include most of the recoded groups. Results also suggest that a change from dowry to bridewealth occurred at the base of the Indo-Iranian clade. The reconstruction for the node representing the split of the Slavonic, Celtic, Germanic, and Romance clades from the others was also marginally affected. However, the inference that dowry was the most probable state at nodes PIH and PIE was not affected.

Discussion

My colleagues and I (Fortunato et al. 2006) used phylogenetic methods to reconstruct the pattern of change in wealth transfers at marriage in societies speaking IE languages, based on the cross-cultural variation in these practices detailed in the ethnographic record. Results suggest that dowry was the prevalent mode of transfer for PIE society, and that it was highly conserved among societies that descended from it.

The comparative philological evidence, based on IE epic narratives and ancient legal codes, suggests that dowry represented the most prestigious mode of initiating a marriage known to the PIE world, followed by bride capture, and brideprice (Allen 1996, 2000b; Dumézil 1979); each mode of marriage represented one of the three functions in the tripartite structure dominating PIE ideology, which related to the domains of religion, force, and wealth, respectively. Ancient Indian matrimonial laws, for example, recommended dowry for priests, bride capture for warriors, and brideprice for merchants (Allen 1996: 14–15; Dumézil 1979: 31–40). Taken together, these two lines of evidence suggest that the association of dowry with the priestly function, which was in charge of maintaining religious and legal order, may be responsible for the persistence of this practice among the descendants of PIE society, and for its higher status in IE societies that recognize both dowry and bridewealth (e.g. Tambiah 1973: 69–71).

The finding that dowry was the prevalent mode of transfer for PIH society finds no support in the comparative linguistic evidence. While there is no clear evidence for a PIH dowry, linguists have reconstructed a PIE word for 'bride-price' (Mallory and Adams 1997: 82–3; 2006: 208); derivatives of the reconstructed PIH term for 'pay' suggest a possible link with a PIH bridewealth. Within the non-monetary economy of PIH society, however, this concept pertained to transactions of exchange rather than purchase, and its interpretation as brideprice seems to rest largely on the reconstructed 'patriarchal organization' (Mallory and Adams 1997: 185) of PIH society.

Within anthropology, dowry has traditionally been regarded as 'a very "Indo-European" institution' (Fox 1967: 328). However, this belief resulted from the skewed geographical focus of the discipline, rather than from systematic analysis of the evidence: anthropologists turned their attention to dowry only in the second half of the twentieth century, following the inclusion of the towns and villages of Eurasia as locations of fieldwork (Schlegel and Eloul 1987). Similarly, discussions of the early development of these practices have been dominated by the assumption of a long-term progression from bridewealth to dowry, but the evidence for such a shift is, for the most part, anecdotal (Goody 1976: 80; 1983: 240–61). Indeed, there is evidence for both practices in the earliest written records, and in many cases the amount of property provided as dowry exceeded the value of the bridewealth (Hughes 1985: 14).

Through the use of simple models, and by making explicit the assumptions that underlie them, the phylogenetic approach provides a formal framework within which to address these questions of the history of cultural traits. Where informed by anthropological, historical, and linguistic analysis, it holds great promise of furthering our understanding of early kinship and marriage practices.

Acknowledgements

I thank Ruth Mace and Clare Holden for comments on previous versions of this chapter. Tom Currie provided the map in Figure 11.2. This work was funded by the Economic and Social Research Council and by the Graduate School of University College London. The Fondazione Aldo Gini and the Centre for the Evolutionary Analysis of Cultural Behaviour provided additional financial support.

12

Reconstructing Ancient Kinship in Africa

Christopher Ehret

Reconstructing the cultural lexicons of anciently spoken languages provides a unique kind of window into past cultures, allowing us a view, as archaeology cannot, into the structure of ideas and the organization of knowledge among peoples of far-off times. In the case of the four major African language families, recent work, combining the evidence of reconstructed subsistence lexicon with palaeoclimatic and archaeological findings, has argued that the first stages of expansion of each of the four recognized African language families – Afroasiatic (Afrasan), Nilo-Saharan, Niger-Kordofanian, and Khoesan – began at a minimum several millennia before 11,000 BP. This dating would take us back more than a quarter of the time-span since the initial dispersal of human-kind out of Africa. So reconstructing the social lexicons of the proto-languages of the African families has the potential to provide specific information on several particular kinship systems as they existed at a deep remove in time from the present.

The lexical reconstruction of material culture in the African language families, particularly in the Nilo-Saharan, Khoesan, and Afroasiatic families, has progressed significantly over the past decade and a half. The evidence of early kinship, though, has been almost completely uninvestigated so far, except for the Southern African Khoesan branch (Barnard 1992 and elsewhere) and the Bantu branch of the Niger-Congo family (Marck and Bostoen in preparation). We will begin here by laying out the chronological backdrop; then move on to consider what in the way of specific kin lexicon has so far been reconstructed; next view some specific kinship structures; and finally explore what possible wider descent reckoning patterns might have characterized the ancestral societies of the different families.

Early History of the African Language Families

Why do we conclude that the proto-languages of each of the African families were most likely spoken close to 15,000 years ago, towards the end of the last glacial age? The relevant evidence consists of two kinds of findings from the reconstructed and provisionally reconstructed lexicons of material culture:

1　The vocabulary of reconstructed subsistence gives us a *terminus post quem* dating three of the proto-languages during or after the period of the adoption of bows and arrows.

The proto-languages of the Afroasiatic, Khoesan, and Nilo-Saharan families each possessed vocabulary relating to the use of bows and arrows (Ehret 1995b forthcoming d; and Orel and Stolbova 1995, for Afroasiatic; Ehret 1986 forthcoming a and b, for Khoesan; proto-Nilo-Saharan *abwa 'bow': unpublished data). It is not yet certain that bow and arrow vocabulary can be traced to the proto-Niger-Kordofanian language, but it does reconstruct to proto-Niger-Congo, the daughter language of proto-Niger-Kordofanian, which was ancestral to all the vastly spread Niger-Congo languages spoken today across West and central, eastern and southern Africa (Greenberg 1964; Westermann 1927). If current ideas about the age of bow technology in Africa prove true, these lexical data would place the ancestral periods of each of the African families in the period between c. 15,000 and 12,000 years ago. If it turns out that certain blades from the archaeology of Africa of the preceding 30,000 years were arrowheads, then our *terminus post quem* for one or more of the proto-languages of the families could have been far earlier.

2　The vocabulary of reconstructed subsistence gives us a *terminus ante quem* for each proto-language, placing its existence in the eras preceding the development of food production.

Food production began earlier in sub-Saharan Africa than is generally recognized by non-specialists in this history, and it had at least three independent, separate origins in the continent: one in West Africa involving Niger-Kordofanian speakers, one by Nilo-Saharans in the southeastern Sahara, and the third in the southern Ethiopian highlands, by the speakers of the Omotic languages of Afroasiatic (Afrasan). The first indications of Nilo-Saharan herding of cattle in the southeastern Sahara, the earliest livestock raising in world history, belong to the period 10,500–10,000 BP (Kuper and Kröpelin 2006; Wendorf and Schild 1998; Wendorf et al. 2001), almost as early as the separate Middle Eastern development of food production.

For two of the families, Nilo-Saharan and Afroasiatic, the lexical evidence clearly places the inception of food production *later* in time than the proto-language of the family, and the correlations of linguistics with archaeology gives calendrical dating to the transitions. In the case of Nilo-Saharan, the match of the linguistic and archaeological stratigraphies is especially detailed. The linguistic geography of the branches of the Nilo-Saharan family places the origin area of the family in the northern Middle Nile Basin, equivalent to the modern-day eastern parts of the southern Sahara. A lexicon of food production – at first, just words relating to cattle raising – began to be created only during the third period of divergence after proto-Nilo-Saharan, as shown in Figure 12.1. Archaeological correlations with independent early southeastern

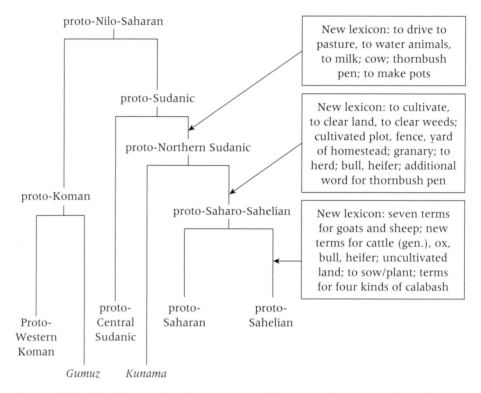

Figure 12.1 Nilo-Saharan family tree: new subsistence lexicon, proto-Sudanic to proto-Sahelian (© Christopher Ehret)

Sahara domestication of cattle place this stage at 10,500–10,000 BP. Two succeeding stages in the history of Nilo-Saharan material cultural lexicon – the development of terms for complex homesteads with granaries followed by the adoption of goat and sheep terminology (Ehret 2001, 2007) – are precisely paralleled in the material cultural evidence for the next two archaeological periods of the southeastern Sahara, dating respectively to 9300–9000 BP and to the ninth millennium BP (Ehret 1993, 1999, 2001; Wendorf and Schild 1998; Wendorf et al. 2001).

The linguistic geography of the branches of Afroasiatic places its proto-language in the Horn of Africa or in the far eastern Sahara just north of the Horn (Ehret 1999, 2006a; also Diakonoff 1998). Each major branch of the family developed its own entirely separate vocabulary of food production well after the early divergences in the family had taken place (Amatruda 1971; Ehret 1979, 1984, Ehret forthcoming d; Ehret et al. 2004; Diakonoff 1998). Proto-Afroasiatic subsistence vocabulary reveals an emphasis on the collection of wild grasses or grains (Ehret 1999, 2007; *contra* the misinterpretations of the evidence by Militarev [2003]). Just this kind of emphasis in subsistence prevailed in areas in the eastern Sahara and in northeastern areas of Ethiopia between 15,000 and 10,000 BP, the very regions in which we must place the proto-Afroasiatic society (Clark 1980; Clark and Williams 1978; Close 1980; Wendorf 1968 and elsewhere).

The inception of food production for Niger-Kordofanian speakers is uncertain, but took place after the proto-Niger-Kordofanian period (Ehret 1984, forthcoming c; Greenberg 1964; cf. Blench 2006 and elsewhere; Williamson 1993). Linguistic and archaeological evidence suggests that practices of cultivation spread along with the spread of one of the deep subgroups of Niger-Congo peoples, the Benue-Kwa, c. 6000 BP or before, into the western parts of West Africa's rain-forest belt (Blench 2006; Ehret 1984; Williamson 1993). Provisional reconstructions of cultivation lexicon support the proposal that the shift to food production began several stages earlier in Niger-Congo language history than the proto-Benue-Kwa era, possibly in the range of 9000–8000 BP (Ehret forthcoming c).

The Khoesan speakers, with the relatively late exceptions of the Sandawe in East Africa and the Khoekhoe in southern Africa, remained food collectors throughout their histories. The commonly accepted archaeological correlation of the Khoesan language family with the 'Wilton' or Eastern African Microlithic complex (Ambrose 1982; Ehret 1997, 2000c; Munson 1977) places the origin areas of the family in East Africa and at a time period dating as much as 18,000 years ago (Phillipson 1977).

The Geographical History of the African Language Families

Strikingly, the most probable origin areas of each of the African families lay in regions within or adjacent to the Horn of Africa. According to the most recent findings (see above), three of the four established families – Nilo-Saharan, Afroasiatic, Niger-Kordofanian, and Khoesan – divide at the deepest level into two primary branches. In each family one of the two primary branches is spoken across large areas of the continent, while the second primary branch occupies a restricted area in eastern or northeastern Africa.

1 Nilo-Saharan's widespread branch, Sudanic, consists of languages spoken right across the African continent, from the Songay language on the bend of the Niger River in the west to the Nilotic languages of Kenya and Tanzania in the east. Its second primary branch, Koman, in sharp contrast, is limited to areas just north and south of the Blue Nile, right at the western fringes of the Ethiopian highlands (Ehret 2001).
2 Afroasiatic, according to several studies (Bender 1975; Ehret 1980b, 1995b, 2000b; Fleming 1969, 1974, 1983), also divides into two branches, Omotic and Erythraic. The Erythraic branch is immensely widespread. It includes the Cushitic languages, found from the Red Sea hills of Sudan to central Tanzania; the Chadic languages of Niger, Nigeria, Chad, and Cameroon; the Berber tongues of the Sahara and North Africa; Ancient Egyptian; and the Semitic languages of far southwestern Asia and parts of northern Africa. In striking contrast, the second primary branch, Omotic, is restricted

entirely to the southwestern Ethiopian highlands – to areas that are in fact immediately adjacent to the Koman primary branch of Nilo-Saharan.

3   Niger-Kordofanian has similarly been held to have two deep primary branches (Greenberg 1963; Williamson and Blench 2000; for an alternative view of the family as having three primary branches, see Bennett and Sterk 1977; Williamson 1989). The Niger-Congo branch, with over 1000 languages, covers more than half of Africa, from Senegal at the far west to the distant eastern and southern coasts of the continent. The Kordofanian branch, on the other hand, is a small cluster of four distinct subbranches, located just west of the middle Nile River, no more than 300 kilometres away from the nearest languages of the Koman branch of Nilo-Saharan and the Omotic branch of Afroasiatic. A possible fifth subbranch of Kordofanian, Kadu, as identified by Greenberg (1963), has been alternatively proposed to belong to Nilo-Saharan (Schadeberg 1983) or to form a sixth African family (Ehret 1995a). The most recent examination of the evidence reaffirms Kadu's membership in Niger-Kordofanian, but as possibly forming another distinct primary branch of the family (Ehret 2000a), and so further reinforcing the arguments placing the origin of the family in the Sudan regions to the west of the Ethiopian highlands.

4   Two classifications of the fourth family, Khoesan, have been proposed, with either two primary branches, East-South Khoesan and Hadza (Ehret 2000b), or else three roughly coordinate branches, Southern African Khoesan, Sandawe, and Hadza. In the first of these classifications, the East-South branch combines Sandawe in East Africa with the southern African branch, spoken in recent millennia all across southern Africa. An alternative classification divides Khoesan into three primary branches, Hadza, Sandawe, and Southern African Khoesan. The Hadza group, like Sandawe, consists today of just a single language. Both the latter are spoken in neighbouring areas of north-central Tanzania, only about 800 kilometres to the south of the nearest languages of the Omotic branch of Afroasiatic. Studies of Khoesan loanwords in other East African languages fill in that geographical gap: they demonstrate that still other, extinct Khoesan-speaking societies, only very distantly related to the extant members of the family, formerly occupied most of the areas between Tanzania and the Ethiopian highlands (Ehret forthcoming a, forthcoming b).

In the global context, the period between 21,000 and 14,000 BP marked the high period of Earth's latest glacial age. In the Northern Hemisphere an initial post-glacial amelioration, the Alleröd Interstadial, took place, c. 13,900–12,800 BP. It was followed by the Younger Dryas, a period of shift back to cooler and drier conditions, and then by renewed, lasting warming of the climate c. 10,500 BP.

The significant question is whether contemporaneous climatic shifts took place in Africa. The eastern Sahara appears to have remained as hyperarid as it had been since the last glacial maximum around 20,000 BP and did not change in climate until 10,500 BP, when the tropical rainfall belts abruptly shifted northward. But the situation farther south and west in Africa remains unclear. The earliest divergences in the existing African language families in each case must be placed before 11,500. Their initial expansions may have come about because their speakers developed ways to cope better with the environmental stress of the often very dry and cooler tropical climates of the terminal Pleistocene. Alternatively, if areas farther south than the Sahara did enter periods of wetter climate concurrently with the Alleröd Interstadial, then new opportunities for growth and expansion of population might have stimulated new expansions and divergences of at least some of the four families as early as 14,000 years ago.

Tracing Old Kinship Words Back in Time and Interpreting Their Semantic Histories

For two of the four language families of Africa, Nilo-Saharan and Khoesan, the comparative evidence available to us already is sufficient for proposing the basic structure of kinship in the proto-society of the family. It is possible, in other words, to provide an initial reconstruction of many features of kinship as it existed in those societies probably on the order of 14,000 or more years ago. In the instance of Nilo-Saharan, we can reconstruct the actual kin terms at a greater variety of levels than for Khoesan, and we can trace changes in the terminology and the structure of kinship in considerable detail over the successive early periods of Nilo-Saharan expansion and divergence. A third family, Afroasiatic, presents an as yet more ambiguous story, but one with notable implications of its own. For the fourth major African family, Niger-Kordofanian, the study of the evidence is only just beginning, and little can as yet be said.

   Kin terms, like any other words in a language, undergo shifts in meaning and usage over time. But the systemic fit of kin terms within overall terminological systems constrains the possible directions and variety of meaning changes. In general, kin relations with concrete individual referents – father, mother, sibling, and child – can be extended to collateral relations of the same or alternate generations; but the opposite direction of shift, extending a term for a secondary relation to apply to a primary one, does not normally take place. Among the different cultures of the world, for example, words for father are widely extended to include father's brothers. Once that extension has taken place, the term can extend further, from father's brother to mother's brother, reflecting a cultural shift from a collateral to a generational identification of parent's brothers. A parallel succession of meaning extensions is possible for parent's sisters. But an opposite expansion of the kin category, in which a word originally referring solely to father's brother developed into the primary term for father, is highly improbable. The same constraints on the directions of semantic extension govern the history of cousin terms. An older root word for 'sibling' can take on the additional meaning 'parallel cousin', and from there can undergo a yet further meaning extension to include cross-cousins as well. But the opposite direction of change is not likely to happen. When sibling terms include cousins, we must normally presume the sibling meaning to have been original.

Let us take a hypothetical instance. We discover that the same root word for a male relative occurs in two related languages, but with different meanings. In language A it refers solely to 'father'; in language B it connotes 'parent's brother' (covering both the paternal and maternal uncles). A particular progression of meaning changes must underlie this outcome. Because meaning extension goes from primary to collateral kin, the root word in most instances would originally have meant 'father' in the ancestral (proto-)language out of which the two languages evolved. In language A it retained that meaning. In language B the meaning first expanded to include the father's brother; subsequently, a further meaning extension of the root, to mother's brother, took place; and finally a new word for 'father' was innovated in language B, with the older root losing its original meaning, 'father'. If the word's original meaning already included 'father's brother' along with 'father', a second, slightly different, although still parallel history is also possible. In that case language A would have had dropped the meaning 'father's brother', while language B would simply have broadened the application to include 'mother's brother', but, as in the first scenario, would subsequently have dropped the application of the word to 'father'.

Now these considerations have to do with the normative directions in *semantic* derivation of new words in languages. The direction of semantic change is *not* necessarily the same thing as the direction of social shift. In the first place, the development or adoption of new words is a recurring process of language history everywhere. Some new terms do come into use in a language because of the speakers' need to express new things or new ways of doing. But the majority of new words arise initially as synonyms of words for already existing items, relations, and behaviours. Secondly, the normative directions of meaning change operate from specific to general and from concrete to metaphor. It is the concrete referents that give power to metaphor and weight to generalization.

In the sphere of kinship, a category of classificatory fathers exists because it has a concrete referent, father. The name of the category can change because the name of its referent changes, but not the other way around. If in a society there already exists a social category of classificatory fathers, when a new word for father comes into use, it can be expected by extension to become also the new term for the category as a whole. The fact that the semantic process is anchored to the term 'father' does not mean that the wider category did not previously exist, and it does not require a society previously structured around nuclear families. Similarly, Hawaiian cousin terminology is anchored to the concrete relations to ego of brother and sister. If a new word replaces the older term for brother or sister, that term will then be extended to the cousins of equivalent gender, providing the society's conceptualization of the cousin relationship remains unchanged.

These perspectives have important implications for inferring kin structure change from changes in particular kin terms. The development of a new term for one of the primary kin relations does not necessarily imply change in the conceptualization of the wider web of relationships. In contrast, secondary or tertiary relationships to ego, such as PG or PGC, are species of the taxon and not the primary referents that give social import to categorizations of close kin or to wider classificatory kin categories. In consequence, the development of new terms for PG or for PGC frequently does reflect changes in kin relations and kinship structure.

Reconstructing the Lexicons of Ancient Nilo-Saharan Kinship

The data for kinship reconstruction from the Nilo-Saharan family are especially rich, allowing for the recovery of many of the key early terms in the evolution of Nilo-Saharan kin terminology and structure. Developments in early cousin terminology remain relatively poorly understood, but the materials relating to other categories of blood relationship and to affinal relations are substantial. In a number of instances, the underlying derivations of kin terms open windows, as well, into early marriage preferences and the history of unilineal descent.

The essential framework for evaluating the evidence is a chronology of the major stages in early Nilo-Saharan cultural evolution. The Nilo-Saharan family tree (Figure 12.2) provides the linguistic stratigraphy of this history. Along the right side of this figure a succession of dates is proposed. The dates *without* question marks come from two sets of published, strong archaeological-linguistic correlations. For the period 10,500–8000 BP, a three-stage sequence of developments – first cattle raising, then sedentary settlement, and finally the addition of ovicaprids – marks the archaeological record of the southeastern Sahara. An exactly parallel three-stage creation of new lexicon relating to the same three successive additions to economy and culture characterizes the proto-Northern Sudanic, proto-Saharo-Sahelian, and proto-Sahelian stages on the Nilo-Saharan tree (as already noted above in Figure 12.1). For the period 3000–2000 BP, a long-established set of correlations (Ambrose 1982) dates the proto-Southern Nilotic society to the early third millennium BP. The dates between those two periods are informed guesses (marked by question marks) as to what the time-spans between the various successive episodes of language divergence might have been.

With the historical stratigraphy plotted (in Figure 12.2), we are able to move on to consider our primary questions. How did the lexicon of kinship evolve in early Nilo-Saharan (at least the portions of the lexicon that we can currently reconstruct)? What does the history of that lexicon imply about developments in kinship among the early Nilo-Saharan-speaking societies? These questions will be posed for the historical sequence of seven nodes in the linguistic stratigraphy of the Nilo-Saharan family (marked by arrows in Figure 12.2):

- proto-Nilo-Saharan;
- proto-Sudanic;
- proto-Northern Sudanic (c. 10,500–9300 BP);
- proto-Saharo-Sahelian (c. 9300–9000 BP);

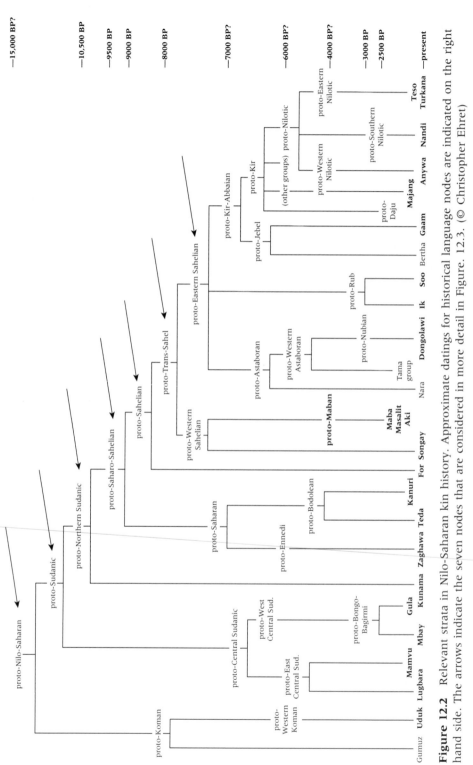

Figure 12.2 Relevant strata in Nilo-Saharan kin history. Approximate datings for historical language nodes are indicated on the right hand side. The arrows indicate the seven nodes that are considered in more detail in Figure. 12.3. (© Christopher Ehret)

- proto-Sahelian (c. ninth millennium BP);
- proto-Trans-Sahel (c. end of ninth millennium BP?);
- proto-Eastern Sahelian.

The published systematic phonological reconstruction of Nilo-Saharan (Ehret 2001, 2003a) provides the framework of regular sound change for (1) validating the reconstruction of early Nilo-Saharan root words, including kinship terms, and (2) tracing the existence of particular root words back to particular periods (linguistic 'strata') preceding those nodes. Appendix 1 presents the terms and their proposed meanings for each of the seven periods, sorting them into sections A–G according to the period in the stratigraphy to which they can be traced. (Appendices to this chapter are to be found at the end of the book.) At each successive period leading down from proto-Nilo-Saharan to proto-Eastern Sudanic, additional terms prove to be reconstructible. In some cases, these may be root words for kinship that actually do go back to the earliest periods but happen to have been retained only in one branch. In other cases, the terms are probable new developments.

Two additional sections of Appendix 1, H and I, list terms that spread though areal contacts postdating the stages in Nilo-Saharan kinship history considered here. Section H contains terms distributed among a set of languages the speakers of which, in the last several thousand years BCE, formed a clutch of interacting societies in the southern parts of the east-central Sahara and adjacent Sahel. Section I adds a further term, limited to languages of the Nubian and Jebel subgroups of Eastern Sahelian, spoken in the northern Middle Nile Basin.

For the actual cognate words on which the roots in Appendix 1 are based, the reader should refer to the numerous kin diagrams available as an on-line adjunct to this chapter (see http://www.sscnet.ucla.edu/history/ehret/kinship/african_kinship_data.htm). The language names in boldface on the Nilo-Saharan family tree, Figure 12.2, identify some of the particular languages, depicted in these diagrams, from which the lexical evidence comes. (Ehret 2001, chapter 2, tabulates the regular sound correspondences that back up the reconstructed root shapes of the kin terms.) The reconstructed meaning of each root has been inferred from the comparative application of semantic historical criteria as described previously, relating to the normative directionalities of meaning change in kin terminology. Appendix 1 provides additional explanatory commentaries for many of the roots. In a number of cases the appendix directs attention as well to the cultural and social implications of particular meaning changes. These implications will figure subsequently in arguments about marriage and descent in Nilo-Saharan history.

The published systematic phonological reconstruction of Nilo-Saharan (Ehret 2001; with further explication in Ehret 2003a) provides the regular sound change criteria for validating each of the particular reconstructed kin terms. The great majority of these root words have not been previously published, so the list in Appendix 1 and the lexical attestations in the on-line kinship diagrams constitute an important new source. (The new data presented in Ehret 2003a also allow correction of errors in the reconstruction of one old kin term found in Ehret 2001, root 844, although reconfirming several other such roots.)

Figure 12.3 displays the succession of kin terminological systems encoded in the reconstructed lexical evidence for the successive early periods of Nilo-Saharan history. This figure shows both the changes and the long-term continuities in these kinship systems. The diagram also helps to locate the significant gaps in our current knowledge.

Parents' Siblings in Early Nilo-Saharan Kinship

The consistent feature of early Nilo-Saharan kinship that stands out in Figure 12.3 is bifurcate collateral reckoning of parents' siblings. The original PNS term for MZ is as yet unreconstructed; and for the last of the seven periods, the proto-Eastern Sahelian (PES) root word for FB is also uncertain. But otherwise the evidence is full: from the proto-Nilo-Saharan period down to the proto-Trans-Sahel period, the consistent pattern was to have separate and distinct terms for each first ascending generation member, FZ, FB, F, M, MZ, and MB. Coincident with the accelerating economic shift to a full livestock-raising economy over the approximately 1000 years from the proto-Saharo-Sahelian to proto-Trans-Sahel periods, new synonyms for FZ and MB came into use alongside the older terms. These additions probably relate to a combination of factors: (1) territorial expansion and divergence, with dialect differences beginning to form, but with the diverging communities still forming an inter-acting network across which new terms could spread; and (2) new pressures on inheritance and kin relations brought on by the growth of movable wealth in livestock. But the bifurcate collateral structure remained.

In later eras bifurcate merging patterns took hold in languages of several distantly related branches of the family (see, for instance, on-line kin diagrams for Mbay, Gula, Songay, and Nandi). Some societies only partially merged P(G) terms, extending the word 'father' to include ego's father's brother, but following other naming patterns for the remaining P(G). In a few cases, MZ and FZ came to be named lineally, with the same term encompassing both (see on-line kin diagrams for Teso, Turkana, Soo, and possibly Maba). In at least one language, Gaam, the same term came to cover both mother's siblings, i.e. MB = MZ, while distinct terms characterized F and FB; and in at least one other language, Majang, one term meant both F and FB, whereas separate words named each of the other three PG. The semantic histories in Appendix 1 indicate, as well, that several languages passed through interme-diate periods in which they, too, adopted the kin equations MB = MZ or MZ = FZ, before changing over to bifurcate merging or back to bifurcate collateral reckoning of parent's siblings. These are each histories deserving of a more extensive consideration than is possible here.

Parents' Siblings' Children in Early Nilo-Saharan

What of cousin terminology? Only one PNS root relating to this aspect of kin-ship, *kaam, can currently be proposed. The tentative proposal (in Appendix 1)

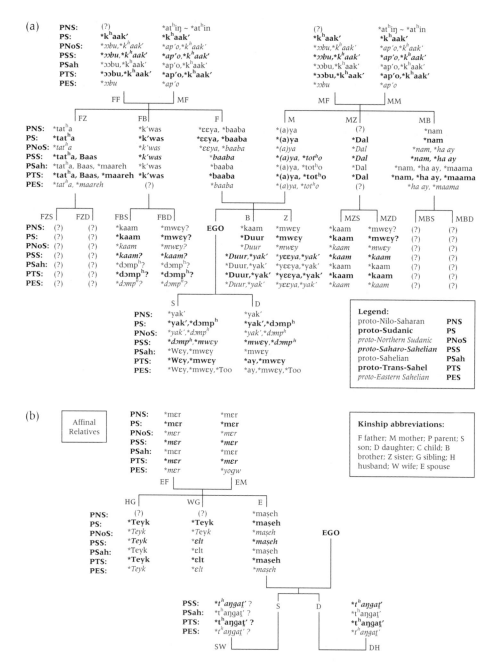

Figure 12.3 Comparison of kin terms at the seven successive proto-language nodes of the Nilo-Saharan language family (the nodes are those indicated by arrows in Figure 12.2) (© Christopher Ehret)

is that *kaam began as a term in PNS for siblings and parallel cousins but not cross-cousins. If that proposal holds, it would indicate that the PNS society had Iroquois cousin reckoning. But the clinching evidence for such a proposal, a separate reconstructed PNS term for cross-cousin, is lacking as yet. So it is possible that *kaam originally included the cross- as well as parallel cousins, in which case PNS would have had a Hawaiian system.

Two systems are relatively common today among Nilo-Saharan societies, Hawaiian and Descriptive (or 'Sudanic'). Iroquois systems exist less commonly, but occur in languages widely separated geographically and relatively distantly related to each other. Interestingly, in a number of cases the terminological evidence implies the former presence of Crow cousin systems, as noted in the second column of Table 12.1, and the presence or former presence of that system has further historical implications, to be returned to below.

Different issues are raised by the relative commonness of Hawaiian and Sudanic cousin terms. The frequency of Hawaiian does not necessarily support its having been the early Nilo-Saharan pattern, since, as Table 12.1 shows, Hawaiian systems in several instances were secondary developments, replacing earlier Crow reckonings. As for Sudanic cousin terminology, although it occurs widely, it does not trace back to the earliest Nilo-Saharan eras. G. P. Murdock (1949) long ago observed that this type of kinship is often associated with more segmentary types of unilineal kinship organization. It seems likely that this type of cousin terminology arose separately among different Nilo-Saharans only after cattle raising and other kinds of food production associated with such segmentary systems in the Sudan belt of Africa had fully developed, hence not until *after* the proto-Eastern Sahelian period.

Cross-Cousin Marriage in Early Nilo-Saharan History

The Nilo-Saharan kin lexicons, in addition, reveal earlier marriage patterns. In particular, the histories of terms for in-laws in different branches and subgroups of the Nilo-Saharan family show a wide development of preferential cross-cousin marriage. In Lugbara, for example, the term for spouse's mother (EM) derives from an older Nilo-Saharan root word for father's sister. This meaning shift makes sense only in a cultural context in which one's spouse customarily was the child of one's actual or classificatory father's sister, i.e. was one's cross-cousin or classificatory cross-cousin. Similar instances, in which the derivations of affinal kin terms imply cross-cousin marriage, occur in languages belonging to various different deep branches of the family. The last column of Table 12.1 cites seven specific instances. The data supporting these inferences are further described in the semantic notes to Appendix 1. Figure 12.4 shows the lines of Nilo-Saharan language descent for which the evidence implies an earlier presence of this practice.

Interestingly, however, none of the five affinal kin terms that can be reconstructed to various of the early Nilo-Saharan eras, from proto-Nilo-Saharan to the proto-Saharo-Sahelian period (Figure 12.3b), shows any such telltale

Table 12.1 Selected cases of Nilo-Saharan kinship organization

Society	Cousin terminology	Parents' siblings terminology	Cross-cousin marriage
Uduk (Koman)	Iroquois	bifurcate collateral, from former lineal, from still earlier bifurcate collateral	
Mbay (Central Sud.)	Sudanic (all terms descriptive?)	bifurcate merging	
Lugbara (Central Sud.)	Hawaiian	bifurcate collateral [but with compound terms reflective of a previous bifurcate merging view of P(G)]	implied: FZ > EM (PS root 3)
Kunama	part Hawaiian (MGC = G), part Eskimo (FGC); but implied earlier Crow (FZ = DH, via FZC: PNS root 6)	mixed bifurcate merging (MZ) and bifurcate collateral (FB)	implied: FZ > FZC > DH (ws) (PNS root 6); also MB > HF(ws) (PNoS root 2)
Kanuri (Saharan)	Hawaiian	bifurcate merging (except that FZ = F, FB)	implied: EP < MB (PNS root 9)
Zaghawa (Saharan)	part Hawaiian (FGC = G), part Eskimo (MGC)	bifurcate collateral	
Teda (Saharan)	Sudanic (all terms descriptive)	bifurcate collateral	
For (Sahelian)	Hawaiian	bifurcate collateral	implied: EM < FZ (PSah root 3)
Songay (W. Sahelian)	Sudanic (some terms descriptive)? FZC/MBC < earlier FZ implies prior Crow system	bifurcate merging	
Maba (W. Sahelian)	Sudanic (attested terms descriptive)	lineal, except for possible FZ = MZ	
Dongolawi (E. Sahelian: Astaboran)	Sudanic (mostly descriptive terms)	bifurcate collateral (all terms descriptive except MB), but from underlying bifurcate merging	

Table 12.1 *Continued*

Society	Cousin terminology	Parents' siblings terminology	Cross-cousin marriage
Gaam (E. Sahelian: Kir-Abbaian)	Hawaiian, but implied earlier Crow (see last column)	bifurcate merging, except that MZ = MB	implied: MB > MBC > H (N. Middle Nile Basin root 1)
Majang (E.Sahelian: Kir-Abbaian)	Eskimo (MGC); Hawaiian (FBC)	bifurcate collateral, except that FB = F	
Anyua (E. Sahelian: Kir-Abbaian: W. Nil)	Sudanic (all terms descriptive)	bifurcate collateral, except that FB = F	implied: FZ = BW(ws) = EZ(ws)
Nandi (E. Sahelian: Kir-Abbaian: S. Nil)	Iroquois; implied earlier pre-SNil Crow (MB = FZC implies earlier MB = FZ = FZC (i.e., Crow), *before* Kalenjin borrowing of Luhya Bantu *-senge FZ)	bifurcate merging	
Turkana (E'rn Sahelian: Kir-Abbaian: E. Nil: Ateker)	Sudanic (all stems simplex, although with prefixes)	lineal (PZ); bifurcate merging (FB = F) (pattern may reflect Western Rub (Soo) contacts with proto-Ateker)	
Teso E. Sahelian: Kir-Abbaian: E. Nil: Ateker	Iroquois, Crow or Hawaiian (FZC, MBC not known)	lineal (PZ); bifurcate merging for FB (not recorded)?	
Ik (E. Sahelian: Rub)	Crow	bifurcate collateral, except for FB = F	
Soo (E. Sahelian: Rub)	Sudanic, except that FBS = B, FBD = Z (all terms except FBS/D are descriptive)	lineal (PZ); bifurcate merging (one term for FB = F)	implied: MB > MBC > HZ (PNS root 6)

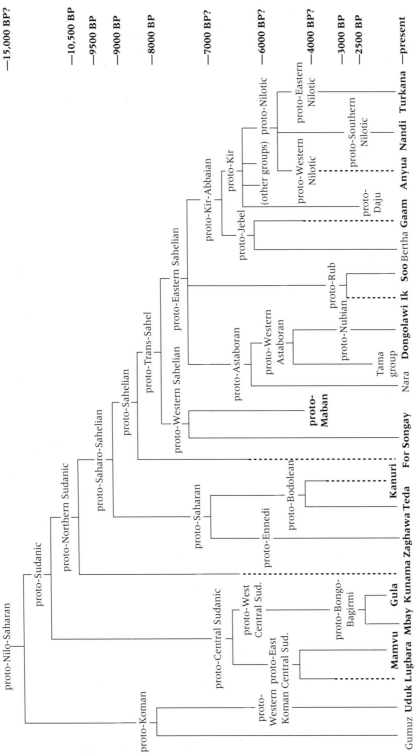

Figure 12.4 Cross-cousin marriage in Nilo-Saharan kin history. Heavy dashed lines identify the instances in which the lexical histories imply the former presence of cross-cousin marriage. Approximate datings for historical language nodes appear along the right-hand side. (© Christopher Ehret)

derivation from parent's sibling terms. The consistent lack of this kind of derivation in the in-law terms of the early strata of Nilo-Saharan history, in contrast to the numerous separate appearances of this kind of semantic link in later descendant languages, suggests that cross-cousin marriage preferences might have come into being in Nilo-Saharan-speaking societies only after the proto-Saharo-Sahelian period and that they may have arisen separately in different regions.

Unilineal Kinship Institutions among the Nilo-Saharans

The developments in Nilo-Saharan kin terminology link up with another old aspect of Nilo-Saharan, the existence far back of unilineal kinship of a particular kind. Relict distributions of matrilinear institutions occur in each of the deep branches of the family, and the presence of this kind of descent and inheritance in societies stemming from the deepest divisions within the family implies the possible existence of matrilineage or matriclan institutions back to the proto-Nilo-Saharan society. The Uduk of the Western sub-branch of the Koman primary branch of the family are matrilineal in descent and inheritance (James 1979), and so apparently are the Gumuz (Hilke and Plester 1955), who form the other sub-branch of Koman. Matrilineal descent persists also in a considerable variety of populations whose languages belong to distant subgroups of the Sudanic primary branch. The Kunama, whose language constitutes one of the two primary divisions of the Northern Sudanic branch of Sudanic, are matrilineal. In the Astaboran subgroup of Eastern Sahelian, the evidence of the previous prevalence of matriliny is pervasive. The Nara, who form one primary branch of Astaboran, are to this day matrilineal, and the presence of matriliny among at least one modern-day Nubian people, the Midob, along with the historical indications of earlier matrilineal institutions among the Nile Nubians, favours the reconstruction of this kind of descent for the proto-Nubian society of the second or first millennium BCE. In the Kir-Abbaian subgroup of Eastern Sahelian, matrilineal descent and inheritance were present up till recent times, or perhaps still are, among the Bertha and at least certain of the Daju.

A second indicator of prior widespread matriliny among Nilo-Saharans is the presence or the implied earlier existence of Crow systems in languages belonging again to several deep branches of the family, including both the Kunama and Saharo-Sahelian primary branches of Northern Sudanic. At least one people, the Ik of the Eastern Sahelian subgroup of Nilo-Saharan, maintain Crow terminology today. This terminology is characteristically connected to matriliny, and when it persists in a patrilineal society, it implies the former presence of matrilineal descent (Murdock 1949, 1959).

Other Nilo-Saharan societies maintain indirect indications that they possibly formerly had matrilineal descent. The For pattern of settlement in matrilocal extended families suggests, as in other such instances, the relatively recent existence of matrilineal principles there (Murdock 1959: 143). Among the Tibu and some Zaghawa-related people of the Saharan sub-branch of Saharo-Sahelian, the custom of an initial period of matrilocal residence after the marriage also makes sense as a feature left over from an earlier matrilineal era.

Figure 12.5 depicts the distribution in the various branches of Nilo-Saharan of features indicative of ancient matriliny. Heavy solid lines mark the lines of descent leading up to societies that in either recent or earlier historical times were matrilineal. Heavy broken lines denote the cases in which the semantic histories of Nilo-Saharan root words reveal the earlier presence of Crow cousin terminology along that line of descent (see the second column of Table 12.1). Heavy dotted lines identify lines of linguistic descent of societies showing features possibly left over from prior eras of matriliny. The dotted parts of all three types of line project these features back into the past, connecting up the nodes of relationship from which come the various lines of descent that have matriliny or are inferred to have had it in the past. The various lines of descent marked in these ways link up, node by node, back to proto-Northern Sudanic, providing strong support for reconstructing matriliny back to that period.

The continuity of this progression back in time is broken at the proto-Sudanic node, intervening between Northern Sudanic and proto-Nilo-Saharan, by the lack of any indication as yet of former matrilineal descent in the Central Sudanic branch.

Did unilineal kinship of a matrilineal kind already exist among the proto-Nilo-Saharans, and simply get fully changed over to patrilineal in proto-Central Sudanic, or did this institution develop separately in Koman and proto-Northern Sudanic? In deference to Ockham's razor, we should not unduly multiply our explanations. The presence of matriliny in both the deep branches of Nilo-Saharan, as shown in Figure 12.5, and the recurrent evidence of former matriliny in Nilo-Saharan societies no longer so organized, is certainly most parsimoniously accounted for if we trace this trait back to the original society. But the second, still relatively parsimonious possibility is that bilateral descent existed down to the second stratum in Nilo-Saharan linguistic history, proto-Sudanic. If we adopt this explanation, two separate creations of unilineal institutions based on matrilineality need be postulated, among the proto-Northern Sudanians and among the proto-Koman – not a perfect parsimony but still economical. This explanation would account in simple fashion for the contrasting universality of patriliny among modern-day Central Sudanic peoples. The proto-Central Sudanic society would, in this view, have taken a different direction of kinship development after the proto-Sudanic period than did the proto-Northern Sudanic people, changing from bilateral to patrilineal rather than matrilineal descent and inheritance.

This proposal intriguingly situates the development of unilineal institutions in a period of major changeover in material circumstances. According to the lexical and correlative archaeological evidence, as previously discussed, the proto-Northern Sudanic people, beginning around 10,500 BP, set in motion the shift from foraging to food production. Food production, by greatly increasing the amount of food that can be extracted from the same amount of land, tends to lead to both growth of population overall and growth in the size of local communities and thus to the need for more formal institutions of cooperation and cohesion. In this situation the reconstitution of obligations to small-scale, personally known kin into the relations of unilineal descent creates persistent

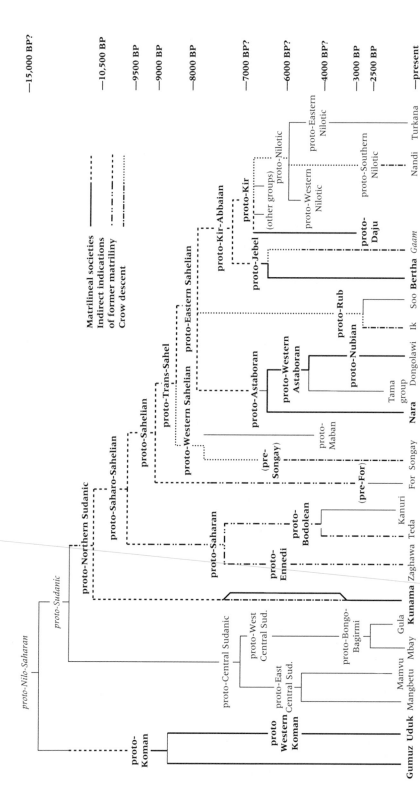

Figure 12.5 Evidence for early matrilineal descent in the Nilo-Saharan language family (© Christopher Ehret)

integrative institutions out of what would otherwise be continually dispersing and dissolving kin links as population grew and expanded with the adoption of the new economy.

The most parsimonious explanation of all – that unilineal matriclan organization goes back to proto-Nilo-Saharan – cannot, on the other hand, be ruled out. Hunter-gatherer societies of more recent millennia, especially those in more productive foraging environments, certainly have not all been bilateral. The Dahalo of the Kenya coast, who were organized in patrilineal clans, come immediately to mind, as do a variety of matrilineal and patrilineal California Indian societies. If the proto-Nilo-Saharan society, in existence significantly before 11,000 BP, was already matrilinear in descent, its people must have exploited a relatively productive set of environments, able to support a denser population than most parts of Africa, despite the Terminal Pleistocene having been a period of very dry environments and low productivity in many parts of the continent. Reliance on the aquatic food resources of the Nile and its tributaries in what is today the southern and eastern Sudan may have been that adaptation.

Early Khoesan Kinship

The Khoesan language family has a great time depth, perhaps greater than that of Nilo-Saharan. The usually accepted correlation of Khoesan with the Eastern African Microlithic complex would place the ancestral period at 18,000 or more years ago. As previously noted, Khoesan loanword sets in non-Khoesan languages of East Africa reveal the ancient existence of several other, now extinct branches of the family, each having the same kind of very deep-time relationship to the still-spoken East African Khoesan languages, Sandawe and Hadza, as these two have to each other and to the Southern African branch. Because the interrelationships among the extinct languages are unclear, several provisional stratigraphical trees of the Khoesan family are possible. Figure 12.6 presents three of those alternative subclassifications.

The three extant branches provide nearly all the currently available evidence for lexical reconstruction of kin terms. A single provisional reconstruction, of a term for younger sibling (see Figure 12.7), rests on loanword evidence from the extinct Khoesan languages of northern East Africa. In analysing this evidence for our purposes here, the three branches, Hadza, Sandawe, and Southern African Khoesan (SAK), are treated as coordinate divisions of the family. Some scholars consider Sandawe and SAK closer related to each other than to Hadza. (Three alternative trees with this configuration of Sandawe relationships appear in the on-line materials as Figures A, B, and C.)

Reconstructing the Lexicons of Ancient Khoesan Kinship

Successively fuller portions of the kin terminology can be reconstructed for the three successive strata in the Khoesan linguistic history attested by still-spoken

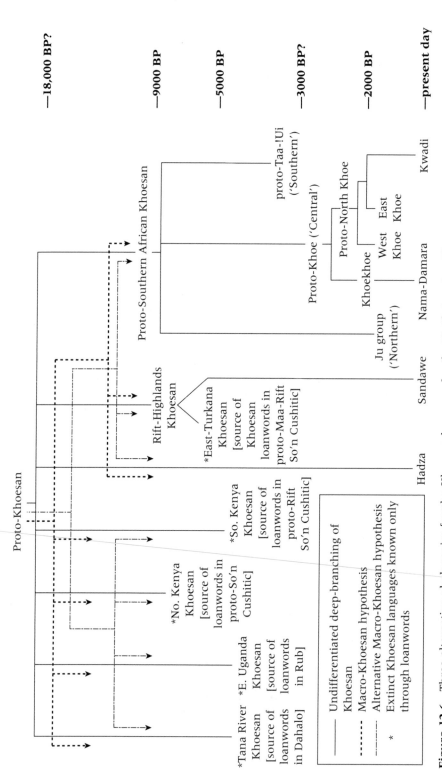

Figure 12.6 Three alternative phylogenies for the Khoesan language family (© Christopher Ehret)

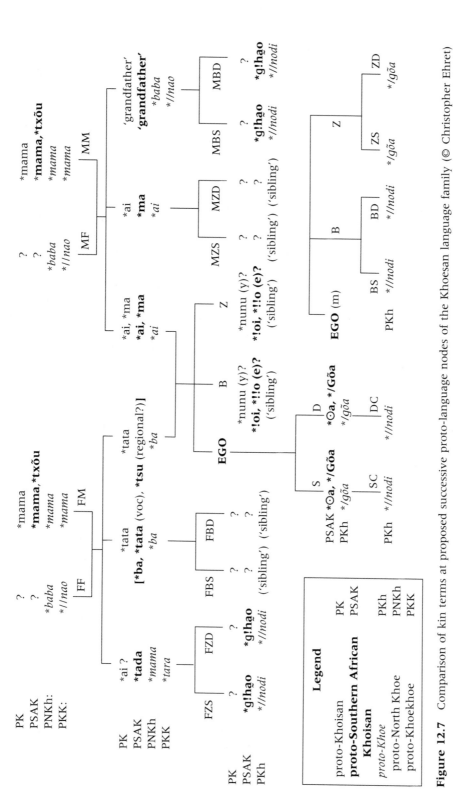

Figure 12.7 Comparison of kin terms at proposed successive proto-language nodes of the Khoesan language family (© Christopher Ehret)

languages – proto-Khoesan (PK), proto-Southern African Khoesan (PSAK), and proto-Khoe (PKh). Appendix 2 lays out the evidence in a fashion comparable to the manner in which Appendix 1 presents the Nilo-Saharan materials. For proto-Khoesan, spoken probably before 15,000 BP, and possibly long before that time, only a few basic terms are yet known. But at the PSAK stage, dating to around the ninth or eighth millennium BP, the reconstructible lexicon includes terminology for cousins as well as parent's siblings, and still further details emerge for proto-Khoe, spoken in the first millennium BC.

How these kin terms combined in the kinship systems at each stage is depicted in Figure 12.7. In several instances, evidence is insufficient to determine the exact word to reconstruct for a particular meaning, but the semantic links of the particular item to other kin terms is so consistently the same throughout the group of languages concerned that this link can be reconstructed. It is unclear, for example, precisely what the word for 'grandfather' was in either the proto-Southern African Khoesan language or its later daughter language proto-Khoe, but we can strongly argue from recurrent semantic patterns in the descendant languages of each that whichever word expressed the relation 'grandfather' in either period also identified 'mother's brother'. In such an instance the English translation of the relationship link, in quotation marks, appears in the figure in place of a particular reconstructed word. The structuring of the system, in other words, can be reconstructed in these cases, even if not the exact word for some of the elements of the structure.

For the Khoesan family, it is possible to propose the likely cousin and parents' siblings systems of the proto-language period, even with the lack as yet of specific reconstructed roots for those particular relations. Comparative analysis of the systems in different branches of the family provides the key. Barnard (1992) gives extensive and detailed presentations of the kin systems among the Southern African Khoesan peoples. In addition, the patterns for Hadza and Sandawe as well as for Zhu and the two best-studied !Ui-Taa languages of the SAK branch are published in the on-line collection of African kin diagrams for this chapter. Table 12.2 sums up the salient characteristics of cousin and parents' siblings terminology and also directs attention to a recurrent feature of grandparent–grandchild terminology in Khoesan languages, of striking strength and frequency almost everywhere in the family.

Kin Patterns of Early Khoesan Societies

These various data allow a variety of proposals about the early evolution of kinship systems among the peoples of the Khoesan language family.

1 Proto-Khoesan society probably had an Iroquois cousin reckoning system. This feature appears in all but a single subgroup of Southern African Khoesan and appears to be present in both Hadza and Sandawe, the other two extant deep branches of the language family.
2 Proto-Southern-African-Khoesan society probably had a bifurcate merging pattern of parents' siblings terminology:

Table 12.2 Khoesan kinship organization

Society	Cousin terminology	Parents' siblings terminology	Grandrelation-collateral links
Hadza	Iroquois (terms for FZC uncertain)	generational, except for distinct word for MB	PF = MB PM = MBD = CD MBS = CS
Sandawe	Iroquois (terms for FZC uncertain)	generational, except for distinct word for MB	Not present
Proto-Khoe	Iroquois	bifurcate merging	PF = MB PM = FZ CC = FZC/MBC = ZC (ms), BC (ws)
Zhu	Eskimo	lineal	PM = PGD = EZ PF = PGS
Eastern ≠Hoã (Taa-!Ui)	Iroquois	lineal	PF = MB/FB PM = CC = FZ/MZ = MBC/FZC = yGC
!Xoõ (Taa-!Ui)	Iroquois	bifurcate merging	PF = MB = CC = ZC (ms) = BC (ws); PM = FZ = EG

   (a)   lineal terminology is limited to two groups;

   (b)   bifurcate merging systems seem present everywhere else and are supported by the reconstructed PSAK kin terminology (Figure 12.7).

3 Proto-Khoesan society may have had a particular unbalanced semantic pattern in its parents' siblings terminology (the Sandawe and Hadza data need rechecking to be sure of this):

   (a)   MZ = FZ = M, FB = F (generational); but

   (b)   MB = PF.

4 The kin equation, MB = PF, not found in the other language family reconstructions – although sporadic instances do occur in individual languages of the other families – is attested in Hadza and in all Southern African Khoesan branches except Zhu. This pattern is therefore to be reconstructed to proto-Khoesan (see Figure 12.7).

5 The corollary identification FZ = PM, postulated for PSAK, can be explained as a logical extension of the original proto-Khoesan PF = MB equation to the corresponding paternal category, thus regularizing a suggested PK part-generational, part-bifurcate-merging system into fully bifurcate merging in the proto-Southern African Khoesan society.

6 The global extension in the Eastern ≠Hoã language of this pattern to all parents' siblings – of MB = PF to FB = PF and of FZ = PM to MZ = PM – accounts for the shift of parents' siblings terminology in that language from bifurcate merging to lineal.

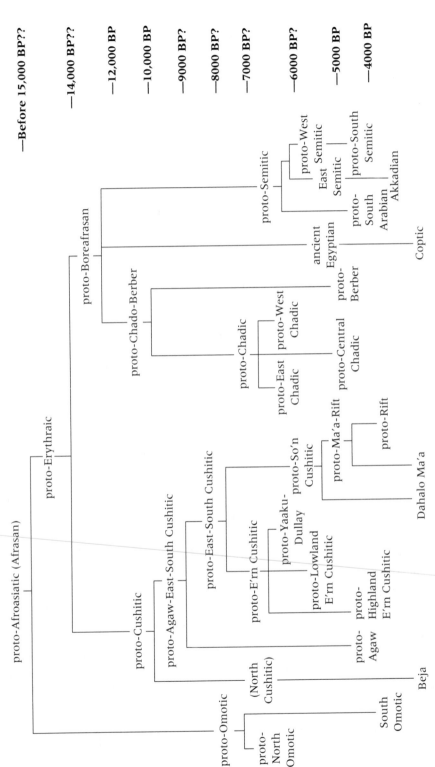

Figure 12.8 Language phylogeny for the Afroasiatic (Afrasan) language family, with approximate datings (© Christopher Ehret)

The double shift in Zhu from Iroquois to Eskimo cousin nomenclature, and from bifurcate collateral to lineal parental sibling terminology (Table 12.2), makes sense as a single systemic shift away from bifurcate reckoning. In pre-proto-Zhu, preliminary to this changeover, the domain of the older Khoesan MB = PF, FZ = PM equation would have expanded to encompass both the parents and their children (ego's cross-cousins), distinguishing them by gender rather than generation, so that in pre-proto-Zhu MB = MBS = FZS = PF and FZ = FZD = MBD = PM. When proto-Zhu subsequently shifted to a lineal system of parent sibling terms, it did so by extending the term for FB to include MB and the term for MZ to include FZ, thus displacing the older terms for MB and FZ. The shift to Eskimo cousin terminology was a parallel extension of the semantic domains of certain older cousin terms to all the collateral lines. In this case, though, it was the existing terms for cross-cousins that expanded their domain to include the parallel cousin slots: the term for FZS/MBS became the word for PGS in general; the term for FZD/MBD became the general word for PGD. In this way the older Southern African Khoesan MB = PF, FZ = PM equation was indirectly preserved, demonstrating that the Zhu system, different as it is, nevertheless developed out of the original PSAK Iroquois and bifurcate collateral naming system.

Unilineal descent groups were surely not present among the early Khoesan. From the comparative ethnography, bilateral descent appears to have been the original rule. Patriclans exist today among the Sandawe, but over the past 2000 years the Sandawe have interacted with and incorporated large numbers of neighbouring people whose much more ancient possession of unilineal institutions probably provided the historical model for this kind of development. In fact, the great majority of Sandawe clans today are of Southern Cushitic or Bantu origin, while still others are of Southern Nilotic provenance. Some Bantu clans may have originally been matrilineal, but the Southern Cushites, the most important earlier influence on the Sandawe, are entirely patrilineal. In southern Africa, complex segmentary patrilineal institutions formerly characterized the Khoekhoe. The original development of these relationships appears to trace back to developments around 2500–2000 years ago, associated with the radical changes in livelihood occasioned by the Khoekhoe adoption of livestock raising (Ehret 1982, 1997; Elphick 1977).

Early Afroasiatic (Afrasan) Kinship

The Afroasiatic (Afrasan) language family is a large one, but considerable information exists on kinship across much of the family. The arguments from linguistic geography and reconstructed subsistence lexicon, reprised above, converge in making the case that the proto-Afroasiatic people were the originators of, or major participants in, the development of wild grasses and/or wild grains as food in northeastern Africa from before 15,000 years ago. Figure 12.8 lays out the linguistic stratigraphy of the family down to the later periods in which food production separately took hold among different Afroasiatic-speaking peoples. Again, as with the Nilo-Saharan and Khoesan stratigraphies, a provisional

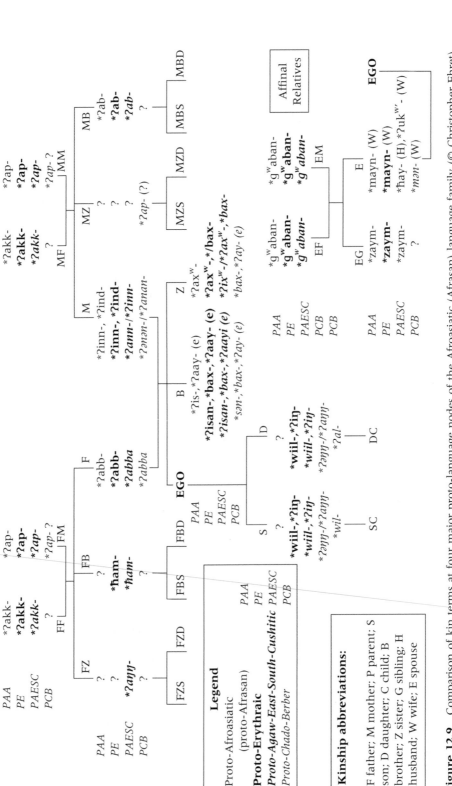

Figure 12.9 Comparison of kin terms at four major proto-language nodes of the Afroasiatic (Afrasan) language family (© Christopher Ehret)

dating scale offers a broad sense of the spans involved in this history. The suggested dating of proto-Afroasiatic rests, of course, on the proposed archaeological correlation with northeastern Africa wild grass collection. A succession of correlations between archaeology, systematic linguistic reconstructions of subsistence lexicon, and the inferences of linguistic geography make the case for the remainder of the proposed dates (most recently surveyed in Ehret 2006a; see also Ehret et al. 2004).

Appendix 3 lists the kinship lexemes currently reconstructed back to the proto-Afroasiatic (PAA), proto-Erythraic (PE), proto-Agaw-East-South-Cushitic (PAESC), and proto-East-South Cushitic periods. Section E of the appendix adds proto-Chadic kin terms. Figure 12.9 displays the overall succession of presently reconstructed kin lexicons, from PAA to PE and from PE to proto-Chado-Berber (PCB) as well as from PE to PAESC. Kin diagrams for proto-Chadic, proto-Eastern Cushitic, proto-Lowland Eastern Cushitic, proto-Southern Cushitic, and proto-Semitic periods, carrying the story to somewhat more recent times, are available in the on-line materials.

Parents' Siblings and Parents' Siblings' Children in Early Afroasiatic

Figure 12.9 gives incomplete evidence on parents' siblings' terms in the early Afroasiatic periods, usually not enough to support firm inferences about the probable overall structures. At the earliest stage, proto-Afroasiatic, all that is clear at this point is that a distinct term existed for mother's brother. Whether FZ, FB, and FM had distinct terms as well or were lineally or generationally denoted, or whether a bifurcate collateral system existed, is not resolvable on the evidence at hand. By the subsequent proto-Erythraic period, however, separate names existed for FB and MB. This evidence might mean that a bifurcate collateral nomenclature for PG existed by this point in time. On the other hand, in a number of the Cushitic languages, separate terms for FB and MB coexist with a lineal reckoning of the aunts, i.e. MZ = FZ, or with a partial bifurcate merging pattern, i.e. M = MZ, but with distinct terms for FZ, FB, and MB.

The later proto-Eastern Cushitic and proto-Southern Cushitic societies most likely did have bifurcate collateral systems; proto-Berber, in contrast, had a bifurcate merging terminology. Different patterns were innovated in different Semitic subgroups. The South Arabian branch developed a bifurcate collateral system, in which the feminine form of the word for MB served as the term for FZ and the feminine of FB named the MZ. Arabic created distinct terms for each aunt and uncle, but did so in opposite fashion by deriving MZ as a feminine of MB and FZ as a feminine of FB.

The specific terms in the early Afroasiatic strata for parents' siblings' children are as yet unknown. The lack of evidence from the Omotic primary branch leaves the proto-Afroasiatic system inaccessible for now. Two terminological patterns predominate in the available evidence from the remainder of the family. Descriptive cousin terminology is virtually universal in the Semitic branch, even among the Ethiopian Semitic subgroup, and must be reconstructed back to proto-Semitic. Descriptive terminologies are present all through the Cushitic-speaking regions as well. The Northern Cushitic people, the Beja, have this pattern, as do the peoples of the Agaw branch, a majority of the Eastern Cushites, and the Dahalo of the Southern Cushitic group. The alternative pattern of any frequency among Afroasiatic speakers is Hawaiian. It was the original proto-Berber system (see Appendix 3, Section B, root 5 for a discussion of the evidence), and it is very widespread among the Chadic peoples. Hawaiian cousin nomenclature is characteristic as well of the Rift branch of Southern Cushitic. Except for a few cases of Iroquois terminology – among the Tuareg of the Berber group, among a small minority of the West Chadic people – descriptive and Hawaiian systems dominate.

What does this evidence suggest about the early cousin naming systems of Afroasiatic societies? The predominance of Hawaiian terminology across the Berber and Chadic groups, and the reconstructibility of this pattern in the proto-Berber case, favours the conclusion that the proto-Chado-Berber society called all cousins by the terms for brother and sister. Descriptive terminology, on the other hand, surely characterized proto-Semitic culture. The wide distribution of the same pattern among the Cushites suggests that this kind of reckoning may separately go back to the proto-Cushitic period as well.

The presence of descriptive cousin terminology has potentially major historical implications. On the whole, if Murdock (1949, 1959) is right, descriptive terminologies tend to be associated with segmentary lineage systems of descent. That association certainly fits both the Semitic and Cushitic cases. The comparative ethnography indicates that the Semites and the Cushites in earlier times, certainly those associated with pastoral economies, both had highly segmentary lineage systems, and these patterns have often continued strongly to persist, not just among Arabs, but among many Cushitic societies as well. Segmentary systems integrate relatively large numbers of people into a hierarchy of unilineal kin relations and therefore tend to evolve only after there exists the subsistence productivity that herding and/or cultivation generate. The development of descriptive cousin terminology among Afroasiatic people must be argued to have arisen separately among the early Cushites and the ancestors of the proto-Semites, thousands of years after the proto-Afroasiatic and proto-Erythraic periods in Afroasiatic history. Proto-Cushitic contained lexicon diagnostic of the herding of cows, sheep, and goats and of the milking of domestic animals (Ehret 1999, 2007), making it possible that segmentary lineage systems along with descriptive cousin terminology could have arisen as early as the proto-Cushitic period of around 10,000 years ago. The proto-Semitic lived in the Middle East several thousand years later, after the beginning of food production there, so the material conditions would also have been met in their case.

What of the cousin terminologies in the earlier, pre-food-production periods in Afroasiatic kinship history? The reconstruction of a Hawaiian system for the proto-Chado-Berber people, who lived in the northern Sahara before food production began to take hold in their regions (Ehret 2007; Ehret et al. 2004), raises the possibility of Hawaiian having been the cousin terminology for the previous proto-Boreafrasan and proto-Erythraic periods. Testing this proposal and seeking to carry the reconstruction farther back in time to proto-Afroasiatic will require extensive collection of cousin terms from the many neglected languages of the family and, especially, from the languages of the Omotic primary branch.

Unilineal Descent among Early Afroasiatic Speakers

For the Cushites, a second kind of evidence exists that further supports the early presence of unilineal descent, if not in the proto-Cushitic period itself, in the immediately subsequent proto-Agaw-East-South Cushitic (PAESC) era. The evidence is a particular named institutional role, *wap'er, traceable to the PAESC language. The comparative ethnographic evidence of recent times consistently shows the bearer of that title, whether among the Iraqw of Tanzania or the Agaw of northern Ethiopia, or in Islamicized form among the Soomaali of the eastern Horn, to have been a hereditary clan ritual chief, a religious intermediary between a clan or a family of related clans and God or a clan deity. The defining social context was the unilineal kin group or family of related lineages over which the *wap'er served as ritual chief. The *wap'er was a clan functionary: the role did not exist outside the context of unilineal descent.

The Cushitic evidence favours the conclusion that from at least the PAESC period the rule of descent was patrilineal. Medieval Arabic records indicate a possible earlier matrilineal pattern among the Beja (Murdock 1959: 314–15). The Beja language contains an early set of loanwords indicating a major cultural impact from a people speaking a Northern Sudanic language. So if the Beja were indeed formerly matrilineal, the Nilo-Saharans who so strongly influenced them were the likely source. But for the rest of the Cushites the evidence is uniform in its indications. No residual evidence exists of any former matrilineality.

Whether unilineal institutions extend farther back in Afroasiatic history than the proto-Cushitic period remains a problem for future investigation. The very old existence of a closely parallel institution of ritual clan chief among the Omotic peoples (Nicolas 1976) does raise the possibility, however, that unilineal descent did have a much older provenance among Afroasiatic speakers. The Omotic group, after all, forms one primary branch of Afroasiatic, coordinate with the Erythraic branch, of which Cushitic is a sub-branch. The presence of a parallel clan-based institution among both Cushites and Omotic peoples may derive from very ancient cross-cultural influences within the Horn of Africa. But it also means that one cannot dismiss out of hand the possibility that these ideas and institutions occurred in both sets of peoples because they date back earlier to the common origins of the Afroasiatic family.

Marriage in Early Afroasiatic History

On the whole, the terminology of affinal relations in Afroasiatic tends not to reveal much about preferential patterns in marriage. Terms for in-laws in most branches of the family lack any indications of their having derived from earlier terms either for cousins or for parents' siblings.

But there is one glaring exception. Uniquely in proto-Semitic, the term for spouse's father (and, with an added feminine suffix, for spouse's mother) derived from the proto-Erythraic root for father's brother (Appendix 3, Section B, root 6). Here is the clearest testimony possible that the custom of preferential marriage to a father's brother's daughter goes back, at the most recent, to the proto-Semitic society of 6000 or more years ago. Taken together, the evidence from Semitic implies that highly segmentary lineage systems, endogamous marriage with preference for FBD, and probably also the strongly patriarchal orientations associated with these customs, were already in effect at the proto-Semitic period.

Just as clearly, the custom of marriage with a FBD does not go back to the very early eras in Afroasiatic history – not to the proto-Boreafrasan period and certainly not to the still earlier proto-Erythraic and proto-Afroasiatic periods (see on-line figures for these periods). It appears to have been a specifically Semitic feature. With the exception of the Beja (North Cushites) – who, under strong Arab influence in recent centuries, have borrowed their word for spouse's parent from Arabic and adopted along with it the idea of preferential marriage with a FBD – no Cushites follow this practice. They generally practise exogamy with respect to the lineage, and most forbid marriage with any first cousins, although cross-cousin marriage is favoured by the Afar of the Eastern Cushitic group. Most Semitic-speaking people of Ethiopia, the major portion of whose genetic ancestry is Cushitic and who have been embedded in the Cushitic milieu for 2000-plus years, also eschew marriage with any first cousins. Many of the Chadic peoples practise preferential cross-cousin marriage, and it appears that, before the arrival of Islam and Arab influence, marriage with FBD did not take place. Similarly, although marriages with FBD occur widely among heavily Arab-influenced Berbers in North Africa, the more isolated Rif were reported to allow marriage with cross-cousins but not parallel cousins (Coon 1931). It seems quite possible from this evidence that preference for cross-cousin marriage dates back to the proto-Chado-Berber society; it seems equally clear that marriage with parallel cousins does not.

Implications for Ancient Human Kinship

From the reconstructions presented here, it apparent that the kin terminological systems anciently present in Nilo-Saharan, Afroasiatic, and Khoesan societies, although differing from each other, were already of kinds widely familiar in the world today. The proto-Nilo-Saharan society, dating to significantly before 11,000 BP and probably as much as 15,000 years ago, had bifurcate collateral terminology for parents' siblings and possibly Iroquois cousin terminology. Very early in Nilo-Saharan history, unilineal descent of a matrilineal type took hold, either already in the proto-Nilo-Saharan period or as two separate developments, one in the Koman branch and the other in the proto-Northern Sudanic society.

The proto-Khoesan people, of 15,000 or more years ago, most likely followed the Iroquois pattern in their cousin terminology. This system seems to have persisted everywhere except in the Zhu branch of Southern African Khoesan. The proto-Khoesan naming system for parents' siblings may have been partially generational, but with a distinct term for mother's brother. The same word used for 'grandfather' also denoted 'mother's brother', and this semantic pattern persisted in a majority of the Khoesan societies down to the present. By the proto-Southern Africa Khoesan stratum of around the ninth millennium BP, the overall system of parents' sibling terms had shifted, if it had not already, to a fully bifurcate collateral one. Bilateral descent was the prevailing pattern through most of Khoesan history.

A still different combination of features marked the proto-Afroasiatic society of 15,000 years ago, or thereabouts. The parents' siblings' nomenclature at the earliest period is not clear, but it seems by the proto-Erythraic period most likely to have been bifurcate merging. An alternative possibility, however, is that PG names followed an unbalanced pattern, with distinct words for MB and FB, but with both the father's and mother's sisters called by the term for 'mother'.

The proto-Afroasiatic cousin terminology is as yet far from being reconstructed. A Hawaiian terminology can be posited for the considerably later proto-Boreafrasan daughter language, and it is possible that this system goes back early in the family. Still later in time, with the rise of food production, the early Cushites and the proto-Semites each separately took up descriptive terminology for cousins, and the social systems in both groups apparently separately evolved from non-complex unilineal descent to segmentary lineage systems.

If the differing kin nomenclatures of these three African language families in the period immediately preceding the end of the last ice age had a common tetradic inspiration, that inspiration lay farther back in time. The value of these findings for our investigation of early human kinship is that they move our base point of knowledge a quarter or more of the way back to the original dispersal of humans out of Africa. If eventually we can undertake this kind of study for enough deep-time language families elsewhere in the world – outside Africa that result may be a long time in coming, though – we may be able, some day, to come much closer to revealing the specific kinship ideas and systems of our last common ancestral period in Africa 60,000-plus years ago.

13

The Co-evolution of Language and Kinship

Alan Barnard

Introduction: On Revolutions and Methods

Social anthropologists frequently lose sight of the really big issues of the discipline, such as cultural difference in the abstract, human universals, and the evolution of human society. This is ironic given that it is often the big issues and difficult questions which lead people into anthropology, even social anthropology, in the first place (see also Layton, this volume). These are also ones which often most inspire anthropology undergraduates. Prehistoric archaeologists, evolutionary psychologists, linguists, and biologists of various kinds have all lent their expertise to the study of human origins, but only rarely have social or cultural anthropologists. I shall try to show here that social anthropology has a place in debating such big issues. For this, we social anthropologists have to look to areas of strength within our own discipline, such as kinship, and to ideas from within the history of social anthropology itself. This has become much more possible than in the past, thanks to advances in genetics, neurology, archaeology, evolutionary psychology, linguistics, and so on. My case rests not simply on social anthropological ideas themselves, but on such ideas in their relation to recent developments in these other fields.

The concern of scholars of human social evolution has been mainly with the last 60,000 or 120,000 years. Little has been done to learn what we can of life before that time. The tendency has been either to assume, at least for the purpose of argument, just one revolution, or to reject the notion of revolutions altogether. In the first category I would put Chris Knight (e.g. 1991), whereas the second characterizes the work of Clive Gamble (e.g. 2007), Alison Brooks (e.g. McBrearty and Brooks 2000), and other recent writers (see also chapters by Knight and Gamble in this volume). This is odd, given the significant changes in brain anatomy, the development of the capacity for language, and the theories about this, which are utterly dependent on revolutionary advances, and given the complexity of social structure and language capacity displayed by *Homo sapiens*. Rather than a mere one revolution or no revolution at all, I think it far more likely that there were several (see also chapter by Gowlett in this volume). Almost certainly, there were at least three. Nearly all prior discussion has been only on the last one, the widely recognized symbolic revolution ('human revolution', 'creative explosion', etc.) that occurred before the migration of Asian and European *Homo sapiens* from Africa.

My argument is based on kinship theory and two theoretical advances within other disciplines, both themselves based on neurological evidence and its relation to fossil finds. The first of these is Robin Dunbar's theory of the relation between neocortex size and social group size among primates, and the second is Derek Bickerton and William Calvin's theory of three stages in the evolution of language. My argument is also consistent with earlier interpretations of the relation between the fossil record and the evolution of cognition, notably by Steven Mithen. Mithen's (1996: 11–16) scheme is itself based in part on Leslie Aiello's (1996) findings on two bursts of brain enlargement, one coinciding with *Homo habilis* (my first revolution) and the other coinciding with early *Homo sapiens* or *Homo heidelbergensis* (my second revolution). This I believe is also consistent with the views of some of those most active recently in the Middle Stone Age excavations at Blombos Cave (Henshilwood and d'Errico 2005), which provide the earliest evidence of the symbolic revolution.

Dunbar (e.g. 1993, 2001, 2003) and Aiello (Aiello and Dunbar 1993) have pointed out that the ratio of neocortex size to group size in non-human primates is constant, and have suggested that it should therefore be possible to predict ideal group sizes for proto-humans and indeed for *Homo sapiens*. The relevant predicted figures are *Australopithecus* group sizes averaging around sixty-five or seventy (before my first revolution); *Homo habilis*, around seventy-five or eighty (the first revolution) and *Homo erectus* typically at around 110; 'archaic' *Homo sapiens* or *Homo heidelbergensis* 120 or 130 (the second revolution); and *Homo sapiens* or Anatomically Modern Humans (AMH) at about 150 (the 'natural' size, at the time of my third revolution). The details are shown in Figure 13.1. As group size increases, so too does the need for language. Whereas grooming forms the basis of communication among chimpanzees, language performs this function among humans – about 20% of our time in each case (grooming for chimpanzees, language for humans). Dunbar (2001: 190–1) estimates that grooming would occupy 43% of time among humans if we had to rely on it instead of language, whereas his proposed threshold beyond which grooming should give way to some sort of language is 30% – in the *Homo erectus* period. Language became a selective advantage, and enabled communication within and between groups. A primitive language should in turn allow migration, including the *Homo erectus* expansion from Africa along the coast to South and Southeast Asia a million years ago.

Linguist Derek Bickerton long argued for two revolutionary advances in the emergence of language (see, e.g., Bickerton 1998), but in a strangely dialogic work co-authored with neurobiologist William Calvin (Calvin and Bickerton 2000) he quite suddenly proposed a new three-phase theory. It is this new theory I follow here. The first linguistic phase is one of proto-language, occurring with the emergence of early *Homo*. In this phase, we have words and phrases, but as yet no real syntax. For example, we might hear 'George

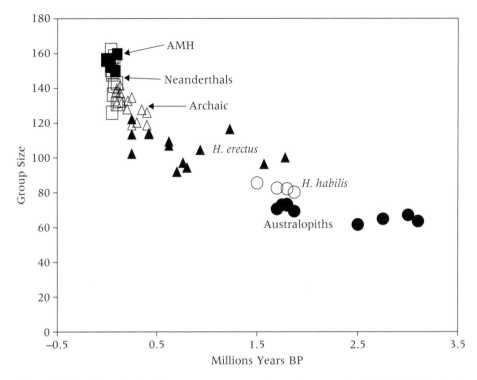

Figure 13.1 The relation between neocortex size and group size (© Robin Dunbar)

meat', without an indication of whether George is eating, whether George is killing edible animals, or indeed whether George is being eaten.

The second linguistic phase is called rudimentary language. It is formed on the basis of proto-language plus what is described as a 'social calculus' entailing reciprocal altruism and distinctions between agent, theme, and goal. Here we do have syntax, but it is not fully developed. It lacks rules such as agreement between subject and verb, or more complex rules of morphology. Thus in this second phase, we can say, for example, 'George eat meat'; but we cannot yet say 'George eats meat', where the 's' in 'eats' refers specifically to 'George' as a grammatically singular subject.

The third phase, that of full language, does have such complex syntax. According to Calvin and Bickerton (2000), it is invented and becomes embedded in organic selection because it enables greater communication, including, I would add, communication for the expression of metaphor and symbolism. Complex syntax enables the reduction of ambiguity and has obvious advantages in the communication of deeper meanings than 'George's' diet.

Although there are technical, philosophical problems in reconciling some of Bickerton's earlier arguments against the slow evolution of syntax with the Calvin and Bickerton model (Botha 2003: 76–81), nevertheless his new three-phase theory makes good sense as the basis of the co-evolution of language and kinship. The three phases proposed by Calvin and Bickerton (2000)

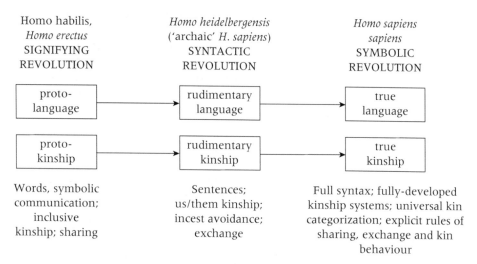

Homo habilis, *Homo erectus* SIGNIFYING REVOLUTION	*Homo heidelbergensis* ('archaic' *H. sapiens*) SYNTACTIC REVOLUTION	*Homo sapiens sapiens* SYMBOLIC REVOLUTION
proto-language	rudimentary language	true language
proto-kinship	rudimentary kinship	true kinship
Words, symbolic communication; inclusive kinship; sharing	Sentences; us/them kinship; incest avoidance; exchange	Full syntax; fully-developed kinship systems; universal kin categorization; explicit rules of sharing, exchange and kin behaviour

Figure 13.2 Calvin and Bickerton's theory of language evolution coupled with the theory of kinship evolution suggested here (© Alan Barnard)

coincide with changes in group size predicted by Dunbar, and with my interpretation of the meaning of both of these theoretical developments for the evolution of kinship structures and other aspects of social organization (see also Barnard in press). This is shown in Figure 13.2.

The Signifying Revolution: Proto-Kinship

To my mind each of the three revolutions bears a passing likeness to a classic formulation in the history of kinship studies, and it helps to envisage them in this way. My vision of the first revolution is of something like Lewis Henry Morgan's (1871: 467–510) stage of primitive promiscuity and subsequent early developments in social evolution. Morgan believed that the earliest human society involved promiscuous sexual intercourse. From this emerged the cohabitation of brothers and sisters, then communal family organization and the sharing of spouses, followed by a classification of cousins in what he called the 'Malayan' style (in the twentieth century, called 'Hawaiian' – all cousins termed as siblings). His later stages involved successively the formation of tribes, 'Ganowanian' or 'Iroquois' classification, marriage between pairs, the 'barbarian' (authority-less) family, polygyny, the patriarchal family, polyandry, private property and lineal succession, the 'civilized' family, and 'descriptive' terminology. These later stages are irrelevant for our purposes here, except in that they hint at his idea of a broad evolutionary trajectory towards patrilineal institutions and descriptive classification. For Morgan, the early phase of classification involved the distinction only of generation and possibly gender, but not yet either what later came to be known as the lineal/collateral distinction or the parallel/cross distinction.

Morgan (1907 [1877]: 5, 35–6) himself held the very modern view that the ability of 'savages' to gesture preceded the development of the vocal apparatus for speech, and held, too, that complex thought preceded language. He makes no claim about kinship terms. However, it is possible that the very first distinctions of the signifying revolution were simply of personal names, with kinship terms following – which some of the classic eighteenth-century writings on the origin of language suggested. In the words of Adam Smith,

> And thus, those words, which were originally the proper names of individuals, would each of them insensibly become the common name of a multitude. A child that is just learning to speak, calls every person who comes to the house, its papa or its mama; and thus bestows upon the whole species those names which it had been taught to apply to two individuals. (1767: 438)

This is the time of the earliest members of the genus *Homo*, either *Homo habilis* or some as yet undiscovered cousin who was the antecedent of *Homo ergaster* and *Homo erectus*. George might mate with Sally, Susan, and Samantha. For whatever reason, he might not mate with Prunella, Patricia, or Pamela. He may or may not come to classify the latter by some relationship category term, by generation (mothers/daughters), or by collateral distance (sisters/not sisters), but the recognition of relationships should follow from the earliest use of proto-language. The ability to classify is one step away from the ability to name, but it accompanies the use of common nouns: we have not just George and Sally, but George, Sally, and 'meat', and maybe 'sex'.

I would suggest further that this stage of evolution is the one in which sharing becomes culturally developed. It is, with *Homo habilis*, a stage accompanied by the production of the earliest stone tools. According to Dunbar's (2003) theory of the social brain, it is also a stage in which grooming gives way to speech or gesture, and some form of language emerges to replace grooming as the primary means of communication. Chimpanzees share, but they lack rules for sharing practices. Morgan would have us believe that 'spouses' were shared, and it is easy to imagine the formalization of society based on family ties, both sexual and non-sexual, in a linguistic milieu which for the first time enables the transmission of knowledge across distances about both people and food. Group size may be seventy-five or eighty, but the population involved in the spread of knowledge, both specific (e.g. on the location of food) and general (e.g. on language, on toolmaking and the cultural transmission of ideas), may have been greater, if not yet marking anything quite like what might be called society. In other words, this was the stage of the family, with society yet to emerge. As in classic evolutionary theory from Sir Henry Maine (1913 [1861]) onwards, I would envisage that society emerged from the family rather than from the pre-familial social contract implied by seventeenth- and eighteenth-century moral philosophers.

It is worth recalling debates of the 1970s, 1980s, and 1990s to put this into perspective. Leslie Aiello and Peter Wheeler (1995) argued that the increased brain size and decreased gut size of *Homo habilis* over the australopithecines accompanied the transition to intensive meat-eating. This in turn was related to increases in group size, and indeed to the intellectual abilities required to

make tools and teach toolmaking skills (see Mithen 1996: 95–114). This suggests that in the great debate between, on the one hand Glynn Isaac (e.g. 1978a,
1978b) and his students and, on the other, Lewis Binford (e.g. 1981), Isaac's
view is at least broadly plausible. In a carefully constructed sequential model
reminiscent of those of nineteenth-century theorists, Isaac argued that early
Homo consumed large amounts of meat, which led in turn to food sharing, a
division of labour, and the acquisition of home bases as opposed to the nests
of fully migratory pre-*Homo* creatures. From this, in his view, developed pair-
bonding and male investment in childrearing, followed by longer dependency
of infants on their parents, and finally enhanced abilities to communicate. Binford
argued that scavenging rather than large-scale hunting was the essence of
Homo habilis subsistence, and therefore that Isaac's model is unsustainable.
Nevertheless, and in spite of the lack of archaeological evidence one way or
the other, the relation between meat-eating, brain size, group size, and communication suggests that sharing, if not necessarily pair-bonding, would form
the basis of *Homo habilis* sociality.

In short, sharing, including possibly the sharing of mates (or spouses), became
important among early *Homo*; pair-bonding possibly came later with increased
time spent in the socialization of children. Early *Homo* had names, and possibly categories of kin as they had categories of other things. If fathers were
unknown, at least mothers would be known. Indeed, we might at such an early
stage see the signification of brothers and sisters, and of mates. Names are
absolute labels, and kinship terms are, in more senses than one, relative labels.
The development of the latter, along with cultural mechanisms of sharing
between categories of relatives, leads directly to a kind of social culture which
no doubt complemented the learning and spread of material culture by *Homo
habilis* and the ancestors of *Homo ergaster*.

The Syntactic Revolution: Rudimentary Kinship

The second revolution is reminiscent of John F. McLennan's theory of the
transition from bride capture to exogamy. McLennan (1970 [1865]: 5–10) begins
Primitive Marriage with an argument that neither 'the geological record'
(archaeology) nor philology can tell us much about the earliest forms of
family life, marriage, and kinship. Archaeology, he says, looks to what people
ate, their weapons and ornaments, while philology does not go far enough back
in time to reconstruct the earliest forms of social structure. Instead, he argues,
we must look to the symbolic meaning of existing customs, of living peoples
at all levels of social evolution, to reconstruct the origins and evolution of human
society. McLennan believed that a shortage of food led to female infanticide,
which in turn led to a shortage of women. Therefore each woman would have
to be married to more than one man. With the polyandrous system that ensued,
the genitor of any given child would be hard to determine. Thus descent came
to be matrilineal. In order for men to gain control over their wives and progeny,
the practice of bride capture came into being. This led to war, which in turn
led to a desire for peace. Exchange of women as wives then replaced bride

capture, paving the way for patrilineality, patriarchy, and, ultimately, nineteenth-century civilization.

Haim Ofek (2001), an economist with an interest in the Palaeolithic, argues that in contrast with other primates, humans communicate with non-kin and strangers, and therefore are mobile, interbreed across boundaries of genetic isolation, and exchange both mates and goods. He even suggests (Ofek 2001: 120–1) that market exchange may have originated as long ago as two million or 1.5 million years ago (the time of *Homo habilis*) and is related both to the earliest use of stone tools and to the subsequent expansion of *Homo erectus* across much of the world. If he is right, it is certainly reasonable to suppose that an age of exogamy might emerge well before a *Homo sapiens* symbolic revolution. To me, this sounds rather like my second revolution in kinship, in between the signifying and the symbolic. It coincides with the emergence of sentence syntax. Syntax would of course have enabled communication to an unprecedented degree of sophistication, and the coupling of noun phrases and verb phrases would have allowed clear and unambiguous descriptions of exogamic practice and the formulation of jural rules for incest avoidance or for enjoining 'marriage' to classes of kin or strangers. In other words, with syntax comes exogamy.

It is worth remembering that whereas McLennan thought kin terms unimportant, Morgan (1871) saw them as essential tools in his method for the reconstruction of the prehistory of kinship and society. I agree with Morgan that all terminology structures collapse into two types. He called them 'descriptive' (those which make a lineal/collateral distinction) and 'classificatory' (those which do not). For me, however, it is not the lineal/collateral distinction which is important but the parallel/cross distinction. In my earlier paper on this subject (Barnard in press), I termed my two types 'genealogical' (those which do not make a parallel/cross distinction or which are purely descriptive such as 'Sudanese' terminologies) and 'classificalogical' (those which divide relatives into the two categories: parallel and cross). The former, genealogical systems, include terminologies of 'Hawaiian', 'Eskimo', and 'Sudanese' types, and in these kinship is reckoned fundamentally on the basis of genealogical distance. These, because of their simplicity, probably characterized the system of the earliest kin-term-using hominins. The latter, classificalogical systems, include terminologies of 'Iroquois', 'Dravidian', 'Crow', and 'Omaha' types, and here category supersedes genealogical distance. This becomes possible when the same-sex sibling link is conceptually 'closer' than that of opposite-sex siblings. Such a structure will emerge if mating structures become important, and of course they are fundamental (after the third revolution, to come) for the alliance structures which characterize tetradic and moiety systems and indeed those of egocentric-defined alliance networks like those of Naro, G/wi, and other central Bushmen (but not Ju/'hoansi or !Kung northern Bushmen). Exactly why and how they emerged are, of course, difficult questions, but nevertheless questions that should be posed (cf. Barnard 1989).

If the first revolution brought the recognition of categories such as mother and maybe father, and of brother, sister, son, daughter, and mate, the second might have brought rather more. With rudimentary syntax comes the ability to formulate complex kin descriptions, and therefore the recognition, for example, of mothers' brothers and mothers' sisters. This in turn may give even at such an early stage the recognition of the relationships, if not the words, that designate the classic kin categories of Proto-World *kaka* (mother's brother, etc.) as well as *mama* (mother) and possibly *papa* (father) (cf. Bancel and Matthey de l'Etang 2002; Matthey de l'Etang and Bancel 2002). It is very difficult to speculate further on the nature of kinship after the second revolution. Yet we can say, if Calvin and Bickerton (2000) are right, that our hominin ancestors, particularly *Homo heidelbergensis* or a related species, had evolved the abilities to describe kin relationships and actions related to kinship, to converse with their neighbours, and therefore probably to enter into exchange and alliance relations with them. We can also say, if Aiello and Dunbar (1993) are right, that group size had increased to 120, within which groups we should certainly envisage smaller bands interacting with other bands of the same group and possibly with bands of other groups. The increase in neocortex size suggests, too, a level of intentionality and a degree of communication enabling the transmission of knowledge about resources, populations, and kinship over geographical distances. Dunbar (2004: 108–37; in press) has suggested that the earliest Archaic *Homo sapiens* or *Homo heidelbergensis*, along with Neanderthals, probably filled what he envisages as a 'bonding gap' via the development of sophisticated communication through chorusing, and possibly dance, prior to the development of full language among Anatomically Modern Humans (AMH). At this pre-Modern stage, we would anticipate, too, the possibility of exogamy, if not yet its full fruition as part of an elementary structure of kinship.

The Symbolic Revolution: Elementary Structures of Kinship

If the first revolution was Morganian and the second McLennanist, the third was Lévi-Straussian. It is my contention that the dawn of true kinship coincides with the emergence of something like elementary structures of kinship. Claude Lévi-Strauss's (1969b [1949]) classic vision of kinship divides the world of kinship into elementary structures (those maintained by a positive rule of marriage, e.g. to marry the category of the 'cross-cousin') and complex structures (those maintained by a negative marriage rule, e.g. to marry someone not classified as a 'sister'). Elementary structures include those of 'direct exchange', where Group A gives women as wives to Group B, and Group B may reciprocate; and those of 'generalized exchange', where Group A gives to Group B and Group B is not allowed to reciprocate, but must give its women to Group C, and so on. Lévi-Strauss argues that kinship is based on a principle of reciprocity, that dual organization (society divided into moieties) is logically simplest. He suggests further that systems of generalized exchange, which characterizes many kinship systems in Asia and some in Australia, are an improvement over direct exchange in that they allow for the expansion of kin networks by bringing new groups into alliance structures. Complex systems are a further development, and in evolutionary terms more advanced than generalized exchange and direct exchange.

The simplest elementary structure in Lévi-Straussian terms, then, and the one which we might imagine to characterize the earliest full kinship, is a moiety structure. However, moiety systems do not allow the formal recognition, in terms of sociocentric categories, of genealogical level (my generation/the one above or below me). The obvious alternative would be to look to four-part, rather than two-part, structures. Nick Allen's model of the logically simplest kind of system is based on this notion (e.g. Allen 2004 and this volume). Much of Allen's concern has been with the evolution of kinship structures since the symbolic revolution, in other words, with the origin of tetradic structures (which he sees as constituting the first complete kinship systems) and with their breakdown (see, e.g. Allen 1989b). In this chapter, I am concerned with earlier periods too, and while I am happy to concede tetradic structures as both logically simple and occurring early in the stage of full language and symbolic thought, they are nevertheless not the only possibility. Even with repeated generational equivalences in terminology and social recognition (in both cases, grandchildren being equated with grandparents), with a parallel/cross distinction, and with universal extension of kin categories, purely egocentric systems (i.e. systems with no sociocentric categories like section or moieties) can be maintained. Naro kinship works in this way (e.g. Barnard 1978b). Allen's assumption is that tetradic structures are prior and tend, ultimately, to break down. The same is true though of other forms of elementary structure, including moiety systems. Either way, we can say almost for certain that the earliest full or elementary kinship structures were 'universal' in the sense that in any given society everyone classified everyone else as 'kin' (Barnard 1978c). In universal kinship systems, any strangers who might have cause to engage in marital alliance or possibly even the trade of material goods would be fitted into kin relations, since society was definable entirely on a kinship basis. This is true today of peoples who practise direct exchange, and of virtually all hunting-and-gathering societies (whether of savannah, deserts, arctic wastes, or rain forests) and small-scale cultivating societies (such as those of the rain forests of South and Southeast Asia and South America).

With the evolution of full kinship, several potential structures were available to our ancestors, but these are all characterized either by making a parallel/cross distinction or not making one. For a great number of reasons, not least the ease in maintaining elementary principles (positive marriage rules), I favour the idea that the earliest full kinship systems did make that distinction. Other reasons include the necessity to differentiate opposite-sex individuals by category, and the likely extension of such categories through links to close kin in a universal system; the probable association of such structures with the evolution of sexual taboos and other aspects of symbolic culture (cf. Knight et al. 1995); and the very widespread occurrence of elementary structures, same-sex sibling joking and opposite-sex sibling avoidance, and the related parallel/cross distinction itself among the world's small-scale societies today. That still leaves the problem of how the parallel/cross distinction is played out. Lévi-Strauss (1969b [1949]) maintained it was a product of moiety structures

reminiscent of those of contemporary South America. Allen maintains classification distinctions through tetradic structures, which may or may not imply
moieties intersecting alternating generations. I maintain a third possibility as
the simplest: the structures can be generated purely by relations among siblings in small social groups and the distinction between possible mates and
those not possible in the next generation (see Barnard 1999). Young people
'marry' their cousins, but only their cross-cousins, and egocentric kinship alone
can do this. In short, neither moieties nor Australian-type sections are needed
– a point noted, too, by Allen (2004), whose vision of tetradic structures is
not dependent on the differentiation of egocentric and sociocentric categories.

Whatever the actual earliest full kinship system, however, it was a product
of the distinction between possible spouses and prohibited spouses, a distinction in kinship theory which after the publication of *The Elementary Structures
of Kinship* (Lévi-Strauss 1969b [1949]) overthrew the then-current notion of
seeing kinship primarily in terms of descent groups. My proposition is that
the earliest system was universal, but of course not all kinship systems are.
What makes a kinship system 'full' is, first, that it recognizes that most crucial
of distinctions, between possible and prohibited, and, secondly, that it allows
for classification of a set of relatives on both sides of the family. In all such
cases, the classification will be uniform, or will rapidly become uniform in the
case of a system in transition, in what we consider a society. The situation is
analogous to that in language: pidgins become creoles; bilingual people, even
children, do not mix English and French indiscriminately; above all, no one
speaks half a language (see also Barnard in press). The point is that no one lives
in a society where there is half a kinship system, or where relatives play by
different rules. Of course, kinship systems change through time, but in order
to maintain the systematic nature of kinship, change has to be rapid – and it
generally is. Kinship systems are, or rapidly become, logical. Like languages,
they are always fully formed. Kinship terminologies are, if not always, at least
usually internally logical, as demonstrated, for example, by the fact that if I
call, say (in an 'Omaha' structure), my FZS '(cross-)nephew' he will call me
'(cross-)uncle'.

The recognition of kinship links beyond the nuclear family, the acquisition
of ties to in-laws as well as to spouses, and classification of society according
to kin categories would undoubtedly give early symbolic people the facility,
and indeed encourage the propensity, for communication through enhanced
rules for exchange and sharing. Add to this the ability, through art, linguistic
metaphor, and symbolic representation, for cultural elaboration, and the
relation between society, culture, and language becomes humanly 'complete'
(cf. Knight et al. 1995).

The Break-Up of Elementary Structures

Later, there would in a sense be a fourth 'revolution' – the Neolithic transition.
In terms of kinship, the Neolithic is marked not by a stone tool tradition or
by the adoption of agriculture, but by the loss of universal kin classification

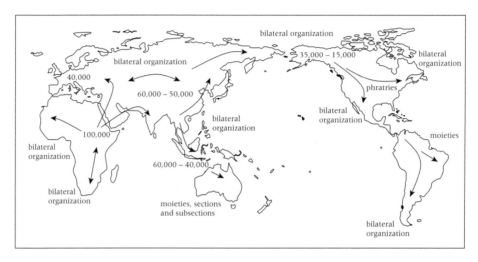

Figure 13.3 The *Homo sapiens* Out of Africa global migration: with kin group structures proposed for relevant dates before the present (© Alan Barnard)

and the change from elementary to complex structures of alliance. These changes did not necessarily occur immediately and were not inevitable (as evidenced today by the persistence of such structures among Dravidian speakers), but they were nevertheless perhaps a logical consequence of neolithization. It may be best to think of the true revolutionary change in mode of thought as occurring, not at the beginning, but at the end of a slow (over a thousand years) Neolithic transition. In other words, the true 'Neolithic revolution' followed rather than accompanied the Neolithic transition (see also Barnard 2007). It is in this period of transition that we still find remnants of direct exchange, for example in South America, where moiety systems occur along with horticulture.

The transition, of course, was preceded by the *Homo sapiens* Out of Africa migration, and it led to the creation of the variety of kinship structures found today. Figure 13.3 illustrates the Out of Africa migration and the kinship group structures now found among hunter-gatherers in the various parts of the world. As shown by both N. J. Allen (1989b) and Maurice Godelier (2004: 511–53), terminology structures eventually evolved (or broke down) from 'Dravidian' and 'Iroquois' forms to forms which do not differentiate parallel from cross-relatives or which simply make all possible distinctions, forms that include 'Hawaiian', 'Eskimo', and 'Sudanese' structures alike. The genealogical emerged again from a long age in which kinship was classificalogical, and we find the disappearance of anything like tetradic structures in most of Asia and the Americas accompanying the gradual transition from Lévi-Straussian elementary to complex structures across the globe.

Conclusion

Elementary structures of kinship mark a pinnacle of form in human sociality, from which, ever since the symbolic revolution, we have retreated. Thanks to a combination of classic kinship theory and modern genetic studies, the prehistory of elementary structures can now be charted not only through the migrations of *Homo sapiens* across the globe, but much earlier in prehistory too. My argument is that Morgan's (1871) theory of group marriage hints at our first revolution (the signifying revolution), McLennan's (1970 [1865]) notion of exogamy at the second (syntactic revolution), and Lévi-Strauss's (1969b [1949]) idea of elementary structures our third (the symbolic revolution). Each is related to increases in neocortex size, group size, and technological advance, and the third with the development of symbolic culture. The first is characterized by sharing, the second by exchange, including possibly the beginnings of marital exchange, and the third undoubtedly by further cultural elaboration of these and by fully formed kinship terminologies, universal kin classification, and alliance structures with moiety or tetradic systems or, more likely in the first instance, in my view, egocentric elementary kinship with parallel/cross distinctions and a recognition of genealogical level or generation as a principle.

Let me conclude with the suggestion that it is time for the full incorporation of social or cultural anthropology into the frameworks of both primary research and intellectual debate on human origins. It is also time for the recognition of the study of human origins as a legitimate sub-discipline within social anthropology, as indeed 130 years ago it was.

Acknowledgements

I would like to thank Nick Allen and Robin Dunbar for their extensive comments on an earlier draft, and Robin Dunbar for permission to use his diagram (my Figure 13.1).

Epilogue

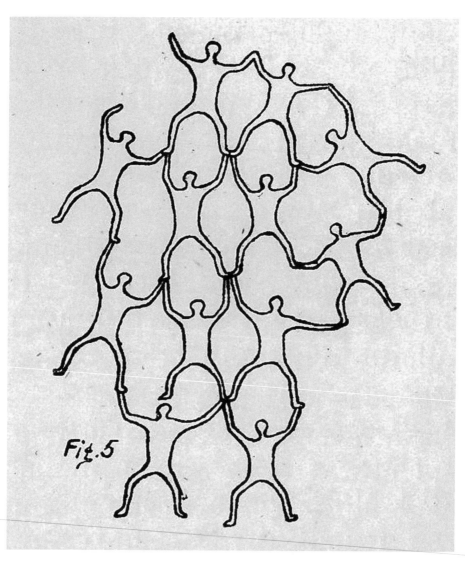

Australian sand drawing: Kamilaroi initiation (R. H. Mathews, *JRAI* 1895: plate XXI)

Reaching across the Gaps

Hilary Callan

Throughout this collection of essays there runs a strong thread of continuity. The workshop on which it is based took place some eleven years after a conference on 'Ritual and the Origins of Culture' (Dunbar et al. 1999), which itself followed on from a series of earlier events organized by the Royal Anthropological Institute, exploring themes common to biological and social anthropology. Several of the contributors to the 1994 workshop and resulting volume also participated in the later one. Focusing on early forms of kinship, the latter event marked a new attempt both to bridge (in a conceptual sense) and to narrow (in a temporal one) the gap between evolutionary and cultural processes as we can understand and represent them. Material presented in these chapters, from a range of methods and research areas, achieves this in impressive detail. My aim here is to highlight some of the continuities and discontinuities in the discussion as they now present themselves; and to suggest how it might be taken forward. What follows is therefore highly selective, and makes no claim to be comprehensive. Where I mention an author without further reference, it is to his or her contribution in this volume.

Returning to 'Big Questions' in Anthropology

Reaching beyond its immediate precursors, this collection has a deeper history. Running through the chapters is a recognition that questions that have been historically constitutive of anthropology as a discipline can now be readdressed in new ways. James in her Introduction sets a bold tone by asking 'Why kinship?' She makes a compelling case, borne out in the other chapters, for the timeliness of drawing on a wealth of new knowledge and methodologies across the domain of anthropology, linguistics, and prehistory, to imagine what the key transitions might have been in the genesis of distinctively human social forms. Taken as a whole, the book takes a journey across the specialisms represented in the chapters: a journey that has also brought a revisitation (and in some cases a re-legitimation) of some of the discipline's founding ideas. Classificatory kinship here becomes interesting in wholly new ways. The Durkheimian notion of 'effervescence' (1915 [1912]) is central to several of the chapters. Allen thinks in terms of vanished tetradic structures leaving 'survivals' within the ethnographic record. Barnard draws substantively on Morgan and McLennan. Knight argues for a rehabilitation of their legacies and that of Bachofen, while presenting a persuasive account of why they largely faded from mainstream view in the twentieth century. Matrilineal and matrilocal patterns are reinvigorated as possibly ancestral forms of kinship organization, in a world emerging as human. There are, naturally, traps to be avoided, and as Layton points out, there was sometimes good reason for the eclipse of early theories based on 'conjectural history'. The authors here do not agree on every point: for example, on the evolutionary status of the 'pair-bond', or matriliny, let alone tetradic organization. That is what 'having a conversation' (James, Introduction) implies. But with the benefit of the information and tools newly available, we begin to see unexpected places in the discipline's history on which to turn the spotlight, and new insights to be drawn from old, and sometimes neglected, arguments and themes.

What Can Evolve? Messy Reality and the Pragmatics of Social Action

In order to take full advantage of the new knowledge becoming available, we need to develop a more sophisticated conception of the social actor in an evolutionary context. We need to be able to think of actors operating strategically within and upon a framework of choices and constraints, having both short- and long-term payoffs attached; and encompassing, crucially, the choices and constraints of others. This collection moves us towards taking seriously the notion of social agency and its evolution as embedded in context and the pragmatics of strategic choice. As Dunbar in particular stresses, choices and their consequences for Darwinian fitness are *intrinsically* context-dependent. Collective accords and strategies in a human world clearly presuppose language, and rest on it. However, material presented here hints at the possibility of a non-language-user gaining Darwinian fitness from a capacity to predict, act with reference to, and possibly manipulate combined and probabilistic effects within a field of social possibilities and constraints. Such a capacity could presumably be a background precondition for language-based forms of collective accord, including those of kinship, within a semantically constituted space.

However, aligning this vision with an evolutionary narrative presents some difficulties on both sides of the story. Here, I shall consider only that of pinning down the facts on the ground on which (or on the genetic substrate of which) Darwinian selection can act. What kinds of phenotype can be present and be subject to selection in a Darwinian environment that is also contextualized? In such a world, what is it that can evolve?

Some Problems with Abstractions

Abstracted 'traits' have often been taken as the appropriate units of analysis and comparison in evolutionary or co-evolutionary modelling of human structures. In some models these are represented as human universals. An example might be the notion of evolved universal 'intuitive theories' of core features of experience: an intuitive physics, engineering, space, biology, ethics, and mind (Pinker 2002: 220ff.). Such 'universals' could yield insights into the transition from pre-human to recognizably human ways of experiencing the world, but tend in practice to display gross ethnocentric bias; the 'we' whose intuitions are generalized to humanity as a whole are, overwhelmingly, historically specific and Western. Elsewhere, as in standard cross-cultural compilations (Murdock 1967), 'traits' appear as variable cultural elements. Here the difficulty is that candidate traits (examples might be particular rules of joking or respect/ avoidance between relatives) are typically not simple or 'surface' descriptions at all. Rather, they come to our attention as abstractions accompanied by their own histories of identification and debate within the ethnographic record. They bring with them their own frames, their contexts, and very often their ideological legacies. Their identification typically rests on categories established at different levels within particular ethnographic traditions. Further, within social anthropology the very notion of 'traits' as conceptual isolates has its own intellectual history linked to the early twentieth-century debates surrounding diffusionism. (For a summary of the historical objections to trait-based forms of diffusionism, and a critical discussion of the relationship between old 'traits' and their new variant, 'memes', see Bloch 2000.)

In order to align such ethnographic constructs with a Darwinian model, we would need to go beyond taking into account the circumstances of original data collection (distortions introduced by the colonial presence, etc.) and the theoretical biases of the ethnographers of particular times and traditions. We would need to deconstruct the categories themselves in order to grasp their relationship to actual social practices and strategies. For a Darwinian model of early human kinship to work, we need to consider how actors with different or shifting interests might move and transact within the genealogical space the emergent rules might give them; and how the contextuality of social action might intersect with a socially generated structure. In a world that is both Darwinian and becoming-human, selection might crucially turn on how and by whom 'rules' of (for example) ownership, production, exchange, distribution of resources, recruitment to groups, are locally understood, rhetorically articulated, and contested. Such detail, though elusive for the deep past, is surely part of Dunbar's search for a 'contextual' account of evolution.

Within evolutionary modelling, a comparable problem confronts abstractions from concrete action that aim to yield units of analysis. A good example is that of 'allocare'. Opie and Power (see also Korstjens) use this construct in an entirely convincing way to evaluate the grandmother hypothesis and its alternatives. At the same time, as everyone knows who has had the care of young children, 'care' itself is an amalgam of many elements – provisioning, actual feeding, protection, socialization, control, cleaning and grooming, comfort, and stimulation, to mention just a few. All incur different demands, can be broken down further, require different trade-offs in other activities forgone, and can in principle be separated. For some purposes – including further elaboration of the grandmother hypothesis itself, as Opie and Power indicate – these may need to be disaggregated before we can fully understand what is going on. To lump them together as 'care' is itself to make a functional judgement on how we expect these actions to be organized; and this may or may not coincide with the realities on the ground. Writers less subtle than our present authors might be tempted to treat a construct such as 'allocare' as if it were a self-evident phenotypic *given* (the analogue here of a cultural 'trait'); and, by failing to deconstruct it, to miss much that is of great interest in prehuman and proto-human strategies of reproduction.

In a comparable way, Knight's summary of contemporary studies of 'partible paternity' (surely a good ethnographic description of what often happens in contemporary Western society's recombined families, despite the hazards of step-parenthood stressed by some evolutionary psychologists) offers a corrective to unexamined notions of 'parental investment'. The 'parental investment' construct is a useful pointer to apparently well established findings that differential parental allocation of resources, including opportunity costs, in sons and daughters occurs in both humans and non-humans; that much of this (though not all) is unconscious even in the human case; and that it is likely to have featured in hominin and early human reproductive strategies. But the problem again is that 'investment' is not a freestanding category of action independent of context and outcome. Knight valuably reminds us of the need to look behind abstracted constructs to underlying strategies and payoffs. We can add that the lesson applies to 'constructs' within both ethnographic and evolutionary discourses.

Multilevel Selection

Multilevel selection as elaborated by Dunbar offers a way through the problem of locating the phenotype on which Darwinian selection can act, in the socially complex world inhabited by some non-human primates and (presumptively) by emergent pre-humans.[1] The critical insight is that 'group living is itself an adaptation carrying costs and benefits in fitness terms'. A consequence of the free-rider problem is that the fitness benefits of sociality are always in tension with those of cheating. Within such a web of tensions, it seems that selection can act at different levels. There can be combined effects, cancelling out, or more complex interaction between the levels. We can imagine context and local circumstance shading the calculus of optimal strategies and producing variable outcomes: a theme elaborated for contemporary hunter-gatherer populations by Layton. In the reproductive environment of *Homo erectus* reconstructed by Opie and Power, which requires contributions to the mother from both female kin and male mates, local conditions, such as resources available for balancing the energy budget, could select for variable strategies, along with the ability to weigh them up. Crucially, within an already social world, Darwinian selection can favour the cognitive capacity to manage the fluid compromises and trade-offs necessary for complex group living: in short, the social brain. The Darwinian phenotype here becomes relative, contextual, and conditional. Without falling into group-selection thinking[2] or departing from the principle that fitness payoffs are scored at genotypic level, multilevel selection enables us to build higher order intentionality and strategy into a Darwinian model of social action (Dunbar 2004: 43ff.). Context-specific structures of opportunity and constraint located at a social level can be the environment in relation to which Hamilton's rule works itself out.

A Sociocentric Shift

Knight analyses some of the reasons – academic and other – behind the naturalization of the ego-centred elementary family in the mainstream anthropology of the twentieth century. As James notes in her Introduction above, a critical shift is made in this collection away from the exclusively ego-centred view of kinship most familiar to Western experience, and hence most readily (by Westerners) represented as rooted in 'nature', to a model that also provides for a sociocentric perspective which may be more representative of kinship structures across the range of ethnography and history. This shift appears clearly in the new treatment given in several chapters to classificatory practices and terminologies; notably in Allen's essay on tetradic kinship. Compared with purely egocentric models, a sociocentric vision of kinship offers a more powerful means to stretch identities and networks across space and time, as Knight argues here for modern Australian Aboriginal section and subsection systems, and Gamble postulates for early expanding groups. Within a sociocentric account of kinship, 'ego' is of course still present as a social actor, but such an account places what James calls the 'ordered character' of human organization squarely at the centre of the analysis. A sociocentric perspective is about coming to agreement on the structuring of social relations; and about ego knowing where he or she stands *vis-à-vis* classes of others and forms of available action in the social universe. And, since structuring is always a dynamic process, it is about coming to agreement on *how* to make future relationships – in other words, about agreeing on rules.

Allen's tetradic structures are an imaginative re-creation of what might be the logically simplest forms of kinship; but the world they inhabit is a human one. If we seek to take a sociocentric vision of kinship a great deal further back in time and use it to shed light on a pre-human or becoming-human world, we are forced to consider how it might be possible to move and transact within a socially created structure whether or not the actors 'in' it could talk about it. Such a scenario would bring us closer to a Darwinian (but also social) world of multilevel selection, context, and choice. What, in such a world, might an actor need to know or grasp? What competences would he or she need to have? How, in turn, might the competences in question be credibly ascribed to actors in such a world? No seamless theory is yet in place, but we begin to see glimpses.

Language and Structure; Structure without Language?

Kinship in a human world is, of course, grounded in language. Ehret's chapter above, while making a clear distinction between evidence for semantic and for social shifts, illustrates the power of historical linguistics as a tool for reconstructing the deep ancestries of kinship terminologies. Fortunato makes effective use of phylogenetic language trees to construct a model for wealth transfers on marriage in early Indo-European societies. New and powerful linguistic tools can extend our knowledge backwards in time towards periods of prehistory where they may add to other kinds of evidence, such as the archaeological record, and so help to reach part of the way across a relatively recent temporal gap.

Looking further back in time, the notion of a sharp division – a red line – demarcating the human world of fully developed language from a non-human, non-linguistic world may be outdated, as James points out in her Introduction (see also Gowlett). Dunbar (2004: 121ff.) brings together fossil anatomical evidence and a calculation of the relationship between group size and the upper limits to grooming time as a means of social bonding to suggest a piecemeal genesis of language: a view elaborated for other periods by Gamble and Barnard. Allen speculates on whether full-blown language is a logical precondition for tetradic structures. It may be productive to envisage an extended period of 'getting it together', with each stage conferring Darwinian advantage. Here, following Gowlett, we can ask: could emergent hominins have 'possessed' structures of kinship in any form without necessarily being able to talk about them in a way that would require full linguistic competence?

A Question of Attribution: How Might 'They' Have Experienced Kinship?

The 'they' here referred to is not intended as an actual or historical 'they'. Whatever model one follows for the emergence of fully modern language, its dating is not certain enough to make any such pinpointing possible.[3] Rather, we can ask whether it is intelligible to credit a hominin actor with a capacity to apprehend structure as a reference for social action without being dependent on language to represent it. What 'knowledge' of the framework of choice, or 'grasp' of structure, can we attribute to non-language-users as a precondition for theorizing about how these would be transformed within a later, semanticized world? Can non-human primates or pre-human hominins be said to have an implicit, non-linguistic 'knowledge' of contextualized pathways of choice in relation to which they could pursue long- and short-term strategies? Could the discussion within contemporary primatology of whether monkeys or apes can have an internal representation of others' awareness (Dunbar 2004; Key and Aiello 1999) be extended to allow them a 'theory' of the networks of relatedness in which they act? Could the great apes be credited with a 'concept' of kinship (Lehmann), or monkeys with a 'grasp' of the apical positioning of grandmothers across daughter-headed matrilines (Korstjens)? In a pre-human context, can we intelligibly credit non-language-users with a capacity to 'perceive' or 'know' a supra-individual *structure* such as one of early kinship, and to move around within it?

The work of Dunbar and others on intentionality and theory of mind (see, for example, Dunbar 2004) provides important cues. Dunbar shows experimentally how successive orders of intentionality in non-human primates and in modern humans form a coherent series. This can be extrapolated to the brain volumes shown in the fossil hominin record to give a good idea when in human evolution the higher orders of intentionality are likely to have emerged. According to this evidence, some orders of intentionality are indeed possible without language. However, mind-reading in this sense is an essentially one-to-one capacity, even where there are several links to the chain and one or more of them is a collective (Shakespeare persuades the audience that Mark Antony knows that his speech will rouse the Roman mob to riot . . . , etc). To attribute an apprehension of *structure* to a non-language-user is a further theoretical step; and it is hard to see how such a claim could be documented experimentally (let alone in the fossil record). Attempts to show individual A acting with respect to an apprehended structure (a dominance *order*, say, or a *category* of potential mates) would be hard to distinguish in practice from theory-of-mind performances (gauging the motivations and intentions of individuals B, C, and D). We need to look in other directions as well.

Whoever and whenever 'they' were, it seems that 'they' were not short of 'things to think with'. As Gamble and Gowlett document from the archaeological record, the conditions of early human life, even before language, will have abounded in objects, technologies, and experiences that would readily lend themselves as metaphors of containment and extension, boundaries, inclusion and exclusion, groups and categories. Archaeological evidence is now impressive for the deep rootedness of the social ordering of the physical world. The body itself has intersubjective rhythms and reciprocities that we can readily imagine forming the basis for social agreement without language. Dancing and rhythmic vocalization are obvious examples of embodied practices on which can be built social accords; as are containers, instruments, and the social ordering of physical space. We can envisage ways in which particular embodied experiences and practices might transform themselves into authoritative metaphors for a socially- and later semantically-constituted sphere. Several of this book's chapters suggest a persuasive scenario for the emergence of publicly recognized categories around which relationships and rules could be negotiated in that indeterminate period (whenever it actually fell) during which space, time, and technology came to be socially ordered in a public way.

Layton reminds us of Bourdieu's concept of *habitus* (a notion not commonly encountered in discussions of evolutionary modelling!) and Giddens's of *agency*. Habitus in particular may offer a pointer to forms of tacit – but often concretely embodied – competence in engaging with structures of choice without necessarily being able to 'talk' about them. Such a construct might prove more fruitful in the long run than others that have been commonly advanced, such as 'symbolic capacity' thought of as an either/or endowment. The interplay of behaviour and rules concerning incest avoidance could, for example, be revisited from this perspective (Fox 1980; cf. Gowlett). A relationship of preadaptation might obtain between habitus in this carefully modified sense, and forms of 'protosymbolic behaviour' such as those described by Mithen (1999). Indeed, forms of embodied competence describable in an imagery of habitus could be thought of as a precursor to Mithen's postulated later sequence in human evolution from domain-specific intelligences to cognitive fluidity (Mithen 1996). Both Gamble and Gowlett, while rightly cautioning us against reading more into the archaeological record than it can support (see also Layton), suggest the possibility of coalition, alliance, and systematic recruitment to social groups without language-based rules of kinship. In comparable fashion, under the grandmother hypothesis explored by Opie and Power, female coalitionary strategies can be envisioned as rooted in a tacit apprehension of the dynamics of giving and receiving help to meet reproductive costs. With later encephalization, we can imagine this creating the conditions for forms of true ritual and symbolic action.

Much of the above is, of course, speculative. However, the newly emerging materials and techniques of interpretation begin to suggest a socially structured world before the appearance of fully modern language. In such a world, the 'they' of our imaginative reconstruction possessed a habitus-like capacity for apprehending, engaging with, and moving within social spaces and categories for which technologies, and the physical experiences of life, offered ready tools for understanding on the part of a hominin already possessing theory-of-mind of a relatively high order. As Wendy James has suggested (pers. comm.), kinship may be a human game with very ancient rules that may in fact pre-date language. In an inherently dynamic system, the object of the game may be as much to make new relationships through ordered exchanges over generational time as it is to classify and label relatives synchronically. This may be neither random nor accidental. The cognitive capacity to engage with higher order dynamic structures, as well as with other individual minds, is readable (we can suggest) as an adaptive package favouring Darwinian fitness in the universe of context-dependency and multilevel selection outlined above.

Time-Reference

A time dimension is integral to the vision taking shape across this collection. Among the competences attributable to our pre-linguistic actor, within a model based on the modified habitus concept, is the social ordering of time. Temporality in a minimal, logical sense is already present in a neo-Darwinian discourse. Behaviour is frequently represented as geared to time without need for either cognition or intentionality, although both may be present. Time-orientation, without any attribution of consciousness, is already implied in notions such as reciprocal altruism and life-history reproductive strategy, in which the actor is represented as, respectively, investing against a future return, and timing reproductive effort according to a best guess of lifetime success (Korstjens). Here, we need to think beyond time-reference in this minimal sense, and consider how social actor-ship might imply harnessing time in an active manner. This seems plausible. Gift exchange is sociality stretched over time, as several contributors point out, and would facilitate the apprehension of enduring relationships and structures. Gamble stresses the importance of extended networks, which would include those based on articulated kinship rules in the human period, in allowing a social life independent of co-presence: '. . . that human trait of distributing our social selves across time and space, and where extended absence . . . does not necessarily result in the collapse of an individual's social networks' (p. 33) He, together with Layton and Allen in different ways, calls attention to the temporal patterning of fission and fusion in putative early human groups, and to the moments of 'effervescence' (Durkheim 1915 [1912]) – heightened interaction with associated endorphin rushes – periodic partying that could very credibly intensify both the particip-ants' experience in, and their apprehension of, socially ordered time, as well as creating the conditions for subsequent symbolic and ritual elaboration. With specific relation to kinship, Dunbar and James stress the intrinsic future-orientation of all kinship structures, both biologically and culturally interpreted. With the advent of language, elaborated structures such as those based on a cyclic alternation of generations in time (Allen, and James in chapter 4) can come into being.

A Question of Representation: How Can 'We' Think about 'Their' Experience of Kinship?

If Gamble and others are right, 'they' both needed and found rich mines of imagery with which to experience relatedness. 'We' in turn need appropriate images with which to represent theoretically what 'they' might have been doing and thinking. Some years ago, one of the debates about the language of what was then called 'sociobiology' focused on the selection of imageries for the representation of evolutionary processes.[4] We were then, it was commonly assumed, dealing with convenient, disposable metaphors of strategic action (selfish genes, trade-offs, investments), notwithstanding the tendency for metaphor to slide into assumed homology. Some of these metaphors are still current; others have faded from view. Part of the argument was about the unstated models of society held to lie behind the choice of those particular images. Now the ground has shifted, largely in consequence of the very much greater sophistication of fields such as behavioural ecology and primatology, and of the new recognition of social complexity itself as an adaptation con-sequential for Darwinian fitness. We now need to consider strategic action in a stronger sense: one involving actual capacity to apprehend the texture of social relations (including those of kinship) and to act in response to opportunities and constraints in a complex social field. It would be helpful to have a toolkit of imageries that would enable us to elaborate the notion of 'tacit' or implicit knowledge or competence available in some form to non-linguistic social actors. What imageries might we now find helpful?

The foregoing chapters, and other recent work, contain indications of what might go into such a toolkit. A carefully modified use of Bourdieu's concept of habitus has already been discussed. Wendy James's formulation (2003) of 'knowing the rules and figures of the dance', though made in the specific context of human (and, here, of kinship) structures, could point to a complex of images with a wider and deeper evolutionary application, as could her image of the 'flow of life'. Knight (1999), developing an evolutionary model of the relationship between language and ritual, makes effective but not reductive use of an imagery of games. Earlier, and in a different theoretical context, Ardener imagined a 'theatre for action' in the form of a non-linguistic, but nonetheless semiotic, system that 'depended, in the absence of the power of speech, upon the apperception by the human participants of contextually defined logical relations among themselves in space . . . [for example] . . . the relative position of each participant to another in a gathering, and to items in a fixed environment' (1989: 25). We can view these representations, and others that will surely follow – cf. Parkin's (2007) image of the 'visceral' – as 'families' of imageries, enabling us to think of a social actor as able to move about within a structure without having a language in which to articulate it. Such an actor could, we can plausibly say, *know how* without having to *know that*.

Taking the Conversation Forward

In bringing together the essays in this collection, the editors and authors have sought to map a new kind of conversation between biological and social anthropologists, archaeologists, and historical linguists. As several contributors acknowledge, it is appropriate that the focus of this conversation should be kinship: a theme that has stood at the heart of anthropology throughout its history, and that, in many theoretical models, marks a point of intersection between 'natural' and 'cultural' processes. The starting point has been the question: what part did kinship play in the long story of our becoming human? As might be expected, this question has led to the many fertile insights into the interweaving of our historical and social nature and our evolutionary inheritance that are set out in the foregoing chapters. From these, the sense emerges of a need to re-establish 'the study of human origins as a legitimate sub-discipline within *social* anthropology' (Barnard, p. 243, emphasis added). At the same time, the discussion has promoted a recognition of context-dependency and multilevel selection in the Darwinian evolution of complex social systems, together with a willingness to imagine the proto-human actor as able to engage actively and strategically with socially generated networks, systems, and structures. This in turn might help to illuminate themes within biological anthropology, primatology, archaeology, and (perhaps more indirectly) linguistics.

But the notion of a 'conversation' is itself, of course, a metaphor as well as a literal description of what occurred as this book took shape. This signals a meta-level at which discourses deriving from different sub-traditions within anthropology can be brought into articulation. These discourses came to be largely detached from one another throughout most of the twentieth century, particularly in the mainstream of anthropology in Britain, although there were submerged currents of continuity throughout the period. There is now a systematic revival of interest, within which this collection can claim to fall, in bringing them into new forms of alignment (Parkin 2007).

Mills and Huber (2005) and others have used the metaphor of a 'trading zone', in contexts such as pedagogy, to represent operations that can be shared and exchanged between separate but related or overlapping disciplines. While caution is needed in extending the mercantile metaphor beyond its original application (and the authors themselves stress its limitations), the idea of trading zones offers a helpful way to understand how ideas and constructs can 'talk to' one another across theoretical territories or jurisdictions – to extend the image – without losing the specificity of each. Put slightly differently, the idea of 'trading zones' may help to build commensurability across intellectual terrains without collapsing them into one another (Knight, pers. comm.).

It is always tempting to dislodge particular units of comparison from the discourses from which they derive in order to hook them together in a direct way. This may often be justified; for example where actual homologies can be claimed or demonstrated. But, as suggested above, this approach risks reifying constructs that are themselves context-dependent relative to particular disciplinary histories. An alternative approach might be based on complexes of imageries such as 'trading zones', and other ways of depicting the travel of knowledge across boundaries that might include the frontiers of related, or divergent, or intermittently estranged, disciplines and sub-disciplines (Strathern 2004).[5] Such an approach would create a more flexible articulation between traditions and discourses. It might, for example, be a helpful way of looking at constructs such as 'bonding', 'coalitions', and 'kinship' itself, as they appear within the terminologies of contrasting but connected fields (Korstjens, Lehmann). Such play in the system, as it were, could allow vocabularies and bodies of knowledge to slide across one another in mutually enlightening ways, without being reductively and distortingly locked together.

There is no denying how much we do not know, and may never know, about early kinship. One of the deep challenges for the future, we can suggest, is to bring the disciplinary frames in which the research is conducted into an open form of alignment, via imageries appropriate to the capacities the evidence leads us to attribute to social actors in worlds that are human, non-human, and becoming-human. Within all these frames, the strategic dimension of the social order is at the centre of what needs to be explained. It may be these very games, dances, choices, and competences, in all their subtlety and contextuality, that evolutionary and cultural theories about human origins need to be interested in – particularly if the focus of the interest is social intelligence. As the conversation continues into the future, parts of it may revolve around the search for an appropriate language that will be a language of science, but also one in which inarticulate things can be articulately imagined.

Notes

1 In fact, the focus on primates may reflect some observer bias in favour of our own part of the phylogenetic tree. A recently published book (de Waal and Tyack 2003) addresses the issue of animal social complexity from a taxonomic base much broader than the primate line. While some of this work is in its pioneer phase, the suggestion is clearly present that in animals with a capacity for individualized relationships, social intelligence may present powerful enough selective advantages to evolve independently in widely separated groups.

2 Interestingly, it appears that Darwin in *The Descent of Man* (cited by Dawkins 2006: 171) adopted a fairly 'soft' version of group selection in relation to human 'tribes', in which groups composed of altruistic individuals would prosper and spread at the expense of those composed of selfish individualists. This contrasts with the 'hard' version of group selection rejected by most contemporary evolutionary biologists, which would require successful groups to generate more 'offspring groups' than their competitors. Because Darwin's account does not treat human groups as singular replicators, it is the more helpful for the model that chapters of this book seek to outline, in which early population expansion is linked to the 'stretching out' of social systems and networks.

3 During the workshop on which this volume is based, there was a lengthy discussion of how we might conceptualize, and label, a period of early human history marked by pre-linguistic capacities to apprehend structure in material, temporal, and spatial form.

4 For an early exposition, see Callan (1984); for an up-to-date discussion of the inevitability and limitations of metaphor, see Knight et al. (1999).

5 I am grateful to Brian Street for drawing my attention to this reference.

Acknowledgements

I am grateful for the valuable comments made by this volume's co-editors on earlier drafts of this Epilogue. Responsiblity for the final version is mine.

Appendix 1: Nilo-Saharan Kinship

A. Kinship terms reconstructed to the proto-Nilo-Saharan (PNS) period

1. PNS *ɛɛya or *eeya 'father': Uduk FB, BC(ms) (recipr); Kunama F
   Semantic note: derivation of Uduk FB from original F indicates earlier pre-Uduk bifurcate merging pattern, as does also the Uduk reflex of #7 below

2. PNS *baab 'father'; var. *baaba 'father (vocative)': 2nd element in Uduk compound for PF (literally 'old father'; Central Sudanic (CSud): Lugbara F; Kunama F, PF (voc.); Kanuri F, FG, FBW; For F, FB; Songay F, FB; Dongolawi F; Gaam F; Surmic: Majangir F (own), FB; [Turkana SC(ms): borrowing of Rub (Ik) PF (as recipr. address)]; Ik PF (sound change regular); [Ik F (voc.): loan from undetermined source]

3. PNS *ya 'mother'; var. *aya 'mother (voc.)'

4. PNS *yak' 'child': Uduk 'son'; Kunama 'child'; Saharo-Sahelian: Kanuri 'elder sibling' (with suffix added: 'sibling'); Gaam 'sister, PGD'
   Semantic note: apparent meaning shift in PSS from 'child' to 'sibling'; narrowing of the meaning in pre-Gaam to just 'sister' explains the Gaam meanings

5. PNS *mwɛy 'sister; girl': Uduk ZC(ms); CSud (*le-mwi) 'sister'; Teda S; Gaam CC, PF (recipr) (plus *ṭ n. suff.); Rub group: Ik 'child,' Soo 'daughter'
   Semantic notes: (a) prefix *a- in Uduk ZC imparts the meaning 'something/someone associated with/characterized by [root word],' i.e., a relation associated with one's sister, implying pre-Uduk Z; (b) generalization of meaning in proto-Saharo-Sahelian from 'girl' to 'child of either sex' would allow for alternative narrowings to S in Teda, to D in Soo

6. PNS *nam 'mother's brother; sister's child (ms)': Uduk ZC(ms); CSud: Mbay MB, ZC(ms), Gula MB; Kunama FZ, DH(ws); Maban: Aiki MB; Ik HZ
   Semantic notes: (a) ZC(ms) is reciprocal relation to MB; thus Uduk ZC(ms) implies former presence of meaning MB for this term in pre-Uduk; (b) Mbay shows same extension of meaning, MB, ZC(ms), retaining both; (c) Kunama FZ

implies pre-Kunama extension of *nam to both parents' 'cross' siblings, MB and FZ, with subsequent narrowing to just FZ; (d) meaning DH in Kunama implies an earlier period of Crow cousin terminology in Kunama as well as preferential cross cousin marriage: i.e., Kunama FZ > FZC = DH(ws); (d) Ik HZ implies earlier MB > MBC (presumably before proto-Eastern Sahelian loss of meaning MB for *nam), with preferential cross cousin marriage

7. PNS *tatʰa 'father's sister': Uduk MB; Kunama FZ; E'rn Sahelian: Ik FZ, Soo FZ (but unexplained irregular vowel ɛ)
    Semantic note: Uduk meaning requires a pre-Uduk generalization of FZ to both 'cross-siblings' of one's parents, i.e., FZ > FZ, MB, followed by a later loss of the meaning FZ and retention only of the meaning MB

8. PNS *k'was 'father's brother': Uduk: combining form in FZC, MBC; Zaghawa FB; Songay MB
    Semantic notes: (a) all reflexes of root 6 above show it to have been the word for MB, hence the choice of FB for this term; (b) Uduk: FB > PB (lineal) > MB (bifurcate collateral), allowing its prefixation to term for parallel cousin to form term for 'cross cousin'; (c) Songay: previous lineal system, FB > PB, with subsequent shift PB > MB as part of change over to bifurcate merging

9. PNS *kam 'sibling; parallel cousin': Uduk G, FBC, MZC (siblings and parallel cousins); second element in compound term for FZC, MBC (cross cousins); Majangir MGC
    Semantic note: proposed history: pre-Majangir FBC/MZC > MZC (narrowing) > Majangir MGC (regeneralization); but this is a weakly attested item, and other histories are possible

10. PNS *atʰiŋ ~ *atʰin 'grandparent': Uduk PM; For CC

11. PNS *maṣeh 'spouse': Uduk WG; Maba H

12. PNS *mɛr 'parent-in-law': Uduk EP; Gaam EF; Surmic: Majangir BW(ms); Turkana 'in-law'

B. Kinship terms reconstructed to the proto-Sudanic (PS) stratum

1. PSS *dɔmpʰ 'child'; CSud *dɔ C; Teda D; Dongolawi FBC; Nandi G, FBC, MZC (parallel cousins)
    Semantic note: semantic shift, C > FBC, MZC (parallel cousins), in proto-Eastern Sahelian would allow for the subsequent Dongolawi and Nandi usages, i.e., narrowing in Dongolawi to FBC and generalization in Kalenjin (Nandi) to FBC, MZC, and G (all parallel cousins and siblings)
    Phonological note: proto-Central Sudanic (CSud) regularly deleted all word-final consonants, hence PNS *dɔmpʰ > CSud *dɔ

2. PS *ɗuur or *duur 'brother': CSud: Lugbara B, MB, MBC, Mangbetu B(ws); Kunama BW; Saharan: Kanuri 'kindred'; E'rn Sahelian: Nuer 'brother'

3. PS *Dal 'mother's sister': East CSud 'father's sister': Mangbetu FZ, Z(ms); Lugbara EM; For ZC
    Semantic notes: this semantic reconstruction posits (a) that the shifts, MZ > PZ > FZ, took place in proto-East Central Sudanic and (b) that For ZC preserves the

original link, i.e., ZC = reciprocal of MZ, implying the meaning MZ in pre-For; Lugbara EM < FZ implies preferential cross cousin marriage

4. PS *yɛɛy 'sister': CSud: PCS *ayi 'spouse's sister': Lugbara HZ; Gula, 1st element in term for EG; Turkana BC(ws); Ik Z, FBD
   Semantic note: Turkana BC (ws) is reciprocal of FZ, implying shift Z > FZ in pre-Turkana

5. PS *kʰaak' 'grandparent': CSud: Mbay, Gula PP; Kanuri PP, CC; Teda PM; Songay 'ancestor; PP'; Surmic: Majangir PM, CC(ws)

6. PS *Teyk 'spouse's sibling': CSud: Lugbara WB; Kanuri EG, GE; Majang HG, BW

C. Kinship terms reconstructed to the proto-Northern Sudanic (PNoS) stratum

1. PNoS *tʰawp' 'sibling's child': Kunama CC; E'rn Sahelian: Gaam GC
   Semantic note: proposed shift as in Italian *nipote*, GC > CC; hence this root is tentatively postulated as the PNoS term for GC

2. PNoS *haɓay 'mother's brother': Kunama HF(ws); Songay FZ; Gaam MZ, MB
   Semantic notes: (a) Kunama HF(ws) implies earlier MB = EF in situation of preferential cross cousin marriage, with later narrowing, EF > HF; (b) Songay: MB > both parent's cross-siblings, MB, FZ, with subsequent narrowing to just FZ; (c) Gaam: MB > MG

3. PNoS *ap'o 'grandmother': Kunama PM; For PM; Dongolawi PM; Surmic: Majangir PF, CC(ms)

4. PNoS *ɔɔbu 'grandfather': Kunama PF; Zaghawa PM; Dongolawi PF; [For PF: loan from early Nubian]

5. PNoS *tʰaŋgaṭ' 'daughter's husband': Kunama DH(ws); Maba DH; Gaam PM
   Semantic note: possible Gaam derivation: extension of DH to DHC, i.e., DC > grandchild, with reciprocal application to PP?

D. Kinship terms reconstructed to the proto-Saharo-Sahelian (PSS) stratum

1. PSS *baas or *ɓaas 'father's sister': Teda FZ; Songay FZC, MBC
   Semantic note: meaning shift in Songay implies pre-Songhay Crow cousin system, i.e., FZ > FZ and FZC = Crow terminology, with generalization to all cross cousins in Songay and subsequent loss of meaning FZ

2. PSS *totʰo 'mother': Teda MZ; [Ateker (E. Nilotic) *toto: Teso, Turkana M, Turkana SC(ws): loanword from Rub (expected *doto)]; Ik MZ, MZC
   Semantic notes: (a) Teda M > M, MZ (bifurcate merging) > MZ only (bifurcate collateral); (b) parallel history in Ik, with extension by Crow reckoning to MZC; (c) borrowing into Ateker from an early Rub language in which meaning M was still present

3. PSS *k'ɛyr or *k'aayr 'parent': Zaghawa M, MZ; Songay P

4. PSS *maŋkʰał or *maŋk'ał 'parent': For EF, DH; [Maba HF: loan from Saharan language (*ł > r /_# is Saharan sound change)]; Gaam M
   Semantic notes: (a) For P > EP > EF; (b) Maba borrowed term shows that parallel meaning shift took place in at least one as yet unidentified language of Saharan subgroup: i.e., this is another attestation of the old central Saharan areal contact zone evidenced in section H below

5. PSS *ɛlt or *hɛlt 'spouse's sibling': Zaghawa WG, ZH, Teda EM; Gaam EG

6. PSS *kʰam 'woman': Kanuri 'wife, woman'; Maba 'woman'; Nandi M, MZ, MBD

E. Kinship terms reconstructed to the proto-Sahelian (PSah) stratum

1. PSah *aɲah 'mother': For FZ (loan from early Nubian?); [Masalit FZ: loan from For, like all Masalit PG terms]; Songay M; Nobiin FZ (loan from pre-For into proto-Nubian?)
   Semantic notes: meaning FZ forms an east-central Sahel areal spread, innovated a single time from M via M > MZ > PZ (lineal PG system) > FZ in either pre-For or pre-proto-Nubian; if For borrowed from Nubian, then the first presence of this root should be moved to the proto-Trans-Sahel period (see section H, East-Central Sahara areal root 4)

2. PSah *maama 'mother's brother': For MB; Maban: Masalit MB (loan from For; F, all PG borrowed by Masalit from For); Gaam FZ; Surmic: Majangir MZ, FBW; Nandi FZC, MB, MBS; Ik MB, MBC
   Semantic note: Nandi FZC and MBS fit with inference of an earlier Crow system, although in this case, influences from the Rub languages may be the cause of this naming pattern in Nandi

3. PSah *maareh 'father's sister': For EM; Majang MB; Anywa MZ
   Semantic notes: (a) EM in For makes sense as a meaning shift, FZ > EM, in a situation of preferential cross cousin marriage; this implies that the pre-For meaning was FZ; (b) Majang MB implies an intermediate generalization of term to the parents' cross-siblings, FZ > FZ/MB, with later re-narrowing, FZ/MB > just MB; (c) Anywa MZ: shift to lineal reckoning of aunts, FZ > PZ, with subsequent narrowing, PZ > MZ

4. PSah *wɛy or *'wɛy 'child': For C; Anywa S, also 'son of'; Ik C (pl.)

F. Kinship terms reconstructed to the proto-Trans-Sahel (PTSah) stratum

1. PTSah *ay 'child'; Aiki D, C (with movable *kʰ- prefix); Turkana FZC, Maasai C

G. Kinship terms reconstructed to the proto-Eastern Sahelian (PES) stratum

1. PES *Too or *Tooh 'child': Dongolawi C; Surmic: Majangir C; Nandi (Kalenjin) *C

2. PES *yogw 'mother-in-law (?)': Dongolawi EM, EZ; Gaam EM; Ik WG, Soo BW

3. PES *kek or *kʰekʰ or *kʰek or *kekʰ 'female relation': Dongolawi -kɛg- in ɛɛn-kɛg-id MZ (ɛɛn M; -id is a noun suffix); Ik W

H. Ennedi-Mara region areally diffused kinship terms

1. *ab(b)a 'father' (loanword from Afroasiatic): Kanuri, Zaghawa, Teda; For

2. *bar 'brother': Zaghawa 2nd element in compound word for B; For B(ms)

3. *bur 'child': Zaghawa C; Dongolawi, Nobiin (Nubian) D

4. *aɲah 'father's sister': For FZ; [Masalit FZ: loan from For, like all Masalit PG terms]; Nobiin FZ (see PSah root 1)

I. Northern Middle Nile Basin areal term

1. PES *gi or *ɟi 'male relative': Gaam H; Dongolawi MB
   Semantic notes: original meaning in Gaam was probably also MB: an earlier meaning extension MB > MB, MBC (Crow pattern?) would allow for the meaning change MBC > H to take place in a situation of preferential cross cousin marriage

Appendix 2: Khoesan Kinship

A. Kinship terms reconstructed to the proto-Khoesan period

1. *ai 'mother; mother's sister': SAK: PKhoe *ai M, MZ; Hadza *aya* M, MZ, also FZ?

2. *ma 'mother; mother's sister': PSAK *ma M; Sandawe mesu (< *ma-isu) M, MZ, FZ

3. *tata 'father, father's brother (voc.)': PSAK *tata F (Taa-!Ui: /Xam *tata* F; Khoe: Damara *dadab* F, FB); also proto-Khoekhoe (PKK) *tara FZ; Sandawe *tata* F, FB
   Semantic note: PKK *tara derives from the same root, but underwent the regular PSAK sound change of *t > PSAK *d (> PKK *r) in non-vocative nouns; the fact that the sound change dates to PSAK shows that the word in this meaning already existed in the proto-Southern African language

4. *mama 'grandmother': PSAK *mama PM; Sandawe *mama* PM; Hadza *mama* CD (recipr).
   Interpretive notes: Sandawe *maame* MB, ZC is not a cognate, but a borrowing from a Rift Southern Cushitic language; Hadza *amama* PM is also probably not a cognate, but appears instead to be a Rift Southern Cushitic loanword

B. Kinship terms reconstructed to the proto-Southern African Khoesan period

1. *ai 'mother; mother's sister': PKhoe *ai M, MZ; Taa-!Ui: /Xam *aiti* 'wife'

2. *ma 'mother; mother's sister': proto-Northern Khoe (PNKhoe) *ma M, MZ; Zhu -*ma* feminine suffix in kin terms, also diminuative; cf. also Taa-!Ui: /Xam *mama* M (voc.), PKK *mama M (loan from Taa-!Ui language?)

3. *ba 'father, father's brother': PNKhoe *ba F, FB; Zhu *ba F; !Xoõ *a̧* F (PSAK *b > !Xoõ Ø /#_); PKhoe *-b(a) masculine suffix)

4.   *tsu 'father, father's brother': regional word?: Zhu *tsu MB, FB; Taa-!Ui: Eastern ≠Hoã *ču* F, FB

5.   */Goa 'child'

6.   *⊙a 'child, offspring'

7.   *!oi 'sibling': Khoe: Naro *!uĩ* 'younger sibling'; Zhu *!ui 'elder sister'; Taa-!Ui: /Xam !koi MG, PP

8.   *ki '(elder?) sibling': some Northern Khoe *ki ~ *gi G(e), also FBC, MZC (parallel cousins); Eastern ≠Hoã ki-si G(e)

9.   *!!o 'older relation (elder sibling?)': Zhu *!ó* 'elder brother'; Taa-!Ui: !Xoõ *!!óo* 'parent of married couple'

10.   *g!hạo 'cross cousin': Khoe: Nama *!hao-s* 'clan, and by extension, tribe, ethnic group'; Taa-!Ui: !Xoõ *-!gạo* 'cross-cousin' when suffixed to 'child': FZC, MBC; 'parallel relation' when suffixed to word for member of alternate ascending or descending generation: suffixed to 'mother': MZ, FBW, ZC(ws), also PPM; suffixed to 'father': FB, MZH, BC(ms), also PPF)

    Semantic note: the primary level of application of this root in !Xoõ, to members of the same generation as ego, identifies its base sense as the cross-cousin relationship

11.   *mama 'grandmother': PKhoe *mama PM (PNKhoe PM, FZ); Zhu *mámà PM (voc.)

12.   *txoũ 'grandmother': Khoe: Naro *tsxõ* PP: loanword (< Eastern ≠Hoã?); Zhu txũ PM, PGD; with dimin. suffix, CD(ms), CS(ws); Taa-!Ui: ≠Hoã *kyxoõ* PM, CC, FZ, MeZ, MBC, FZC, yGC, GCC

13.   */'u(i) 'parent-in-law': PKhoe */'ui 'in-law'; Zhu */'ù-dshù* EM (*dshù*, meaning uncertain), */'ùì* 'to marry into a family,' */'ùì-sì* 'in-laws'

Appendix 3: Kinship Terms Reconstructed to Early Afroasiatic Strata

A. Kinship terms reconstructed to the proto-Afroasiatic (proto-Afrasan) period

1. PAA *ʔabb- 'father': Omotic; Cushitic; Chadic; Berber; Semitic

2. PAA *ʔinn- 'mother (voc.?)': Omotic: Yemsa *into* M (stem plus *-t fem. suff.); Cushitic: Beja M; Eastern Cushitic: Afar *ina* M; proto-Chado-Berber (PCB) *ʔinn-/*ʔann- M: Tuareg *anna* M, MZ; Chadic *nan/*nən M: West Chadic (WCh): Angas *nən* M, MZ, FZ; Tangale none, Ngamo *no*, Dera *nana*, etc., M; Central Chadic (CCh): Njanye *nana*, Jaku *naan*, etc., M, Daba *nana* MB, ZC(ms), East Chadic (ECh): Tumak MB.

3. PAA *ʔind- 'mother': Omotic: Kafa M; Aari M; Cushitic: Beja M

4. PAA *ʔis- 'brother': proto-Omotic *ʔis-im- B; proto-Erythraic (PE) *ʔis-an- B

5. PAA *ʔaxʷ- 'sister'; Omotic 'sibling': Gonga (Kafa, Sheko) B in compound term for FB; Bench FZ; Cushitic *ʔaxʷ-/*ʔixʷ- 'sister': Beja Z; proto-North Agaw *əxʷ-əra C (stem plus AA *r noun suffix); Boreafrasan: PSem *ʔax- B, *ʔax-t- Z

6. PAA *ʔaay- 'elder brother': Omotic: Yemsa *ày-* B; Cushitic: proto-Southern Cushitic (PSC: for the PSC roots see Ehret 1980) *ʔaayi B(e); Eastern Cushitic: Saho G(e); Boreafrasan (BA): Chadic: pre-WCh *ʔayaʔay- (redup. stem) > WCh *yaaya B(e): Hausa B(e), Bade B

7. PAA *ʔab- 'mother's brother': Omotic: Bench *àbm̀* MB; Cushitic: proto-East-South Cushitic (PC) *ʔabu MB

8. PAA *ʔakk- 'grandfather': Omotic: Bench PF; Aari PP; proto-Eastern Cushitic (PEC) 'grandfather'; PSC 'grandmother'

9. PAA *ʔap- 'grandmother': Omotic: Yemsa *appo* PF, *afa* PM; Bench *ap* PM; Cushitic: PEC *ʔaboo- PM; BA: Chadic: ECh: *ʔap-: Migama MZ, FZ

10. PAA *mayn- 'woman, wife': Omotic: Bench *main*; Cushitic: Southern Cushitic: proto-Rift *amayn- (stem with *a- noun pref.); Chadic: PCh *mən 'woman, wife'

11. PAA *gʷaban- 'in-law': Omotic: Yemsa *gùbànō*; Cushitic: North Agaw *gʷäbän- EZ; Cushitic loanword in some Ethiopic Semitic

12. PAA *zaym- 'spouse's sibling': Omotic: Bench EG; Cushitic: LEC: Saho EG, Afar 'in-laws'

13. PAA *ʔiz-/*ʔaz- 'male relative older than ego': Omotic: Bench B(e); Cushitic: Agaw: Kemant F; Cushitic: EC: Dhaasanac ʔið-aam 'fathers'; proto-Soomaali *ʔaz-eer- FB

B. Kinship terms reconstructed to the proto-Erythraic period

1. PE *ʔiŋ- 'child': proto-Cushitic (PC) *ʔiŋ- C; Chado-Berber: PBC *ʔəŋŋ-/*ʔaŋŋ-; proto-Semitic (PS) *ʔin- C (Soqotri 'children')

2. PE *wiil- 'child': Cushitic: Soomaali S; NE: proto-Berber (PBB) *wilt- 'sister' (adds *-t fem. suff. to non-gendered root to feminize its referent); Tuareg Z, FBD, MZD; Chadic *wul- 'child': PWCh *wun-; ECh: Mokilko ʔulo

3. PE *bar- 'offspring, young': Cushitic: EC: Saho S, D; Soomaali 'lamb'; Boreafrasan: PS *bar-/bart- 'son/daughter'; Berber: Tuareg *barar S; Chadic: WCh: Angas par C

4. PE *bax- 'sibling': Cushitic: SC: Maʼa 'classificatory sibling'; ECush: Soomaali 'child of the same mother'; Boreafrasan: Berber: Tuareg MBC, FZC (Iroquois); Chadic: WCh: Ngamo báʔà Z, Fyer bèt B pl., Kariya vàyán B, Diri ávíyà C; CCh: Lame vai G, Masa ba B, Zime vay C
   Semantic note: primary relation is G; application of this root to just cross cousins in Tuareg therefore requires previous extension in pre-Tuareg of root first to all PGC before narrowing to just cross-cousins; in other words, the meaning of this root in Tuareg implies a prior Hawaiian system in pre-Tuareg, a finding in keeping with the wide occurrence of Hawaiian terminology elsewhere in Berber

5. PAA *ħam- 'father's brother': Cushitic: PSC *ħam- FB; Boreafrasan: PS *ħam- 'spouse's father'; also relatively recent Arabic loanword for Beja EF
   Semantic note: semantic history of this root can be accounted for only by a shift from original FB to EF in a cultural context in which preferred marriage partner is FBD; the PS meaning EF (with extension to EM by addition of *-t fem.) demonstrates that the customary preference for marriage to the daughter of FB, notable in Arab cultures, goes back to at least the proto-Semitic period of 6,000-plus years ago.

6. PAA *ʔaama 'female relation' (probably originally vocative).
   Interpretive note: This root takes on a wide range of specific meanings in different branches of the family, including D, Z, PM, W, M, MZ, and MB; some examples: Cushitic: Agaw: Chamir aɲa 'mother' (PC *m > Agaw *ŋ); Highland ECush: Burji W, North HEC M; Southern Cushitic: proto-Rift PM; Burunge Z; Kwadza M; Dahalo MB; Tuareg PM; Chadic: WCh: 'woman, wife'; ECh: Musgu M; Semitic *ʔam-t- 'girl'

7. PE *ħay- 'male relation': Cushitic: PC *ħay- 'husband'; SCush: Iraqw B; Boreafrasan: Berber: Tuareg CS, CD (plus *-t fem. suff.), ZS(ms), ZD(ms) (plus *-t fem. suff.)
   Semantic note: addition of fem. suffix to Tuareg CD and ZD implies that the original reference was to a male child

8. PE *ʔad- 'relative on father's side': Cushitic: PEC *ʔad- FZ; Berber: Kabyle FB (redup.); Chadic: WCh: Gwandara F, FB (FZ, with added *-y suff.); CCh: Gude, Jari, Kilba, Malgwa F

9. PE *ʔal-, ʔalaw- 'girl': Cushitic: ECush: Burji D; Dullay *ʔalaw-Z; PSC *ʔal- 'older girl'; Berber D; Chadic: WCh, CCh *law- C; Musgu *ali* 'boys'

C. Kinship terms reconstructed to the proto-Agaw-East-South-Cushitic period

1. PC *ʔukʷˈ- 'wife': PNAgaw W; Eastern Cushitic: Yaaku W

D. Kinship terms reconstructed to the proto-East-South Cushitic period

1. Proto-East-South Cushitic (PESC) *ʔayy- 'mother'
    Interpretive note: some Chadic languages have *ya 'mother' or similar; the phonological shapes indicate that they are probable Nilo-Saharan loanwords (Ehret 2006b), rather than retentions of the root seen in Eastern and Southern Cushitic

2. PESC *ʔaŋŋ-/*ʔiŋŋ- 'father's sister': Cushitic: PSC *ʔaŋŋ-FZ; E. Cush: Arbore *ʔiŋgo*; MZ; Afar *anna* MZ, FZ

4. PESC *taata 'male relation older than ego' (probably originally vocative): ECush: Harso F, Gollango B(e); SCush: Iraqw, Burunge F (vocative), Dahalo Z(e)

5. PESCS *maama 'female relative older than ego' (probably originally vocative): Eastern Cushitic: Gollango, Harso FZ; SCush: Burunge FZ, MB, PM, Iraqw MB, Ma'a M(Ds)

E. Kinship terms reconstructed to the proto-Chadic period

1. Proto-Chadic (PCh) *baba 'father': WCh: Dera *baba*, Tangale *baba*, etc.; CCh: Bachama *baba*, Glavda *baba*, etc.
    Derivational note: This is a probable Nilo-Saharan loanword: see Appendix I, Section A, root 1

2. PCh *ʔafa 'father': WCh: Ngizim F; ECh: Migama PZ; Masa: Musgu F

3. PCh *mal- 'sister': WCh: Angas Z, PGD; ECh: Mokilko EZ

4. PCh *ɗyəm 'child': WCh: Angas *dyɛm* S, GS, PGCS; CCh: Matakam *dəm* D; Masa: Musgu -*ɗam* G

5. PCh *k'ən- 'mother's brother': WCh: Angas MB; Masa Ch: Kotoko PB, Musgu MB; Masa EP, GE

6. PCh *gigi 'grandfather': WCh: Buli *gigi*, Pero *jiji*; CCh: Bachama *žiži*, etc.

7. PCh *kaka 'grandmother': ECh: Tumak PF; Mokilko PF; CCh: Migama (?) PF
    Interpretive note: This is a probable Nilo-Saharan loanword: see Appendix 1, Section B, root 5

8. PCh *səkʷar- 'parent-in-law': WCh: Gwandara 'in-law'; CCh: Mafa EM, SW, Malgwa 'in-law,' Daba HP; Masa Ch: Musgu EP

9. PCh *məs- 'husband': WCh: Angas H, HG, Ngizim H; CCh: Mafa EF, DH
   Interpretive note: This is another probable Nilo-Saharan loanword: see Appendix 1, section A, root 11, for the likely source

10. PCh *dada 'female relative (voc.)': WCh: Bole D, Bade Z, Ngizim M (voc.); CCh: Gisiga, etc., M; Musgu PM; ECh: Mokilko PM

F. Kin term of uncertain provenance

1. *baaba 'father (vocative)'
   This root, despite its widely scattered occurrence in different Afroasiatic groups, in all likelihood should *not* be reconstructed back to proto-Afroasiatic. In Semitic it has a limited areal distribution, in Arabic and Soqotri, where it can be suspected to be an Arabic loanword. It is also attested in the deeply Arabic-influenced northern Berber languages, but not in the less influenced Tuareg farther south, and so can be included among the set of Arabic kin terms borrowed into those languages (the italicized terms for PG in the on-line kin diagrams for Kabyle, Baamarani, and Shawiya are the notable examples). Among the Cushitic languages, it can be reconstructed only to proto-Southern Cushitic. In the Eastern Cushitic branch it is reported in only those Cushitic languages strongly influenced by Arabic, i.e., Afar and the Soomaali group, and in Yaaku, which was deeply influenced earlier in its history by its Southern Cushitic neighbors. Finally, the root can separately be reconstructed in proto-Chadic as *baba, but there it most probably belongs to the set of Nilo-Saharan loanwords in that language (Ehret 2006b cites additional such loans).

Bibliography

Abbott, D. H., W. Saltzman, N. J. Schultz-Darken, and T. E. Smith, 1997. Specific Neuroendocrine Mechanisms Not Involving Generalized Stress Mediate Social Regulation of Female Reproduction in Cooperatively Breeding Marmoset Monkeys. *Annual of the New York Academy of Science* 807: 219–38.

Aberle, D. F., 1961a. Navaho. In *Matrilineal Kinship*. D. M. Schneider and K. Gough, eds, 96–201. Berkeley and Los Angeles: University of California Press.

—— 1961b. Matrilineal Descent in Cross-Cultural Perspective. In *Matrilineal Kinship*. D. M. Schneider and K. Gough, eds, pp. 655–727. Berkeley and Los Angeles: University of California Press.

Aiello, L. C., 1996. Terrestriality, Bipedalism and the Origin of Language. In *Evolution of Social Behaviour Patterns in Primates and Man*. Proceedings of the British Academy 88. J. Maynard-Smith, ed., pp. 269–89. London: The British Academy.

—— and R. I. M. Dunbar, 1993. Neocortex Size, Group Size and the Evolution of Language. *Current Anthropology* 34: 184–93.

—— and C. Key, 2002. Energetic Consequences of Being a *Homo erectus* Female. *American Journal of Human Biology* 14: 551–65.

—— and P. Wheeler, 1995. The Expensive Tissue Hypothesis: The Brain and the Digestive System in Human and Primate Evolution. *Current Anthropology* 36: 199–221.

Alexander, R. D., 1974. The Evolution of Social Behavior. *Annual Review of Ecological Systematics* 5: 325–83.

—— and K. Noonan, 1979. Concealment of Ovulation, Parental Care, and Human Social Evolution. In *Evolutionary Biology and Human Social Behavior*. N. Chagnon and W. Irons, pp. 436–53. North Scituate, MA: Duxbury Press.

Allen, N. J., 1982. A Dance of Relatives. *Journal of the Anthropological Society of Oxford* 13: 139–46.

—— 1986. Tetradic Theory: An Approach to Kinship. *Journal of the Anthropological Society of Oxford* 17: 87–109 (revised as Allen 2004).

—— 1989a. Assimilation of Alternate Generations. *Journal of the Anthropological Society of Oxford* 20: 45–55.

—— 1989b. The Evolution of Kinship Terminologies. *Lingua* 77: 173–85.

—— 1996. The Hero's Five Relationships: A Proto-Indo-European Story. In *Myth and Myth-Making: Continuous Evolution in Indian Tradition*. J. Leslie, ed., pp. 1–20. London: Curzon.

—— 1998a. The Prehistory of Dravidian-Type Terminologies. In *Transformations of Kinship*. M. Godelier, T. R. Trautmann, and F. E. Tjon Sie Fat, eds, pp. 314–31. Washington, DC: Smithsonian Institution.

—— 1998b. Effervescence and the Origins of Human Society. In *On Durkheim's Elementary Forms of Religious Life*. N. J. Allen, W. S. F. Pickering, and W. Watts Miller, eds, pp. 148–61. London: Routledge (revised in Allen 2000a).

—— 2000a. *Categories and Classifications: Maussian Reflections on the Social*. Oxford: Berghahn.

—— 2000b. Cúchulainn's Women and Some Indo-European Comparisons. *Emania* 18: 57–64.

—— 2004. Tetradic Theory: An Approach to Kinship. In *Kinship and Family: An Anthropological Reader*. R. Parkin and L. Stone, eds, pp. 221–35. Oxford: Blackwell.

—— 2005. Tetradic Theory and the Origin of Human Kinship Systems. Paper presented to The Evolution of Kinship, Gregynog, Royal Anthropological Institute.

Allen, H., 1972. Where the Crow Flies Backwards: Man and Land in the Darling Basin. Unpublished Ph.D. thesis, Department of Prehistory, Research School of Pacific Studies, Australian National University, Canberra.

Alvard, M., 2000. Kinship, Lineage Identity, and an Evolutionary Perspective on the Structure of Cooperative Big Game Hunting Groups in Indonesia. *Human Nature* 14: 129–63.

—— 2003. The Adaptive Nature of Culture. *Evolutionary Anthropology* 12: 136–49.

Alvarez, H. P., 2004. Residence Groups among Hunter-Gatherers: A View of the Claims and Evidence for Patrilocal Bands. In *Kinship and Behavior in Primates*. B. Chapais and C. Berman, eds, pp. 420–42. New York: Oxford University Press.

Amatruda, W. T., 1971. Linguistic Evidence for Cereal Plow Agriculture in Ethiopia and the Horn. Unpublished paper for University of California at Los Angeles, African History Seminar.

Ambrose, S. J., 1982. Archaeological and Linguistic Reconstructions of History in East Africa. In *The Archaeological and Linguistic Reconstruction of African*, C. Ehret and M. Posnansky, eds, pp. 104–57. Berkeley: University of California Press.

Ames, K., and H. Maschner, 1999. *The Peoples of the Northwest Coast: Their Archaeology and Prehistory*. London: Thames and Hudson.

Ardener, E. W., 1989. *The Voice of Prophecy and Other Essays*. Oxford: Blackwell.

Asfaw, B., W. H. Gilbert, Y. Beyene, W. K. Hart, P. R. Renne, G. Woldegabriel, E. S. Vrba, and T. D. White, 2002. Remains of *Homo erectus* from Bouri, Middle Awash, Ethiopia. *Nature* 416: 317–19.

Axelrod, R., 1990. *The Evolution of Co-operation*. Harmondsworth: Penguin.

Bachofen, J., 1973 [1861]. *Myth, Religion and Mother-Right: Selected Writings*. Princeton, NJ: Princeton University Press.

Bancel, P. J., and A. M. de l'Etang, 2002. Tracing of the Ancestral Kinship System: The Global Etymon KAKA. Part I: A Linguistic Study. *Mother Tongue* 7: 209–44.

Barber, N., 1994. Machiavellianism and Altruism: Effects of Relatedness of Target Person on Machiavellian and Helping Attitudes. *Pyschological Report* 75: 403–22.

Barham, L. S., 1998. Possible Early Pigment Use in South-Central Africa. *Current Anthropology* 39: 703–10.

Barkai, R., A. Gopher, S. E. Lauritzen and A. Frumkin, 2003. Uranium Series Dates from Qesem Cave, Israel, and the End of the Lower Palaeolithic. *Nature* 423: 977–79.

Barnard, A., 1978a. Universal Systems of Kin Categorization. *African Studies* 37: 69–81.

—— 1978b. The Kin Terminology System of the Nharo Bushmen. *Cahiers d'Etudes africaines* 18: 607–29.

—— 1978c. Universal Systems of Kin Categorization. *African Studies* 37: 69–81.

—— 1989. Kinship, Language and Production: A Conjectural History of Khoisan Social Structure. *Africa* 58: 29–50.

—— 1992. *Hunters and Herders of Southern Africa: A Comparative Ethnography of the Khoisan peoples*. Cambridge: Cambridge University Press.

—— 1999. Modern Hunter-Gatherers and Early Symbolic Culture. In *The Evolution of Culture: An Interdisciplinary View*. R. I. M. Dunbar, C. Knight, and C. Power, eds, pp. 50–68. Edinburgh: Edinburgh University Press.

—— 2007. From Mesolithic to Neolithic Modes of Thought. In Going Over: The Mesolithic–Neolithic Transition in North-West Europe. *Proceedings of the British Academy, London* 144. A. Whittle and V. Cummings, eds, pp. 5–19. London: The British Academy.

—— in press. Social Origins: Sharing, Exchange, Kinship. In *The Cradle of Language, Volume 2: African Perspectives*. R. P. Botha and C. Knight, eds, Oxford: Oxford University Press.

Barrett, L., R. I. M. Dunbar, and J. E. Lycett, 2002. *Human Evolutionary Psychology*. Basingstoke: Palgrave/Macmillan.

Bar-Yosef, O. 1998. On the Nature of Transitions: The Middle to Upper Palaeolithic and the Neolithic Revolution. *Cambridge Archaeological Journal* 8: 141–63.

—— 2001. From Sedentary Foragers to Village Hierarchies: The Emergence of Social Institutions. *Proceedings of the British Academy London* 110: 1–38.

—— 2002. The Upper Palaeolithic Revolution. *Annual Review of Anthropology* 31: 363–93.

—— and A. Belfer-Cohen, 1989. The Origins of Sedentism and Farming Communities in the Levant. *Journal of World Prehistory* 3: 447–98.

Bateson, P. P. G., 1983. Rules for Changing the Rules. In *Evolution from Molecules to Men*. D. S. Bendall, ed., pp. 483–507. Cambridge: Cambridge University Press.

Beckerman, S., and P. Valentine, 2002. Introduction: The Concept of Partible Paternity among Native South Americans. In *Cultures of Multiple Fathers: The Theory and Practice of Partible Paternity in Lowland South America*. S. Beckerman and P. Valentine, eds, pp. 1–13. Gainesville, FL: University Press of Florida.

—— R. Lizarralde, C. Ballew, S. Schroeder, C. Fingelton, A. Garrison, and H. Smith, 1998. The Bari Partible Paternity Project: Preliminary Results. *Current Anthropology* 391: 164–7.

Bender, M. L., 1975. *Omotic: A New Afroasiatic Family*. Carbondale: University Museum, Southern Illinois University.

Bennett, P. R., and J. R. Sterk, 1977. South-Central Niger-Congo: A Reclassification. *Studies in African Linguistics* 8: 241–65.

Bereczkei, T., 1998. Kinship Network, Direct Childcare, and Fertility among Hungarians and Gypsies. *Evolution and Human Behaviour* 19: 83–98.

—— and R. I. M. Dunbar, 1997. Female-Biased Reproductive Strategies in a Hungarian Gypsy Population. *Proceedings of the Royal Society, London* 264B: 17–22.

Bergman, T. J., J. C. Beehner, D. L. Cheney, and R. M. Seyfarth, 2003. Hierarchical Classification by Rank and Kinship in Baboons. *Science* 302: 1234–6.

Berndt, C., and R. M. Berndt, 1951. *Sexual Behaviour in Western Arnhem Land*. Viking Fund Publications in Anthropology 16. New York: Wenner–Gren.

Bernstein, I. S., P. G. Judge, and T. E. Ruehlmann, 1993. Kinship, Association, and Social Relationships in Rhesus-monkeys (*Macaca mulatta*). *American Journal of Primatology* 31: 41–53.

Berté, N. A., 1988. K'ekchi' Horticultural Labor Exchange: Productive and Reproductive Implications. In *Human Reproductive Behaviour*. L. M. Betzig, M. Borgerhoff Mulder, and P. Turke, eds, pp. 83–96. Cambridge: Cambridge University Press.

Betzig, L. M., and P. Turke, 1986. Food Sharing on Ifaluk. *Current Anthropology* 27: 397–400.

Bickerton, D., 1998. Catastrophic Evolution: The Case for a Single Step from Proto-language to Full Human Language. In *Approaches to the Evolution of Language: Social and Cognitive Bases*. J. R. Hurford, M. Studdert-Kennedy, and C. Knight, eds, pp. 341–58. Cambridge: Cambridge University Press.

Binford, L. R., 1981. *Bones: Ancient Men and Modern Myths*. New York: Academic Press.

Blench, R., 1996. *Archaeology, Language, and the African Past*. Lanham, MD: AltaMira Press.

Bliege Bird, R., 1999. Cooperation and Conflict: The Behavioral Ecology of the Sexual Division of Labor. *Evolutionary Anthropology* 8: 65–75.

Bloch, M. E. F., 1998. *How We Think They Think: Anthropological Approaches to Cognition, Memory, and Literacy*. Boulder, CO: Westview Press.

—— 2000. A Well-Disposed Social Anthropologist's Problems with Memes. In *Darwinizing Culture: The Status of Memetics as a Science*. R. Aunger, ed., pp. 163–73. Oxford: Oxford University Press.

—— and D. Sperber, 2002. Kinship and Evolved Psychological Dispositions: The Mother's Brother Controversy Reconsidered. *Current Anthropology* 43: 723–48.

Blurton Jones, N. G., K. Hawkes, and J. F. O'Connell, 1989. Studying Costs of Children in Two Foraging Societies: Implications for Schedules of Reproduction. In *Comparative Socioecology: The Behavioural Ecology of Humans and Other Mammals*. V. Standen and R. A. Foley, eds, pp. 365–90. Oxford: Blackwell.

—— L. C. Smith, J. F. O'Connell, K. Hawkes, and C. L. Kamuzora, 1992. Demography of the Hadza, an Increasing and High Density Population of Savanna Foragers. *American Journal of Physical Anthropology* 89: 159–82.

—— F. W. Marlowe, K. Hawkes, and J. F. O'Connell, 2000. Paternal Investment and Hunter-Gatherer Divorce Rates. In *Adaptation and Human Behavior*. L. Cronk, N. Chagnon, and W. Irons, eds, pp. 69–90. New York: Aldine de Gruyter.

—— K. Hawkes, and J. F. O'Connell, 2005. Older Hadza Men and Women as Helpers: Residence Data. In *Hunter-Gatherer Childhoods*. B. S. Hewlett and M. E. Lamb, eds, pp. 214–36. New Brunswick, NJ, and London: Aldine Transaction.

Boas, Franz, 1891. The Indians of British Columbia. *Sixth Report of the Committee on the North-Western Tribes of Canada*. Report of the British Association for the Advancement of Science 1890, pp. 801–903.

—— 1897. *The Social Organization and the Secret Societies of the Kwakiutl Indians*. Washington, DC: Report of the US National Museum, 1895.

Boesch, C., and Boesch-Achermann, H., 2000. *The Chimpanzees of the Taï Forest: Behavioural Ecology and Evolution*. Oxford: Oxford University Press.

—— G. Kohou, H. Néné, and L. Vigilant, 2006. Male Competition and Paternity in Wild Chimpanzees of the Taï Forest. *American Journal of Physical Anthropology* 130: 103–15.

Boone, J. L., 1988. Parental Investment, Social Subordination and Population Processes amongst the 15th- and 16th-Century Portuguese Nobility. In *Human Reproductive Behaviour*. L. M. Betzig, M. Borgerhoff Mulder, and P. Turke, eds, pp. 83–96. Cambridge: Cambridge University Press.

Borgerhoff Mulder, M., M. George-Cramer, J. Eshleman, and A. Ortolani, 2001. A Study of East African Kinship and Marriage Using a Phylogenetically Based Comparative Method. *American Anthropologist* 103: 1059–82.

Borries, C., and A. Koenig, 2000. Infanticide in Hanuman Langurs: Social Organization, Male Migration, and Weaning Age. In *Infanticide by Males and Its Implications*. C. P. van Schaik and C. H. Janson, eds, pp. 99–122. Cambridge: Cambridge University Press.

Botha, R. P., 2003. *Unravelling the Evolution of Language*. Amsterdam: Elsevier.

Bourdieu, P., 1977. *Outline of a Theory of Practice*. R. Nice, trans. Cambridge: Cambridge University Press.

Boyd, R., and P. J. Richerson, 1985. *Culture and the Evolutionary Process*. Chicago: University of Chicago Press.

—— and J. Silk, 1997. *How Humans Evolved*. New York: Norton.

Boyer, P., 2001. *Religion Explained*. London: William Heinemann.

Bradley, B. J., D. M. Doran-Sheehy, D. Lukas, C. Boesch, and L. Vigilant, 2004. Dispersed Male Networks in Western Gorillas. *Current Biology* 14: 510–13.

—— M. M. Robbins, E. A. Williamson, D. Steklis, N. G. Steklis, N. Eckhardt, C. Boesch, and L. Vigilant, 2005. Mountain Gorilla Tug-of-War: Silverbacks Have Limited Control over Reproduction in Multimale Groups. *Proceedings of the National Academy of Sciences of the United States of America* 102: 9418–23.

Braidwood, R., 1957 [1948]. *Prehistoric Men*. Chicago: Chicago Natural History Museum Popular Series Anthropology 37. 3rd edition.

Brown, P., M. J. Sutikna, R. P. Morwood, Jatmiko Soejono, E. W. Saptomo, and Rokus Awe Due, 2004. A New Small-Bodied Hominin from the Late Pleistocene of Flores, Indonesia. *Nature* 431: 1055–61.

Brunet, M., F. Guy, D. Pilbeam, H. T. Mackay, A. Likius and D. Ahounta, 2002. A New Hominid from the Upper Miocene of Chad, Central Africa. *Nature* 418: 145–51.

Bryant, D., F. Filimon, and R. D. Gray, 2005. Untangling Our Past: Languages, Trees, Splits and Networks. In *The Evolution of Cultural Diversity: A Phylogenetic Approach*. R. Mace, C. J. Holden, and S. Shennan, eds, pp. 67–83. London: UCL Press.

Buchan, J. C., S. C. Alberts, J. B. Silk, and J. Altmann, 2003. True Paternal Care in a Multi-male Primate Society. *Nature* 425: 179–81.

Burch, E. S., 1975. *Eskimo Kinsmen: Changing Family Relationships in Northwest Alaska*. American Ethnological Society Monograph 59. New York: West Publishing.

Burton, L. M., 1990. Teenage Childbearing as an Alternative Life-Course Strategy in Multigeneration Black Families. *Human Nature* 1: 123–43.

Buss, D., 1994. *The Evolution of Desire: Strategies of Human Mating*. New York: Basic Books.

Butler, R. W. H., E. McClelland, and R. E. Jones, 1999. Calibrating the Duration and Timing of the Messinian Salinity Crisis in the Mediterranean: Linked Tectono-climatic Signals in Thrust-Top Basins of Sicily. *Journal of the Geological Society, London* 156: 827–35.

Butynski, T., 1982. Harem-Replacement and Infanticide in the Blue Monkey *Cercopithecus mitis stuhlmanni* in the Kibale Forest, Uganda. *American Journal of Primatology* 3: 1–22.

Callan, H., 1970. *Ethology and Society: Towards an Anthropological View*. Oxford: Clarendon Press.

—— 1984. The Imagery of Choice in Sociobiology. *Man* 19: 404–20.

Calvin, W. H., and D. Bickerton, 2000. *Lingua ex Machina: Reconciling Darwin and Chomsky with the Human Brain*. Cambridge, MA: MIT Press.

Cann, R., M. Stoneking, and A. Wilson, 1987. Mitochondrial DNA and Human Evolution. *Nature* 325: 31–6.

Carbonell, E., and M. Mosquera, 2006. The Emergence of a Symbolic Behaviour: The Sepulchral Pit of Sima de los Huesos, Sierra de Atapuerca, Burgos, Spain. *Comptes Rendus Palevol* 5: 155–60.

Caro, T. M., D. W. Sellen, A. Parish, R. Frank, D. M. Brown, E. Voland, and M. Borgerhoff Mulder, 1995. Termination of Reproduction in Nonhuman and Human Primate Females. *International Journal of Primatology* 16: 205–20.

Carsten, J., 2004. *After Kinship*. Cambridge: Cambridge University Press.

—— and S. Hugh-Jones, eds, 1995. *About the House: Lévi-Strauss and Beyond*. Cambridge: Cambridge University Press.

Caspari, R., and S.-H. Lee, 2004. Older Age Becomes Common Late in Human Evolution. *Proceedings of the National Academy of Sciences* 101: 10895–900.

Cauvin, J. 2000. *The Birth of the Gods and the Origins of Agriculture*. Cambridge: Cambridge University Press.

Cavalli-Sforza, L. L., 1971. Similarities and Differences in Sociocultural and Biological Evolution. In *Mathematics in the Archaeological and Historical Sciences*. F. R. Hodson, D. G. Kendall and P. Tautu, eds, pp. 535–41. Edinburgh: Edinburgh University Press.

—— and F. Cavalli-Sforza, 1995. *The Great Human Diasporas: The History of Diversity and Evolution*. Reading, MA: Perseus Books.

—— P. Menozzi, and A. Piazza, 1994. *The History and Geography of Human Genes*. Princeton, NJ: Princeton University Press.

Chagnon, N. A., 1981. Terminological Kinship, Genealogical Relatedness, and Village Fissioning among the Yanomamö Indians. In *Natural Selection and Social Behavior*. R. Alexander and D. Tinkle, eds, pp. 490–508. New York: Chiron Press.

—— and P. E. Bugos, 1979. Kin Selection and Conflict: An Analysis of a Yanomamö Ax Fight. In *Evolutionary Biology and Human Social Behavior*, N. A. Chagnon and W. Irons, eds, pp. 213–37. North Scituate, MA: Duxbury.

Chapais, B., and C. M. Berman, eds, 2004. *Kinship and Behavior in Primates*. New York: Oxford University Press.

Chapman, J. 2000. *Fragmentation in Archaeology: People, Places and Broken Objects in the Prehistory of South-eastern Europe*. London: Routledge.

Cheney, D. L., 1987. Interactions and Relationships between Groups. In *Primate Societies*. B. B. Smuts, D. L. Cheney, R. M. Seyfarth, R. W. Wrangham, and T. T. Struhsaker, eds, pp. 267–81. Chicago: University of Chicago Press.

—— and R. M. Seyfarth, 1999. Recognition of Other Individuals' Social Relationships by Female Baboons. *Animal Behaviour* 58: 67–75.

Childe, V. G., 1942. *What Happened in History*. Harmondsworth: Penguin.

Chimpanzee Sequencing and Analysis Consortium, 2005. Initial Sequence of the Chimpanzee Genome and Comparison with the Human Genome. *Nature* 437: 69–87.

Clark, J. D., 1980. The Origins of Domestication in Ethiopia. In *Proceedings of the Eighth Panafrican Congress of Prehistory and Quaternary Studies*. R. E. Leakey and B. A. Ogot, eds, pp. 268–70. Nairobi: Louis Leakey Memorial Institute for African Prehistory.

—— and M. A. J. Williams, 1978. Recent Archaeological Research in Southeastern Ethiopia (1974–1975): Some Preliminary Results. *Annales d'Ethiopie* 11: 19–44.

—— Y. Beyenne, G. Wolde Gabriel, W. K. Hart, P. Renne, H. Gilbert, A. Defleur, G. Suwa, S. Katoh, K. R. Ludwig, J.-R. Boisserie, B. Asfaw, and T. D. White, 2003. Stratigraphic, Chronological and Behavioural Contexts of Pleistocene *Homo sapiens* from Middle Awash, Ethiopia. *Nature* 423: 747–52.

Close, A. ed., 1980. *Loaves and Dishes: The Prehistory of Wadi Kubbaniya*. Dallas: Southern Methodist University.

Clottes, J., and D. Lewis-Williams, 1996. *Les chamanes de la préhistoire: transe et magie dans les grottes ornées*. Paris: Seuil.

Clutton-Brock, T. H., 1989. Female Transfer and Inbreeding Avoidance in Social Mammals. *Nature* 337: 70–2.

Coale, A. J., and P. Demeny, 1983. *Regional Model Life Tables and Stable Populations*. New York and London: Academic Press.

Colmenares, F., 1992. Clans and Harems in a Colony of Hamadryas and Hybrid Baboons: Male Kinship, Familiarity and the Formation of Brother-Teams. *Behaviour* 121: 61–94.

Coon, C. S., 1931. Tribes of the Rift. *Harvard African Studies* 9: 1–417.

Cords, M., B. J. Mitchell, H. M. Tsingalia, and T. E. Rowell, 1986. Promiscuous Mating among Blue Monkeys in the Kakamega Forest, Kenya. *Ethology* 72: 214–26.

Cosmides, L., and J. H. Tooby, 1992. Cognitive Adaptations for Social Exchange. In *The Adapted Mind*. J. H. Barkow, L. Cosmides, and J. H. Tooby, eds, pp. 163–228. Oxford: Oxford University Press.

Cowlishaw, G., and R. Mace, 1996. Cross-cultural Patterns of Marriage and Inheritance: A Phylogenetic Approach. *Ethology and Sociobiology* 17(2): 87–97.

Cresswell, T., 2006. *On the Move*. London: Routledge.

Crockett, C. M., and C. H. Janson, 2000. Infanticide in Red Howlers: Female Group Size, Male Membership, and a Possible Link to Folivory. In *Infanticide by Males and Its Implications*. C. P. van Schaik and C. H. Janson, eds, pp. 75–98. Cambridge: Cambridge University Press.

—— and R. Sekulic, 1984. Infanticide in Red Howler Monkeys (*Allouatta seniculus*). In *Infanticide: Comparative and Evolutionary Perspectives*. G. Hausfater and S. B. Hrdy, eds, pp. 173–91. New York: Aldine.

Cronk, L., and A. Gerkey, 2007. Kinship and Descent. In *Oxford Handbook in Evolutionary Psychology*. R. I. M. Dunbar and L. Barrett, eds, pp. 463–78. Oxford: Oxford University Press.

Crook, J. H., 1980. *The Evolution of Human Consciousness*. Oxford: Clarendon Press.

—— and S. J. Crook, 1988. Tibetan Polyandry: Problems of Adaptation and Fitness. In *Human Reproductive Behaviour*. L. Betzig, M. Borgerhoff-Mulder, and P. Turke, eds, pp. 97–114. Cambridge: Cambridge University Press.

Darwin, C., 1871. *The Descent of Man, and Selection in Relation to Sex*. 2 vols. London: Murray.

Dawkins, R., 2006. *The God Delusion*. London: Transworld Publishers.

de Miguel, C., and M. Henneberg, 2001. Variation in Hominid Brain Size: How Much is Due to Method? *Homo* 52: 3–58.

Deacon, H. J., and J. Deacon, 1999. *Human Beginnings in South Africa: Uncovering the Secrets of the Stone Age*. Walnut Creek, CA: AltaMira Press.

Deacon, T., 1997. *The Symbolic Species: The Co-evolution of Language and the Human Brain*. London: Penguin.

Deady, D., M. Law Smith, J. Kent, and R. I. M. Dunbar, 2006. Is Priesthood an Adaptive Strategy? Evidence from a Historical Irish Population. *Human Nature* 17: 393–404.

Dennell, R. W., 1998. Grasslands, Tool Making and the Hominid Colonization of Southern Asia: A Reconsideration. In *Early Human Behaviour in Global Context*. M. D. Petraglia and R. Korisettar, eds, pp. 280–303. London: Routledge.

—— 2003. Dispersal and Colonisation, Long and Short Chronologies: How Continuous is the Early Pleistocene Record for Hominids outside East Africa? *Journal of Human Evolution* 45: 421–40.

d'Errico, F., C. S. Henshilwood, G. Lawson, M. Vanhaeren, A.-M. Tillier, M. Soressi, F. Bresson, B. Maureille, A. Nowell, J. Lakarra, L. Backwell, and M. Julien, 2003. Archaeological Evidence for the Emergence of Language, Symbolism, and Music: An Alternative Multidisciplinary Perspective. *Journal of World Prehistory* 17: 1–70.

Destro-Bisol, G., F. Donati, V. Coia, I. Boschi, F. Verginelli, A. Caglia, S. Tofanelli, G. Spedini, and C. Capelli, 2004. Variation of Female and Male Lineages in Sub-Saharan Populations: The Importance of Sociocultural Factors. *Molecular Biology and Evolution* 21: 1673–82.

de Waal, F., and P. Tyack, eds, 2003. *Animal Social Complexity*. Cambridge MA and London: Harvard University Press.

Diakonoff, I. M., 1998. The Earliest Semitic Society. *Journal of Semitic Studies* 43: 209–19.

Di Fiore, A., and C. J. Campbell, 2007. The Atelines: Variation in Ecology, Behavior, and Social Organization. In *Primates in Perspective*. C. J. Campbell, A. Fuentes, K. C. MacKinnon, M. Panger, and S. K. Bearder, eds, pp. 155–85. New York, Oxford: Oxford University Press.

Digby, L. J., S. F. Ferrari, and W. Saltzman, 2007. Callithrichines: The Role of Competition in Cooperatively Breeding Species. In *Primates in Perspective*. C. J. Campbell, A. Fuentes, K. C. MacKinnon, M. Panger, and S. K. Bearder, eds, pp. 85–105. New York, Oxford: Oxford University Press.

Dole, G. E., 1960. The Classification of Yankee Nomenclature in the Light of Evolution in Kinship. In *Essays in the Science of Culture in Honour of Leslie A. White*. G. E. Dole and R. L. Carneiro, eds, pp. 162–78. New York: Crowell.

Domínguez-Rodrigo, M., and T. Rayne Pickering, 2003. Early Hominid Hunting and Scavenging: A Zooarchaeological Review. *Evolutionary Anthropology* 12: 275–82.

Doran-Sheehy, D. M., and C. Boesch, 2004. Behavioral Ecology of Western Gorillas: New Insights from the Field. *American Journal of Primatology* 64: 139–43.

—— D. Greer, D., P. Mongo, and D. Schwindt, 2004. Impact of Ecological and Social Factors on Ranging in Western Gorillas. *American Journal of Primatology* 64: 207–22.

Dousset, L., 2002. Accounting for Context and Substance: The Australian Western Desert Kinship System. *Anthropological Forum* 12: 193–204.

—— 2005. Structure and Substance: Combining 'Classic' and 'Modern' Kinship Studies in the Australian Western Desert. *Australian Journal of Anthropology* 16: 18–30.

Dow, M. M., 1993. Saving the Theory: On Chi-Square Tests with Cross-Cultural Survey Data. *Cross-Cultural Research* 27: 247–76.

Dumézil, G., 1979. *Mariages indo-européens*. Paris: Payot.

Dunbar, R. I. M., 1984. *Reproductive Decisions: An Economic Analysis of Gelada Baboon Social Strategies*. Princeton, NJ: Princeton University Press.

—— 1988. *Primate Social Systems*. London: Croom Helm.

—— 1992a. Neocortex Size as a Constraint on Group Size in Primates. *Journal of Human Evolution* 20: 469–93.

—— 1992b. Time: A Hidden Constraint on the Behavioural Ecology of Baboons. *Behavioural Ecology and Sociobiology* 31: 35–49.

—— 1993. The Coevolution of Neocortical Size, Group size and Language in Humans. *Behavioral and Brain Sciences* 16: 681–735.

—— 1995. The Mating System of Callitrichid Primates: I Conditions for the Coevolution of Pair Bonding and Twinning. *Animal Behaviour* 50: 1057–70.

—— 1996a. *Grooming, Gossip and the Evolution of Language*. London: Faber and Faber.

—— 1996b. On the Evolution of Language and Kinship. In *The Archaeology of Human Ancestry: Power, Sex and Tradition*. J. Steele and S. Shennan, eds, pp. 380–96. London: Routledge.

—— 1998. The Social Brain Hypothesis. *Evolutionary Anthropology* 7: 178–90.

—— 2000. Male Mating Strategies: A Modeling Approach. In *Primate Males: Causes and Consequences of Variation in Group Composition*. P. M. Kappeler, ed., pp. 259–68. Cambridge: Cambridge University Press.

—— 2001. Brains on Two Legs: Group Size and the Evolution of Intelligence. In *Tree of Origin: What Primate Behavior Can Tell Us about Human Social Evolution*. F. B. M. de Waal, ed., pp. 173–92. Cambridge, MA: Harvard University Press.

—— 2003. The Social Brain: Mind, Language and Society in Evolutionary Perspective. *Annual Review of Anthropology* 32: 163–81.

—— 2004. *The Human Story: A New History of Mankind's Evolution*. London: Faber and Faber.

—— and M. Spoors, 1995. Social Networks, Support Cliques, and Kinship. *Human Nature* 6: 273–90.

—— A. Clark, and N. L. Hurst, 1995. Conflict and Cooperation among the Vikings: Contingent Behavioural Decisions. *Ethology and Sociobiology* 16: 233–46.

—— C. Knight, and C. Power, eds, 1999. *The Evolution of Culture*. Edinburgh: Edinburgh University Press.

—— L. Barrett, and J. E. Lycett, 2005. *Evolutionary Psychology: A Beginner's Guide*. Oxford: OneWorld Books.

—— in press. Why Only Humans Have Language. In *The Cradle of Language, Volume 1: Multidisciplinary Perspectives*. R. P. Botha and C. Knight, eds, Oxford: Oxford University Press.

Dunn, M., A. Terrill, G. Reesink, R. A. Foley, and S. C. Levinson, 2005. Structural Phylogenetics and the Reconstruction of Ancient Language History. *Science* 309(5743): 2072–5.

Durham, W. H., 1991. *Coevolution: Genes, Culture and Human Diversity*. Stanford, CA: Stanford University Press.

Durkheim, É., 1915 [1912]. *The Elementary Forms of the Religious Life*. J. W. Swain, trans. London: Allen and Unwin.

—— and M. Mauss, 1963 [1903]. *Primitive Classification*. R. Needham, trans. London: Cohen and West.

Dyen, I., J. B. Kruskal, and P. Black, 1992. An Indo-European Classification: A Lexicostatistical Experiment. *Transactions of the American Philosophical Society* 82(5): 1–132.

Dyson-Hudson, N., 1966. *Karimojong Politics*. Oxford: Clarendon Press.

Eggan, F., 1950. *Social Organization of the Western Pueblos*. Chicago: University of Chicago Press.

Ehret, C., 1979. On the Antiquity of Agriculture in Ethiopia. *Journal of African History* 20: 161–77.

—— 1980a. *The Historical Reconstruction of Southern Cushitic Phonology and Vocabulary*. Berlin: Reimer.

—— 1980b. Omotic and the Subclassification of the Afroasiatic Language Family. In *Proceedings of the Fifth International Conference on Ethiopian Studies, Session B*. R. Hess ed., pp. 51–62. Chicago: University of Illinois.

—— 1982. The First Food Production in Southern Africa. In *The Archaeological and Linguistic Reconstruction of African History*. C. Ehret and M. Posnansky, eds, pp. 158–81. Berkeley, Los Angeles: University of California Press.

—— 1984. Historical/Linguistic Evidence for Early African Food Production. In *From Hunters to Farmers*. J. Desmond Clark and S. Brandt, eds, pp. 26–35. Berkeley, Los Angeles: University of California Press.

—— 1986. Proposals on Khoisan Reconstruction. *Sprache und Geschichte in Afrika* 7(2): 105–30.

—— 1993. Nilo-Saharans and the Saharo-Sudanese Neolithic. In *The Archaeology of Africa: Food, Metals and Towns*. T. Shaw, P. Sinclair, B. Andah, and A. Okpoko, eds, pp. 104–25. London: Routledge.

—— 1995a. Do Krongo and Shabo Belong in Nilo-Saharan? In *Fifth Nilo-Saharan Linguistics Colloquium, Nice 24–29 August 1992 Actes/Proceedings*. R. Nicolai and F. Rottland, eds, pp. 165–93. Cologne: Rüdiger Köppe Verlag.

—— 1995b. *Reconstructing Proto-Afroasiatic (Proto-Afrasian): Vowels, Tone, Consonants, and Vocabulary*. Berkeley, Los Angeles: University of California Press.

—— 1997. Transformations in Southern African History: Proposals for a Sweeping Overview of Change and Development, 6000 BC to the present. *Ufahamu* 26: 54–80.

—— 1999. Who Were the Rock Artists? Linguistic Evidence for the Holocene Populations of the Sahara. Symposium: Rock Art and the Sahara. In *Proceedings of the International Rock Art and Cognitive Archaeology Congress.* A. Muzzolini and J.-L. Le Quellec, eds. Turin: Centro Studie Museo d'Arte Prehistorica. [Published as a CD].

—— 2000a. Is Krongo After All a Niger-Congo Language? In *'Mehr als nur Worte…' Afrikanistische Beiträge zum 65. Geburtstag R. von Franz Rottland.* R. Vossen, A. Mietzner, and A. Meissner, eds, pp. 225–67. Cologne: Rüdiger Köppe Verlag.

—— 2000b. Language and History. In *African Languages: An Introduction.* B. Heine and D. Nurse, eds, pp. 272–97. Cambridge: Cambridge University Press.

—— 2000c. Testing the Expectations of Glottochronology against the Correlations of Language and Archaeology in Africa. In *Time Depth in Historical Linguistics.* C. Renfrew, A. McMahon, and L. Trask, eds, Volume 2, pp. 373–99. Cambridge: McDonald Institute for Archaeological Research.

—— 2001. *A Historical-Comparative Reconstruction of Proto-Nilo-aharan.* Cologne: Rüdiger Köppe Verlag.

—— 2003a. Language Contacts in Nilo-Saharan Prehistory. In *Language Contacts in Prehistory: Studies in Stratigraphy.* H. Andersen, ed., pp. 135–57. Amsterdam, Philadelphia: John Benjamins Publishing Company.

—— 2003b. Language Family Expansions: Broadening Our Understanding of Cause from an African Perspective. In *Language and Agricultural Dispersals.* P. Bellwood and C. Renfrew, eds, pp. 163–76. Cambridge: McDonald Institute for Archaeological Research.

—— 2006a. Linguistic Stratigraphies and Holocene History in Northeastern Africa. In *Archaeology of Northeastern Africa.* M. Chlodnicki and K. Kroeper, eds, pp. 1019–55. Posnan: Posnan Archaeological Museum, Studies in African Archaeology, Vol. 9.

—— 2006b. The Nilo-Saharan Background of Chadic. In *West African Linguistics: Studies in Honor of Russell G. Schuh.* P. Newman and L. Hyman eds, pp. 56–66, *Studies in African Linguistics*, Suppl. 11. Columbus: Ohio State University.

—— forthcoming a. Extinct Khoisan Languages in East Africa. In *The Khoisan Languages of Africa.* R. Vossen, ed. Richmond, Surrey: Curzon.

—— forthcoming b. Khoisan Languages and Late Stone Age Archaeology. In *Proceedings of 12th Congress of the Pan African Association for Archaeology and Related Studies, Gaborone, 3–10 July 2005.*

—— forthcoming c. Linguistic Evidence and the Origins of Food Production in Africa: Where Are We Now? In *African Flora, Past Cultures and Archaeobotany.* D. Q. Fuller and M. Murray, eds. Walnut Creek, CA: Left Coast Press.

—— forthcoming d. *Reconstructing Proto-Afroasiatic,* Vol. 2.

—— online: http://www.sscnet.ucla.edu/history/ehret/kinship/african_kinship_data.htm

—— S. O. Y. Keita, and P. Newman, 2004. The Origins of Afroasiatic. *Science* 306: 1680–1.

Ellison, P. T., 1994. Extinction and Descent. *Human Nature* 5: 155–66.

Elphick, R., 1977. *Kraal and Castle.* New Haven: Yale University Press.

Ember, C. R., 1978. Myths about Hunter-Gatherers. *Ethnology* 17: 439–48.

Embleton, S., 1986. *Statistics in Historical Linguistics.* Bochum: Studienverlag Brockmeyer.

Emery Thompson, M., N. E. Newton-Fisher, and V. Reynolds, 2006. Probable Community Transfer of Parous Adult Female Chimpanzees in the Budongo Forest, Uganda. *International Journal of Primatology* 27: 1601–17.

Engels, F., 1972a [1891]. Preface to the Fourth Edition. *The Origin of the Family, Private Property and the State.* New York: Pathfinder Press, pp. 27–38.

—— 1972b [1884]. *The Origin of the Family, Private Property and the State.* New York: Pathfinder Press.

Euler, H. A., and B. Weitzel, 1996. Discriminative Grandparental Investment as a Reproductive Strategy. *Human Nature* 7: 39–59.

Evans-Pritchard, E. E., 1940. *The Nuer: A Description of the Modes of Livelihood and Political Institutions of a Nilotic People*. Oxford: Clarendon Press.

—— 1951. *Kinship and Marriage among the Nuer*. Oxford: Clarendon Press. Reissued 1990 with new introduction by Wendy James.

—— 1965. *Theories of Primitive Religion*. Oxford: Clarendon Press.

Fagan, B. ed., 2004. *The Seventy Great Inventions of the Ancient World*. London: Thames and Hudson.

Fashing, P. J., 2005. African Colobine Monkeys. In *Primates in Perspective*. C. J. Campbell, A. F. Fuentes, K. C. MacKinnon, M. Panger, and S. Bearder, eds, pp. 201–24. Oxford: Oxford University Press.

Fehr, E., and S. Gaechter, 2002. Altruistic Punishment in Humans. *Nature* 415: 137–40.

Felsenstein, J., 1985. Phylogenies and the Comparative Method. *The American Naturalist* 125: 1–15.

—— 2004. *Inferring Phylogenies*. Sunderland: Sinauer Associates, Inc.

Ferguson, A. 1995 [1767]. *An Essay on the History of Civil Society*. Cambridge: Cambridge University Press.

Fisher, J. W., and H. C. Strickland, 1991. Dwellings and Fireplaces: Keys to Efe Pygmy Campsite Structure. In *Ethnoarchaeological Approaches to Mobile Campsites*. C. S. Gamble and W. A. Boismier, eds, pp. 215–36. Ann Arbor: International Monographs in Prehistory.

Fisher, R. A., 1930. *The Genetical Theory of Natural Selection*. Oxford: Clarendon Press.

Fleming, H. C., 1969. The Classification of West Cushitic within Hamito-Semitic. In *Eastern African History*. J. Butler, ed., pp. 3–27. New York: Praeger.

—— 1974. Omotic as an Afroasiatic Family. *Studies in African Linguistics* Supplement 5: 80–94.

—— 1983. Chadic External Relations. In *Studies in Chadic and Afroasiatic Linguistics*. H. Ekkehard Wolff and H. Meyer-Bahlburg, eds, pp. 17–31. Hamburg: Buske.

Foley, R. A., 1987. *Another Unique Species*. Harlow: Longman.

—— 1991. How Many Hominid Species Should There Be? *Journal of Human Evolution* 20: 413–27.

—— and P. C. Lee, 1989. Finite Social Space, Evolutionary Pathways and Reconstructing Hominid Behaviour. *Science* 243: 901–6.

—— and P. C. Lee, 1991. Ecology and Energetics of Encephalization in Hominid Evolution. *Philosophical Transactions of the Royal Society, London* Series B 334: 223–32.

Forster, P., 2004. Ice Ages and the Mitochondrial DNA Chronology of Human Dispersals: A Review. *Philosophical Transactions of the Royal Society of London*, Series B 359: 255–64.

Fortes, M., 1970. *Kinship and the Social Order*. London: Routledge.

Fortunato, L., and R. Mace, in press. Testing Functional Hypotheses about Cross-Cultural Variation: A Maximum-Likelihood Comparative Analysis of Indo-European Marriage Practices. In *Pattern and Process in Cultural Evolution*. S. Shennan, ed. Berkeley: University of California Press.

—— C. Holden, and R. Mace, 2006. From Bridewealth to Dowry? A Bayesian Estimation of Ancestral States of Marriage Transfers in Indo-European Groups. *Human Nature* 17: 355–76.

Fox, R., 1967. *Kinship and Marriage: An Anthropological Perspective*. Harmondsworth: Penguin.

—— 1980. *The Red Lamp of Incest*. London: Hutchinson.

Fried, M., 1967. *The Evolution of Political Society: An Essay in Political Anthropology*. New York: Random House.

Friedl, E., 1978. Society and Sex Roles. *Human Nature* 1(4): 68–75.

Furuichi, T., 1989. Social Interactions and the Life History of Female *Pan paniscus* in Wamba, Zaïre. *International Journal of Primatology* 10: 173–97.

Galdikas, B. M. F., and J. W. Wood, 1990. Birth Spacing Patterns in Humans and Apes. *American Journal of Physical Anthropology* 83: 185–91.

Gamble, C. S., 1993. *Timewalkers: The Prehistory of Global Colonization.* Cambridge MA: Harvard University Press.

—— 1998. Palaeolithic Society and the Release from Proximity: A Network Approach to Intimate Relations. *World Archaeology* 29: 426–49.

—— 1999. *The Palaeolithic Societies of Europe.* Cambridge: Cambridge University Press.

—— 2001. Modes, Movement and Moderns. *Quaternary International* 75: 5–10.

—— 2004a. Materiality and Symbolic Force: A Palaeolithic View of Sedentism. In *Rethinking Materiality: The Engagement of Mind with the Material World.* E. DeMarrais, C. Gosden, and C. Renfrew, eds, pp. 85–95. Cambridge: McDonald Institute of Archaeological Research.

—— 2004b. Social Archaeology and the Unfinished Business of the Palaeolithic. In *Explaining Social Change: Studies in Honour of Colin Renfrew.* J. F. Cherry, C. Scarre, and S. Shennan, eds, pp. 17–26. Cambridge: McDonald Institute Monographs.

—— 2007. *Origins and Revolutions: Human Identity in Earliest Prehistory.* New York: Cambridge University Press.

Gaulin, J. C., D. H. McBurney, and S. L. Brakeman-Wartel, 1997. Matrilateral Biases in the Investment of Aunts and Uncles: A Consequence and Measure of Paternity Uncertainty. *Human Nature* 8: 139–51.

Geary, D. C., and M. V. Flinn, 2001. Evolution of Human Parental Behavior and the Human Family. *Parenting: Science and Practice* 5: 5–61.

Gell, A., 1998. *Art and Agency: Towards a New Anthropological Theory.* Oxford: Clarendon Press.

Geissler, W., E. Alber, and S. Whyte, eds, 2004. Grandparents and Grandchildren. *Africa* 74 (special issue): 1–120.

Ghiglieri, M. P., 1987. Sociobiology of the Great Apes and the Hominid Ancestor. *Journal of Human Evolution* 16: 319–57.

Giddens, A. 1984. *The Constitution of Society.* Cambridge: Polity Press.

Gilby, I. C., L. E. Eberly, L. Pintea, and A. Pusey, 2006. Ecological and Social Influences on the Hunting Behaviour of Wild Chimpanzees, *Pan troglodytes schweinfurthii. Animal Behaviour* 72: 169–80.

Godelier, M., 2004. *Métamorphoses de la parenté.* Paris: Fayard.

—— T. R. Trautmann, and F. E. Tjon Sie Fat, eds, 1998. *Transformations of Kinship.* Washington, DC: Smithsonian Institution.

Goldberg, T. L., and R. W. Wrangham, 1997. Genetic Correlates of Social Behaviour in Wild Chimpanzees: Evidence from Mitochondrial DNA. *Animal Behaviour* 54: 559–70.

Goldizen, A. W., 1987. Tamarins and Marmosets: Communal Care of Offspring. In *Primate Societies.* B. B. Smuts, D. L. Cheney, R. M. Seyfarth, R. W. Wrangham, and T. T. Struhsaker, eds, pp. 112–20. Chicago: University of Chicago Press.

Goldschmidt, W., 1979. A General Model for Pastoral Social Systems. In *Pastoral Productions and Society.* Équipe Ecologique, ed., pp. 15–28. Cambridge: Cambridge University Press.

Goodall, J., 1986. *The Chimpanzees of Gombe: Patterns of Behaviour.* Cambridge: Cambridge University Press.

Goodman, M., B. F. Koop, J. Czelusniak, D. H. A. Fitch, D. A. Tagle, and J. L. Slighton, 1989. Molecular Phylogeny of the Family of Apes and Humans. *Genome* 31: 316–35.

Goody, J., 1973. Bridewealth and Dowry in Africa and Eurasia. In *Bridewealth and Dowry.* J. Goody and S. J. Tambiah, eds, pp. 1–58. Cambridge: Cambridge University Press.

—— 1976. *Production and Reproduction: A Comparative Study of the Domestic Domain*. Cambridge: Cambridge University Press.

—— 1983. *The Development of the Family and Marriage in Europe*. Cambridge: Cambridge University Press.

Gordon, R. G., ed., 2005. *Ethnologue: Languages of the World*. Dallas: SIL International.

Goren-Inbar N., N. Alperson, M. E. Kislev, O. Simchoni, Y. Melamed, A. Ben–Nun, and E. Werker, 2004. Evidence of Hominin Control of Fire at Gesher Benot Ya'aqov, Israel. *Science* 304: 725–7.

Gouzoules, S., and H. Gouzoules, 1987. Kinship. In *Primate Societies*. B. B. Smuts, D. L. Cheney, R. M. Seyfarth, R. W. Wrangham, and T. T. Struhsaker, eds, pp. 297–305. Chicago: University of Chicago Press.

Gowaty, P., 1997. Sexual Dialectics, Sexual Selection, and Variation in Mating Behavior. In *Feminism and Evolutionary Biology: Boundaries, Intersections, and Frontiers*. P. Gowaty, ed., pp. 351–84. New York: Chapman and Hall.

Gowlett, J. A. J., 2006. The Early Settlement of Northern Europe: Fire History in the Context of Climate Change and the Social Brain. In *Climats, cultures et sociétés aux temps préhistoriques, de l'apparition des Hominidés jusqu'au Néolithique*. H. de Lumley, ed., *C.R. Palevol*. 5: 299–310.

—— in press. The Longest Transition or Multiple Revolutions? Curves and Steps in the Record of Human Origins. In *A Sourcebook of Paleolithic Transitions: Methods, Theories and Interpretations*. M. Camps and P. Chauhan, eds. Hamburg: Springer Verlag.

—— J. Hallos, S. Hounsell, V. Brant, and N. C. Debenham, 2005. Beeches Pit – Archaeology, Assemblage Dynamics and Early Fire History of a Middle Pleistocene Site in East Anglia, UK. *Journal of Eurasian Prehistory* 3: 3–43.

Gray, J. P., 1999. A Corrected *Ethnographic Atlas*. *World Cultures* 10: 24–136.

Gray, R. D., and Q. D. Atkinson, 2003. Language-Tree Divergence Times Support the Anatolian Theory of Indo-European Origin. *Nature* 426(6965): 435–39.

—— and F. M. Jordan, 2000. Language Trees Support the Express-Train Sequence of Austronesian Expansion. *Nature* 405(6790): 1052–5.

Grayson, D. K., 1993. Differential Mortality and the Donner Party Disaster. *Evolutionary Anthropology* 2: 151–9.

Greenberg, J. H., 1963. *The Languages of Africa*. Bloomington: Indiana University Press.

—— 1964. Historical Inferences from Linguistic Research in Sub–Saharan Africa. In *Boston University Papers in African History*. J. Butler, ed., 1: 1–15.

Greenwood, P. J., 1983. Mating Systems and the Evolutionary Consequences of Dispersal. In *The Ecology of Animal Movement*. I. R. Swingland and P. J. Greenwood, eds, pp. 116–31. Thetford: Thetford Press.

Griffin, A. S., and S. A. West, 2002. Kin Selection: Fact and Fiction. *Trends in Ecology and Evolution* 17: 15–21.

Gürerk, Ö., B. Irlenbusch, and B. Rockenbach, 2006. The Competitive Advantage of Sanctioning Institutions. *Science* 312: 108–11.

Gurven, M., and K. Hill, 1997. 'Comment' on Hawkes et al. *Current Anthropology* 38: 566–7.

Hage, P., 2002. The Ancient Maya Kinship System. *Journal of Anthropological Research* 59: 5–21.

—— 2006. Dravidian Kinship Systems in Africa. *L'Homme* 177–8: 395–408.

Hallowell, A. I., 1955 [1949]. Psychosexual Adjustment, Personality, and the Good Life in a Nonliterate Culture. Reprinted in *Culture and Experience*, A. I. Hallowell, ed., pp. 291–305. Philadelphia: University of Pennsylvania Press.

Hamai, M. with T. Nishida, H. Takasaki, and L. A. Turner, 1992. New Records of Within-Group Infanticide and Cannibalism in Wild Chimpanzees. *Primates* 33: 151–62.

Hames, R., 1987. Garden Labor Exchange among the Ye'Kwana. *Ethology and Sociobiology* 8: 259–84.

Hamilton, W. D., 1964. The Genetical Evolution of Social Behaviour I, II. *Journal of Theoretical Biology* 7: 1–52.

—— 1984. Significance of Paternal Investment by Primates to the Evolution of Adult Male–Female Associations. In *Primate Paternalism*. D. M. Taub, ed., pp. 309–35. New York: Van Nostrand Reinhold.

Hammer, M. F., T. M. Karafet, A. J. Redd, H. Jarjanazi, S. Santachiara-Benerecetti, H. Soodyall, and S. L. Zegura, 2001. Hierarchical Patterns of Global Human Y-chromosome Diversity. *Molecular Biology and Evolution* 18: 1189–203.

Harcourt, A. H., 1979. Social Relationships among Adult Female Mountain Gorillas. *Animal Behaviour* 27: 251–64.

—— K. J. Stewart, and D. Fossey, 1976. Male Emigration and Female Transfer in Wild Mountain Gorilla. *Nature* 263: 226–7.

Harris, M., 1969. *The Rise of Anthropological Theory*. London: Routledge.

Hart, C., and A. Pilling, 1960. *The Tiwi of North Australia*. New York: Holt, Rinehart. 1st edition.

—— A. Pilling, and J. Goodale, 1988. *The Tiwi of North Australia*. New York: Holt, Rinehart. 3rd edition.

Harvey, P. H., and M. D. Pagel, 1991. *The Comparative Method in Evolutionary Biology*. Oxford: Oxford University Press.

Hawkes, K., 2004. The Grandmother Effect. *Nature* 428: 128–9.

—— and R. Bliege Bird, 2002. Showing Off, Handicap Signalling and the Evolution of Men's Work. *Evolutionary Anthropology* 11: 58–67.

—— J. F. O'Connell, and N. G. Blurton Jones, 1989. Hardworking Hadza Grandmothers. In *Comparative Socioecology: The Behavioural Ecology of Humans and Other Mammals*. V. Standen and R. A. Foley, eds, pp. 341–66. Oxford: Blackwell.

—— J. F. O'Connell, and N. G. Blurton Jones, 1991. Hunting Income Patterns among the Hadza: Big Game, Common Goods, Foraging Goals, and the Evolution of the Human Diet. *Philosophical Transactions of the Royal Society, London* Series B 334: 243–51.

—— J. F. O'Connell, and N. G. Blurton Jones, 1995a. Hadza Children's Foraging: Juvenile Dependency, Social Arrangements and Mobility among Hunter-Gatherers. *Current Anthropology* 36: 688–700.

—— A. Rogers, and E. L. Charnov, 1995b. The Male's Dilemma: Increased Offspring Production is More Paternity to Steal. *Evolutionary Ecology* 9: 662–77.

—— J. F. O'Connell, and N. G. Blurton Jones, 1997. Hadza Women's Time Allocation, Offspring Provisioning, and the Evolution of Long Postmenopausal Life Spans. *Current Anthropology* 38: 551–77.

—— J. F. O'Connell, N. G. Blurton Jones, H. P. Alvarez, and E. L. Charnov, 1998. Grandmothering, Menopause, and the Evolution of Human Life Histories. *Proceedings of the National Academy of Sciences of the United States of America* 95: 1336–9.

—— J. F. O'Connell, and N. G. Blurton Jones, 2001. Hunting and Nuclear Families: Some Lessons from the Hadza about Men's Work. *Current Anthropology* 42: 681–709.

Heath, J., F. Merlan, and A. Rumsey, 1982. *The Languages of Kinship in Aboriginal Australia*. Oceania Linguistic Monographs 24. Sydney: University of Sydney.

Helms, M. W., 1988. *Ulysses' Sail: An Ethnographic Odyssey of Power, Knowledge, and Geographical Distance*. Princeton, NJ: Princeton University Press.

Henry, J., 1941. *Jungle People: A Kaingang tribe of the Highlands of Brazil*. New York: J. J. Augustin.

Henshilwood, C. S., and Francesco d'Errico, 2005. Being Modern in the Middle Stone Age: Individuals and Innovation. In *The Hominid Individual in Context: Archaeological*

Investigations of Lower and Middle Palaeolithic Landscapes, Locales and Artefacts. C. Gamble and M. Porr, eds, pp. 244–64. London: Routledge.

—— and C.W. Marean, 2003. The Origin of Modern Human Behaviour: Critique of the Models and Their Test Implications. *Current Anthropology* 44: 627–51.

—— J. C. Sealy, R. Yates, K. Cruz-Uribe, P. Goldberg, F. E. Grine, R. G. Klein, C. Poggenpoel, K. van Niekerk, and I. Watts, 2001. Blombos Cave, Southern Cape, South Africa: Preliminary Report on the 1992–1999 Excavations of the Middle Stone Age Levels. *Journal of Archaeological Science* 28: 421–48.

—— F. d'Errico, R. Yates, Z. Jacobs, C. Tribolo, G. A. T. Duller, N. Mercier, J. C. Sealy, H. Valladas, I. Watts, and A. G. Wintle, 2002. Emergence of Modern Human Behavior: Middle Stone Age Engravings from South Africa. *Science* 295: 1278–80.

Henzi, S. P., J. E. Lycett, and S. E. Piper, 1997. Fission and Troop Size in a Mountain Baboon Population. *Animal Behaviour* 53: 525–35.

Hepper, P. G., 1986. Kin Recognition: Functions and Mechanisms. *Biological Reviews of the Cambridge Philosophical Society* 61: 63–93.

Hilgen, F. J., L. Bissoli, S. Iaccarino, W. Krijgsman, R. Meijer, A. Negri, and G. Villa, 2000. Integrated Stratigraphy and Astrochronology of the Messinian GSSG at Oued Akrech (Atlantic Morocco). *Earth and Planetary Science Letters* 182: 237–51.

Hilke, H., and D. Plester, 1955. Forschungsreise in das Land der Präniloten. *Zeitschrift für Ethnologie* 80: 178–86.

Hill, D. A., 2004. The Effects of Demographic Variation on Kinship Structure and Behavior in Cercopithecines. In *Kinship and Behavior in Primates.* B. Chapais and C. M. Berman, eds, pp. 132–50. New York: Oxford University Press.

Hill, K., and A. M. Hurtado, 1996. *Aché Life History: The Ecology and Demography of a Foraging People.* New York: Aldine de Gruyter.

Hinde, R. A., 1979. The Nature of Social Structure. In *The Great Apes.* D. A. Hamburg and E. R. McCown, eds, pp. 295–315. Menlo Park, CA: Benjamin.

Hiraiwa-Hasegawa, M., and T. Hasegawa, 1994. Infanticide in Non-Human Primates: Sexual Selection and Local Resource Competition. In *Infanticide and Parental Care.* S. Parmigiani and F. S. vom Saal, eds, Langhorne, PA: Harwood Academic.

Hodder, I., 1990. *The Domestication of Europe: Structure and Contingency in Neolithic Societies.* Oxford: Blackwell.

Hohmann, G., U. Gerloff, D. Tautz, and B. Fruth, 1999. Social Bonds and Genetic Ties: Kinship, Association and Affiliation in a Community of Bonobos (*Pan paniscus*). *Behaviour* 136: 1219–35.

Holden, C. J., 2002. Bantu Language Trees Reflect the Spread of Farming across Sub-Saharan Africa: A Maximum-Parsimony Analysis. *Proceedings of the Royal Society of London* Series B 269(1493): 793–9.

—— and R. Mace, 1997. Phylogenetic Analysis of the Evolution of Lactose Digestion in Adults. *Human Biology* 69: 605–28.

—— and R. Mace, 1999. Sexual Dimorphism in Stature and Women's Work: A Phylogenetic Cross-Cultural Analysis. *American Journal of Physical Anthropology* 110: 27–45.

—— and R. Mace, 2003. Spread of Cattle Led to the Loss of Matrilineal Descent in Africa: A Coevolutionary Analysis. *Proceedings of the Royal Society of London* Series B 270(1532): 2425–33.

—— and R. Mace, 2005. 'The Cow is the Enemy of Matriliny': Using Phylogenetic Methods to Investigate Cultural Evolution in Africa. In *The Evolution of Cultural Diversity: A Phylogenetic Approach.* R. Mace, C. J. Holden, and S. Shennan, eds, pp. 217–34. London: UCL Press.

—— R. Sear, and R. Mace, 2003. Matriliny as Daughter-Biased Investment. *Evolution and Human Behavior* 24: 99–112.

Holder, M., and P. O. Lewis, 2003. Phylogeny Estimation: Traditional and Bayesian Approaches. *Nature Reviews Genetics* 4(4): 275–284.

Holmes, W. G., and P. W. Shermann, 1982. Kin Recognition in Animals. *American Scientist* 71: 46–55.

Hovers, E., S. Ilani, O. Bar-Yosef, and B. Vandermeersch, 2003. An Early Case of Color Symbolism. *Current Anthropology* 44: 491–522.

Howell, N., 2000. *Demography of the Dobe !Kung.* New York: Aldine de Gruyter.

Hrdy, S. B., 1974. Male–Male Competition and Infanticide among the Langurs (*Presbytis entellus*) of Abu, Rajasthan. *Folia Primatologica* 22: 19–58.

—— 1979. Infanticide among Animals – Review, Classification, and Examination of the Implications for the Reproductive Strategies of Females. *Ethology and Sociobiology* 1: 13–40.

—— 1981. *The Woman that Never Evolved.* Cambridge, MA: Harvard University.

Huelsenbeck, J. P., and B. Rannala, 2003. Detecting Correlation between Characters in Comparative Analysis with Uncertain Phylogeny. *Evolution* 57(6): 1237–47.

—— F. Ronquist, R. Nielsen, and J. P. Bollback, 2001. Bayesian Inference of Phylogeny and Its Impact on Evolutionary Biology. *Science* 294(5550): 2310–14.

Hughes, A., 1988. *Evolution and Human Kinship.* Oxford: Oxford University Press.

Hughes, D. O., 1985. From Brideprice to Dowry in Mediterranean Europe. In *The Marriage Bargain: Women and Dowries in European History.* M. A. Kaplan, ed., pp. 13–58. New York: The Institute for Research in History and the Haworth Press, Inc.

Hurd, J. P., 1983. Kin Relatedness and Church Fissioning among the 'Nebraska' Amish of Pennsylvania. *Social Biology* 30: 59–63.

Isaac, G. L., 1978a. The Food Sharing Behavior of Proto-Human Hominids. *Scientific American* 238(4): 90–108.

—— 1978b. Food Sharing and Human Evolution: Archaeological Evidence from the Plio-Pleistocene of East Africa. *Journal of Anthropological Research* 34: 311–25.

—— 1989. Stone Age Visiting Cards: Approaches to the Study of Early Land-Use Patterns. In *The Archaeology of Human Origins: The Isaac Papers,* B. Isaac, ed., 206–27. Cambridge: Cambridge University Press.

Isbell, L. A., 1991. Contest and Scramble Competition: Patterns of Female Aggression and Ranging Behaviour among Primates. *Behavioral Ecology* 2: 143–55.

—— 2004. Is There No Place Like Home? Ecological Bases of Female Dispersal and Philopatry and Their Consequences for the Formation of Kin Groups. In *Kinship and Behavior in Primates.* B. Chapais and C. M. Berman, eds, pp. 71–109. New York: Oxford University Press.

—— and D. van Vuren, 1996. Differential Costs of Locational and Social Dispersal and Their Consequences for Female Group Living Primates. *Behaviour* 133: 1–36.

—— and T. P. Young, 1996. The Evolution of Bipedalism in Hominids and Reduced Group Size in Chimpanzees: Alternative Responses to Decreasing Resource Availability. *Journal of Human Evolution* 30: 389–97.

Ivey, P., 2000. Cooperative Reproduction in Ituri Forest Hunter-Gatherers: Who Cares for Efe Infants? *Current Anthropology* 41: 856–66.

Jackson, G. B., and A. Kimball Romney, 1973. Historical Inference from Cross–Cultural Data: The Case of Dowry. *Ethos* 1: 517–20.

Jamard, J.-L., 2000. La Passion de la Parenté: derniers échos ou retour de la flamme? *L'Homme* 154–5: 733–48.

James, W. R., 1979. *'Kwanim Pa: The Making of the Uduk People. An Ethnographic Study of Survival in the Sudan–Ethiopian Borderlands.* Oxford: Clarendon Press.

—— 1998a. The Treatment of African Ethnography in *L'Année sociologique* (I–XII). *L'Année sociologique* 48: 193–207.

—— 1998b. Mauss in Africa: On Time, History, and Politics. In *Marcel Mauss: A Centenary Tribute*. W. James and N. J. Allen, eds, pp. 226–48. New York and Oxford: Berghahn Books.

—— 2000a. Kuria and the Passages of Life. Review artricle. *Journal of Religion in Africa* 30: 121–6.

—— 2000b. Placing the Unborn: On the Social Recognition of New Life. *Anthropology and Medicine* 7: 169–89.

—— 2003. *The Ceremonial Animal: A New Portrait of Anthropology*. Oxford: Oxford University Press.

—— 2007. *War and Survival in Sudan's Frontierlands: Voices from the Blue Nile*. Oxford: Oxford University Press.

—— N. J. Allen, and H. Callan, 2005. Unpublished notes for the RAI workshop on 'Early Human Kinship', held at Gregynog, Wales.

Janson, C. H., and C. P. van Schaik 2000. The Behavioural Ecology of Infanticide by Males. In *Infanticide by Males and Its Implications*. C. P. van Schaik and C. H. Janson, eds, pp. 469–94. Cambridge: Cambridge University Press.

Jarman, M. R., 1972. A Territorial Model for Archaeology: A Behavioural and Geographical Approach. In *Models in Archaeology*. D. L. Clarke, ed., pp. 705–33. London: Methuen.

Johanson, Donald, C., Maurice Taieb, and Yves Coppens, 1982. Pliocene Hominids from the Hadar Formation, Ethiopia (1973–1977): Stratigraphic, Chronologic, and Paleoenvironmental Contexts, with Notes on Hominid Morphology and Systematics. *American Journal of Physical Anthropology* 57: 373–402.

Johnson, A. W., and T. K. Earle, 2001. *The Evolution of Human Societies: From Foraging Group to Agrarian State*. Stanford: Stanford University Press. 2nd edition.

Johnson, S. B., and R. C. Johnson, 1991. Support and Conflict of Kinsmen in Norse Earldoms, Icelandic Families and the English Royalty. *Ethology and Sociobiology* 12: 211–20.

Jones, S., 1997. *The Archaeology of Ethnicity: Constructing Identities in the Past and Present*. London: Routledge.

—— R. Martin, and D. Pilbeam, eds, 1993. *The Cambridge Encyclopaedia of Human Evolution*. Cambridge: Cambridge University Press.

Jordan, F. M., 2007. A Comparative Phylogenetic Approach to Austronesian Cultural Evolution. Ph.D. dissertation, University College London.

Jorde, L. B., M. Bamshad, and A. R. Rogers, 1998. Using Mitochondrial and Nuclear DNA Markers to Reconstruct Human Evolution. *BioEssays* 20: 126–36.

Judge, D. S., 1995. American Legacies and the Variable Life Histories of Women and Men. *Human Nature* 6: 291–323.

Julien, M., C. Karlin, and P. Bodu, 1987. Pincevent: Où en est le modèle théorique aujourd'hui? *Bulletin de la Société Préhistorique Française* 84: 335–42.

Junod, H., 1912. *The Life of a South African Tribe*, Vol. 1. Neuchatel.

Kaplan, H., and K. Hill, 1985. Food Sharing Among Aché Foragers: Tests of Explanatory Hypotheses. *Current Anthropology* 26: 223–46.

—— and A. J. Robson, 2002. The Emergence of Humans: The Coevolution of Intelligence and Longevity with Intergenerational Transfers. *Proceedings of the National Academy of Sciences* 99: 10221–6.

—— K. Hill, and A. M. Hurtado, 1990. Risk, Foraging and Foodsharing among the Aché. In *Risk and Uncertainty in Tribal and Peasant Economies*. E. Cashdan, ed., pp. 107–43. Boulder, CO: Westview.

—— K. Hill, J. Lancaster, and A. M. Hurtado, 2000. A Theory of Human Life History Evolution: Diet, Intelligence, and Longevity. *Evolutionary Anthropology* 9: 156–85.

—— K. Hill, A. M. Hurtado, and J. Lancaster, 2001. The Embodied Capital Theory of Human Evolution. In *Reproductive Ecology and Human Evolution*. P. T. Ellison, ed., pp. 293–317. New York: Aldine de Gruyter.

Kapsalis, E., 2004. Matrilineal Kinship and Primate Behavior. In *Kinship and Behavior in Primates*. B. Chapais and C. M. Berman, eds, pp. 153–76. New York: Oxford University Press.

Kennedy, G., 2003. Palaeolithic Grandmothers? Life History, Theory and Early *Homo*. *Journal of the Royal Anthropological Institute* (New Series) 9: 549–72.

Key, C., 2000. The Evolution of Human Life History. *World Archaeology* 31: 329–50.

—— and L. C. Aiello, 1999. The Evolution of Social Organisation. In *The Evolution of Culture*. R. I. M. Dunbar, C. Knight, and C. Power, eds, pp. 15–33. Edinburgh: Edinburgh University Press.

—— and L. C. Aiello, 2000. A Prisoner's Dilemma Model of the Evolution of Paternal Care. *Folia Primatologica* 71: 77–92.

—— and C. Ross, 1999. Sex Differences in Energy Expenditure in Non-Human Primates. *Proceedings of the Royal Society, London*, B Series 266: 2479–85.

Kinderman, P., R. I. M. Dunbar, and R. P. Bentall, 1998. Theory-of-Mind Deficits and Causal Attributions. *British Journal of Psychology* 89: 191–204.

Klein, R. G., 1995. Anatomy, Behavior, and Modern Human Origins. *Journal of World Prehistory* 9: 167–98.

—— 2000. Archaeology and the Evolution of Human Behaviour. *Evolutionary Anthropology* 9: 17–36.

Knappett, C., 2005. *Thinking Through Material Culture: An Interdisciplinary Perspective*. Pittsburgh: University of Pennsylvania Press.

Knight, C., 1991. *Blood Relations: Menstruation and the Origins of Culture*. New Haven, CT: Yale University Press.

—— 1999. Sex and Language as Pretend-Play. In *The Evolution of Culture*. R. I. M. Dunbar, C. Knight, and C. Power, eds, pp. 228–47. Edinburgh: Edinburgh University Press.

—— and C. Power, 2005. Grandmothers, Politics and Getting Back to Science. In *Grandmotherhood: The Evolutionary Significance of the Second Half of Life*. E. Voland, A. Chasiotis, and W. Schiefenhövel, eds, pp. 81–98. New Brunswick, NJ and London: Rutgers University Press.

—— C. Power, and I. Watts, 1995. The Human Symbolic Revolution: A Darwinian Account. *Cambridge Archaeological Journal* 5(1): 75–114.

Koenig, A., 2002. Competition for Resources and Its Behavioral Consequences among Female Primates. *International Journal of Primatology* 23: 759–83.

Koertvelyessy, T., 1995. Ethnicity, Isonymic Relationships, and Biological Distance in Northeastern Hungary. *Homo* 46: 1–9.

Konigsberg, L. W., and N. P. Herrmann, 2005. The Osteological Evidence for Human Longevity in the Recent Past. In *The Evolution of Human Life History*. K. Hawkes and R. R. Paine, eds, pp. 267–306. Santa Fe, NM, and Oxford: School of American Research Press/James Currey.

Korchmaros, J. D., and D. A. Kenny, 2001. Emotional Closeness as a Mediator of the Effect of Genetic Relatedness on Altruism. *Psychological Science* 12: 262–5.

Korstjens, A. H., and R. Noë, 2004. The Mating System of an Exceptional Primate, the Olive Colobus (*Procolobus verus*). *American Journal of Primatology* 62: 261–73.

—— E. H. M. Sterck, and R. Noë, 2002. How Adaptive or Phylogenetically Inert is Primate Social Behaviour? A Test with Two Sympatric Colobines. *Behaviour* 139: 203–25.

—— E. C. Nijssen, and R. Noë, 2005. Inter-Group Relationships in Western Black-and-White Colobus, *Colobus polykomos polykomos*. *International Journal of Primatology* 26: 1267–89.

—— K. Bergmann, C. Deffernez, M. Krebs, E. C. Nijssen, B. A. M. van Oirschot, C. Paukert, and E. Ph. Schippers, 2007. How Small-Scale Differences in Food Competition Lead to Different Social Systems in Three Closely Related Sympatric Colobines. In *Monkeys of the Taï Forest, Ivory Coast: An African Primate Community*. S. McGraw, K. Zuberbühler, and R. Noë, eds, pp. 72–108. Cambridge: Cambridge University Press.

Kramer, K. L., 2005. Children's Help and the Pace of Reproduction: Cooperative Breeding in Humans. *Evolutionary Anthropology* 14: 224–37.

Kuper, A., 1988. *The Invention of Primitive Society: Transformations of an Illusion*. London: Routledge.

Kuper, R., and S. Kröpelin, 2006. Climate-Controlled Holocene Occupation in the Sahara: Motor of Africa's Evolution. *Science* 313: 803–7.

Kurland, J., 1979. Paternity, Mother's Brother, and Human Sociality. In *Evolutionary Biology and Human Social Behavior: An Anthropological Perspective*. N. A. Chagnon and W. Irons, eds, pp. 145–77. North Scituate, MA: Duxbury.

Lafitau, J. F., 1724. *Moeurs des sauvages amériquaines, comparées aux moeurs des premiers temps*, Vol. 1. Paris: Saugrain l'aîné.

Lahdenperä, M., V. Lummaa, S. Helle, M. Tremblay, and A. F. Russell, 2004. Fitness Benefits of Prolonged Post-Reproductive Lifespan in Women. *Nature* 428: 178–81.

Lahr, M. M., and R. Foley, 1994. Multiple Dispersals and Modern Human Origins. *Evolutionary Anthropology* 3: 48–60.

Lakoff, G., and M. Johnson, 1980. *Metaphors We Live By*. Chicago: University of Chicago Press.

Langergraber, K. E., J. C. Mitani, and L. Vigilant, 2007. The Limited Impact of Kinship on Cooperation in Wild Chimpanzees. *Proceedings of the National Academy of Sciences of the United States of America* 104: 7786–90.

Lawrence, W. E., 1937. Alternating Generations in Australia. In *Studies in the Science of Society*. G. P. Murdock, ed., pp. 319–54. New Haven, CT: Yale University Press.

Layton, R., 1995. Relating to the Country in the Western Desert. In *The Anthropology of Landscape: Perspectives on Place and Space*. E. Hirsch and M. O'Hanlon, eds, pp. 210–31. Oxford: Clarendon Press.

—— 1997a. The Alawa Totemic Landscape: Ecology, Religion and Politics. In *The Archaeology and Anthropology of Landscape: Perspectives on Place and Space*. P. Ucko and R. Layton, eds, pp. 220–39. London: Routledge.

—— 1997b. Small Tools and Social Change. In *Archaeology and Linguistics*. P. McConvell and N. Evans, eds, pp. 377–84. Oxford: Oxford University Press.

—— 2005. Are Hunter-Gatherer Immediate Return Strategies Adaptive? In *Property and Equality, Vol. 1: Ritualization, Sharing, Egalitarianism*. T. Widlok and W. Tadesse eds, pp. 130–50. New York: Berghahn.

—— and R. Barton, 2001. Warfare and Human Social Evolution. In *Ethnoarchaeology of Hunter-Gatherers: Pictures at an Exhibition*. K. J. Fewster and M. Zvelebil, eds, pp. 13–24. BAR International Series 955. Oxford: Archaeopress.

Leach, E., 1961. *Rethinking Anthropology*. LSE Monographs in Anthropology 22. London: University of London Press.

Leakey, M. G., F. Spoor, F. H. Brown, P. N. Gathogo, C. Kiarie, L. N. Leakey, and I. McDougall, 2001. New Hominin Genus from Eastern Africa Shows Diverse Middle Pliocene Lineages. *Nature* 410: 433–40.

Lederer, J., 1672. *The Discoveries of John Lederer, in three several marches from Virginia, to the West of Carolina and other parts of the Continent. Begun in March 1669, and ended in September 1670*. London: Samuel Heyrick.

Lee, R. B., 1979. *The !Kung San: Men, Women and Work in a Foraging Society*. Cambridge: Cambridge University Press.

—— and I. DeVore, 1968. Problems in the Study of Hunters and Gatherers. In *Man the Hunter*. R. Lee and I. DeVore, eds, pp. 3–12. Chicago: Aldine.

Legesse, A., 1973. *Gada: Three Approaches to the Study of African Society*. New York: Free Press.

Lehmann, J., and C. Boesch, 2008. Sex Differences in Sociality. *International Journal of Primatology* 28: in press.

—— and C. Boesch, submitted. Sociality of the Dispersing Sex: The Nature of Social Bonds in West African Female Chimpanzees (*Pan troglodytes*).

—— G. Fickenscher, and C. Boesch, 2006. Kin Biased Investment in Wild Chimpanzees. *Behaviour* 143: 931–55.

—— A. H. Korstjens, and R. I. M. Dunbar, 2007. Fission–Fusion Social Systems as a Strategy for Coping with Ecological Constraints: A Primate Case. *Evolutionary Ecology* 21: 613–34.

Leonard, W. R., and M. L. Robertson, 1997. Comparative Primate Energetics and Hominid Evolution. *American Journal of Physical Anthropology* 102: 265–81.

Leonetti, D. L., D. C. Nath, N. S. Hemam, and D. B. Neill, 2005. Kinship Organization and the Impact of Grandmothers on Reproductive Success among the Matrilineal Khasi and Patrilineal Bengali of Northeast India. In *Grandmotherhood: The Evolutionary Significance of the Second Half of Life*. E. Voland, A. Chasiotis, and W. Schiefenhövel, eds, pp. 194–214. New Brunswick, NJ. and London: Rutgers University Press.

Leroi-Gourhan, A., and M. Brézillon, 1972. Fouilles de Pincevent. Essai d'analyse ethnographique d'un habitat magdalénien (La Section 36). *Gallia Préhistoire, VII Supplément*. Paris: Éditions CNRS.

Levinson, D., 1994. *Encyclopedia of World Cultures*. New York: G. K. Hall and Co.

—— and M. J. Malone, 1980. *Toward Explaining Human Culture: A Critical Review of the Findings of Worldwide Cross-Cultural Research*. New Haven: HRAF Press.

Lévi-Strauss, C., 1969a [1962]. *Totemism*. Harmondsworth: Penguin.

—— 1969b [1949]. *The Elementary Structures of Kinship*. London: Eyre and Spottiswoode.

—— 1977–8 [1958, 1972]. *Structural Anthropology*, 2 vols, C. Jacobsen and B. G. Schoepf, trans. (Vol. 1); M. Layton, trans., Vol. 2. Harmondsworth: Penguin.

—— 1979. *La Voie des Masques*. Paris: Plon.

Lordkipanidze, D., A. Vekua, R. Ferring, G. P. Rightmire, J. Agusti, G. Kiladze, A. Mouskhelishvili, M. Nioradze, M. S. Ponce de León, M. Tappen, and C. P. E. Zollikofer, 2005. The Earliest Toothless Hominin Skull. *Nature* 434: 717–18.

Lovejoy, C. O., 1981. The Origin of Man. *Science* 211: 341–50.

Lowie, R., 1920. *Primitive Society*. New York: Harper.

—— 1937. *The History of Ethnological Theory*. New York: Holt, Rinehart and Winston.

—— 1960a [1914]. Social Organization. In *Lowie's Selected Papers in Anthropology*. Cora du Bois, ed., pp. 17–47. Berkeley and Los Angeles: University of California Press.

—— 1960b [1919]. Family and Sib. In *Lowie's Selected Papers in Anthropology*. Cora du Bois, ed., pp. 82–94. Berkeley and Los Angeles: University of California Press.

Lukas, D., V. Reynolds, C. Boesch, and L. Vigilant 2005. To What Extent Does Living in a Group Mean Living with Kin? *Molecular Ecology* 14: 2181–96.

McBrearty, S., and A. S. Brooks, 2000. The Revolution That Wasn't: A New Interpretation of the Origin of Modern Humans. *Journal of Human Evolution* 39: 453–563.

McConvell, P., 1997. Long Lost Relations: Pama-nyungan and Northern Kinship. In *Archaeology and Linguistics*. P. McConvell and N. Evans, eds, pp. 207–35. Oxford: Oxford University Press.

McCullough, J. M., and E. York Barton, 1991. Relatedness and Mortality Risk During a Crisis Year. Plymouth Colony, 1620–21. *Ethology and Sociobiology* 12: 195–209.

McDougall, I., F. H. Brown, and J. G. Fleagle, 2005. Stratigraphic Placement and Age of Modern Humans from Kibish, Ethiopia. *Nature* 433: 733–6.

Mace, R., 1996. Biased Parental Investment and Reproductive Success in Gabbra Pastoralists. *Behavioral Ecology and Sociobiology* 38: 75–81.

—— and M. Pagel, 1994. The Comparative Method in Anthropology. *Current Anthropology* 35: 549–64.

—— and M. Pagel, 1997. Tips, Branches and Nodes: Seeking Adaptation through Comparative Studies. In *Human Nature: A Critical Reader*. L. Betzig, ed., pp. 297–310. New York: Oxford University Press.

—— and C. Holden, 1999. Evolutionary Ecology and Cross-Cultural Comparison: The Case of Matrilineal Descent in Sub-Saharan Africa. In *Comparative Primate Socioecology*. P. C. Lee, ed., pp. 387–405. Cambridge: Cambridge University Press.

—— and F. Jordan, 2005. The Evolution of Human Sex Ratio at Birth: A Bio-Cultural Analysis. In *The Evolution of Cultural Diversity: A Phylogenetic Approach*. R. Mace, C. Holden, and S. Shennan, eds, pp. 207–16. London: UCL Press.

—— and R. Sear, 2005. Are Humans Cooperative Breeders? In *Grandmotherhood: The Evolutionary Significance of the Second Half of Life*. E. Voland, A. Chasiotis, and W. Schiefenhövel, eds, pp. 143–59. New Brunswick, NJ, and London: Rutgers University Press.

—— F. Jordan, and C. Holden, 2003. Testing Evolutionary Hypotheses about Human Biological Adaptation Using Cross-Cultural Comparison. *Comparative Biochemistry and Physiology* Series A 136(1): 85–94.

McElreath, R., and J. Henrich, 2007. Modelling Cultural Evolution. In *Oxford Handbook of Evolutionary Psychology*. R. I. M. Dunbar and L. Barrett, eds, pp. 571–85. Oxford: Oxford University Press.

McGrew, W. C., 1992. *Chimpanzee Material Culture: Implications for Human Evolution*. Cambridge: Cambridge University Press.

McHenry, H. M., 1996. Sexual Dimorphism in Fossil Hominids and its Socioecological Implications. In *The Archaeology of Human Ancestry*. J. Steele and S. Shennan, eds, pp. 91–109. London: Routledge.

—— and K. Coffing, 2000. *Australopithecus* to *Homo*: Transformations in Body and Mind. *Annual Review of Anthropoogy* 29: 125–46.

McKinnon, J. R., 1974. The Behaviour and Ecology of Wild Orang-Utans (*Pongo pygmaeus*). *Animal Behaviour* 22: 3–74.

McLennan, J. F., 1970 [1865]. *Primitive Marriage: An Inquiry into the Origin of the Form of Capture in Marriage Ceremonies*. Chicago: University of Chicago Press.

Maddock, K., 1974. *The Australian Aborigines: A Portrait of Their Society*. Harmondsworth: Penguin.

Madsen, E. A., R. J. Tunney, G. Fieldman, H. C. Plotkin, R. I. M. Dunbar, J. Richardson, and D. J. McFarland, 2007. Altruism and Kinship: A Cross-Cultural Experimental Study. *British Journal of Psychology* 98: 339–59.

Maine, H. S., 1883. *Dissertations on Early Law and Custom*. London.

—— 1913 [1861]. *Ancient Law: Its Connection with the Early History of Society and Its Relation to Modern Ideas*. London: George Routledge and Sons.

Malinowski, B., 1930. Kinship. *Man* (New Series) 30(2): 19–29.

—— 1932. *The Sexual Life of Savages in North-Western Melanesia*. London: Routledge. 3rd edition.

—— 1954. *Magic, Science and Religion*. New York: Doubleday.

—— 1956 [1931]. *Marriage: Past and Present. A Debate between Robert Briffault and Bronislaw Malinowski*. M. F. Ashley Montagu, ed. Boston: Porter Sargent.

Mallory, J. P., and D. Q. Adams, eds, 1997. *Encyclopaedia of Indo-European Culture*. London: Fitzroy Dearborn.

—— and D. Q. Adams, 2006. *The Oxford Introduction to Proto-Indo-European and the Proto-Indo-European World*. Oxford: Oxford University Press.

Marck, J., and K. Bostoen, in preparation. Proto–Oceanic (Austronesian) and Proto-East Bantu (Niger-Congo) Kin Terms ca. 1000 BC. In *Kinship and Language*. B. Milicic, ed.

Marks, J., 2002. *What It Means to be 98% Chimpanzee: Apes, People, and Their Genes*. Berkeley: University of California Press.

Marlowe, F., 2001. Male Contribution to Diet and Female Reproductive Success among Foragers. *Current Anthropology* 42: 755–60.

—— 2004. Marital Residence among Foragers. *Current Anthropology* 45: 277–84.

Martins, E. P., and E. A. Housworth, 2002. Phylogeny Shape and the Phylogenetic Comparative Method. *Systematic Biology* 51(6): 873–80.

Marx, K., 1930 [1867]. *Capital*. E. and C. Paul, trans., Vol 1. London: Dent.

—— 2000a [1844]. Economic and Philosophical Manuscripts. In *Karl Marx: Selected Writings*. D. McLellan ed., pp. 83–121. Oxford: Oxford University Press. 2nd edition.

—— and F. Engels, 2000b [1846]. The German Ideology. In *Karl Marx: Selected Writings*. D. McLellan ed., pp. 175–208. Oxford: Oxford University Press.

Matthey de l'Etang, A., and P. J. Bancel, 2002. Tracing of the Ancestral Kinship System: The Global Etymon KAKA. Part II: An Anthropological Study. *Mother Tongue* 7: 245–58.

Mauss, M. 1954 [1925]. *The Gift: Forms and Functions of Exchange in Archaic Societies*. Ian Cunnison, trans. London: Cohen and West.

Maynard Smith, J., 1964. Group Selection and Kin Selection. *Nature* 201: 1145–7.

—— 1976. Group Selection. *Quarterly Review of Biology* 51: 277–83.

Mead, M., 1935. *Sex and Temperament in Three Primitive Societies*. New York: Aldine.

Mealey, L., C. Daood, and M. Krage, 1996. Enhanced Memory for Faces of Cheaters. *Ethology and Sociobiology* 17: 120–7.

Megerssa, G., and A. Kassam, 2005. The 'Rounds' of Time: Time, History and Society in Borana Oromo. In *The Qualities of Time: Anthropological Approaches*. W. James and D. Mills, eds, pp. 251–65. Oxford and New York: Berg.

Mellars, P., 1990. Comment on Lindly and Clark: Symbolism and Modern Human Origins. *Current Anthropology* 31: 245–6.

—— 1994. The Upper Palaeolithic Revolution. In *The Oxford Illustrated Prehistory of Europe*. B. Cunliffe, ed., pp. 42–78. Oxford: Oxford University Press.

—— 2005. The Impossible Coincidence: A Single-Species Model for the Origins of Modern Human Behaviour in Europe. *Evolutionary Anthropology* 14: 12–27.

—— and C. Stringer, eds, 1989. *The Human Revolution: Behavioural and Biological Perspectives on the Origins of Modern Humans*. Edinburgh: Edinburgh University Press.

Milardo, R. M., 1992. Comparative Methods for Delineating Social Networks. *Journal of Social and Personal Relationships* 8: 447–61.

Militarev, A., 2003. The Prehistory of a Dispersal: The Proto-Afrasian (Afroasiatic) Farming Lexicon. In *Examining the Farming/Language Dispersal Hypothesis*, P. Bellwood and C. Renfrew, eds, pp. 135–50. Cambridge: The MacDonald Institute.

Miller, G., 2000. *The Mating Mind: How Sexual Selection Shaped the Evolution of Human Nature*. London: Heinemann.

Mills, D., and M. T. Huber, 2005. Anthropology and the Educational 'Trading Zone': Disciplinarity, Pedagogy and Professionalism. *Arts and Humanities in Higher Education* 4(1): 9–32.

Milton, K., 1999. A Hypothesis to Explain the Role of Meat-Eating in Human Evolution. *Evolutionary Anthropology* 8: 11–21.

Mitani, J. C., and D. Watts, 1997. The Evolution of Non-Maternal Caretaking among Anthropoid Primates: Do Helpers Help? *Behavioral Ecology and Sociobiology* 40: 213–20.

—— D. A. Merriwether, and C. B. Zhang, 2000. Male Affiliation, Cooperation and Kinship in Wild Chimpanzees. *Animal Behaviour* 59: 885–93.

Mithen, S., 1996. *The Prehistory of the Mind: A Search for the Origins of Art, Religion and Science*. London: Thames and Hudson.

—— 1999. Symbolism and the Supernatural. In *The Evolution of Culture*. R. I. M. Dunbar, C. Knight, and C. Power, eds, pp. 147–69. Edinburgh: Edinburgh University Press.

Moore, J., and R. Ali, 1984. Are Dispersal and Inbreeding Avoidance-Related? *Animal Behaviour* 32: 94–112.

Morgan, C. J., 1979. Eskimo Hunting Groups, Social Kinship and the Possibility of Kin Selection in Humans. *Ethology and Sociobiology* 1: 83–6.

Morgan, L. H., 1871. *Systems of Consanguinity and Affinity of the Human Family*. Washington, DC: Smithsonian Institution.

—— 1907 [1877]. *Ancient Society: Researches into the Lines of Human Progress from Savagery through Barbarism to Civilization*. London: Macmillan.

—— 1881. *Houses and House-Life of the American Aborigines*. Chicago and London: University of Chicago Press.

Morris, D., 1967. *The Naked Ape*. London: Cape.

Morwood, M. J., R. P. Soejono, R. G. Roberts, T. Sutikna, C. S. M. Turney, K. E. Westaway, W. J. Rink, J.-X. Zhao, G. D. van den Bergh, R. A. Due, D. R. Hobbs, M. W. Moore, M. I. Bird, and L. K. Fifield, 2004. Archaeology and Age of a New Hominin from Flores in Eastern Indonesia. *Nature* 431: 1087–91.

Munson, P. J., 1977. Africa's Prehistoric Past. In *Africa*. P. O'Meara, ed., pp. 62–82. Bloomington: Indiana University Press.

Murdock, G. P., 1949. *Social Structure*. New York: Macmillan.

—— 1959. *Africa: Its Peoples and Their Culture History*. New York: McGraw-Hill.

—— 1967. *Ethnographic Atlas*. Pittsburgh, PA: University of Pittsburgh Press.

Myers, F., 1986. *Pintupi Country, Pintupi Self*. Washington, DC: Smithsonian Institution.

Nakhleh, L., D. Ringe, and T. Warnow, 2005. Perfect Phylogenetic Networks: A New Methodology for Reconstructing the Evolutionary History of Natural Languages. *Language* 81(2): 382–420.

Nash, C., 2004. Genetic Kinship. *Cultural Studies* 18: 1–33.

Needham, R., 1974. *Remarks and Inventions*. London: Tavistock.

Nettle, D., 1999. *Linguistic Diversity*. Oxford: Oxford University Press.

—— and R. I. M. Dunbar, 1997. Social Markers and the Evolution of Reciprocal Exchange. *Current Anthropology* 38: 93–9.

Nicolas, G., 1976. The Dizzu of Southwest Ethiopia: An Essay in Cultural History Based on Religious Interactions. Ph.D. dissertation, University of California at Los Angeles.

Nicolson, N. A., 1987. Infants, Mothers and Other Females. *In Primate Societies*. B. B. Smuts, D. L. Cheney, R. M. Seyfarth, R. W. Wrangham, and T. T. Struhsaker, eds, pp. 330–42. Chicago: University of Chicago Press.

Nishida, T., H. Takasaki, and Y. Takahata, 1990. Demography and Reproductive Profiles. In *The Chimpanzees of the Mahale Mountains: Sexual and Life History Strategies*. T. Nishida, ed., pp. 63–98. Tokyo: University of Tokyo Press.

Noble, W., and I. Davidson, 1996. *Human Evolution, Language and Mind*. Cambridge: Cambridge University Press.

Noë, R., and A. A. Sluijter, 1995. Which Adult Savanna Baboons Form Coalitions? *International Journal of Primatology* 16: 77–105.

O'Connell, J. F., K. Hawkes, and N. G. Blurton Jones, 1988. Hadza Scavenging: Implications for Plio-Pleistocene Hominid Subsistence. *Current Anthropology* 29: 356–63.

—— K. Hawkes, and N. G. Blurton Jones, 1999. Grandmothering and the Evolution of *Homo erectus*. *Journal of Human Evolution* 36: 461–85.

—— K. Hawkes, K. D. Lupo, and N. G. Blurton Jones, 2002. Male Strategies and Plio-Pleistocene Archaeology. *Journal of Human Evolution* 43: 831–72.

Oates, K., and M. Wilson, 2002. Nominal Kinship Cues Facilitate Altruism. *Proceedings of the Royal Society, London*, B Series 269: 105–9.

Ofek, H., 2001. *Second Nature: Economic Origins of Human Evolution*. Cambridge: Cambridge University Press.

Onderdonk, D. A., 2000. Infanticide of a Newborn Black-and-White Colobus Monkey (*Colobus guereza*) in Kibale National Park, Uganda. *Primates* 41: 209–12.

Opie, K., 2004. Testing the Grandmothering Hypothesis: The Provisioning of *Homo erectus* Infants and Juveniles. M.Sc. dissertation, University of London.

Orel, V., and O. Stolbova, 1995. *Hamito-Semitic Etymological Dictionary: Materials for a Reconstruction*. Leiden and New York: E. J. Brill.

Ostrom, E., 1990. *Governing the Commons: The Evolution of Institutions for Collective Action*. Cambridge: Cambridge University Press.

Pagel, M., and A. Meade, 2004. A Phylogenetic Mixture Model for Detecting Pattern-Heterogeneity in Gene Sequence or Character-State Data. *Systematic Biology* 53(4): 571–81.

—— and A. Meade, 2005. Bayesian Estimation of Correlated Evolution across Cultures: A Case Study of Marriage Systems and Wealth Transfer at Marriage. In *The Evolution of Cultural Diversity: A Phylogenetic Approach*. R. Mace, C. J. Holden, and S. Shennan, eds, pp. 235–56. London: UCL Press.

—— and A. Meade, 2006. Bayesian Analysis of Correlated Evolution of Discrete Characters by Reversible-Jump Markov Chain Monte Carlo. *American Naturalist* 167(6): 808–25.

—— A. Meade, and D. Barker, 2004. Bayesian Estimation of Ancestral Character States on Phylogenies. *Systematic Biology* 53(5): 673–84.

Palmer, C. T., 1992. Kin-Selection, Reciprocal Altruism and Information Sharing Among Maine Lobstermen. *Ethology and Sociobiology* 12: 221–35.

Palombit, R. A., 2000. Infanticide and the Evolution of Male–Female Bonds in Animals. In *Infanticide by Males and Its Implications*. C. P. van Schaik and C. H. Janson, eds, pp. 239–68. Cambridge: Cambridge University Press.

Panter-Brick, C., 1989. Motherhood and Subsistence Work: The Tamang of Rural Nepal. *Human Ecology* 17: 205–28.

Parish, A., R., and F. B. M. de Waal, 2000. The Other 'Closest Living Relative' – How Bonobos (*Pan paniscus*) Challenge Traditional Assumptions about Females, Dominance, Intra- and Intersexual Interactions, and Hominid Evolution. *Evolutionary Perspectives on Human Reproductive Behavior* 907: 97–113.

Parkin, D., 2007. The Visceral in the Social: The Crowd as Paradigmatic Type. In *Holistic Anthropology: Emergence and Convergence*. D. Parkin and S. Ulijaszek, eds. Oxford and New York: Berghahn Books.

Parkin, R. 1997. *Kinship: An Introduction to Basic Concepts*. Oxford and Malden, MA: Blackwell.

Pashos, A., 2001. Does Paternal Uncertainty Explain Discriminative Grandparental Solicitude? A Cross-Cultural Study in Greece and Germany. *Evolution and Human Behavior* 21: 97–109.

Pasternak, B., C. R. Ember, and M. Ember, 1997. *Sex, Gender, and Kinship: A Cross-Cultural Perspective*. Upper Saddle River, NJ: Prentice Hall.

Paul, A., and J. Kuester, 2004. The Impact of Kinship on Mating and Reproduction. In *Kinship and Behavior in Primates*. B. Chapais and C. M. Berman, eds, pp. 271–91. New York: Oxford University Press.

Paul, A., S. Preuschoft, and C. P. van Schaik, 2000. The Other Side of the Coin: Infanticide and the Evolution of Affiliative Male–Infant Interactions in Old World Primates. In *Infanticide by Males and Its Implications*. C. P. van Schaik and C. H. Janson, eds, pp. 269–92. Cambridge: Cambridge University Press.

Pavelka, M. S. M., L. M. Fedigan, and S. Zohar, 2002. Availability and Adaptive Value of Reproductive and Postreproductive Japanese Macaque Mothers and Grandmothers. *Animal Behaviour* 64: 407–14.

Peatrik, Anne-Marie, 2005. Old System, New Conflicts: Age, Generation and Discord among the Meru, Kenya. In *The Qualities of Time: Anthropological Approaches*. W. James and D. Mills, eds, pp. 285–300. Oxford and New York: Berg.

Peccei, J. C., 2001. Menopause: Adaptation or Epiphenomenon? *Evolutionary Anthropology* 10: 43–57.

Pennington, R., and H. Harpending, 1993. *The Structure of an African Pastoralist Community: Demography, History and Ecology of the Ngamiland Herero*. New York: Oxford University Press.

Peterson, N., 1976. *Tribes and Boundaries in Aboriginal Australia*. Canberra: Institute of Aboriginal Studies.

Phillipson, D. W., 1977. *The Later Prehistory of Eastern and Southern Africa* London: Heinemann.

Pinker, S., 1997. *How the Mind Works*. London: Penguin.

—— 2002. *The Blank Slate*. London: Penguin.

Pope, T. R., 1990. The Reproductive Consequences of Male Cooperation in the Red Howler Monkey: Paternity Exclusion in Multimale and Single-Male Troops Using Genetic Markers. *Behavioral Ecology and Sociobiology* 27: 439–46.

—— 2000a. The Evolution of Male Philopatry in Neotropical Monkeys. In *Primate Males: Causes and Consequences of Variation in Group Composition*. P. M. Kappeler, ed., pp. 219–35. Cambridge: Cambridge University Press.

—— 2000b. Reproductive Success Increases with Degree of Kinship in Cooperative Coalitions of Female Red Howler Monkeys (*Alouatta seniculus*). *Behavioral Ecology and Sociobiology* 48: 253–67.

Power, C., 1999. Beauty Magic: The Origins of Art. In *The Evolution of Culture*. R. I. M. Dunbar, C. Knight, and C. Power, eds, 92–112. Edinburgh: Edinburgh University Press.

—— and I. Watts, 1996. Female Strategies and Collective Behaviour: The Archaeology of Earliest *Homo sapiens*. In *The Archaeology of Human Ancestry*. J. Steele and S. Shennan, eds, pp. 306–30. London and New York: Routledge.

—— and L. C. Aiello, 1997. Female Proto-Symbolic Strategies. In *Women in Human Evolution*. L. D. Hager, ed., pp. 153–71. New York and London: Routledge.

Proctor, R. N. 2003. Three Roots of Human Recency: Molecular Anthropology, the Refigured Acheulean, and the UNESCO Response to Auschwitz. *Current Anthropology* 44: 213–39.

Purvis, A., 1995. A Composite Estimate of Primate Phylogeny. *Philosophical Transactions of the Royal Society of London Series B – Biological Sciences* 348: 405–21.

Pusey, A. E., and C. Packer, 1987. Dispersal and Philopatry. In *Primate Societies*. B. B. Smuts, D. L. Cheney, R. M. Seyfarth, R. W. Wrangham, and T. T. Struhsaker, eds, 250–66. Chicago: University of Chicago Press.

Radcliffe-Brown, A. R., 1924. The Mother's Brother in South Africa. *South African Journal of Science* 21: 542–55.

—— 1931. The Social Organization of Australian Tribes. *Oceania Monographs* No. 1. Melbourne: Macmillan.

—— 1950. Introduction. In *African Systems of Kinship and Marriage*. A. R. Radcliffe-Brown, ed., pp. 1–85. London: Oxford University Press.

—— 1952. *Structure and Function in Primitive Society*. London: Cohen and West.

Reich, D. E., and D. B. Goldstein, 1998. Genetic Evidence for a Paleolithic Human Population Expansion in Africa. *Proceedings of the National Academy of Sciences of the United States of America* 95: 8119–23.

Reichard, U., 1995. Extra-Pair Copulations in a Monogamous Gibbon (*Hylobates lar*). *Ethology* 100: 99–112.

Rendall, D., 2004. 'Recognizing' Kin: Mechanisms, Media, Minds, Modules, and Muddles. In *Kinship and Behavior in Primates*. B. Chapais and C. M. Berman, eds, pp. 295–316. New York: Oxford University Press.

Renfrew, C., 1996. The Sapient Behaviour Paradox: How to Test for Potential? In *Modelling the Early Human Mind*. P. Mellars and K. Gibson, eds, pp. 11–14. Cambridge: McDonald Institute for Archaeological Research.

—— 2001. Symbol before Concept: Material Engagement and the Early Development of Society. In *Archaeological Theory Today*. I. Hodder, ed., pp. 122–40. Cambridge: Polity Press.

Rexová, K., D. Frynta, and J. Zrzavý, 2003. Cladistic Analysis of Languages: Indo-European Classification Based on Lexicostatistical Data. *Cladistics* 19(2): 120–7.

—— Y. Bastin, and D. Frynta, 2006. Cladistic Analysis of Bantu Languages: A New Tree Based on Combined Lexical and Grammatical Data. *Naturwissenschaften* 93(4): 189–94.

Reynolds, V., 2005. *The Chimpanzees of the Budongo Forest: Ecology, Behaviour, and Conservation*. Oxford: Oxford University Press.

Richards, A. I., 1932. *Hunger and Work in a Savage Tribe*. London: Routledge.

—— 1969. *Land, Labour and Diet in Northern Rhodesia*. Oxford: Oxford University Press.

Rightmire, P., 2001. Patterns of Hominid Evolution and Dispersal in the Middle Pleistocene. *Quaternary International* 75: 77–84.

Rijksen, H. D., 1978. *A Field Study on Sumatran Orang-Utans (Pongo pygmaeus abelii): Ecology, Behavior, and Conservation*. Wageningen: H. Veenmann.

Ringe, D., T. Warnow, and A. Taylor, 2002. Indo-European and Computational Cladistics. *Transactions of the Philological Society* 100(1): 59–129.

Roberts, R. G., R. Jones, and M. A. Smith, 1990. Thermoluminescence Dating of a 50,000-Year-Old Human Occupation Site in Northern Australia. *Nature* 345: 153–6.

Rocek, T., and O. Bar-Yosef, eds, 1998. *Seasonality and Sedentism: Archaeological Perspectives from Old and New World Sites*. Cambridge, MA: Peabody Museum of Archaeology and Ethnology. Peabody Museum Bulletin No. 6.

Rodseth, L., R. W. Wrangham, A. M. Harrigan, and B. B. Smuts, 1991. The Human Community as Primate Society. *Current Anthropology* 32: 221–54.

Roebroeks, W., J. Kolen, and E. Rensink, 1988. Planning Depth, Anticipation and the Organization of Middle Palaeolithic Technology: The 'Archaic Natives' Meet Eve's Descendants. *Helinium* 28: 17–34.

Rolland, N., 2004. Was the Emergence of Home Bases and Domestic Fire a Punctuated Event? A Review of the Middle Pleistocene Record in Eurasia. *Asian Perspectives* 43: 248–80.

Ronquist, F., 2004. Bayesian Inference of Character Evolution. *Trends in Ecology and Evolution* 19(9): 475–81.

Rousseau, J.-J., 1963 [1767]. *The Social Contract and Discourses*. G. D. H. Cole, ed. London: Dent.

Ruel, M., 1962. Kuria Generation Classes. *Africa* 132: 14–37.

—— 1997. *Belief, Ritual and the Securing of Life: Reflexive Essays on a Bantu Religion.* Leiden: Brill. [See especially Appendix 1, 'A Note on Kuria Generation Classes', pp. 241–51.]

—— 2002. The Structural Articulation of Generations in Africa. *Cahiers d'Études africaines* 42: 51–81.

Ruff, C. B, E. Trinkaus, and T. W. Holliday, 1997. Body Mass and Encephalization in Pleistocene Homo. *Nature* 387: 173–6.

Ruhlen, M., 1991. *A Guide to the World's Languages.* London: Edward Arnold.

Sackett, J. R., 1982. Approaches to Style in Lithic Archaeology. *Journal of Anthropological Archaeology* 1: 59–122.

Salter, E., 1972. *Daisy Bates.* Sydney: Angus and Robertson.

Salter, F. K., ed., 2002. *Risky Transactions: Trust, Kinship and Ethnicity.* Oxford: Berghahn.

Schadeberg, T., 1983. The Classification of the Kadugli Language Group. In *Nilo-Saharan.* T. Schadeberg and M. L. Bender, eds, pp. 291–305. Dordrecht: Foris Publications.

Schaller, G., 1968. *The Serengeti Lion.* Chicago: University of Chicago Press.

Schick, K. D., and N. Toth, 1993. *Making Silent Stones Speak: Human Evolution and the Dawn of Technology.* New York: Simon and Schuster.

Schlegel, A., and R. Eloul, 1987. A New Coding of Marriage Transactions. *Cross-Cultural Research* 21(1–4): 118–40.

Schneider, D., 1961. Introduction: The Distinctive Features of Matrilineal Descent Groups. In *Matrilineal Kinship.* D. M. Schneider and K. Gough, eds, pp. 1–29. Berkeley: University of California Press.

Schürmann, C. L., and J. A. R. A. M. van Hooff, 1986. Reproductive Strategies of the Orang-Utan: New Data and a Reconsideration of Existing Socio-sexual Models. *International Journal of Primatology* 1: 265–87.

Sear, R., R. Mace, and I. A. McGregor, 2000. Maternal Grandmothers Improve Nutritional Status and Survival among Children in Rural Gambia. *Proceedings of the Royal Society of London*, Series B, 267: 1641–7.

Searle, J., 1996. *The Construction of Social Reality.* London: Penguin.

Seielstad, M., T. E. Minch, and L. L. Cavalli–Sforza, 1998. Genetic Evidence for Higher Female Migration Rate in Humans. *Nature Genetics* 20: 278–88.

Semaw, S., P. Renne, J. W. K. Harris, C. S. Feibel, R. L. Bernor, N. Fesseha, and K. Mowbray, 1997. 2.5-Million-Year-Old Stone Tools from Gona, Ethiopia. *Nature* 385: 333–6.

—— M. J. Rogers, J. Quade, P. R. Renne, R. F. Butler, M. Domínguez-Rodrigo, D. Stout, W. S. Hart, T. Pickering, and S. W. Simpson, 2003. 2.6-Million-Year-Old Stone Tools and Associated Bones from OGS-6 and OGS-7. Gona, Afar, Ethiopia. *Journal of Human Evolution* 43: 169–77.

Service, E., 1962. *Primitive Social Organization.* New York: Random House.

Shavit, Y., C. S. Fischer, and Y. Koresh, 1994. Kin and Nonkin under Collective Threat: Israeli Networks during the Gulf War. *Social Forces* 72: 1197–215.

Shultz, S., R. Noë, S. McGraw, and R. I. M. Dunbar, 2004. Predator-Specific Risks and the Evolution of Mammalian Prey Group Size. *Proceedings of the Royal Society, London*, Series B 271: 725–32.

Sicotte, P., and A. J. MacIntosh, 2004. Inter-Group Encounters and Male Incursions in *Colobus vellerosus* in Central Ghana. *Behaviour* 141: 533–53.

Silk, J., 1990. Human Adoption in an Evolutionary Perspective. *Human Nature* 1: 25–52.

—— 2002. Kin Selection in Primate Groups. *International Journal of Primatology* 23: 849–75.

—— S. Alberts, and J. Altmann, 2003. Social Bonds of Female Baboons Enhance Infant Survival. *Science* 302:1231–4.

Skinner, M. M., and B. Wood, 2005. The Evolution of Modern Human Life History: A Paleontological Perspective. In *The Evolution of Human Life History*. K. Hawkes and R. R. Paine, eds, pp. 331–400. Santa Fe, NM, and Oxford: School of American Research Press/James Currey.

Smith, A., 1767. Considerations Concerning the First Formation of Languages, and the Different Genius of Original and Compound Languages. In *The Theory of Moral Sentiments, to Which is Added a Dissertation on the Origin of Languages*, pp. 437–78. London: Printed for A. Millar, A. Kincaid, and J. Bell in Edinburgh, and sold by T. Cadell in the Strand. 3rd edition.

Smith, B. H., 1993. The Physiological Age of KNM-WT 15000. In *The Nariokotome Homo erectus Skeleton*. A. Walker and R. Leakey, eds, pp. 195–220. Cambridge, MA: Harvard University Press.

Smith, M. S., B. Kish, and C. Crawford, 1987. Inheritance of Wealth as Human Kin Investment. *Ethology and Sociobiology* 8: 171–82.

Smith, M. A., 1989. The Case for a Resident Human Population in the Central Australian Ranges during Full Glacial Aridity. *Archaeology in Oceania* 24: 93–105.

—— 2005. Moving into the Southern Deserts: An Archaeology of Dispersal and Colonisation. In *23°S: Archaeology and Environmental History of the Southern Deserts*. M. A. Smith and P. Hesse, eds, pp. 92–107. Canberra: National Museum of Australia Press.

—— M. Spriggs, and B. Frankhauser, 1993. *Sahul in Review: Pleistocene Archaeology in Australia, New Guinea and Island Melanesia*. Canberra: Department of Prehistory Research School of Pacific Studies.

Smuts, B. B., and R. W. Smuts, 1993. Male Aggression and Sexual Coercion of Females in Nonhuman Primates and Other Mammals: Evidence and Theoretical Implications. *Advances in the Study of Behavior* 22: 1–63.

Sosis, R., and C. Alcorta, 2003. Signalling, Solidarity and the Sacred: The Evolution of Religious Behavior. *Evolutionary Anthropology* 12: 264–74.

Stack, C. B., 1975. *All Our Kin: Strategies for Survival in a Black Community*. New York: Harper and Row.

Stanford, C. B., 1998. Predation and Male Bonds in Primate Societies. *Behaviour* 135: 513–33.

Starin, E. D., 1994. Philopatry and Affiliation Among Red Colobus. *Behaviour* 130: 253–70.

Sterck, E. H. M., and A. H. Korstjens, 2000. Female Dispersal and Infanticide Avoidance in Primates. In *Infanticide by Males and Its Implications*. C. P. van Schaik and C. H. Janson, eds, pp. 293–321. Cambridge: Cambridge University Press.

—— D. P. Watts, and C. P. van Schaik, 1997. The Evolution of Female Social Relationships in Nonhuman Primates. *Behavioural Ecology and Sociobiology* 41: 291–309.

Steward, J., 1936. The Economic and Social Basis of Primitive Bands. In *Essays on Anthropology in Honour of Alfred Louis Kroeber*. R. H. Lowie, ed., pp. 311–50. Berkeley: University of California Press.

—— 1955. *Theory of Culture Change*. Urbana: University of Illinois Press.

Stewart, F. H., 1977. *Fundamentals of Age-Group Systems*. New York and London: Academic Press.

Stiller, J., and R. I. M. Dunbar, 2007. Perspective-Taking and Social Network Size in Humans. *Social Networks* 29: 93–104.

Stout, D., J. Quade, S. Semaw, M. J. Rogers, and N. E. Levin, 2005. Raw Material Selectivity of the Earliest Stone Toolmakers at Gona, Afar, Ethiopia. *Journal of Human Evolution* 48: 365–80.

Strathern, M., 2004. *Commons and Borderlands: Working Papers on Interdisciplinarity, Accountability and the Flow of Knowledge.* Oxford: Sean Kingston Publishing.

Stringer, C., and P. Andrews, 1988. Genetic and Fossil Evidence for the Origin of Modern Humans. *Science* 239: 1263–8.

—— and C. Gamble, 1993. *In Search of the Neanderthals: Solving the Puzzle of Human Origins.* London: Thames and Hudson.

—— and E. Mackie, 1996. *African Exodus.* London: Cape.

Struhsaker, T. T., 1975. *The Red Colobus Monkey.* Chicago: University of Chicago Press.

Tambiah, S. J., 1973. Dowry and Bridewealth, and the Property Rights of Women in South Asia. In *Bridewealth and Dowry.* J. Goody and S. J. Tambiah, eds, pp. 59–169. Cambridge: Cambridge University Press.

Tattersall, I., 1995. *The Fossil Trail.* Oxford: Oxford University Press.

Tax, S., 1955. *From Lafitau to Radcliffe-Brown.* In *Social Anthropology of North American Tribes.* F. Eggan, ed., pp. 445–84. Chicago: University of Chicago Press. 2nd edition.

Testart, A., 1978. *Des classifications dualistes en Australie.* Lille: Maison des Sciences de l'Homme, Université de Lille.

—— 2000. Quelques considérations sur le temps dans la parenté et le mariage entre cousins croisés. *L'Homme* 154–5: 547–58.

—— 2006. La question du sujet dans la parenté. *L'Homme* 179: 165–99.

Thieme, H., 2005. The Lower Palaeolithic Art of Hunting: The Case of Schöningen 13 II–4, Lower Saxony, Germany. In *The Hominid Individual in Context.* C. Gamble and M. Porr, eds, pp. 115–132. London: Routledge.

Thornhill, N. W., 1991. An Evolutionary Analysis of Rules Regulating Human Inbreeding and Marriage. *Behavioural and Brain Sciences* 14: 247–293.

Tilley, C., 1999. *Metaphor and Material Culture.* Oxford: Blackwell.

Toren, C., 1999. *Mind, Materiality and History: Explorations in Fijian Ethnography.* London: Routledge.

Torun, B., P. S. W. Davies, M. B. E. Livingstone, M. Paolisso, R. Sackett, and G. B. Spurr, 1995. *Energy Requirements and Dietary Energy: Recommendations for Children and Adolescents 1 to 18 Years.* Tokyo: United Nations University Press.

Trautmann, T. R., 2001. The Whole History of Kinship Terminology in Three Chapters: Before Morgan, Morgan, and After Morgan. *Anthropological Theory* 1: 268–87.

Trivers, R. L., 1971. Evolution of Reciprocal Altruism. *Quarterly Review of Biology* 46: 35–55.

—— 1972. Parental Investment and Sexual Selection. In *Sexual Selection and the Descent of Man.* B. Campbell, ed., pp. 136–79. London: Heinemann Educational Books Ltd.

—— 1985. *Social Evolution.* Menlo Park, CA: Benjamin/Cummings.

Troeng, J., 1993. *Worldwide Chronology of Fifty-Three Prehistoric Innovations.* Stockholm: Acta Archaeologica Lundensia 21.

Tryon, C., and S. McBrearty, 2002. Tephrostratigraphy and the Acheulian Middle Stone Age Transition in the Kapthurin Formation, Kenya. *Journal of Human Evolution* 42: 211–35.

Turnbull, C. M., 1965. *Wayward Servants: The Two Worlds of the African Pygmies.* Westport, CT: Greenwood.

—— 1972. Demography of Small-Scale Societies. In *The Structure of Human Populations.* G. A. Harrison and A. J. Boyce, eds, pp. 283–312. Oxford: Oxford University Press.

Turner, A., 1986. Species, Speciation and Human Evolution. *Human Evolution* 1: 419–30.

Turner, J. H., and A. Maryanski, 1991. Network Analysis. In *The Structure of Sociological Theory.* J. H. Turner, ed., pp. 540–72. Belmont, CA: Wadsworth.

Tutin, C. E. G., 1996. Ranging and Social Structure of Lowland Gorillas in the Lopé Reserve, Gabon. In *Great Ape Societies*. W. C. McGrew, L. F. Marchant, and T. Nishida, eds, pp. 58–70. Cambridge: Cambridge University Press.

Tylor, E. B., 1889. On a Method of Investigating the Development of Institutions: Applied to Laws of Marriage and Descent. *The Journal of the Anthropological Institute of Great Britain and Ireland* 18: 245–72.

UNESCO, 1997. Universal Declaration on the Human Genome and Human Rights. *http://portal.unesco.org*.

Utami, S. S., S. A. Wich, E. H. M. Sterck, and J. van Hooff, 1997. Food Competition between Wild Orangutans in Large Fig Trees. *International Journal of Primatology* 18: 909–27.

—— B. Goossens, M. W. Bruford, J. R. de Ruiter, and J. van Hooff, 2002. Male Bimaturism and Reproductive Success in Sumatran Orang-Utans. *Behavioural Ecology* 13: 643–52.

van den Berghe, P. L., 1979. *Human Family Systems: An Evolutionary View*. New York: Elsevier.

van Schaik, C. P., 1989. The Ecology of Social Relationships amongst Female Primates. In *Comparative Socioecology: The Behavioural Ecology of Humans and Other Mammals*. V. Standen and R. A. Foley, eds, pp. 195–218. Oxford: Blackwell.

—— and R. I. M. Dunbar, 1990. The Evolution of Monogamy in Primates: A New Hypothesis and Some Crucial Tests. *Behaviour* 115: 30–62.

—— and C. H. Janson, eds, 2000. *Infanticide by Males and Its Implications*. Cambridge: Cambridge University Press.

—— J. K. Hodges, and C. L. Nunn, 2000. Paternity Confusion and the Ovarian Cycles of Female Primates. In *Infanticide by Males and Its Implications*. C. P. van Schaik and C. H. Janson, eds, pp. 361–87. Cambridge: Cambridge University Press.

Vekua, A., D. Lordkipanidze, G. P. Rightmire, J. Agusti, R. Ferring, G. Maisuradze, A. Mouskhelishvili, M. Nioradze, M. Ponce de León, M. Tappen, M. Tvalchrelidze, and C. Zollikofer, 2002. A New Skull of Early *Homo* from Dmanisi, Georgia. *Science* 297: 85–9.

Voland, E., A. Chasiotis, and W. Schienfenhövel, eds, 2005. *Grandmotherhood: The Evolutionary Significance of the Second Half of Female Life*. New Brunswick, NJ: Rutgers University Press.

Wadley, L., 2001. What is Cultural Modernity? A General View and a South African Perspective from Rose Cottage Cave. *Cambridge Archaeological Journal* 11: 201–21.

Walker, A., 1981. Dietary Hypotheses and Human Evolution. *Philosophical Transactions of the Royal Society, London*, Series B, 292: 57–64.

Waser, N. M., S. N. Audstad, and B. Keane, 1986. When Should Animals Tolerate Inbreeding? *The American Naturalist* 128: 529–37.

Washburn, S., and C. S. Lancaster, 1968. The Evolution of Hunting. In *Man the Hunter*. R. B. Lee and I. DeVore, eds, pp. 293–303. Chicago: Aldine.

—— and I. DeVore, 1961. Social Behavior of Baboons and Early Man. In *The Social Life of Early Man*. S. Washburn, ed., pp. 91–105. London: Methuen.

Watkins, T., 2004. Building Houses, Framing Concepts, Constructing Worlds. *Paléorient* 30: 5–24.

Watts, D., 1988. Environmental Influences on Mountain Gorilla Time Budgets. *American Journal of Primatology* 15: 195–211.

—— 1994. Social Relationships of Immigrant and Resident Female Mountain Gorillas, II: Relatedness, Residence, and Relationships between Females. *American Journal of Primatology* 32: 13–30.

Watts, I., 1999. The Origin of Symbolic Culture. In *The Evolution of Culture*. R. I. M. Dunbar, C. Knight, and C. Power, eds, pp. 113–46. Edinburgh: Edinburgh University Press.

—— 2002. Ochre in the Middle Stone Age of Southern Africa: Ritualised Display or Hide Preservative? *South African Archaeological Bulletin* 57: 1–14.

Wendorf, F., 1968. Late Paleolithic Sites in Egptian Nubia. In *The Prehistory of Nubia*. F. Wendorf, ed., 791–953. Dallas: Southern Methodist University.

—— and R. Schild, 1998. Nabta Playa and Its Role in the Northeastern African History. *Anthropological Archaeology* 20: 97–123.

—— R. Schild, 'and Associates', 2001. *Holocene Settlement of the Egyptian Sahara, Vol. 1: The Archaeology of Nabta Playa*. New York: Kluwer Academic/Plenum Publishers.

Wengrow, D. 1998. 'The Changing Face of Clay': Continuity and Change in the Transition from Village to Urban Life in the Near East. *Antiquity* 72: 783–95.

Westermann, D., 1927. *Die westlichen Sudansprachen und ihre Beziehungen zu Bantu*. Berlin: W. de Gruyter.

Westermarck, E., 1926. *A Short History of Marriage*. London: Macmillan and Co., Ltd.

White, F. J., 1992. Pygmy Chimpanzee Social Organization: Variation with Party Size and between Study Sites. *American Journal of Primatology* 26: 203–14.

—— 1996. Comparative Socio-ecology of *Pan paniscus*. In *Great Ape Societies*. W. C. McGrew, L. F. Marchant, and T. Nishida, eds, pp. 29–41. Cambridge: Cambridge University Press.

White, R., 1997. Substantial Acts: From Materials to Meaning in Upper Palaeolithic Representation. In *Beyond Art: Pleistocene Image and Symbol*. M. W. Conkey, O. Soffer, D. Stratmann, and N. G. Jablonski, eds, pp. 93–122. San Francisco: Wattis Symposium Series in Anthropology, Memoirs of the California Academy of Sciences 23.

White, T. D., B. Asfaw, D. DeGusta, H. Gilbert, G. D. Richards, G. Suwa, and F. C. Howell, 2003. Pleistocene *Homo sapiens* from Middle Awash, Ethiopia. *Nature* 423: 742–7.

Widdig, A. P., P. Nürnberg, M. Krawczak, W. J. Streich, and F. B. Bercovitch, 2001. Paternal Relatedness and Age Proximity Regulate Social Relationships among Adult Female Rhesus Macaques. *Proceedings of the National Academy of Sciences of the United States of America* 98: 13769–73.

—— P. Nürnberg, M. Krawczak, W. J. Streich, and F. B. Bercovitch, 2002. Affiliation and Aggression among Adult Female Rhesus Macaques: A Genetic Analysis of Paternal Cohorts. *Behaviour* 139: 371–91.

Wiessner, P., 1983. Style and Social Information in Kalahari San Projectile Points. *American Antiquity* 48: 253–76.

Williamson, K., 1989. Niger-Congo Overview. In *The Niger-Congo Languages*. J. Bendor-Samuel and R. L. Hartell, eds, pp. 3–45. Lanham, MD: University Press of America.

—— 1993. Linguistic Evidence for the Use of Some Tree and Tuber Food Plants in Southern Nigeria. In *The Archaeology of Africa: Food, Metals and Towns*. T. Shaw, P. Sinclair, B. Andah, and A. Okpoko, eds, pp. 139–53. London: Routledge.

—— and R. M. Blench, 2000. Niger-Congo. In *African Languages: An Introduction*. B. Heiner and D. Nurse, eds, pp. 11–42. Cambridge: Cambridge University Press.

Wingfield, C., 2005. Historical Time versus the Imagination of Antiquity: Critical Perspectives from the Kalahari. In *The Qualities of Time: Anthropological Approaches*. W. James and D. Mills, eds, pp. 119–35. Oxford and New York: Berg.

Winterhalder, B. 1990. Open Field, Common Pot: Harvest Variability and Risk Avoidance in Agricultural and Foraging Societies. In *Risk and Uncertainty in Tribal and Peasant Economies*. E. Cashdan, ed., pp. 67–87. Boulder, CO: Westview.

—— 1996. Social Foraging and the Behavioural Ecology of Intragroup Resource Transfers. *Evolutionary Anthropology* 5: 46–57.

Wobst, H. M., 1974. Boundary Conditions for Palaeolithic Social Systems: A Simulation Approach. *American Antiquity* 39: 147–78.

Wood, B. A., and M. Collard, 1999. The Changing Face of Genus *Homo*. *Evolutionary Anthropology* 8: 195–207.

Woodburn, J., 1968a. Stability and Flexibility in Hadza Residential Groupings. In *Man the Hunter*. R. B. Lee and I. DeVore, eds, pp. 103–10. Chicago: Aldine.

—— 1968b. An Introduction to Hadza Ecology. In *Man the Hunter*. R. B. Lee and I. DeVore, eds, pp. 49–55. Chicago: Aldine.

—— 1988. African Hunter-Gatherer Social Organization: Is It Best Understood as a Product of Encapsulation? In *Hunters and Gatherers: History, Evolution and Social Change*. T. Ingold, D. Riches, and J. Woodburn, eds, pp. 31–64. Oxford: Berg.

Wrangham, R. W., 1979. Sex Differences in Chimpanzee Dispersion. In *The Great Apes*. D. A. Hamburg and E. R. McCown, eds, pp. 481–99. Menlo Park, CA: Benjamin.

—— 1980. An Ecological Model of Female-Bonded Primate Groups. *Behaviour* 75: 262–30.

—— 1987. The Significance of African Apes for Reconstructing Human Social Evolution. In *The Evolution of Human Behavior*. W. G. Kinzey, ed., pp. 51–71. Albany: New York State University Press.

—— and D. Peterson, 1996 *Demonic Males: Apes and the Origins of Human Violence*. London: Bloomsbury.

—— C. A. Chapman, A. P. Clark-Arcadi, and G. Isabirye-Basuta, 1996. Social Ecology of Kanyawara Chimpanzees: Implications for Understanding the Costs of Great Ape Groups. In *Great Ape Societies*. W. C. McGrew, L. F. Marchant, and T. Nishida, eds, pp. 45–57. Cambridge: Cambridge University Press.

—— J. H. Jones, G. Laden, D. Pilbeam, and N. Conklin-Brittain, 1999. The Raw and the Stolen: Cooking and the Ecology of Human Origins. *Current Anthropology* 40: 567–94.

Wylie, A., 2002. *Thinking from Things: Essays in the Philosophy of Archaeology*. Berkeley: University of California Press.

Zhou, W.-X., D. Sornette, R. A. Hill, and R. I. M. Dunbar, 2004. Discrete Hierarchical Organization of Social Group Sizes. *Proceedings of the Royal Society London*, Series B, 272: 439–44.

Index

Note: page numbers in italics denote figures, tables or illustrations